# LINCOLN'S NAVY

# LINCOLN'S NAVY

## The Ships, Men and Organization, 1861-65

Donald L Canney

CONWAY
MARITIME PRESS

*To My Mother*

Text © Donald L Canney, 1998
Volume © Conway Maritime Press,
1998

First published in Great Britain in 1998
by Conway Maritime Press,
an imprint of Brassey's UK Ltd,
33 John Street,
London WC1N 2AT
Telephone: 0171 753 7777
Fax: 0171 753 7795
E-mail: brasseys@dial.pipex.com
Web: hhtp://www.brasseys.com

A CIP catalogue record for this book is
available from the British Library.

ISBN 0 85177 669 8

**Frontispiece:** The battle between Union
steam sloop *Kearsarge* and Confederate
cruiser *Alabama*. Painting by Xanthus
Smith.

Designed by Peter Champion
Printed and bound in Italy by
LEGO SpA

# Acknowledgements

A project of this magnitude cannot be completed without significant aid from others in the field who have gone before. They have been generous enough to lend expertise and advice, as well as suggest ideas and sources.

The following people have been of special assistance: Dr Bill Still, formerly of East Carolina University, and editor of Conway Maritime Press's companion volume on the Confederate Navy; Kevin Foster, of the National Maritime Initiative, who lent expertise on Civil War vessels of all sorts, particularly those of the 'Rebel' navy and blockade runners; Chuck Haberlein, long-time friend at the Naval Historical Center photo collection, and John Reilly, also at the NHC; Dr Robert Browning Jr, US Coast Guard Historian and author of *Cape Charles to Cape Fear: The North Atlantic Blockading Squadron during the Civil War*, and a great source of bibliography and other source materials.

Notes of thanks also go to Harold Langley of the Smithsonian Institution, Frank McGrane at the Army Museum of Transportation, Fort Eustis, Virginia, and to the respondees on the Internet for ideas on the nineteenth-century use of oatmeal in steam engine firerooms.

A particular note of appreciation goes to Steve Selenfriend, who graciously permitted me to study and handle his magnificent collection of Civil War naval firearms and equipment.

I would like to express my gratitude to the staffs of the libraries at the Navy Historical Center, the Coast Guard Academy and Library of Congress Manuscript Division.

On a more personal level, thanks to my co-worker, Gail Fuller, Coast Guard Curator, for her continued support and encouragement; also, to the congregation of Capitol Baptist Church for their interest, support and spiritual uplifting through this long process.

To my wife Janice and son Brendan I owe much for their long-suffering and understanding of the pressures and work involved in this – and previous – projects.

**Donald L Canney**
Bowie, Maryland, January 1998.

# CONTENTS

A NOTE ON SOURCES AND THE
UN-FILLED GAPS IN CIVIL WAR
NAVAL HISTORY .................................. VI

INTRODUCTION ............................. VII

*Chapter One*
HISTORIC BACKGROUND AND THE
INTERNATIONAL SCENE.......................... 1

*Chapter Two*
ORGANIZATION AND ADMINISTRATION ................. 22

*Chapter Three*
NAVAL SHORE FACILITIES ...................... 33

*Chapter Four*
THE SHIPS OF LINCOLN'S NAVY...................... 56

*Chapter Five*
SHIPBUILDING IN IRON AND WOOD ................. 82

*Chapter Six*
NAVY UNIFORMS, EQUIPMENT AND
SMALL ARMS ...................................... 99

*Chapter Seven*
THE ENLISTED SAILOR................................ 117

*Chapter Eight*
THE NAVAL OFFICER CORPS ............................. 140

*Chapter Nine*
THE CIVIL WAR MARINE CORPS ........................ 153

*Chapter Ten*
SHIPHANDLING UNDER STEAM AND SAIL ............ 161

*Chapter Eleven*
NAVAL ORDNANCE AND GUNNERY ....................... 169

*Chapter Twelve*
UNION NAVAL STRATEGY AND LOGISTICS OF
THE CIVIL WAR.............................................. 178

*Chapter Thirteen*
CIVIL WAR NAVAL TACTICS................................ 186

*Chapter Fourteen*
ASSOCIATED UNION MARITIME SERVICES............. 206

*Chapter Fifteen*
US NAVAL CASUALTIES AND VESSEL LOSSES ......... 216

SOURCES ................................... 221

INDEX ..................................... 229

# A Note on Sources and the Un-filled Gaps in Civil War Naval History

Because of the nature of this work, it is for the most part based on secondary published material, though many of the sources are somewhat obscure and rare. A smattering of primary materials has been culled from the previous research I have done on the nineteenth-century steam navy, and a few of the more obscure issues were the subjects of limited research at the National Archives and Library of Congress.

Recently Charles Dana Gibson quoted a popular narrative historian who declared that 'the gaps are filled' in the telling of the American Civil War. Merely in terms of numbers of books, one would expect this to be abundantly true. The fascination of Americans – and others – with the War of the Rebellion has spawned probably thousands of books and articles, and yet the popular interest continues to support efforts like this one.

Amazingly obvious 'gaps' do remain, and they are significant ones, particularly in the area of naval history. Example: in attempting to locate any pre-digested statistics or even general information on Civil War navy desertions, I found almost nothing. Of course the raw, original muster rolls and vessel logs exist, and probably general reports from vessel commanders to the judge advocate or provost marshall on the subject. But, as interesting and potentially significant as the subject is, no one seems to have seriously studied it.

Along similar lines, I was able to find very little on vessel loss-es and casualties. My listing of naval ship losses of the war is orig-inal – though it benefitted from a database being prepared by the Naval Historical Center on all Civil War vessel losses.

Of course many of the more mundane aspects of the war have not been scrutinized to any extent. Logistics, for instance, is nearly a blank slate, with the exception of Dr Robert Browning's *From Cape Charles to Cape Fear*, which relates in depth the North Atlantic Blockading Squadron's logistical situation.

Another neglected, and less sedate, subject area is that of ves-sel histories. Excepting works on *Monitor*, *Hartford*, and *Cairo*, few writers have studied individual Union naval ships, even those which participated in many of the major naval actions of the war. *Richmond* comes to mind – a vessel which was at New Orleans, Vicksburg, Port Hudson and Mobile Bay. On the western rivers, ironclads such as *Benton* and *Essex* come to mind – mainstays of the Mississippi River campaigns.

Finally, the entire relationship of the navy with the army's Northern Virginia campaigns is ripe for study, with the potential of significant insights into the navy's effect on that critical theatre of operations.

Fortunately for the historian, records of the war are volumi-nous, and of course the 30-volume *Official Records* is invaluable, and not yet plumbed for many aspects of the war, including those list-ed above.

It is encouraging to see these sources being used, in a current study on the contributions of the Black sailor during the war. I am writing this as a reminder that there are indeed significant 'gaps' yet to be filled, as well as abundant resources to supply those miss-ing pieces of Civil War naval history.

# INTRODUCTION

Few historical subjects have attracted the number of chroniclers as the American Civil War. And, nearly 150 years after the fact, the number of books continues to mushroom. However, as is common with other military subjects, the bulk of the published works deal with the combat itself, right up to minute-by-minute descriptions of the great battles, to the neglect of the more mundane, but possibly more significant, subject areas.

This work is a survey of the United States Navy during that internecine conflict, concentrating on the certainly less glamorous, and perhaps less exciting but no less necessary subjects. Among the areas covered will be personnel, including training, discipline, and shipboard life; the ships and their acquisition and construction; small arms, uniforms, equipment and ship's ordnance; supply and logistics; tactics and strategy; administration and logistics; and yards and stations. It opens with a short history of the service and a comparison with other contemporary navies, including, of course, that of the Confederate States of America, together with a summary of the naval history of the Civil War. There is also an overview of the associated naval forces of the conflict: the United States Revenue Marine (Revenue Service), the army's Quartermaster Department, and the Coast Survey, all of which contributed ships and men to the common effort.

This is not intended to be a presentation of great depth or with significant original scholarship. Rather, I have sought to collect, under one cover, a wide spectrum of subjects heretofore only available from widely scattered sources.

As will be deduced by the reader who scans bibliographies and sources, there remain fairly substantial areas of Civil War naval history only lightly touched by serious scholarship. Logistics, for instance, has been studied thoroughly only by Dr Robert Browning Jr in his recent book *Cape Charles to Cape Fear: The North Atlantic Blockading Squadron during the Civil War*, and this only deals with one of the Union squadrons. Another lack is a detailed study of the seagoing characteristics and handling of the transitional steam-and-sailing vessels. There apparently was no prominent nineteenth-century work on the subject, which leaves the modern student even less well informed.

It is worth noting at this juncture that, in many instances, scholarship on the Confederate Navy is more extensive and available than that concerning its victorious adversary. This despite the comparative sparsity of original material available on that short-lived but heroic service. Certainly the mystique of the 'Lost Cause' is a contributing factor to this rather odd state of affairs.

In any event, I hope that this presentation will shed some light where little has been previously and bring together some of the more obscure aspects of the navy side of the War of the Rebellion. At the same time, I hope it might inspire some new scholarship where it is obviously needed.

# Chapter One
# HISTORIC BACKGROUND AND THE INTERNATIONAL SCENE

The American Civil War, as far as the United States Navy was concerned, was an aberration. The entire history and tradition of the service had little bearing on the conflict of the 1860s and no other war – before or since – caught the service so thoroughly unadapted to its requirements.

Despite the decades of increasing sectional tensions, there seems to have been few who foresaw the ultimate tragedy to which it led. In the naval context, when the Confederate forces fired on Fort Sumter the navy was still cruising on station and preparing for a repeat – in strategy and execution – of the War of 1812.

The US Navy of 1861 was prepared – as it had been for five decades – to harass the commerce of an enemy, and fight single-ship encounters with inferior foes à la *Constitution* versus *Guerriere*. In contrast, there were no vessels designed for long-term coastal blockade, for riverine warfare, or for attacking coastal fortifications; tasks which became crucial in the conflict at hand.

Whether the navy could be held accountable for this unpreparedness is a question beyond our scope here. However, it is difficult to surmise the kinds of actions which could have been taken, given the mixed sectional composition of the officer corps, and the domestic reaction that sectionally-biased actions may have engendered. In fact, it may well be said that the South was probably restrained in its reaction to many activities of the pre-war navy which may have been construed as reflecting an anti-Southern bias. In point of fact, spirited enforcement of the anti-slave trade laws by the African squadron certainly would have inspired a lack of trust in Southern minds. The fact that the steam sloops of 1857-59 were built with the stated purpose of entering shallow southern ports (in contrast to the earlier deep-hulled steam frigates) also may well have raised some questions among some of the disaffected in those harbor towns.

The air of unpreparedness, both in the navy and other areas, is still astounding to this writer. It seems that there was a spirit of naivety at play in the mid nineteenth-century mind: a disparity between high goals and ideals – unionism on one side and 'states rights' on the other – and the ultimate practical outgrowth of their unrestrained expression into physical conflict and war. Somehow, the rose-colored chivalry of the day filtered out the blood that was the ultimate price to be paid.

In any event, any study of the US Navy during the War Between the States must begin by describing that force as it stood in April 1861. This involves more than enumerating vessels, guns and personnel: it must explain the causal factors. If these forces and men were so ill-suited, what were they intended for and what were the historic precedents which made the navy what it was? The following is a capsulized look at the Mr Lincoln's fleet in 1861 and its history.

For reasons which are peculiarly American, the navy of the United States had two beginnings. The Continental Navy, organized in 1775, was allowed to lapse with the coming of peace with England in 1783. The American distrust of military and naval force, which had been an instrument of repression in the colonial years, far outweighed the perceived need to protect commerce on the high seas. Over a decade passed after Cornwallis surrendered at Yorktown before a department of the navy was formed and vessels were obtained and seamen shipped.

In the popular mind John Paul Jones embodied the navy of the American Revolution. In numbers the Continental Navy was never more than a nuisance to the British, and a significant number of its officers were political appointees – further diluting its effectiveness. But Jones was one of the few truly gifted leaders and left the service with a heroic legacy. (US Navy)

In any case, the Continental Navy had not been a particularly rousing proposition, John Paul Jones aside. Most authorities agree this navy itself had little effect on the outcome of the conflict, despite the fact that many of the purpose-built frigates were of excellent design (and were significantly larger than their counterparts in the British fleet). Numbering some fifty ships, the majority of its vessels found little purpose except as something to be burned before capture by British forces. Given the overwhelming odds in the British favor, this fate was not at all a shameful one. On the other hand a multitude of privateers captured some 3000 merchant ships, raising havoc with the shipping interests and contributing to the unpopularity of the war in Britain.

As to Captain Jones, his attributes as a seaman and naval officer are manifest and justifiably celebrated in the iconography of US naval history. His victory over HMS *Serapis* even as his own command was sinking beneath him, as well as other truly heroic exploits during his short career made him a legend to generations

yet unborn who would conn American warships in harms way.

The sole American naval ship to survive the war was sold out in 1785, leaving a burgeoning national sea trade without protection. The Barbary powers of North Africa took particular note of this, and, as was their wont, demanded their medieval 'tribute' (bribe) to allow American merchant vessels safe passage along their Mediterranean coasts. When the American government refused, the adversaries obtained – with little effort – hostages. Cash and goods were then the only resort for the humiliated government of the thirteen states.

Not long into Washington's first administration, it seems to have occurred to some that the expense of a navy might be preferable and, in the long run, cheaper, than that demanded by foreign extortionists and Congress authorized construction of six frigates to deal with the Barbary 'pirates'. The names of the six vessels would pass into legend: *Constitution, Constellation, Congress, President, United States,* and *Chesapeake.*

The same act which authorized the men-of-war called for a naval establishment of fifty-four commissioned officers (the highest rank: captain), eighty-four warrant officers, and 1922 petty officers, seamen and marines. Early on, this was administered under the War Department, but by 1798 a separate navy department was organized.

The years without a navy, as well as the dilatory process by which one was obtained – even when the need was blatantly self-evident – illuminate prominent features of the American attitude towards the seagoing service. Not even when the passage of enabling legislation was certain did active opposition to the concept of the navy desist, particularly by representatives from the far west who saw no use for such a fleet. More fundamentally, the debates on the issue turned up two major themes which would surface in future legislative congeries. First, a navy was expensive. In contrast to the army, which could be disbanded when the danger abated, the navy required a large capital investment in ships and facilities and absorbed continuing maintenance costs. This argument was quite effective in the money-lean days of the new republic (and it has held its own quite well since).

Then there was the philosophical theme. How did a self-proclaimed egalitarian society justify an elitist organization whose highest officers acted indeed as petty tyrants on their quarterdecks? The word Admiralty smacked of royalty and privilege; anathema to the democratically high minded in the new nation – men of no less clout than Thomas Jefferson. Indeed, the creation of the navy was part of that furious internecine era of the

Federalist/anti-Federalist conflict and the new service was considered a child of the likes of Alexander Hamilton and the pro-British, pro-royalty, pro-oppressive big government clique. 'True' egalitarians such as Jefferson saw their stars in the goings on in Revolutionary France – or at least in the levelling of the aristocracy and the ideals adhered to early on in that cataclysm – and viewed navies as tools of oppression and bastions of privilege.

Such was the political milieu into which the new service was born. And, by the time the new ships were ready for sea, the Barbary powers were overshadowed by a new and more potent enemy: France. In mid 1798 an undeclared war had broken out on the high seas and the new frigates already mentioned were quickly at sea and in its midst.

It is not the author's intent to enumerate all the vessels of the navy. However, the frigate *Constitution* and sister vessels, were more influential than any other group in the history of the navy, and their hold on the psyche of the corps, especially in the area of warship design, was still palpable at least until the Civil War. Their design thus deserves a short description here.

Most sources credit Joshua Humphreys of Philadelphia with the design theory behind these vessels, if not the actual lines. He was the official given charge of their development by War Secretary Henry Knox (whose army service had not prepared him for such an assignment). Humphreys essentially ceded numbers of vessels to the European navies, arguing that the US could not hope to equal such fleets already in being. 'I would build them of larger size than theirs, and take the lead of them...' he wrote, and proceeded to draft 44-gun frigates some 20 feet longer and 2 or 3 feet wider than vessels of like rate in the British navy. In fact, the '44's' commonly carried over 50 guns each.

Outgunning enemy vessels of the same rate proved one half of Humphreys' formula. The second was sufficient speed to allow these men-of-war to escape anything larger than themselves. This was accomplished by incorporating relatively sharp lines, which in itself was facilitated by the extra hull length. It has been estimated that *Constitution* and *President* could turn out 13½ knots, a rate not often exceeded in the age of sailing warships.

The Napoleonic Wars found the United States attempting a harried neutrality, a stance rendered impossible by the arrogance and aggression of the French Directorate. By mid 1798 the undeclared 'Quasi-War' was under way, with fourteen American war vessels at sea, in addition to hundreds of letter of marque privateers. Four squadrons combed the seas from Caracas northward, and American vessels quickly made their mark.

The action off Flamborough Head between Jones's *Bonhomme Richard* and *Serapis* was one of the most horrific single-ship duels in American history taking 3½ hours with 300 casualties on each side. Jones refused to yield and prevailed – though it was his ship which sank from her wounds two days later. Despite Jones and a few others who took the war to the British home islands, American privateers had a greater economic impact on the war than the navy. (US Navy)

**US** frigate *Constellation* defeats French *L'Insurgente*, February 1799. American naval vessels performed well, ending the careers of eighty-five French ships in the space of the two-year war. (US Navy)

**S**ecretary of the Navy Benjamin Stoddert, first to hold that office under President John Adams. Stoddert saw to it that the re-born navy under the Constitution was available to meet the challenge of the French Directory in the undeclared Quasi-War. At the close of his term, Stoddert laid the basis for the shore establishment with the purchase of land for six navy yards. (US Navy)

The frigate *Constellation*, Captain Thomas Truxton, was first, capturing the French *L'Insurgente* in February 1799, then bringing the *Vengeance* to heel a year later. In all, some ninety-three armed French vessels were captured, at a small cost to the new navy. By the war's end, there were over fifty American men-of-war.

More important than mere numbers, the quality of the new officer corps was such as to bode well for the future. Edward Preble, Isaac Hull, William Bainbridge, Stephen Decatur, David Porter and Thomas Macdonough all served in this undeclared war, and went on to make themselves heroes of the new republic against other foes.

Furthermore, using the leverage provided by naval victories, Secretary of the Navy Benjamin Stoddert had the foresight to consolidate the naval establishment by purchase of land for six navy yards, an act for which he had questionable statutory authority. Additionally, in 1798, Congress authorized the building of the navy's first 74-gun ships of the line as well as numerous smaller vessels to round out the squadrons.

This ambitious building program, it transpired, was not to be tolerated by the next administration, but the success of the new service probably played a large part in preventing its complete dismantling with the elevation of Thomas Jefferson to the presidency in 1801.

Jefferson advocated a coastal defense force only, fearing a seagoing fleet would 'implicate' the nation in 'eternal' wars. The

The bombardment of Tripoli, 1804. Until the formation of the American fleet, American merchant vessels were subject to harassment and capture by the Barbary powers of north Africa. After years of paying protection money in the form of a 'tribute', the new American naval squadron delivered a less subtle form of response. (US Navy)

resulting reduction in force included selling the majority of the vessels and laying up the remainder (seven). The navy yards were generally ignored, with most losing their appointed constructors, clerks and storekeepers. Only Washington Navy Yard grew during this period, and only because Jefferson could easily monitor its activities for incipient Federalist leanings. Of course, the 74-gun ships were never built and materials gathered for them were used elsewhere; and numbers of all categories of personnel were reduced by about half. Naval expenses dropped to $946,000 in 1802 from $3.3 million two years before.

Two antithetical factors now dominated naval policy: Jefferson's coastal defense ideas and the depredations and humiliations of the Barbary powers. The year 1802 proved the lowest point for naval appropriations as the Tripolitan conflict, which continued until 1806, escalated the need for warships.

Jefferson's solution to a big navy and big appropriations was essentially a naval militia: dozens of small gunboats stationed on the coasts, stored easily in peacetime and quickly put into service when a threat appeared on the horizon. In part inspired by similar vessels in Neapolitan and other Mediterranean navies, each of these 60-foot or smaller vessels had a crew of twenty-five to forty-five men and one or two cannon. One-hundred-and-seventy-six were built at a cost of $1.5 million (about the cost of six frigates). In terms of national defense, they were useless; in terms of political patronage, they provided government contracts to builders as far

west as Kentucky and Ohio. In any event, the gunboat program did not entirely replace the seagoing navy. Jefferson retained a squadron to deal with the continued depredations of the Barbary powers.

Long used to American toothlessness, the North African extortionists paid little heed to the nation's growing naval trucu-lence, and were soon faced with a new phenomenon: an American naval squadron made up of frigates and sloops bombarding their fortifications. This, plus the capture of a Tripolitan town by a combined Arab-American land force, including several US Marines, brought the pasha to terms. The troubles then faded until 1815, when yet another American squadron was sent to set-tle the matters.

As the fight against Napoleon raged in Europe, its American overspill, meriting little more than a footnote in world history texts, was the War of 1812, fought ostensibly because of British seizures of American maritime commerce as well as impressment of seamen from American vessels. In fact, New England shipping interests actively opposed the war, while the congressional 'war hawks' were westerners swift to imagine British influence foment-ing Native American hostilities on the expanding northwestern frontier. What better excuse to seize coveted Canada?

While the conquest of that vast territory made for wonderful political grist, it did little to galvanize the American armies. Conversely, the naval encounters at sea and on the northern lakes produced victories which yet resound in American naval mythology.

Frigate *Constitution* and HM frigate *Guerriere*, August 1812. The typical American frigate outgunned her British counterpart, and wrought a series of American single-ship victories on the high seas. Though wonderful morale boosts to the American public, these had little strategic impact on the course of the war. (US Navy)

At sea, before the inevitable British blockade immobilized the small American fleet, single-ship engagements were the rule: the nation could ill afford any fleet action that could potentially annihilate the entire navy. The numbers bear this out: besides some sixty-three patently useless gunboats, the American navy listed eighteen vessels, the largest of which were the Humphreys-designed 44-gun frigates. In theory the Royal Navy could array over 700 vessels, 200 of which were ships of the line (60 guns or more). In practice, given the low priority of this war in comparison with that being waged in Europe, the numbers of British vessels engaged on the western verge of the Atlantic were few. But

with the defeat of Napoleon, the year 1814 brought overwhelming naval strength to bear on the American conflict.

The first six months of the war saw a series of single-ship actions the likes of which had never been seen by the British navy. First and, for American posterity, foremost, was the loss of *Guerriere* (38 guns) to *Constitution* in August 1812. The Americans, smarting after years of submitting to impressment and the insult delivered to the frigate *Chesapeake* by *Leopard* in 1807 in that regard, as well as the disparagement of the American frigates as large, 'fir-built' contraptions, had a score to settle.

*Constitution*, nicknamed Old Ironsides, followed up this success by taking *Java* later that year. In succession, *United States* took the frigate *Macedonian*, *Hornet* took *Peacock*, *Enterprise* triumphed over *Boxer*, *Wasp* versus *Reindeer*, etc. Later *Constitution* took *Cyane* and *Levant*, vessels whose aggregate batteries equalled hers in number. In short, the American navy, long an unknown quantity, and with a dubious Revolutionary War heritage, was now an adversary not to be underestimated, even by the heirs of Lord Nelson.

This string was not to be unbroken. Captain Philip Broke, HMS *Shannon*, took on *Chesapeake* in a set-piece challenge off Boston. Captain James Lawrence unwisely rushed into a well-made trap with a poorly trained crew. Broke's topmen did his bidding well, taking out most of the American quarterdeck officers, leaving a mortally wounded Lawrence imploring, to no avail: 'Don't give up the ship!' The navy had a new catch phrase, but had lost a frigate and its short-lived victorious mystique. The Admiralty had learned, however, the efficacy of the big frigates and, by extension, validated constructor Humphreys' principles they incorporated. Orders went out that single-ship actions with American frigates were not to be entered into. (Broke either had not received this directive, or had ignored it.)

The American naval single-ship offensive was of little account when the weight of the British fleet took on the blockade of the east coast. By 1814, the Royal Navy could cull out their targets with seeming impunity, and proceeded to do so, with incursions at New Orleans, New England and Chesapeake Bay. The last saw the burning of Washington; one of whose more stalwart defenders was Commodore Joshua Barney, who had been forced to burn his gunboats and defend the capitol's approaches on foot. There would appear to be some shade of irony, as well as instruction, in his crew's heroism on that day, when Jefferson's gunboats proved exactly how useful they were in the test of war.

On the open sea, the most consistently effective American vessels were the privateers. There were some 500 at large, ranging as far as the English Channel and the Irish Sea. These fast vessels accounted for 1350 merchantmen captured or destroyed. Lloyd's testified to their effectiveness by refusing insurance to un-convoyed ships in the Irish Sea. They boosted morale at home, disrupted British supply lines, and, as in the War of Independence, brought the war home to the merchant classes.

The only fleet actions of the war occurred on Lake Erie and Lake Champlain, the latter located between New York and Vermont. Unlike the single-ship actions, these had a decided impact on the war itself.

On Lake Erie, Master Commandant Oliver Hazard Perry set out to counter a British fleet fronting an army advance into Ohio. Perry's ten hastily built vessels stanched this invasion of the American northwest, and moved Castlereagh to propose a peace conference.

The Battle of Lake Champlain brought an end to yet another British invasion of the former colony. Commodore Thomas Macdonough, with four ships and ten row galleys, met four British ships and a dozen galleys in September 1814.

**B**attle of Lake Erie, 1813. A scratch-built American flotilla commanded by Oliver Hazard Perry defeated the British, ending Britain's attempt to invade the United States via Ohio. This and a later victory on Lake Champlain were the two most important strategic naval victories of the war. (US Navy)

MacDonough's small fleet prevailed, sending the invading army back to Canada.

Of all the naval victories of the War of 1812, by far the most strategic was that on Lake Erie. However, to the populace at large, the open sea one-on-one victories, despite their lack of strategic impact, loomed large. Those victories, in particular those of *Constitution* early in the war when the army was suffering a series of ignominious reverses, electrified public opinion as nothing else had. Only General Andrew Jackson's lopsided defeat of the regulars at New Orleans and the news of that victory, arriving nearly simultaneously with the news of the Treaty of Ghent, engendered a similar response. In fact the latter circumstance gave rise to the popular notion that the United States had won the 'Second War of Independence'. This legend of victory was commonly believed in the US for nearly a century.

The outpouring of nationalistic fervor which accompanied the cessation of hostilities could not but benefit the navy. Even before the war ceased, a book was published on the *Distinguished Officers in the American Navy*, followed the next year by *American Naval Biography*, introducing a spate of hagiographical and popular naval literature that would continue through the pre-Civil War decades. The navy's performance during the war had ensured its future — one which had been in considerable doubt during Jefferson's administration less than a decade before.

Within the service, the war had also had an impact far greater than the events themselves. Even today, 'Old Ironsides' (*Constitution*) overshadows all. From the day she demolished *Guerriere*, she became the ultimate American naval fighting machine; the measure by which all other pretenders were judged. From the standpoint of warship design, Humphreys' 'bigger and faster' principles were assiduously applied through the remaining decades of the sailing fleet and beyond. The vessel became a tangible object lesson in the American way of war: overwhelming power applied via Yankee technology. Indeed, her characteristics were conscientiously followed, though not entirely effectively, in the steam frigates *Merrimack* and sisters as late as 1854.

Furthermore, in terms of naval strategy, the American victories seemed to validate the status quo. Therefore, there was never an attempt to build an American sailing line-of-battle fleet. Small squadrons, single-ship actions, coastal defense and commerce raiding were for decades to come the naval givens of any potential external conflict. These principles dismissed out of hand the less than palatable facts: the navy had accomplished little beyond eliminating twenty-three warships — a small and easily replaceable percentage of the British navy. None were larger than some 40 guns. Strategically, this was of no account. The navy, or its individual vessels, failed to prevent a blockade which annihilated American commerce. More to the point, the American coast was left defenseless, allowing British invaders access at will, resulting in the burning of the capitol, among other depredations.

Another fact obscured by the euphoria was that there had been no strategic planning whatsoever on the part of the Navy Department. For some time after war was declared, the Secretary of the Navy dithered and eventually asked for advice from senior officers on the value of squadron versus individual ship actions. By the time a decision was reached, Captain Hull was already at sea angling for the *Guerriere*. The series of ship-to-ship victories soon shunted aside other approaches to the war at sea, and the pattern was set.

The end of the War of 1812 found the navy with seventy-five warships and 240 small craft. Two of the new vessels were the navy's first line-of-battle ships, the 74-gun *Washington* and *Independence*. On the Great Lakes four vessels were on the stocks — two frigates and two ships of the line. These were never completed. Wartime naval expenditures rose from $1.9 million in 1811 to $8.6 million in 1815. In personnel, the total of seamen and boys rose from about 4000 to over 10,000. Officer levels rose from about 500 to 629. The marine force increased from 1800 to around 2600.

The end of the war brought about two major developments in naval administration and long term growth. The first of these was the creation of the Board of Naval Commissioners in 1815; the second was the congressional Act for the Gradual Increase of the Navy of 1816.

The Navy Department heretofore had been the sole responsibility of the Secretary of the Navy. This administrator personally dealt with the gamut of departmental tasks, from strategic policy down to supervising the purchase of supplies for yards and vessels. At this time, other than the naval officers and men, the department consisted of the Secretary of the Navy (and clerk) and the constructors, clerks and naval agents at the yards and stations.

In peacetime, particularly under the reduction-in-force Jeffersonians, the work of the department was relatively light. The War of 1812 revealed shortcomings of the system. In addition to the Secretary's stringent workload, it was found that abuses were common among the navy agents in the field.

The Board of Naval Commissioners was the upshot. Three senior naval officers were appointed to give expert advice to the Secretary as well as handle the more mundane tasks such as procurement of supplies and the specifics involved in overseeing naval vessel design and construction. This board sat from 1815 to 1842, when it was replaced by a bureau system.

The department in Washington during this era typically numbered about thirty from the Secretary down to the clerks and messengers. The clerical force by 1842 was eight clerks and a draftsman. Accounting for the department, beginning in 1817, was vested in an auditor of the Treasury Department.

The year 1816 brought the navy's first long term vessel construction plan. Congress voted $1 million annually for eight years to be applied to vessel construction. The program called for nine ships of the line, at 74 guns and over, and twelve 44-gun frigates.

These vessels, in addition to those already in service, were to form the basis of the fleet for the remaining years of the sailing navy. All of the liners were under construction by 1819, with two never launched and one completed as a storeship. The largest was the *Pennsylvania*.

The first of the frigates was launched in 1821, while the last was begun five years later. The last of the series was *Santee*, completed in 1855 – long after steam had usurped the dominance of sail at sea.

These frigates and ships of the line were not the definitive list of larger naval vessels during this period. The *Hudson* (44), for instance, was built for the Greeks, but purchased by the navy. Then there was the last large sailing vessel built for the navy: *Constellation* of 1854. Ostensibly a rebuilding of the original 1797 frigate, the resulting ship was a sloop of war quite different to her predecessor. The newer vessel still exists in Baltimore.

The decades between the War of 1812 and the Civil War were marked by the explosive expansion of American seaborne trade, accompanied by the rapid geographical growth of the nation. Estimates place American imports at $113 million in 1815 and $362 million by 1860 – a tripling in value. Exports ballooned from $52 million to $400 million in the same period. The high point came in 1861, when American vessels in the carrying trade measured 2.6 million tons, second only to that of Great Britain, which measured 3.2 million merchant marine tons.

American vessels could be found in every place a dollar could be made. Whales and furs beckoned on the Pacific; tea and other commodities from China, the East Indies and India; sandalwood from the Pacific islands; gold from California.

The expansion of the nation's borders accompanied these commercial ventures. The port of New Orleans, long under threat from foreign interference, was finally free to funnel goods from the Mississippi Valley to the world, and quickly became America's second largest exporter. The Floridas were annexed and the contiguous continental United States was completed with the territories gained from Mexico. This, as well as the gold in California, spurred trade between the two coasts, whether by way of Cape Horn or the Isthmus of Panama.

For the most part – the main exception being the Mexican War – American naval operations of this era were centered around the various squadrons. Each was concerned with showing the flag and protection of trade and other interests in their particular segment of the world's oceans.

The Mediterranean squadron had its inception with the troubles with the Barbary powers of North Africa. After an Anglo-Dutch bombardment, these piratical kingdoms lost their potency and the appearance of a strong American squadron in 1815 soon quelled any further belligerence on their part. Stationed at Minorca, this was the prestige squadron of the navy, with not infrequent diplomatic duties, as well as the sorting out of American interests in the tangled affairs between the Ottomans and rebelling Greeks.

The West India squadron was formed in 1822 with a long and arduous task ahead: to suppress piracy in the Caribbean. Between 1815 and 1823, as the power of Spain faded in the region, some 3000 cases of piracy had been reported from the Bahamas to the coasts of Central and South America. The new fifteen-vessel squadron faced not only pirates, but tropical climes and accompanying yellow fever. Complicating the task was that of gaining cooperation from local authorities.

Using small boat tactics and raiding parties, the anti-piracy operations continued until 1829 and succeeded in ferreting out the outlaw lairs. The navy's first operational steamer was employed in the process, as well as certain vessels of the US Revenue Marine.

The squadron's next combat came in the mid 1830s in Florida. The navy cooperated with the army in its war against the Seminole Indians, a vicious guerilla-style conflict which rumbled on until 1842.

In the Pacific, a squadron was formed in 1822 for protection of South Seas trade. The forerunner of this squadron was the sloop of war *Ontario*, which officially took possession of the

The brig *Perry* takes the slave ship *Martha*. The peacetime navy was composed of six squadrons, five of which were on foreign station. The Africa squadron cooperated with the British in interdicting slavers and repatriating blacks to their homeland. The American squadron was also intrumental in the establishment of Liberia by former slaves. (US Navy)

Oregon Territory in 1818 and remained in the Pacific to protect American interests in the war between Spain and Chile.

A Brazil squadron was formed in 1826, and an East Indies command in 1835. The latter followed an 1831 punitive expedition by *Potomac* against Sumatran tribesmen for injuries to American traders.

The home squadron was formed in 1841, and originally consisted of eight vessels. This was a direct result of an Anglo-American war crisis of 1840 when it was noted that the entire fleet was scattered world-wide, leaving the east coast without protection.

The African squadron had its antecedents in 1819, with the establishment of an agency for resettling American slaves on the west coast of that continent. One of the outstanding outgrowths of this was the founding of Liberia in 1823. The navy continued visits to that nation during the process of enforcing the American anti-slave trade laws, and returning blacks to Africa. Certain naval officers, in particular Matthew Calbraith Perry and Andrew H Foote, took an influential role in the early years of the new nation.

The following list shows the composition of American cruising squadrons in 1849 and 1855, taken from the Secretary of the Navy's annual reports. Note that the 1849 listing is shortly after the Mexican War and before great reductions in appropriations came into effect. The listings do not include store, supply and receiving ships, or the steamer *Michigan* permanently stationed on the Great Lakes.

## COMPOSITION OF AMERICAN SQUADRONS

### 1849

Home – 6 vessels: 1 frigate; 2 sloops of war; 2 steamers; 1 schooner.
Pacific – 8 vessels: 1 liner; 1 frigate; 6 sloops.
Mediterranean – 6 vessels: 3 frigates; 1 steamer; 1 sloop.
Brazil – 2 vessels: 1 frigate; 1 sloop.
Africa – 6 vessels: 3 sloops; 3 brigs.
China – 2 vessels: 1 sloop; 1 brig.

### 1855

Home – 4 vessels: 1 frigate; 2 sloops; 1 steamer.
Pacific – 4 vessels: 1 frigate; 3 sloops.
Mediterranean – 3 vessels: 1 frigate; 1 steamer; 1 sloop.
Brazil – 3 vessels: 1 frigate; 1 sloop; 1 brig.
Africa – 4 vessels: 3 sloops; 1 brig.
E. India – 3 vessels: 1 sloop; 1 steamer; 1 sloop.

**N**aval steamers support army operations in the Mexican War, 1846-1848. This war saw successful – though unopposed – amphibious landings at Vera Cruz, a blockade of the Mexican Gulf coast and naval protection for army supply lines to the United States. (US Navy; drawing by Henry Walke)

The Mexican War provided significant and varied operational experiences for the navy, though the enemy lacked an efficient naval force. It was also the first in which steam warships played a significant role.

On the west coast, the navy provided forces in support of local 'Bear Flag' revolutionaries in California until American troops arrived overland. American warships under John Sloat seized Monterey and San Francisco early on, and naval and marine forces under Robert Stockton assisted in taking Los Angeles and San Diego.

The main theatre of operations was in the Gulf of Mexico, where the navy maintained an effective blockade, controlling the sea and allowing free movement of troops and supplies for the armies. Steam vessels, particularly the pioneering screw-propelled *Princeton*, were found quite effective holding station in this effort. At Vera Cruz, the navy organized and carried out its first major amphibious landing, setting 10,000 men ashore in the space of four hours. In this and other similar operations, steamers were utilized to tow invasion boats and hold them in position while all rendezvoused at the jump-off point. The boats then rowed to shore on signal. Though unopposed, the landings were carried out without a hitch and on schedule, and became part of Marine Corps amphibious studies before the Second World War.

The navy then bombarded the fortress of San Juan de Uloa and assisted in beseiging the town of Vera Cruz. Both fell with minimal American casualties, ending the major naval involvement on the Gulf coast.

Though the Mexican War did not involve ship-to-ship actions, the navy's control of the seas and communications between the army and the US were essential to carrying out the army's strategic plan. Certainly the capture of Vera Cruz would have been impossible without naval amphibious expertise, and naval forces made possible the seizure of a great part of California.

To complete this sketch of the pre-Civil War navy, three other major topics must be reviewed. First were the minor armed encounters which typically occurred when American citizens or interests were endangered overseas. Second were the expeditions mounted to explore relatively unknown areas of the globe in the interest of science as well as to encourage American commerce and trade. Third was the impact of emerging technology on the vessels, personnel and operations of the navy.

Three examples from the 1850s serve to illustrate the navy's armed encounters in this era. The first was the most unusual. In 1856, American settlers in the relatively new Washington Territory were subjected to Native American Indian uprisings and sought refuge on the coast. A landing force from sloop of war *Decatur*, accompanied by gunfire from the vessel, drove back a substantial Native American attack on the settlement of Seattle. Three other naval vessels actively assisted the army during this period of unrest.

The disorders in China brought about by their war with Britain and exacerbated by widespread piracy resulted in a succession of American interventions. In 1854, for example, American naval forces assisted the British in destroying sixty-eight piratical junks and their depots near Hong Kong. Other similar expeditions followed.

Despite official American neutrality, forces led by Commander A H Foote and, later, Josiah Tattnall, actively aided the British in actions against the 'barrier forts' below Canton. In one instance, American boats withdrawing a protective landing force were fired upon by the Chinese, subsequently drawing American return fire from sloops *Portsmouth* and *Levant*. Later, under Tattnall, a British force in small boats faced decimating Chinese fire and possible annihilation until the American commander towed them out of the line of fire. This was the event which elicited Tattnall's famous quotation: 'Blood is thicker than water.'

Closer to home, a major punitive expedition against Paraguay was mounted in 1859. The US steamer *Water Witch* had been fired upon while on an officially sanctioned survey of the Parana River in 1855, and one seaman was killed. This, and other indignities against American citizens and trade without diplomatic satisfaction resulted in a powerful squadron – 1700 men and 78 heavy guns – being dispatched to the La Plata River. The show of force brought a sudden reversal of Paraguayan attitudes and a new treaty resulted.

Exploring expeditions were popular in this era when expanding commercial interests were searching for new markets and products. Improved navigation and charting techniques and the quest for scientific knowledge also made strong motives for dispatching skilled mariners to unknown and dangerous quarters.

The most extensive American effort in this era was led by Lieutenant Charles Wilkes. In 1838, he led five vessels to the Antarctic and the far reaches of the Pacific. Beginning at Hampton Roads, Virginia, the little fleet rounded Cape Horn, called at Honolulu and Sydney, then skirted the Antarctic ice barrier for over 1000 miles, with ice and winds playing hob with men and vessels. From thence they saw the southwest Pacific again, Hawaii, and the northwestern coast of the United States, exploring and charting both coasts and rivers of the latter. Wilkes then returned home, by way of Honolulu, Manila, Cape Town and Brazil, arriving in New York in 1842.

Other efforts were less ambitious, usually having a specific limited objective. One of the earliest was the cruise of the *Alligator* in 1821, sent to Africa to search out sites for a homeland for former slaves under the auspices of the American Colonization Society. Liberia was the result. Other expeditions explored the

**M**atthew Calbraith Perry. One of the major reformers in the pre-war navy, Perry agitated for steam-powered vessels, shell guns, and improved education for officers. (US Navy)

Dead Sea and Jordan River, searched for the lost Arctic expedition of Sir John Franklin, charted the western Pacific, studied possible routes for an Isthmuthian canal, and surveyed for the future Atlantic cable.

Of course, the single most memorable expedition was that of Matthew Calbraith Perry. Arriving in Yedo Bay with his 'black ships" guns run out, Perry, taking a page from the handbook of oriental potentates, remained high and unseen, refusing to treat with any but a direct representative of the Emperor. Taken aback and uncertain of the power vested in these smoking black vessels, the Japanese reluctantly treated, ending their centuries of self-imposed isolation. Perry, imposing and aristocratic, had been perfect for the part.

Diplomacy aside, the expedition itself was nearly flawless in execution. The logistics alone were daunting: four vessels made the initial contact, two steam frigates and two sailing vessels; seven returned the next year, including three coal-hungry steamers. Considering the American 'empire' of 1853 ended in California, sending this group across the Pacific was no mean feat.

Perry's paddle frigates — *Mississippi*, *Powhatan* and *Susquehanna* — were in fact the first steam-powered vessels to appear in Japan, and were the product of a reluctant and convoluted transition in the navy. Steam propulsion, of course, was accompanied by major innovations in gunnery, the introduction of iron hulls and, later, iron armor. The propulsion issue itself was complicated by development of the screw propeller. It was the beginning of the era when technological obsolescence overtook age in determining a vessel's usefulness.

On paper, the navy's first steam vessel was *Demologos*, or *Fulton*, donated for New York Harbor defense as early as 1815. Built by Robert Fulton, she barely stemmed the tide and lay idle until her accidental destruction in 1829. Despite the quick mercantile adoption of river steamboats, the navy did not design and build a steamer until 1837, with *Fulton II*, another poorly designed 'harbor defense' ship.

Opposition to steam at this stage was not merely irrational sailing ship sentimentality, despite the fact that Hiram K Paulding, Secretary of the Navy 1838-1841, stated that he would 'never consent to let our ships perish and transform our navy into a fleet of sea monsters'. More rather there were significant practical considerations: maintaining a fuel starved steamer on foreign station was expensive; machinery and side paddle wheels consumed significant hull and broadside space; and machinery located high in the hull invited crippling enemy shot.

The screw propeller solved some of these problems, and the US Navy initially led the field in this new technology, with John Ericsson's *Princeton* of 1843. This lead was squandered due to a technological dead end involving horizontal (merry-go-round style) paddle wheels. These were as unlikely as they sounded, but their introduction, (im-)perfection and after effects stymied US naval steam progress for most of the 1840s. Thus, the service's first class of screw-propelled ships did not appear until 1856. By

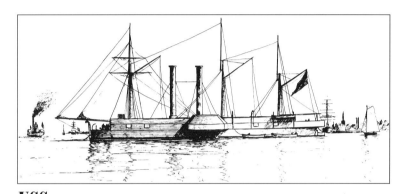

USS *Fulton II*, 1837, the first navy-built and designed steamer. Intended as a harbor defense vessel, she proved fast but uneconomical, and so was useless in the cruising navy. Matthew C Perry used her as test-bed for new shell guns. (US Navy)

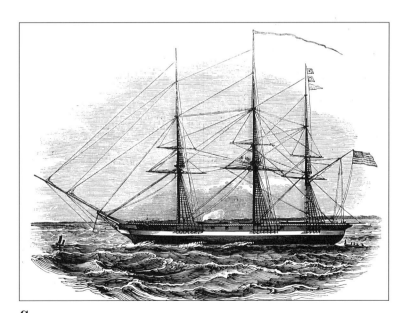

Screw steamer *Princeton*, 1843. As the first result of navy negotiations with inventor John Ericsson, *Princeton* was the first naval vessel designed and built to be powered by the submerged screw propeller. Note the small puff of smoke between fore and main masts, indicating location of her telescoping funnel. Ericsson designed the ship, engines and her shell guns. (Library of Congress)

Abel P Upshur, Secretary of the Navy 1841-1843. Upshur was an innovator, supporting the navy's first screw steamer, *Princeton*, its first iron ship, *Michigan*, and funding for an ironclad steamer, the Stevens Battery.

Iron steamer *Michigan*, 1844. This vessel was conceived as an effort to encourage American iron manufacture. Her components were built in Pittsburg and assembled in Erie, Pennsylvania. She remained on duty on the Great Lakes until the 1920s. (US Navy)

the outbreak of the Civil War the navy was committed to steam screw propulsion and there were thirty-four active steamers, twenty-eight of which were screw propelled.

American naval ordnance had in the meantime been advancing steadily, under the leadership of Captain John Dahlgren. As will be presented in a subsequent chapter, his smoothbore shell guns and Robert Parrott's rifled ordnance placed the US in the forefront of ordnance development in the 1850s.

The use of iron to construct warship hulls was not lost on the navy either. As early as 1841, Secretary of the Navy Abel P Upshur, insisted on building the steamer *Michigan* for the Great Lakes, with an eye on encouraging the American iron industry. The discovery that shards of brittle iron were more dangerous than wooden splinters, and the fact that there were no facilities for iron hull construction at the navy yards, effectively ended this American foray into iron warship construction. During the upcoming war, iron hulled vessels, including the monitors, would be built by civilian firms.

The short tenure of Secretary of the Navy Upshur also saw the laying down of what might have been the world's first ironclad. The 'Stevens Battery', the brainchild of entrepreneur and inventor Robert Stevens of Hoboken, New Jersey, was to be an iron-hulled

and armored steam vessel for the protection of New York harbor. An occasional infusion of federal money kept the project viable through the 1940s and 1950s, though actual construction was sporadic and hampered by advances in ordnance which necessitated major design changes. At the beginning of the Civil War when ironclads were being evaluated, a naval inspection team declared the vessel would be far to deep for naval use on southern coasts. The vessel was never completed.

As technology drove the development of vessels and ordnance, it contributed to significant administrative and educational changes in the navy of this era. Both the founding of the Naval Academy and the re-organization of the Navy Department had aspects emanating from the growth of technology in the service.

The Board of Naval Commissioners, in place since 1815, had become a common scapegoat for those critical of the navy, particularly in the 1830s. Generally, the board was blamed for lack of economy, poorly designed vessels, delays in fitting out ships, and nearly every shortcoming perceived in the navy. Critics suggested that their collective responsibility over the navy be supplanted by a system in which specialized areas of responsibility were assigned to individuals. The commissioners were replaced by a bureau system in 1842.

**The new system included five bureaus:**
Construction, Equipment and Repair; Yards and Docks; Ordnance and Hydrography; Provisions and Clothing; Medicine and Surgery.

At the same time a steam engineering office was established as well as an engineer corps. The bureau form of organization, with some modifications, remained in place until long after the Civil War.

The navy's methods of obtaining officers also came under increased scrutiny during the 1840s, particularly after the mutiny on the brig *Somers* (1842) and its aftermath. In this instance, a summary court martial had resulted in the hanging of two of the accused – both young naval apprentices on a practice cruise – under controversial circumstances. The apprentice program, which was intended to supplant or at least supplement the traditional midshipmen's on-the-job education, then came under fire. The program was popularly characterized as a method of palming off the family 'black sheep' on the service.

This event, plus the increasingly specialized, and technological nature of naval science brought more pressure to establish a systematic education for midshipmen. Under the urgings of men such as Matthew C Perry and others, a Naval Academy was organized in 1845 at Annapolis, Maryland. For the first time, a systematized education was available to would be naval officers.

By 1861 the United States Navy had achieved much since its baptism of fire in the French conflict of 1798. In many areas, such as the education of officers and the organization of the department, much needed structure had replaced traditional, but often erratic methods and ideas. It's officer corps had developed an esprit based on decades of cruising on station and the independence of action this engendered. They had explored much of the oceans of the world and excelled in seamanship to the extent that such vast opportunities had allowed. In fact, though this has not been studied systematically, the navy now had a core of seamen who also had faced the rigors of decades of serving in a small group of vessels on foreign station – a coterie of hardened 'salts' around which the navy would grow during the war years.

Finally, the navy had at last caught up to the current technology of steam propulsion, and was in the vanguard of the ordnance revolution of this era. These factors would weigh heavily in the service's response to the impending conflict.

On the negative side, two things were lacking. First was the

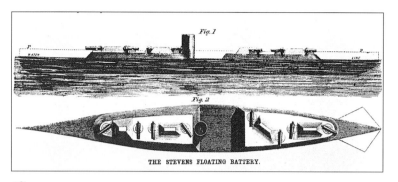

THE STEVENS FLOATING BATTERY.

'Stevens Battery'. Robert L Stevens and family, of New Jersey, were noted for their industry and inventions, and proposed an iron, armored, screw steamer to defend New York City. She was to attain 16 knots, be over 400 feet long, have water tanks to fill and lower her profile, and shell guns which loaded from apertures through the deck. Sporadic congressional funding did not keep up with the technology and resulting re-designs. By the Civil War the project had stalled and the vessel was never completed (*Scientific American*, February 1861)

reliance on single-ship duels and commerce raiding. The second shortcoming was less general but nearly fatal, and became obvious on 8 March 1862 at Hampton Roads, Virginia. The navy had too long ignored the technology of ironclad vessels and its late recognition of this nearly left the best of the old unarmored steam battlefleet at the mercy of an enemy ironclad, the ex-USS *Merrimack*, now CSS *Virginia*. Only the services of John Ericsson and the arrival of his *Monitor* – literally in the nick of time – saved the squadron at Hampton Roads and the Union blockade there.

The irony of the situation was dramatic: the staid old service was harried into meeting the challenge of a technology they had previously discounted, thrown at them by a navy which had not existed a year before. The naval aspect of the Civil War was the outworking of factors such as these.

# The navy and mid nineteenth-century US foreign policy

Both policy and the unbendable facts of geography served as fundamental pillars of American foreign policy for the first century of the nation's history. George Washington himself had sounded the theme of 'no entangling alliances' and neutrality had been vociferously defended particularly amidst the Napoleonic Wars when partisans of the French and English sought to sway the nation to their respective viewpoints.

Non-alignment was further strengthened in 1823, with President James Monroe's declaration that European interference in the western hemisphere would be unwelcome. This can be seen in context with the smoldering Latin American anti-monarchical and anti-colonial revolutions of that decade. That British policy echoed this sentiment was no coincidence, and therefore there was little danger that the small American navy would be called to enforce Mr Monroe's doctrine. In fact, the only serious nineteenth-century breech would be Maximilian's foray into Mexico while the United States was obsessed with the Civil War.

The salient geographical fact impinging on the role of the navy – and even its existence at all – was the protection provided by the oceans. Indeed, the distances had been part and parcel of the failure of Britain to retain – or regain – the colonies in the War of Independence and War of 1812 respectively. The geographical reality was sufficient to fuel the fires of those who saw navies as wasted expenses. President John Quincy Adams, for one, when dismissing the need for steam warships, questioned the necessity of having a navy at all. And that gentleman was from the seafaring state of Massachusetts. Thus there is little wonder that congressmen representing newly created states farther and farther into the hinterland echoed this view.

In any case, with no colonial empire, no formal international alliances, and little realistic expectation that a major European power would arrive as an enemy on an American beach, the navy's responsibilities were limited. The flag followed American citizens and mercantile interests abroad, and the navy stood by to insure that the rights, persons and property were unmolested in foreign jurisdictions. Along with this task came the less tangible one of maintaining an American presence and 'showing the flag' among the nations of the world.

# Foreign Navies: 1860

Though no foreign (i.e. European) adversary arose during the Civil War years, there was, at least up until late 1862, a distinct possibility that either Britain or France might ally themselves with the Confederacy, in part due to the much ballyhooed 'cotton diplomacy', as well as British and French complicity in fitting out raiders such as *Alabama*. Fortunately, this did not materialize.

However, as late as 1864, Secretary of the Navy Welles still felt it necessary to begin a program for a significant number of fast steam sloops designed specifically as commerce raiders. As the Confederacy had no commerce to speak of, these ships were obviously intended for a foreign conflict. When Emperor Maximilian appeared in Mexico, the bête noir of European interference in the hemisphere seemed to be at the doorstep.

With these factors in view, it might be well to present a short description of a selected group of foreign navies, as they were in 1860.

Great Britain in 1860 was not yet the ally she would become in the twentieth century. She was not, on the other hand, the ogre of the era of George III. Between these two extremes there was a certain affinity, yet not complete trust.

Merely a name list of the British navy's vessels in 1860 would be sufficient to make the point that their fleet was an overwhelming force. In specifics, the inventory included fifty-three steam ships of the line (60 to 131 guns and 2400 to 4200 tons), plus twenty-one on the ineffective list. (The United States had no steam liners.) There were 128 steam cruising vessels – corvettes, sloops and frigates – plus ten sailing ships of the line and an equal number of sailing frigates and sloops. Screw and paddle-wheel gunboats of 2 to 6 guns numbered 197.

During the years of the Civil War, twelve new ironclads were commissioned, totalling approximately 212 guns. These were ocean-going ships with broadside batteries. As will be seen, the American ironclads were almost exclusively coastal or river vessels.

In France, the fleet numbered thirty-seven screw liners of up to 130 guns each; fifteen screw frigates and eighty-four steam corvettes and sloops, plus at least twenty-five gunboats. The sailing fleet included eight ships of the line, twenty-seven frigates, and thirty-four corvettes and brigs.

Beginning with *Gloire* (1860), the French would have eleven ironclads in commission by 1865. Additionally, there would be seven new coastal defense floating batteries, over and above the five batteries constructed for the Crimean War. Finally, during the Civil War years, some thirteen new screw cruisers would be commissioned.

Again, the French navy was a formidable force. Though the US fleet would outnumber them in vessels by 1865, as will be seen, the majority of the American ships were hastily converted merchant ships suited for little more than their intended role: maintaining the blockade of southern coasts.

The Imperial Russian Navy was considered the third largest in this era. There were ten screw line-of-battle ships, nine screw frigates, and twenty-six screw sloops and corvettes. Between 1862 and 1865, four ironclads were built, two of which were coastal vessels. It is noteworthy that ten monitors based on John Ericsson's design were begun in 1863 and completed three years later.

In the western hemisphere, the most formidable navy other than that of the United States was that of Brazil. This consisted of fifteen steam sloops and twenty sailing ships. Eight steamers were under construction in 1860, and five ironclads were completed by 1865.

## THE UNION FLEET, MARCH 1861 (Serviceable Vessels)

| Vessel | Type | Guns | Location |
| --- | --- | --- | --- |
| Pawnee | screw sloop | 8 | Washington |
| Crusader | screw steamer | 8 | New York |
| Mohawk | screw steamer | 5 | New York |
| Supply | sail/storeship | 4 | New York |
| Sabine | sail/frigate | 50 | Pensacola |
| St Louis | sail/sloop | 20 | Pensacola |
| Brooklyn | screw sloop | 25 | Pensacola |
| Wyandotte | screw steamer | 5 | Pensacola |
| Macedonian | sail/sloop | 22 | Vera Cruz |
| Cumberland** | sail/sloop | 24 | Ord/Norfolk |
| Pocahontas | screw steamer | 5 | Ret fm Vera Cruz |
| Powhatan | paddle steamer | 11 | Ret fm Vera Cruz |
| Richmond | screw sloop | 16 | Medit. sqdn |
| Susquehanna | paddle sloop | 15 | Medit. sqdn |
| Iroquois | screw sloop | 6 | Medit. sqdn |
| Constellation | sail/sloop | 22 | Africa sqdn |
| Portsmouth | sail/sloop | 22 | Africa sqdn |
| Mohican | screw sloop | 6 | Africa sqdn |
| Mystic | screw steamer | 5 | Africa sqdn |
| Sumter | steamer | 5 | Africa sqdn |
| San Jacinto | screw sloop | 13 | Africa sqdn |
| Relief | storeship | 2 | Africa sqdn |
| Congress | sail/frigate | 50 | Brazil sqdn |
| Seminole | steam sloop | 5 | Brazil sqdn |
| John Adams | sail/sloop | 18 | East Indies |
| Hartford | screw sloop | 25 | East Indies |
| Dakota | screw sloop | 6 | East Indies |
| Niagara | steam sloop | 12 | Ret. fm Japan |
| Saratoga | sail/sloop | 18 | Africa |
| Pulaski | screw steamer | 1 | Brazil |

| Vessel | Type | Guns | Location |
| --- | --- | --- | --- |
| Saginaw | paddle steamer | 3 | East Indies |
| Michigan* | paddle steamer | 1 | Great Lakes |
| Saranac | paddle sloop | 9 | Pacific Sqdn |
| Lancaster | screw sloop | 25 | Pacific Sqdn |
| Potomac | sail/frigate | 50 | Ord/New York |
| St Lawrence | sail/frigate | 50 | Ord/New York |
| Santee | sail/frigate | 50 | Ord/New York |
| Savannah | sail/sloop | 24 | Ord/New York |
| Jamestown | sail/sloop | 22 | Ord/Philadelphia |
| Vincennes | sail/sloop | 18 | Ord/Boston |
| Marion | sail/sloop | 15 | Ord/Portsmouth |
| Dale | sail/sloop | 15 | Ord/Portsmouth |
| Preble | sail/sloop | 10 | Ord/Boston |
| Bainbridge | brig | 6 | Ord/Boston |
| Perry | brig | 9 | Ord/New York |
| Roanoke | steam frigate | 46? | Ord/New York |
| Colorado | steam frigate | 48 | Ord/Boston |
| Minnesota | steam frigate | 48 | Ord/Boston |
| Wabash | steam frigate | 48 | Ord/New York |
| Pensacola | screw sloop | 24 | Not Complete |
| Mississippi | paddle sloop | 12 | Ord/Boston |
| Water Witch | paddle sloop | 3 | Ord/Philadelphia |

\* Vessel remained on Great Lakes during war.

\*\* Towed from yard before yard was destroyed.

Ord: In ordinary at navy yard

## VESSELS IN ORDINARY/LOST AT NORFOLK NAVY YARD, APRIL 1861

| Vessel | Type | Guns |
| --- | --- | --- |
| Merrimack | steam frigate | 40 |
| Germantown | sail/sloop | 22 |
| Plymouth | sail/sloop | 22 |
| Dolphin | brig | 4 |
| Pennsylvania | ship of the line | 120 |
| United States | frigate | 44 |
| Columbus | ship of the line | |
| Delaware | ship of the line | |
| Raritan | frigate | |
| Columbia | frigate | |
| New York | unfinished ship of the line | |

**U**SS *Stonewall*. Lack of industrial infrastructure forced the Confederacy to look overseas for additional armored ships. *Stonewall* was the only one of several contracted vessels to reach American shores – and she was too late for the war.

## Confederate naval forces

The navy of the Confederate States of America was begun in late 1860 with a conglomerate of state navies. This 'force' amounted to little more than a few ex-United States revenue cutters, seized at the various port cities.

It is a matter of record that naval secretary Stephen A Mallory opted to build ironclads of an unknown quantity in 1860. He was convinced, however, that a great deal of resources would be wasted if used to construct a navy of conventional wooden ships, each of which might be less formidable than a likely Union adversary. Because the Union navy was at that juncture entirely composed of wooden vessels, Mallory concluded, despite opposition within the naval hierarchy, that a fleet of ironclads would automatically put the Union navy at a great, and possibly fatal, disadvantage.

A second emphasis was to be on commerce raiders on the high seas. Given the size of the Union merchant fleet (comparable to Great Britain's in that era), Mallory expected ocean cruisers to drive Union commerce from the oceans and result in pressure from commercial interests to end the war.

Finally, at the instigation of the more conservative elements

of the department, the Confederates began construction of a large number of unarmored, wooden gunboats. These were to number around one hundred and be available to defend the South's port cities.

These ambitious plans snagged on the paucity of resources – both of raw materials and industrial capacity – in the seceded states. Engines, boilers, and iron armor quickly became difficult to obtain, and slowed all aspects of warship construction significantly.

In an effort to overcome these problems, Mallory entered into a program whereby the Confederacy had numerous vessels, both armored and conventional, built in foreign yards. Though shortages of funds and effective diplomatic moves by the United States effectively short-circuited this program, a few exceedingly effective, or at least highly feared, vessels resulted; the most infamous being the Laird-built cruiser *Alabama*.

Blockade runners added another dimension to the Confederate naval effort. These fast vessels were important for the supplies they delivered to the Confederate army and civilian populace, as well as for the pressure they put upon the Union naval blockade forces.

The total number of vessels in the Confederate naval force remains a matter of judgement. A recent listing indicated over 400 vessels were in service, though most were hastily converted merchant ships or riverboats. Though a majority of the domestically built ironclads were not completed, and therefore cannot be counted as 'commissioned' vessels, the fact of their existence – finished or not – was often sufficient to cause major problems for the Union navy. Certainly the building of ironclads served to delay Union operations in several port cities until Union monitors were available to counter them. Similarly, the existence of commerce raiders, regardless of their effectiveness, served to draw forces away from the blockade and from other Union coastal operations.

In all categories, except possibly riverboats, the number of Confederate effectives was numbered in the hands-full. Of about twenty-nine ironclads laid down, less than a dozen actually saw service, and fewer actually encountered a Union foe. The four most effective were the first *Virginia* (ex-*Merrimack*), the *Tennessee*, the *Albemarle* and the *Arkansas*. The first mounted 10 guns, and sank two major warships before being countered by Ericsson's *Monitor*. It is also claimed that her very existence immobilized the Union army for two months in early 1862. The *Tennessee* took on the entire Union fleet at Mobile Bay, the *Arkansas* traumatized the Union's Mississippi squadron for a short time in July 1862, and the *Albemarle* accomplished the same in eastern North Carolina in 1864.

About nine commerce raiders made the high seas dangerous for American merchant vessels, as well as for a few US Navy warships. *Alabama* never entered a Confederate port and took sixty-four merchant prizes worth $6.5 million in her two-year career. Though ordered not to engage naval vessels, she sank the gunboat *Hatteras* off Galveston, then met her match in the USS *Kearsarge* off Cherbourg in 1864. Second most dangerous was *Shenandoah*, whose year-long world cruise netted thirty-eight prizes. She surrendered only after the Confederate government collapsed. Both of these were built in Great Britain.

In a program initiated by Matthew Fontaine Maury, former Union navy scientist and major figure in the Confederate Navy Department, some one hundred conventional steam gunboats were to be built. These were to defend the port cities and were 100 feet long mounting 2 guns each. In the end only about a dozen gunboats of any kind were completed and most of these were conversions from merchant steamers.

Numbering the blockade runners would be impossible, as any ship fast or lucky enough to elude the blockaders qualified, whether privately or government owned. It is estimated that 200 vessels were built to be blockade runners. Of these, around 120 actually saw service in that role.

In a spate of technological innovation, the Confederacy sponsored several semi-submersibles, usually termed 'Davids', and armed with spar torpedoes. These were no more than 60 feet long and accomplished little of significance, with one exception: *H L Hunley* attacked and sank the steam sloop *Housatonic* at Charleston in 1864 – that vessel becoming the first victim of a 'submarine'.

The balance of the Confederate forces were either small gunboats or riverboats. The latter were hastily converted from merchant steamers and sometimes given rams. Several of the latter were sunk during the Battle of Memphis in 1862.

If many of the vessels were substandard, the caliber of the men was not. Charles Read, of the raider *Tacony*, entered the harbor of Portland, Maine, and captured the revenue cutter *Caleb Cushing*. Henry K Stevens took the ram *Arkansas* through thirty vessels of the Union river fleet near Vicksburg in 1862. Only an engine breakdown finally doomed that vessel. Franklin Buchanan – with no hope of victory – took the *Tennessee* into the bay against Farragut's fleet, wooden and iron.

In all, the Confederate Navy was marked by accomplishments far out of proportion to its numbers, both of men and ships. In spirit, if not materiel, they were a fitting match for Abraham Lincoln's navy.

# A summary of the naval history of the Civil War

## *1861*

On 12 April 1861 Confederate forces fired on federal-held Fort Sumter in the harbor of Charleston, South Carolina. President Lincoln then called for volunteers to put down the rebellion and for a blockade of the southern coast. At that moment, available Union naval forces in Atlantic coastal waters numbered less than ten, with the balance of the active fleet – less than thirty vessels – returning from foreign stations. Under Secretary of the Navy Gideon Welles and Assistant Secretary Gustavus V Fox, a vast expansion was undertaken, including conversion of merchant ships for blockade duty and construction of purpose-built warships for the blockade, coastal and river operations and cruising at sea. The former two objectives were part and parcel of the so-called Anaconda Plan: a strict blockade of Southern commerce accompanied by a major thrust aimed at dividing the south along the line of the Mississippi River. Cruising vessels were found necessary early on, when the Confederacy commissioned commerce raiders to prey on the Union merchant fleet.

In the Mississippi Valley the Union army initiated the campaign which eventually wrested that river from the Confederate States. Inevitably, river transport and gunboats were needed for this campaign, and, with ad hoc advice from naval experts, gunboats were built or converted from merchant riverboats. In accord with the latest technology, many of these were iron-armored, and, in fact were in action before the appearance of Ericsson's more famous *Monitor*.

Along the southern coast, the war began with minor naval clashes along the Potomac River, as well as the initiation of the blockade itself. The latter began with token forces stationed at the entrance to each major port city, with vessels added as they were acquired. Eventually the navy numbered around 600 ships, a majority of which were blockading vessels. This summary is not an appropriate place to discuss the details and effectiveness of the blockading squadrons, only to relate that over 1500 vessels were taken, valued at over $30 million. Furthermore, it resulted in forcing the Confederates to develop faster and 'stealthier' runners to elude the Union gauntlet.

The only major naval operations of 1861 were the capture of

potential naval bases near Hatteras, North Carolina, and Port Royal, South Carolina. Both were taken by Union fleets which met little opposition.

The need for these bases was underlined by the capture of the massive Union navy yard at Norfolk, Virginia, a loss made more ominous by the presence of the modern steam frigate *Merrimack* at that place. Though partially burned, her hull and engine became the basis for the building of the Confederate casemate ironclad *Virginia*. This turn of events forced the Union navy to respond with the construction of three disparate, experimental ironclads, one of which was Ericsson's turret vessel *Monitor*. As 1861 ended, a virtual race existed to complete these vessels. For the Union, the stakes were immense: with no ironclads to counter the threat, their wooden-hulled blockading squadrons would be short work for any iron-armored vessel.

## 1862

The combined army-navy campaign in the west began with the capture of Fort Henry and Fort Donelson in northern Tennessee. Navy-commanded ironclads and other converted gunboats played key parts in these engagements, under Andrew H Foote, with army forces commanded by Ulysses S Grant. These forces cooperated, forcing their way south towards the Confederate stronghold of Vicksburg, Mississippi; in the process taking river fortifications at such places as Island No. 10 and Fort Pillow, and defeating a rebel fleet at Memphis, Tennessee, in mid 1862.

During the same period, a fleet under David G Farragut threatened New Orleans, the most important southern port. Supported by mortar boats, Farragut's squadron fought past the defending forts and captured the city in April 1862. Shortly thereafter, Baton Rouge fell, leaving the stretch of river between Port Hudson, Louisiana and Vicksburg still in Confederate hands. The campaign for Vicksburg now absorbed most of the Union resources on the river. Though the city's defending batteries could be passed by on the river, a land-side approach was necessary to besiege the town. Grant, with navy forces under David Dixon Porter, cooperated in a year-long series of stratagems to bring about surrender of the city. Further impeding Federal efforts was the *Arkansas*, a crude but effective rebel ironclad, which at one point took on nearly the entire flotilla. She was finally destroyed in mid 1862.

In the east, the ironclad 'race' ended with the appearance of the *Virginia* (ex *Merrimack*) among the blockading fleet at Hampton Roads, Virginia. The 8 March battle was a Union disaster, with

*Virginia* destroying two sailing frigates with impunity and threatening the balance of the wooden-hulled Union fleet. The impending catastrophe was averted by the arrival of the *Monitor*, fresh from her builders. In a remarkable three-hour engagement – the first between ironclad vessels – neither adversary was seriously damaged and the Battle of Hampton Roads was over. Though the blockade was saved, *Virginia*'s existence stymied Union forces, both army and navy, for two months, contributing to the failure of George B McClellan's Peninsula Campaign, the object of which was the Confederate capital of Richmond, Virginia.

The success of the *Monitor* had a major effect on the course of the naval war. 'Monitor fever' claimed the north and resulted in the construction of many improved versions of the original, to the exclusion of any other types of ironclad vessels. Unrealistically, the monitors were expected to be the naval panacea for the war – able to take on both enemy ironclads as well as fortifications.

On the high seas, two of the most dangerous Confederate commerce raiders began their careers in 1862. The CSS *Alabama* went to sea in July 1862, and the *Florida* followed a month later. Both were built for the Confederacy in Britain, technically circumventing neutrality laws. The resulting diplomatic crisis nearly brought about war between the US and Britain.

## 1863

Coastal operations for the latter part of 1862 had been hampered by the construction of Confederate ironclads in various port cities – threats for which the Union as yet had only one answer, the original *Monitor*. It was not until late 1862 that the first of the 'improved' *Passaic* class monitors was commissioned and plans were begun for a major effort against Charleston, South Carolina. In April 1863, Samuel F Dupont took nine ironclads, seven of them monitors, into the strongly defended harbor. The vessels were heavily outgunned – 32 versus 70 on shore – and withdrew with significant damage. Later in the year renewed efforts were made, using combined naval and ground forces. The city did not fall until early 1865.

In the west, the year began with a Union setback. Galveston, Texas, which had been captured by a combined naval and army force in October 1862 was re-taken by a well executed surprise attack on the first day of 1863. Two Union vessels were lost and over 400 men in the attack, and the city remained in rebel hands for the balance of the war.

Along the Mississippi, the Vicksburg Campaign continued,

with Grant's forces at one point digging a canal to facilitate troop movements. Naval forces closely supported all these operations and diverted enemy forces with engagements such as that at Grand Gulf, Mississippi in April. Vicksburg was besieged by both army ordnance and naval mortars in May 1863 and surrendered on 4 July 1863. This defeat, along with that on the previous day at Gettysburg, Pennsylvania, marked the turning point in the war for the Confederacy.

## 1864

The Red River Campaign involved a large portion of the river fleet in early 1864. Ostensibly mounted to destroy enemy supply depots and the cotton industry in Louisiana and Texas, the effort, which also involved over 25,000 men, nearly dissolved when the level of the Red River fell precipitously, threatening to ground the fleet. The construction of a makeshift dam prevented that disaster but the campaign itself accomplished little.

Mobile, Alabama, the last major port still open on the Gulf of Mexico, was the next Union objective. On 5 August, David G Farragut took his wooden vessels and a vanguard of monitors past Fort Morgan and Confederate floating mines into Mobile Bay, then met and defeated the ram *Tennessee*. Along with his victory at New Orleans, this triumph sealed Farragut's reputation for posterity.

On the Atlantic, the Union met another setback with the appearance of the rebel ironclad *Albemarle*. In April, this vessel defeated a four-vessel Federal squadron and allowed the re-capture of Plymouth, North Carolina. *Albemarle* remained dominant in the area until October, when a small boat expedition under William B Cushing sunk her in a brazen point-blank spar torpedo attack.

Once *Albemarle* was removed, plans were set in motion to take the last major port on the Atlantic coast: Wilmington, North Carolina. Blockade runners had favored Wilmington due to the short run to Bermuda and her rail connections to Richmond. In December 1864, a combined army-navy force attacked the city's defences at Fort Fisher. Though this was the largest American naval fleet assembled to that date, it failed due to poor interservice cooperation. A second attempt would come early in 1865.

This year also saw the first successful wartime use of undersea warfare. In July, a hand-powered semi-submersible *H L Hunley* attacked and sank the Union sloop *Housatonic* at anchor off Charleston, using a spar torpedo. Unfortunately, the Confederate vessel sank with her victim.

At sea, the last of the major cruisers, *Shenandoah*, became active

Confederate 'David'. Several semi-submersibles were built for Confederate service, intended to be armed with spar torpedoes. Only one, *H L Hunley*, successfully sank a Union vessel. This example was photographed at Charleston after the war. (US Navy)

in October, some four months after the end of the infamous *Alabama*. *Alabama*, in twenty-one months, had taken sixty-four prizes and driven hundreds of ships to foreign flags. She was finally confronted by the steam sloop *Kearsarge* at Cherbourg in June 1864, and was sunk in battle within sight of the French coast. After the war, an international tribunal on the '*Alabama* claims' declared that 'neutral' Britain was liable for the losses incurred by the British-built vessel.

## 1865

A second attack on Fort Fisher initiated this year. In this instance the huge fleet methodically destroyed the fort, accompanied by both army and navy ground forces. This ended Wilmington's career as a blockade runner's haven and shut down the South's last major port city (other than besieged Charleston).

In Virginia at Trent's Reach, Confederate ironclads made their final sortie. Two of the three ironclads grounded during the attack and fire from shore batteries and the monitor Onondaga completed the rout. This marked the last major naval fight of the War Between the States. A final postscript came with the surrender of the last Confederate vessel – the cruiser *Shenandoah* – in European waters in November 1865.

# Chapter Two
# ORGANIZATION AND ADMINISTRATION

The growth of the Navy Department to its present immensity has been virtually a twentieth-century phenomenon. It was presaged by the 'new navy' of the 1880s and its technology, and necessitated by the emergence of the true blue-water battlefleet and its role in an active foreign policy.

From the establishment of the department in the 1790s to the late 1880s the organization varied somewhat in structure, but little in actual numbers of individuals – employees and office holders. As will be seen, even the enormous undertaking of putting down the secession in 1861 through 1865 saw relatively little growth in the department. Certainly the organizational growth did not reflect in proportion the number of men and ships employed for that conflict.

Amazingly, the Secretary of the Navy had operated the department single-handedly until 1815, when Congress decreed the appointment of a Board of Naval Commissioners as advisors to the Secretary. Until replaced by the bureau system, these three appointees were charged with the 'civil' affairs of the department: mainly the building, repair and equipping of ships, as well as superintending the various yards and stations. The Secretary retained operational control of the squadrons and looked to the board members for advice on naval matters.

The somewhat amorphous character of the commissioners' duties gave way to the more structured bureau system in 1842. Of the five bureau chiefs, two could be civilians: the head of the Bureau of Construction, Equipment and Repairs, was to be an experienced naval constructor and that of the Bureau of Provisions and Clothing could be either a civilian or naval officer

(the post reverted to naval officers only in 1849.) The chief of the Bureau of Medicine and Surgery was appointed from the ranks of naval physicians, and the heads of the Bureau of Navy Yards and Docks, and the Bureau of Ordnance and Hydrography, were both naval officers. There were no set term limits to these appointments, which were made by the President and confirmed by Congress.

Thirty employees rounded out the Navy Department staff in Washington at the time of the creation of the bureaux. Twenty-four were clerks, nine in the Secretary's office itself. Two draftsmen were hired, one for yards and docks, one for the construction and repair bureau. A civil engineer was employed for the Bureau of Yards and Docks, and an assistant surgeon was appointed for the medical arm of the department. By 1860 the clerical staff had been increased to forty-two.[1]

The responsibilities of the individual bureau were denoted by their names. Administration of the yards and docks was carried out through the yard commandants who were senior naval officers. The chief subordinate officers of the Bureau of Construction, Equipment, and Repairs were the naval constructors at the yards, who designed and supervised the building of vessels and saw to their equipping, fitting out and repair. Timber agents in the south also fell under the chief of this department, as well as the Naval Asylum in Philadelphia. The steam engineering corps began its administrative life under this bureau. Navy agents on shore – at yards, stations and depots – carried out the field work for the Bureau of Provisions and Clothing, dealing with civilian suppliers and contracts. Their shipboard counterparts were the pursers.

Naval charts and information was disseminated by the Bureau of Ordnance and Hydrography, which also was responsible for the ammunition magazines and other supplies at the yards. The Naval Observatory and the Naval Academy, both created in the 1840s, fell under the purview of this bureau. Naval medicine, including purchasing of supplies, supervising of personnel and operating the naval hospitals fell under the Bureau of Medicine and Surgery.

Though not part of the Navy Department proper, the administration of fiscal responsibility should be mentioned here. In 1817, the work of auditing the government's departmental accounts was concentrated in the Treasury Department. Specifically, the office of the Fourth Auditor was tasked with maintaining scrutiny over disbursements of appropriated navy funds. This arrangement held throughout the Civil War era.

A final pair of naval policy-related bodies were the naval affairs committees of the Senate and House of Representatives in the US Congress. Though standing committees, they were called into session sporadically, usually to the irritation of the department. The members of the committees had no direct authority over the navy, but of course had significant power in terms of public influence and wielded votes which could approve or deny congressional appropriations for the department. Often the force of the committees was exerted indirectly, sometimes in the form of public hearings held to investigate some alleged abuse or irregularity in the department, or, more specifically, in the navy yards. The yards, and the amount of work done in them, drew considerable congressional attention, particularly in election years, as the employees of these establishments were also voting constituents. Of course, it goes without saying that there were times that the committee's activities, dominated by a certain political agenda or party, were merely cudgels aimed at the party in power.

Influential constituents also targeted their particular committee members when the navy was not responding as readily to their desires as they wished. In this era, these constituents were often inventors or entrepreneurs seeking to foist their inventions or schemes on the service. More often than not the result of such interference was counterproductive, though the navy's resentment at outside interference did nothing to ameliorate these situations.

The above describes the organization and administration of the navy at the outbreak of the Civil War. Before the war, the only variations on its administrative character were committees, usually composed of naval officers, detailed to a particular short term project or need. As examples, the 1850s had seen committees charged with investigating alleged improprieties in the navy yards,

and with recommending reductions in force in the officer ranks. There were no standing committees in the department.

On 4 March 1861 Gideon Welles took office as Secretary of the Navy, and within six weeks Confederate guns had opened the conflict at Fort Sumter. Welles, a dour Connecticut Yankee, found the department in disarray. In addition to the growing number of resignations of pro-Southern employees and naval officers, the administrative organization itself was not large or flexible enough to deal with a crisis of the magnitude to come.

Gideon Welles himself, though a competent administrator, had had limited naval experience, having been a newspaperman – though a politically astute one – at the time of his appointment. He had, from 1846 to 1849, been chief of the Bureau of Provisions and Clothing, a position in which he no doubt became familiar with naval terminology, and purchasing and contract pro-

Gideon Welles, Secretary of the Navy. A former newspaperman with experience as a naval bureau chief in the 1840s, Welles was a competent administrator, who compensated for his limited knowledge of in-depth naval affairs by selecting efficient subordinates. (USAMHI)

cedures. But these had little bearing on the demands being made upon him now. His political acumen and, among other things, his ability to write, would work to his advantage in Lincoln's cabinet. His weaknesses in other areas would have to be compensated by selecting knowledgeable and efficient subordinates. Fortunately, Welles, for the most part, was a good judge of character and abilities, and was not hampered by any compulsion to micro-manage. Only this aptitude in delegating authority enabled him to accomplish what the war required of the navy.

At the time of his appointment, the Secretary's staff consisted entirely of clerks, numbering fourteen, plus two messengers. Heading the staff, was the Chief Clerk, making some $2200 per year. William Faxon filled this position from August 1861 through the end of the war. The Chief Clerk was in charge of the records of the department, its correspondence, and handled personnel matters within the staff. With the subordinant disbursing clerk, he handled the department's budget and spending. Though a long-time friend of Welles, Faxon was one of the few civilian employees who qualified for his position by examination; in contrast to straightforward political appointees.[2] (The civil service examination, government-wide, was decades in the future at this juncture in American history.)

The department was housed in a building immediately west of the White House. During the war, a third storey and new wing were added to the building, to house the growing number of staff. In addition to Welles, the Assistant Secretary (discussed below) and Faxon, the number of clerks and draftsmen grew from thirty-nine to sixty-six during the war years.

The proximity to the President's home is mentioned here to point out that President Lincoln was a frequent visitor to the department during the war. He would often be seen in one of the bureaux, as one eyewitness described, in his 'carpet slippers' and shawl, particularly when major events were in the offing or one of the ranking officers was reporting. Thus Lincoln's role in the navy's war may well have been more influential than a formal organizational chart would have indicated. It is known that at times of great activity, the President would issue naval orders in his own hand.[3]

Lincoln's frequent and unheralded presence also serves to illustrate the level of complexity of the American government and its war effort during the conflict. It would be the next century before the layers of bureaucracy — military and civilian — so common today, would be ensconced in Washington and its environs.

One of Welles' first acts as Secretary was to augment the small bureaucracy he had inherited, with the appointment of an 'office of detail' to assist him in determining the most appropriate assignments for the senior naval officers, particularly in regard to their sympathies with the seceding states. Commodore Silas Stringham, a solid New Englander, filled this need initially, then was replaced by a board of three officers, who not only advised in this area, but were charged with training the hundreds of volunteer officers who poured into the service during the emergency.

While the office of detail dealt with the indirect repercussions of the impending conflict, the next organizational creation was strictly in response to the war itself. This was officially denominated the Commission of Conference, popularly known as the Blockade Strategy Board, which proved to be one of the most important boards of the naval war.

This group was composed of Professor Alexander Dallas Bache, eminent scientist and superintendent of the Coast Survey, Major J G Barnard of the Army Engineering Corps, Captain Samuel F DuPont, and Commander Charles H Davis. They reported on hydrographic, geographic and topographic characteristics of the southern coast in relation to proposed naval operations, and made recommendations on implementation of the blockade, including possible locations for coaling and watering depots. It met several times through September 1861 and submitted information and recommendations to both the cabinet and Chief of the Army, General Winfield Scott. One of the less productive recommendations of this board was the Stone Fleet — the sinking of old sailing vessels to block various southern ports — done despite the warnings that the currents would swiftly dislodge the hulks and nullify the effort.

With the outbreak of fighting and Lincoln's call for a blockade of the southern coast, Secretary Welles found himself foundering in a deluge of work, attempting to get the navy moving despite decades of peacetime encrustation. The 3500 miles of southern coast, riddled with inlets, bays and estuaries, required blockading vessels. These ships were to be acquired by construction or purchase, and Welles looked for agents familiar with merchant ships to act for the department at the major ports. After one expensive mistake with a dishonest middleman, Welles turned to his brother-in-law, George D Morgan, a successful New York merchant, for assistance. Morgan was exceedingly effective in this task, purchasing over ninety vessels from sixty-five different firms in six months. When Congress later 'investigated' the alleged impropriety and nepotism in this temporary appointment (as well as the small commission Morgan received for his work), it was proved that Morgan had gotten extremely reasonable prices for his purchases, and that the vessels were proving useful to the navy. Welles' trust in him had not been misplaced.[4]

With Morgan and others acting for the department in vessel purchases, Welles could turn to pressing needs elsewhere. However, as was reflected by his reliance on Morgan, Welles found that he was in need of a right-hand man to deal with the more technical aspects of the office. As is the American tradition, the cabinet officers were political appointees rather than professionals in the requisite field, and Welles was a journalist, not a trained naval officer. Fortunately for the Union cause, the Secretary found help near at hand.

Early in 1861, Gustavus Vasa Fox, a woollen mill executive and former naval officer, had submitted a proposal for an expedition to relieve Fort Sumter in Charleston Harbor. Through no fault of his own the effort was a fiasco. However, his aggressiveness and knowledge of naval affairs had impressed Welles and he was subsequently appointed Chief Clerk of the department. Fox's family

Gustavus Vasa Fox, Assistant Secretary of the Navy. Fox was the perfect complement to Welles: a man with considerable practical maritime experience and the ability, and energy, to deal with the many aspects of the daily affairs of the department. A confirmed supporter of monitors, his enthusiasm possibly overrode caution in that area. (US Navy)

connections did him no harm either: his brother-in-law was Lincoln's Postmaster General. Welles saw to it that the post of Assistant Secretary of the Navy was created by Congress, and on 1 August, Fox was appointed to that position.

Fox proved to be the perfect complement to Welles, with the latter dealing with the political and general policy areas, and Fox playing in effect the 'Chief of Naval Operations'. At times Fox, who had had eighteen years in the navy including sea service during the Mexican War, actually overruled Welles and indeed had a closer hand in both determining strategy and implementing it than did the Secretary.

Despite this, it appears that neither Fox nor Welles considered Fox's actions in any way insubordinate. In fact, Welles appears to have positively welcomed Fox's input and expertise. It is also evident that their contemporaries quickly recognized the respective roles of each man in the department, though they were never officially defined.

Shortly after Fox's appointment, a series of significant executive bodies were created to deal with wartime exigencies. As it was self-evident that the navy facilities could furnish only a small percentage of the war vessels needed, contracting through civilian shipbuilders would supply the balance of the purpose-built warships. Consequently, in July 1861 the navy set up an office in New York City specifically to oversee dealings with engine and vessel builders. This office would draft and supply plans and specifications to contractors, and periodically inspect progress at the various yards and manufactories. Later, as operations and construction burgeoned on the western rivers, a comparable office was opened in St Louis, Missouri. In each instance, the office was headed by a senior retired officer. The New York office was run by Rear Admiral Francis Gregory; the western office by Commodore J B Hull. These offices would abruptly mushroom in significance after the appearance of *Monitor*, as none of the navy yards had the machinery to build iron-hulled vessels or Ericsson turrets. Eventually the original purpose would become lost on the public, and the New York office at least would be dubbed the 'monitor bureau'. It employed as many personnel as the remainder of the navy's bureaux combined. In addition there were forty-five to fifty naval officers stationed as liaisons and inspectors at the various contractor's shipyards or engineering firms.[5]

These offices were an anomaly, both geographically and organizationally. Though tasked with steam-vessel design responsibilities, they were not part of, or answerable to, the Bureau of Construction, Equipment and Repair (or later, to the Bureau of Construction and

Repair and the Bureau of Steam Engineering). This situation remained benign as long as the bureau dealt with routine matters such as the copying and transmitting of machinery plans and quality control at the builders. It was when the New York office began designing its own vessels that this lack of oversight reared its head. The result was the disaster of the Light Draft Monitors.

This cautionary tale began with the need for monitors for the western rivers, where extremely light draft was of prime importance on shallow streams. John Ericsson submitted a rough plan for a turretted vessel to meet these needs, leaving the details to be worked out by the department. Alban Stimers, a young and ambitious engineer attached to the 'monitor bureau', proceeded to complete the working drawings.

Beginning with Ericsson's drawings, Stimers proceeded to 'improve' on what Ericsson had intended to be a simple, inexpensive vessel, introducing water tanks and a pumping system intended to raise or lower the vessel's profile and freeboard. These and other changes were introduced, later investigations revealed, with only cursory review by more senior engineers. Apparently the heads of both the Bureau of Steam Engineering and of the Bureau of Construction and Repair assumed that John Ericsson had studied and approved Stimers' work. Ericsson, on the contrary, felt that his original concept had been destroyed and had disassociated himself with Stimers' version of his plans.[6]

In any event, it was found after the first launch that the entire class of twenty vessels was exceedingly overweight, and would require extensive modifications just to float. At no less than $500,000 for each vessel – more than the cost of a major warship of that era – this miscarriage cost the government no less than $10 million, a fantastic sum for the time.

Fortunately, the implications of this imbroglio for the department were mooted by the end of the war. It seems that the situation may well have been prevented had the 'monitor bureau' fallen directly under one of the established arms of the department.

Another instance of a body independent of the bureaux was a temporary committee on ironclads. The genesis of this group can be traced to the loss of Gosport (Norfolk) Navy Yard and the steam frigate *Merrimack* at that place. The department had paid little attention to the subject of ironclads until it was bruited about that the Confederacy had begun the reconstruction of the steam frigate into the casemate ironclad *Virginia*. In point of fact, actual construction on the vessel was begun in July, and the Union's board was formed on 3 August 1861.

In this context it is instructional to note the contrasting meth-

ods of the Confederate and Union naval departments. It seems that the rebel leadership, in the person of Stephen Mallory, simply made straightforward decisions, with little resort to bureacratic skulduggery. Welles, in contrast, inevitably formed a committee. In the case of the Ironclad Board, in July Welles asked Congress to authorize a committee to investigate the subject and authorization came a month later.

This board was composed of Commodore Joseph Smith, Captain Hiram Paulding, and Commander C H Davis. These gentlemen were to study the armored floating batteries used at the Crimea, and other previous ironclad ideas, and evaluate proposals for ironclads to be built for the navy.

Given the technological aspect of their mandate, the composition of this board is puzzling. For one, the aging Paulding had a reputation for opposition to steam technology in the navy. Equally aged was Smith, who would later press Ericsson to erect a complete sailing rig on the *Monitor*. Also, no naval constructors were included, nor were men such as Captain John Dahlgren, an expert on modern ordnance and certainly one who was cognizant of the latest in armored vessel development.

The committee completed their work and reported on 16

**C**ommander Charles H Davis was one of the members of the 'Blockade Board' – Welles' committee dedicated to studying the southern coast and recommending the navy's strategy in instituting the blockade. (US Navy)

September. Though couching their report in extremely diffident terms, reiterating their general unfamiliarity with the subject, etc, they selected three of seventeen proposed vessels for contracts. One of these was Ericsson's *Monitor*; a second would become the *New Ironsides*. These two selections belie their collective claims of lack of expertise. Certainly their confidence in Ericsson's exceedingly strange ship was an act of faith, and one which would have an astonishing impact on the course of the war.[7] Furthermore, *New Ironsides* proved to be probably the most useful single armorclad of the conflict. The third choice was not as felicitous: it would become the *Galena*, a total failure as an armored vessel. In all, the committee made some astounding achievements in six weeks, while the iron adversary grew in Norfolk. The committee's celerity enabled Ericsson to follow with his speedy, nearly miraculous construction of the *Monitor* in time to meet and parry the CSS *Virginia* at Hampton Roads the following March.

Yet another ironclad committee was formed in 1861: in this instance to study and report on the Stevens Battery. Five men composed this board, among them Joseph Henry, Secretary of the Smithsonian Institute. The object of their enquiries was an experimental iron-hulled armorclad begun in the 1840s by the prominent and inventive Stevens family of New Jersey, and partially underwritten with tax money. The original plan was advanced for its day, and the vessel, had it been completed, would have been the most powerful warship in existence. However, advances in iron and steam engineering and gunnery in the next decades had outstripped the Stevens' ability to update the vessel even on the stocks.

The committee was to evaluate the utility of completing the vessel for wartime use. Their report was negative, noting, among other things, that the ship would be too deep for operating on the southern coast and that its length to breadth ratio was excessive. The project was shelved, as far as the navy was concerned, though the inventors continued to press their claims for another ten years.[8]

With these matters of ships and ironclads in hand, yet another board was formed to deal with a sensitive personnel matter: enforced retirement. To date, there had not been a statutory retirement age, resulting in an increasingly superannuated officer list. Some commanders were over sixty; some lieutenants as old as fifty. In peacetime, such men could be shunted to light duty; in wartime, they stood in lieu of younger, more efficient officers.

Welles' Retirement Board met in October, 1861 and proceeded to implement a retirement act, which included voluntary retirement at forty years service, and reduced pay (and ineligibility for promotion) for retirees. In December 1861, further legislation

**J**ohn Ericsson, inventor and designer of the *Monitor*. Though not part of the department, his influence, as well as that of his followers, permeated the entire Union naval effort. (US Navy)

instituted mandatory retirement at sixty-two or forty-five years service. Shore duty was available for retirees.[9]

With these boards in place in mid 1861, the department dealt with the immediate wartime contingencies: meeting the legalities of the blockade with newly acquired vessels; putting in motion a response to the Confederate ironclad building in Virginia; instituting an entity to deal with the coming deluge of contracts for new vessels and their machinery; determining the outlines of blockade strategy and proposing outposts on the southern coasts; and, on the personnel front, determining the loyalty of the officer corps, and relieving that body of the aged and infirm.

Another year would pass until further needs would arise which would require special dispensations by the department. This time the needs would reflect wartime experience, as well as longer term goals for the department and the navy.

The fight at Hampton Roads, and the success of a vessel built in a civilian shipyard, at one and the same instant pointed up both a long term direction for the department as well as the deficiency which could (and, as history shows, did) impede the progress of the navy on that course. The *Monitor* was an iron vessel, only the

Commodore Silas Stringham. A solid New Englander, Stringham assisted Welles in sorting out the strengths and sympathies of the men in the officer corps and later commanded the Atlantic Blockading Squadron. (US Navy)

fourth such in the history of the US Navy.[10] All were built in civilian shipyards because the service had no facilities for iron shipbuilding. Though this war could be fought with wood, and hybrid iron and wood steam vessels, it was evident that any future foreign conflict would call for vessels to match such behemoths as Britain's iron-hulled *Warrior*, a ship which would have been impossible to construct in a US Navy dockyard.

With this in mind, Welles lobbied Congress to accede to the idea of establishing a new navy yard, one which could be established and planned from the outset to contain the foundries, machine shops and machinery for the building of iron ships and ironclads. The city of Philadelphia had offered to donate 900-acre League Island for that purpose, and two sites in New England were also under consideration, with each of the three supported by influential friends in Congress.

A six-member board was appointed to consider all the proposed sites. Despite Welles' stated bias towards League Island, the support of the board was split between this and another tract at New London, Connecticut. Though the majority favored the latter place, Welles tabled their recommendation, and Congress was equally unable to agree. The Pennsylvania site was approved in the

end, but only as the war was drawing to a close, and, consequently, the new yard contributed little to the war effort.

Of more importance to the immediate needs of the service was an act dated 16 July 1862, designed to overhaul the navy's rank structure, and bring it into line with the army's system, as well as provide higher ranks commensurate with the growing size of the fleet. For the first time in the navy's history, the title of admiral was authorized, with nine rear admirals to be made service-wide. Additionally, the ranks of ensign, lieutenant commander and commodore were created, totalling nine grade levels, the same number as the army, which at this time ended with lieutenant general. Before the end of the war, the vice admiral rank was created.

Another provision of this act was the institution of a Promotion Board, to determine the men qualified for the new grades. The board, composed of five captains, was to use seniority as their major consideration for all grades below rear admiral. Other criteria, among them genius and skill were to play larger roles in the selections for the highest ranks during wartime. According to the act, a promotion board was to sit every four years. Later, in 1864, examinations were added to the requirements for all promotions below the grade of commodore, and advancement within the grade was allowed on the basis of heroism in combat.[11]

Even as the increase in grade levels enhanced the navy's ability to assign ranks commensurate with the number of levels of responsibility in the fleet, Secretary Welles saw that an expansion in the number of administrative bureaux would enable the service to deal more efficiently with growing specialities in the department. Consequently, with the passage of an act of 5 July 1862, the number of bureaux was increased to eight. From the old Bureau of Equipment and Repairs came three entities: Equipment and Recruiting; Construction and Repair; and Steam Engineering. The Bureau of Ordnance and Hydrography, surely a mismatch in any case, was reorganized into two: the Bureau of Ordnance and the Bureau of Navigation. Only one of the bureaux was to have a civilian head: that of Construction and Repair was to be a naval constructor. A paymaster of over ten years service was to head the Provisions and Clothing department; a chief engineer was to fill the leading position at the steam engineering branch.

The act further provided for an assistant chief for the Bureau of Ordnance and a civil engineer in the Bureau of Yards and Docks. A small increase in number of draftsmen and clerks was also part of the act, making a total of fifty.

Each of the wartime department heads, as one authority put it, was 'safe and conservative, rather than brilliant and aggressive'.[12]

John Lenthall, Chief of the Bureau of Construction and Repair. Lenthall remained at his post until after the war, although he was not a acolyte of John Ericsson and his monitors. (US Navy)

Admiral John A Dahlgren, Chief of the Bureau of Ordnance, pioneered the guns bearing his name, from 12-pounders to 20-inch shell guns. He later commanded the South Atlantic Blockading Squadron in its operations against Charleston, South Carolina. (US Navy)

Joseph Smith had the longest tenure, serving from 1846 to 1869 at the Bureau of Yards and Docks. Horatio Bridge was chief of Provisions and Clothing from 1854 to 1869; William Whelan remained at Medicine and Surgery from 1853 through the war. The only major changes in leadership occurred in the Ordnance branch, which was led first by G A Magruder, who resigned to join the Confederacy, then by John A Dahlgren, followed by Henry A Wise.

By far the most controversial head was Benjamin F Isherwood, the engineer-in-chief. He was by all accounts, an energetic and dynamic leader, with both a scientific and practical mind. This combination enabled him to realize that the strict application of scientific principles in steam propulsion was likely to produce more complexities in the steam plant than the wartime influx of poorly educated engineers could deal with efficiently. Unfortunately, Isherwood was also ambitious, outspoken and not a friend of John Ericsson. Despite this, he remained at his post, though under fire, until 1869.[13]

The creation of Isherwood's Bureau of Steam Engineering acknowledged the navy's new dependence on machinery to propel its vessels and heralded the role science and technology were playing in the mid nineteenth-century navy.

The interaction between science and the tools of war became more tangible as the nation of tinkerers began to deluge the department with ideas, inventions and schemes intended to help the war effort. Other than John Dahlgren's work with ordnance, the department obviously had no 'research and development' arm per se, and it's top scientifically minded men were sorely stressed merely carrying out the war. To evaluate this influx of well intentioned, though sometimes harebrained ideas, Welles called upon the good offices of, among others, Joseph Henry, Secretary of the still young Smithsonian Institution, to act as consultant to the department. Acting with Henry were Charles H Davis and Alexander Dallas Bache, the latter of the Coast Survey and a descendant of Benjamin Franklin. The group, called the Permanent Commission, was to report and advise on all scientific questions brought to it by the navy. With great foresight, Welles envisioned this organization as one with national significance, not merely to serve the navy. It was the nation's first government-sponsored research organization and would become the forerunner of the National Academy of Sciences.[14]

Among the department's snowballing war responsibilities was

Benjamin F Isherwood, Chief of the Bureau of Steam Engineering. Energetic and scientifically minded, Isherwood was criticized for building an 'empire' within his bureau, and accused of designing inefficient steam machinery for the navy's warships. (US Navy)

a mounting workload in the legal and financial areas. The reliance on a myriad contractors, for items ranging from treenails to twin-turretted ironclads, naturally brought the possibility of financial conflict among the contracting parties. Wartime pressures – labor shortages, strikes, inflation, acts of war – exacerbated the problems many contractors faced in carrying out their obligations, and litigation was often the result. The impossibility of close scrutiny by overworked departmental inspectors also allowed for fraud and malfeasance on the part of less scrupulous suppliers of naval materiel. Furthermore, the vast increase in personnel during the conflict added to the numbers of court martial necessary to maintain discipline in the ranks.

Such factors induced Welles, in February 1865, to ask Congress to create the office of Solicitor and Judge Advocate General for the service. The office was created on 2 March 1865 and was filled by William A Chandler, who would later become Secretary of the Navy. In 1870, the office was eliminated and the responsibilities moved to the Justice Department.[15]

# Contract administration

Having presented the varied developments in the administration of the Navy Department during the course of the war, some subjects require a general explanation rather than chronological approach. One of these was the handling and administration of contracts and contractors.

At the outset of the war, Congress had mandated that all government purchases and contracts for services and supplies be advertised and awarded to the lowest bidder. Welles found some latitude in a clause allowing variances in emergency situations, as well as in earlier statutes which allowed department heads discretion in acceptance of open bids. However, for the general run of purchases, the lowest bid ruled.

To give a sampling of the wartime reliance on outside work, it is instructive to look at the ninety-day gunboats of 1861. Each of these twenty-three vessels cost between $88,000 and $103,000, and each represented two contracts: one for the hull; another for the machinery. Thirty-four contracts were written, seven of which went to the Novelty Iron Works of New York, for engines. Three other firms had multiple obligations for providing machinery: Morgan Iron Works (3 contracts); I P Morris (2); and Allaire Co. (2).[16]

In the course of the war, some 171 vessels were built, or at least begun, with either machinery or hull, or both, by contract. In some instances, there was one contractor for a vessel, who subcontracted for her engines and boilers. The vessels ranged in cost (with machinery) from that of the ninety-day gunboats up to $1.5 million for some of the larger monitors.

Contracts for ships and machinery made up a small proportion, at least in raw numbers, of the gamut of goods and services which were let out to civilian providers. Coal may have been one of the most consumed commodities. In 1864, for example, the blockaders in Virginia waters alone required 2000 tons per week. It is estimated that over $18 million was spent on coal during the war. Other commodities included bricks, lime, hair, hay, files, pig iron, timber, paint, litharge (red lead putty), stone, clothing, provisions, canvas, and so forth; every item the navy could not make itself.[17]

The actual number of contracts and contractors, plus the amounts spent, would require a major study and computer database to calculate with any accuracy, suffice it to say here that contracting was a vast subject and undertaking even during the Civil War. Given the few resources in the department devoted to overseeing this, it is no surprise that problems arose.

The initial problem for the department was simply finding firms to undertake the required work. To be more precise, finding companies which had the capabilities – capital equipment and skills – to accomplish the tasks was sometimes nearly an impossibility.

Of course, the most critical areas were ironclad vessels and engines, both of which required specialized machinery and skilled work forces. Early in the war a survey revealed that only thirty-eight engines could be built in the Union states in four months hence, and that six of the surveyed firms were in financial difficulty.[18] Probably the major difficulty was that most of the available shops were geared to production for the railroads, for which the valve gear for one cylinder on each side of the locomotive was the most complicated job. Marine engines, particularly for screw vessels, were far more complex and demanded higher standards of precision.

These factors did not necessarily deter firms from bidding on marine engines. It was, therefore, not unusual for two related events to occur: an ill-equipped shop with inexperienced mechanics would enter the lowest bid and receive the contract, and then, some time into the specified term, conclude that they had sorely underestimated their capabilities, costs and time requirements. As the war continued, such situations became more common, as the government was finding it increasingly problematic to engage contractors not already overburdened with other war work, particularly for the army.

Another negative factor as far as the machine shops were concerned, was the necessity of investing substantial amounts for specialized machinery, particularly for making iron armor. The possibility that this capital outlay would pay for itself in course of the war was small, and the likelihood was that the close of hostilities, and consequent end to government contracts, would leave the company with a significant loss on their investment.

Once contracts were let, another series of difficulties ensued. First, the government payment policy was awkward and, particularly for small firms, fraught with cash-flow troubles. Rather than a lump sum, the department paid in installments, each based on progress made. If there were unexpected expenses early on which absorbed the installment at hand, and prevented completion of the requirements to receive the next installment, and if there were no other sources of cash available, work would stop. Only a special dispensation from the department would allow early disbursement of the needed funds.

Feeding into the above scenario were changes made in the vessel or machinery plans and specifications after the construction had begun. Particularly troublesome to the contractors were the monitors, which underwent significant design alterations as the result of combat experience. In one instance, a builder had expeditiously sped ahead with the hull erection, only to be informed three months later that the entire stern section was affected by a departmental redesign and had to be dismantled completely and re-built to new specifications.[19]

To eliminate or prevent some of the more prevalent contractor-related problems, Welles devised a 'yardstick' of costs. With the twenty-three ninety-day gunboats, for instance, bids were initially accepted for four vessels. The mean of these figures was used and contracts for the remaining ships were offered at that cost. This method was used for most of the other vessels built during the war, excepting experiments such as the first ironclads.

In this regard, the department also made use of the performance bond. For example, Ericsson's original *Monitor* was required to prove itself in combat before the government would pay for its construction. So, in effect, the ship was owned by its inventor until after the Battle of Hampton Roads. If she had been sunk, Ericsson would have lost his $175,000 investment.[20]

The department, while protecting itself with a performance bond or specific contractual requirements in the performance of the completed vessel, was sometimes overruled. An example, shortly after the war, was the steam sloop *Idaho*, which failed by 4 knots to meet its requisite speed (11 knots versus 16 knots). The department rejected the vessel, but the contractor, through congressional influence, forced the navy to accept the ship.[21]

Finally, in the construction of iron ships and machinery, the department supplied all plans and specifications, including, for example, tensile strength of all the ironwork. In most instances, these specifications and plans were provided at the request of the potential bidders, and, especially for the monitors, these were exhaustive. Even today, in the National Archives, there are plans – to the last bolt – for some of the Civil War vessels.

Despite the department's efforts, of course, contract litigation became common during the course of the war. Disputes arose due to all of the above mentioned factors, plus the unexpected and uncontrollable, and those directly or indirectly war-related. Probably the most widely heard complaints in the latter categories were wartime inflation which increased contractors' costs, shortage of labor brought on by the military draft, shortage of materials, particularly iron, and labor strikes. More singular problems were caused, for instance, by the New York City riots of 1864, and the sinking of a vessel carrying most of the parts of a monitor hull to the west coast.

In most instances, settlements were made. However, unsatisfied contractors with much cash at stake sometimes took their cases to congress for redress, resulting in various investigatory boards and commissions. The last of these cases was finally settled in the first decade of the twentieth century.

# Operational organization: the squadrons

At the outbreak of the war, the overseas squadrons were dismantled, losing the majority of their ships, which were ordered to the Atlantic and Gulf coasts. Originally there were two blockading squadrons – Atlantic and Gulf – with their dividing point at Key West. Additionally, there was the Potomac flotilla, which was essentially for the defense of Washington and its vicinity, and operated on the Potomac and Rapahannock Rivers and in Chesapeake Bay.

It was soon found that the size of the blockading fleet was outstripping the two-squadron organization and both were subdivided. The North Atlantic and South Atlantic Blockading Squadrons were formed on 29 October 1861; the East and West Gulf squadrons, on 21 February 1862. The boundary between the two Atlantic units was the border between North and South Carolina. The demarcation between the Gulf squadrons was St Andrew's Bay, in north Florida; the line between the Atlantic and Gulf squadrons was Cape Canaveral on the Floridas Atlantic coast.

On the western rivers, the original Mississippi River flotilla was under the US Army until transferred to the Navy on 1 October 1862.

The Confederate commerce raiders received special attention by the department. At various times individual vessels were ordered out to search for them. On 8 September 1862, an entire squadron was formed for the purpose of hunting down the *Alabama* and *Florida*. This consisted of seven fast ships under Captain Charles Wilkes. Popularly called the Flying Squadron, it ranged mainly in the West Indies and south as far as the Yucatan Peninsula. It was disbanded in 1863. In 1864, the Bahamas and Cuban waters were added to the East Gulf squadron.

The Navy Department in the Civil War was amazingly efficient given its size and composition. Welles and Fox provided energetic and knowledgeable leadership, both in terms of operations and in personnel. Organizationally, the prevailing shortcoming of the department, both before and after the war, was the independent

The Navy Department, Washington. This plain structure was home to the naval administration during the war – a bureaucracy numbering less than a hundred souls. It was within walking distance of the White House and Lincoln himself was a frequent visitor there, usually unnannounced and sometimes in his 'carpet slippers'. (USAMHI)

bureau system. There was no requirement for the bureaux to coordinate their activities except through the office of the Secretary or Assistant Secretary. Indeed, each bureau was jealous of its perquisites and boasted of its own adherents in Congress. This was particularly awkward at the navy yards, where the Bureau of Yards and Docks controlled the facilities, but could not require cooperation on the part of their other bureaus represented there.

The Light Draft Monitor debacle, the most visible materiel failure of the war, can in part be laid to the bureau system's influence. When the 'Ironclad Bureau' was created, it exercised as much independence as the other established branches, with dire results.

The rather loosely defined role of the Assistant Secretary of the Navy may well have been a negative aspect of the wartime administration. The office was basically as Fox made it, with obvious areas sacrosanct to Welles. Where Fox's instincts were correct, this arrangement was fruitful. However, when Fox was off the mark, he carried the department down with him. Apparently Fox was instrumental in the creation of the 'Ironclad Bureau', and, indeed, it was largely due to Fox that the navy fell in lock step with the 'monitor lobby' (see Chapter Thirteen). Fox believed, with numerous others, in the monitor for all reasons, ignoring their impotence against fortifications. In a different leadership arrangement, it may have been possible that more versatile ironclads might have resulted. This may be useless speculation, however, in view of the powerful 'monitor lobby' of the time.

# Chapter Three
# NAVAL SHORE FACILITIES

The United States naval shore establishment was geared to a peacetime service, both prior to and after the Civil War. That is, the navy yards and other facilities were sufficient to support the needs of a home squadron plus those vessels on station with Mediterranean, Brazil, Pacific, East Indian and African squadrons. (Post-war squadrons were re-named but remained in these cruising areas.) Rarely did the aggregate number of vessels in commission number over sixty, and the yards were chiefly in the business of preparing replacements for the vessels on station.

The sudden onset of the Civil War and the concomitant massive force increase clogged the yards with new construction, conversions of purchased vessels, and increased maintenance and refit responsibilities. Despite these factors, the war saw only moderate expansion in the yards themselves, and the new wartime-acquired facilities were geared towards operational support, rather than ship construction. Another factor in limiting the usefulness of the navy yards during the war was the emphasis on ironclads and iron vessels: ships for which the yards had only limited construction capabilities. Therefore, much of the new construction was contracted out to civilian shipyards.

After the war's end, the ironclads were laid up, and the antebellum status quo reasserted itself. With niggardly congressional appropriations and no potential adversary, the yards settled back into a refit and rebuild mode.

The naval infrastructure ranged from the naval dockyards (in American parlance 'navy yards') downward in size and importance. Usually the navy yards were those that had significant ship repair and construction capabilities. Below this were the stations, which normally did not build vessels, but provided maintenance, repair and provisions. A third category was the naval rendezvous which was a recruiting establishment, often temporary in nature. Besides these, there were the other special purpose facilities such as hospitals, the Naval Observatory, an asylum for the mentally unsound, and the Naval Academy. These latter will be dealt with in later chapters.

By 1861 there were eight navy yards, spread from Portsmouth, New Hampshire (on the border with Maine) to San Francisco, California. The system of yards had seen its beginning in 1800, through the efforts of the first Secretary of the Navy, Benjamin Stoddert, who took it upon himself – without statutory authority – to acquire land in Washington, DC; Philadelphia; New York; Boston; Portsmouth; New Hampshire; and Norfolk, Virginia for the establishment of these facilities. He utilized funds voted for six ships of the line, on the grounds that the six yards were needed for construction of these vessels.[1] (It is noteworthy that, since the re-establishment of the navy in 1794, all its purpose-built vessels, including the celebrated frigates *Constitution* and *Constellation*, had been constructed in private shipyards.)

By the outbreak of the Civil War, two yards had been added to the original six: the bases at Pensacola, Florida and Mare Island (San Francisco), California. Pensacola had been established in 1825, and Mare Island in the early 1850s. Before the war, only two ships had been built at Pensacola, and one at Mare Island. Additionally, there had been a navy yard at Memphis, Tennessee, from 1844 to 1853 and a naval facility at Sackets Harbor on the Great Lakes in New York state.[2] The latter was centered around a ship of the line on the stocks, but was offi-

Post-war view of Washington Navy Yard. The former Confederate ironclad *Stonewall* is center, mid-distance. To the right are three monitors. (US Navy)

cially termed a naval station, while the former had no shipbuilding facilities whatever, and had been intended for rope making with American hemp.

Any study of the naval facilities during the Civil War must allude to the two yards captured by the Confederates during the conflict: Pensacola and Norfolk. In the first instance, the yard was destroyed by the Confederates before its re-capture by Union forces; in the second, the yard was partially burned by the Union before the Confederates took the facility, and burned again when the rebels abandoned it. The yards were thus seriously hampered in supporting the navy's war effort.

Several other facilities played special roles in the conflict, among them Mare Island; Mound City, Illinois; Baltimore; and Port Royal, South Carolina. Mare Island was outside the scope of the main campaigns, but was important in supporting the

US cruisers in their search for far-ranging Confederate raiders. One monitor was assembled at the yard, but was completed long after the war ended.

A naval station was established at Mound City, Illinois in 1862. This establishment, on the Ohio River near its confluence with the Mississippi, was specifically intended for the riverine fleet and closed in 1875. Additionally, for most of the war, a small facility was operated at Baltimore. This was primarily for repairing blockaders and was particularly useful following the loss of Norfolk. Port Royal, South Carolina, the site of one of the Union Navy's first successful inroads on the southern coast, also became a makeshift, but important supply and repair base. Finally, a supply station was set up at New Orleans in 1862 and smaller facilities were set up at various points along the coast.

The facilities enumerated above formed the core of the navy's shore establishment.Unlike the British navy, there were no major overseas bases, simply conveniently located coaling stations or supply depots leased for long terms and designated for the various cruising squadrons.

On the western rivers, the first naval facility was at Mound City, Illinois, on the Ohio River. This was a supply and repair facility, without ways for hauling out vessels. (USAMHI)

# The work of the navy yards

In theory, the navy yards were the sources, or at least the conduits, for all the needs of the fleet. For the purposes of this work, these necessities can be divided into the areas of personnel; supplies and equipment; ordnance; ship construction and repair; information and communications; and maintenance and support for the yard infrastructure itself.

Needless to say, ship repair and construction were the prime reasons for the yards' existence. Of these two, the former was the continuous staple of the workforce, while the latter was more subject to factors as diverse as national policy, availability of funds and congressional whim.

For the wooden navy, the time span between a new vessel and one in need of repair or refit was understandably brief. Indeed, early into a vessel's first commission the flaws would be revealed. There followed an immediate rash of modifications or additions, most generally in her rig or internal arrangements. It was not unusual for a ship's commander to demand relocation of her masts, though such requests were subject to the opinion of the naval constructor on site. On warships, probably the next most common problem was armament, in particular the location or number of guns, the weight and position of which would significantly effect the ship's trim and

seaworthiness. All such matters were tended to at the dock or under the masting shears.

From the steam engineering standpoint, the term 'new' when applied to an engine was pejorative, and the initial 'running in' of the engine was a highly critical period. There were trials at the dock and under weigh, with engines at slow speed. This was an agonizing process because new and rough bearing surfaces generated immense heat until they wore themselves smooth. The potential for severe damage was great, and it was not unusual to have a crew pouring literally buckets of lubricant on the red-hot engine bearings to prevent them from seizing up, resulting in major engine repairs even before it went into service.

Once the vessel had emerged from the shakedown phase and gone to sea, major repair and refit, in peacetime, came roughly in six year cycles, usually after two three-year cruises on foreign stations. By contrast, in wartime few vessels underwent periodical major repairs except in the case of significant battle damage. Everything possible was done to keep the ship on station and perform repairs there. For example, the ironclad *New Ironsides* survived a spar torpedo attack off Charleston, but remained in place for six months before returning to Philadelphia for repair.[3]

This is not to say that work was scarce at the yards during wartime. With new ship construction, conversion of merchant vessels for blockade work, and a steady stream of minor repairs, both battle related and due to normal maintenance, the yards were congested with vessels and work.

The major difference between wartime yard repairs and peacetime work was the turnaround time. Wartime exigencies, limited yard facilities, and the pressure from blockade squadron commanders made short yard stays a priority. In the peacetime cruising milieu, however, a vessel would return from her station and be replaced by another, and so there was not necessarily a pressing need to have the first vessel completed and back in service expeditiously. Furthermore, the miserly annual congressional peacetime appropriations further cut into funds available for repairs. The result, in the post-war years, was exceedingly long yard stays, not atypically measured in years rather than months. To illustrate this point, the steam sloop *Richmond* was out of service from 1865 to 1869 at Boston having new engines installed. In 1871, less than three years later, she had a less drastic refit at Philadelphia, requiring a year's work. She had major refits beginning in 1877 (13 months), and 1884 (two years and four months), before becoming a receiving ship and ending her active service.

In stark contrast were the war years for the same ship. An enemy torpedo attack in mid October 1861 required temporary repairs at Pensacola for two weeks in the November. An engagement later that month put her in repairs at New York until February 1862. Her only other time out of service was three months at New York in 1863 after heavy damage in the New Orleans and lower Mississippi campaigns. Thus *Richmond* was out of service and under repair for six months of the war, compared to a total of nearly seven years thereafter.[4]

*Richmond* was not an isolated example in this regard, emphasizing the fact that major refits were results of normal wear and tear, rather than battle-related damage. It should be noted here that the extent of these peacetime repairs became something of a scandal in that era, when a major 'repair' could mean stripping the vessel to her frames, and result in expenses which frequently were beyond the original cost of the ship.

If vessel repair provided a steady stream of shipyard work, new vessel construction was a sporadic deluge. It was, of course, usually dependent on congressional largess. And, surveying the various classes of vessels both before and after the war, it is obvious that every effort was made to spread the wealth with the construction of one ship of each class being assigned to each yard. In peacetime, new warship construction was in the main a continual round of replacing worn out ships, rather than adding to the size of the fleet. During the war, the patterns changed drastically. Enlargement of the fleet was suddenly a priority. That, plus the loss of two yards to the Confederates, resulted in utilizing every available ship house and building slip, and the overflow was contracted to outside shipyards.

In general, the larger the vessel, the more likely it would be built in a navy facility – reflecting the traditional naval distrust of civilian shipbuilders. (Ironclads and iron-hulled vessels, were, of course, almost exclusively contract built.) Further, most of the civilian-built ships were those more numerous classes where the government could supply standard plans to each contracting firm. Naval officers were then assigned to periodically inspect their construction.

The coming of steam engines and their appurtenances complicated the entire shipbuilding process. Though the naval shipyards gradually obtained the tools and equipment for engine repairs, before the Civil War only Washington Navy Yard had the capability of building entire engines. Of some thirty naval marine engines built before the war, three were built at Washington. Though the Bureau of Steam Engineering regularly plied Congress for funds to build marine engine shops, other priorities prevailed. It was a question of relative economy:capital expenditures for machinery and tools, versus as-needed engine contracts in the private sector. Though Boston, Portsmouth, New York and Mare Island yards also built a few engines during the 1860s, the bulk of such work continued to be done outside, with politicians quite cognizant of the benefits such contracts brought to their industrial constituencies.[5]

At this point, the yards will be descibed. The yard at Portsmouth, New Hampshire will be presented in some detail as an example of all the American yards. The remaining shipyards will be presented in more general terms, with particular attention to the unique features of each. Following this I will attempt to give a general picture of their aggregate capabilities and contributions to the navy's Civil War effort.

# Portsmouth Navy Yard

Portsmouth Navy Yard was the first of the original six yards to be established, in 1800. It was sited on 66 acres of Fernald's Island, near the mouth of the Piscataqua River, which forms the boundary between Maine and New Hampshire. Another 171 acres was available for naval use at adjacent Seavey's Island. It is and was

Waterfront view, Portsmouth Navy Yard, about 1898. The building to the right is the Mast and Spar shop, dating from the 1830s, and still in existence. The steam sloop in the background is the USS *Essex*, built in the 1870s and painted grey for the Spanish American War. (Portsmouth Naval Shipyard Historical Society)

sometimes referred to as Kittery Yard, due to its proximity to the town of that name in Maine. If the Seavey's Island property was taken into account, the yard was the largest on the east coast; if not, it was fourth largest, behind New York, Boston and Norfolk.

Here there was easy access to the vast New England forests, and abundant stone for building construction. The area had a long seafaring tradition, and in fact the first naval warship built in North America (HMS *Falkland* of 54 guns) was constructed and commissioned here in 1695. By 1861 the yard had built ten sailing warships, including two 74-gun ships of the line, and two steam sloops. (A thirteenth ship, the steam frigate *Franklin* was building there throughout the war.)[6]

Before the war, the civilian workforce had numbered as high as 775 in 1858, but generally fluctuated significantly. In April 1861, eighty-five were employed; one month later that number was 820 as the demands of the war began to be felt. The peak was 2455, reached in May 1865, to fall precipitately with the return to peacetime endeavours. These numbers did not include naval and marine contingents, or management and professional personnel.[7]

The physical plant was subdivided under the various naval bureaux as set up in the reorganization of the navy in 1842 and as

modified in 1862: Yards and Docks, Equipment and Recruiting, Navigation, Ordnance, Construction and Repair, Steam Engineering, Provisions and Clothing, and Medicine and Surgery.

The Department of Yards and Docks was responsible for general maintenance and facilities in the yard itself, including sewers, fencing, fire reservoirs and fire fighting apparatus, and the waterfront wharves. The department oversaw a carpentry shop, smithery, general and lumber storage areas, and stables. The derricks and masting shears also fell under its purview. At this time there was no railroad on the yard.

Some 25,000 square feet was dedicated to the shops, storage and stables, with the largest proportion devoted to storage. The fire department consisted of four hand-operated and two steam fire engines. There were eight cranes (five more than any other yard) and two masting shears, with the largest of the latter 126 feet high and capable of handling 60-ton loads.

Portsmouth had the largest waterfront area of the six east coast yards: over 4000 yards long. Of this total, 1866 were in the yard itself, with the remainder at adjacent Seavey's Island.[8]

The Department of Construction at Portsmouth was the third largest behind the Boston and Norfolk yards, at over

132,000 square feet of space. Of this, some 46,000 square feet were in various types of storage: metal and iron, furniture, tanks, oils and paints, etc. The largest of the shops were, of course, the masting shops and mould lofts, totalling some 17,000 square feet each. Other buildings housed smitheries, copper, tin, boat, block and joinery shops, plus iron plating and paint shops, and sawmills. These all could employ some 390 journeymen, the largest proportion of which were joiners, platers, machinists, and mast and spar makers.

A standard array of tools outfitted the woodworking shops and smithery. These included drilling machines, lathes, jig and circular saws, treenail machines, planers, and mortise and tenon machinery. The sawmill included various cutting machines as well as a steam box for bending timber. The smithery had sixteen forge fires, punches, steam hammers, shears, and bolt cutters. Power for these shops came from a steam engine and boilers in the saw mill.

Also under this department were pitch and oakum storage, timber sheds and ship houses and docks. Timber storage amounted to 78,000 square feet in six structures, the third largest such storage in any of the other yards. There were three ship houses and one floating dry dock.[9]

Portsmouth's floating 'balance' dry dock was one of four floating decks in the navy yards, with others at Pensacola, Philadelphia, and Mare Island. It was completed in 1852 and was 350 feet long by 105 feet, 4 inches wide, with walls 38 feet high, built entirely of yellow pine. There were eight water chambers and two steam engines with twelve pumps enabling equilibrium to be maintained while raising vessels as large as 5000 tons. (Hence the term 'balance' dock). First, water was introduced as ballast, dropping the dock below the level of the keel of the vessel to be taken in. Once the vessel was towed into place, pumping out the water raised both the dock and the ship. The entire process could dock a 2000-ton ship in two hours. The dry dock was then towed onto its basin

and the ship was aligned with the keel and bilge 'rails' of a marine railway. There a steam-driven hydraulic cylinder mechanism drew the hull and its cradle on to dry ground. This dock was large enough for even the *Merrimack* class steam frigates and remained in active use until 1907.[10]

The three ship houses ranged from 300 to 330 feet in length and were of typical wood and slate construction. The oldest was built in 1814, the second in 1819, and the third was completed in 1838. The latter, in which the steam frigate *Franklin* was built in the Civil War years, was named after that vessel and survived to house submarine construction in the twentieth century, finally burning in 1936.[11]

The Steam Engineering department at Portsmouth was relatively small compared with that at other yards, and was able to employ less than four hundred workers. There were boiler shops, coppersmiths, iron and brass founderies, machine and pattern shops. These occupied some 48,000 square feet of building space in the yard.

Steam Engineering tools were more specialized than those of the Yards and Dock shops. These included flanging forges and punches, steam rivetting machines, various sizes of shears, bolt heading machines, rolls for iron plates, and specialized drills. Tools directly associated with building steam engines were cylinder boring machines, gear cutters, crank shaft lathes, and shaft straightening machines. It should be noted here that these machinery lists are taken from an 1869 survey of the yards, and it is not clear whether all the items listed were in place during the war years. However, given the drastic post-war cutbacks, it is likely that most of the machinery was installed during the war.

While Steam Engineering dealt with machinery, and Construction handled the hulls, sails and rigging fell under the Department of Equipment and Recruiting. Some 16,000 square feet comprised the rigging and sail lofts at Portsmouth, providing

**P**erspective view of the floating dry dock. Two steam engines pumped water into eight chambers in the base of the dock, which enabled the dock and vessel to be raised evenly. From Stuart's *The Naval Drydocks of the United States*, 1852.

Floating dry dock, 1884. Here the base of the dock has been lowered to below water level in preparation for receiving a ship. (Portsmouth Naval Shipyard)

employment for about one hundred riggers and sail makers. The yard had no facilities for making anchors, chain, or rope.

The Bureau of Ordnance was also small at this yard and included an armory, gun carriage shop, machine shop and riggers loft. Seventy-five could be employed in this area, which included storage for carriages and lumber.

Rounding out the facilities were offices and storage for the Department of Navigation and Hydrography, and storage overseen by the Department of Provisions and Clothing. Last were the barracks for the marine contingent (about fifty-two men and officers in 1860), a small hospital and a recruiting rendezvous.[12]

The yard began or completed a total of twenty-three vessels during the Civil War, including the *Franklin* which was begun prior to the conflict and was not commissioned until afterwards. Of the twenty-three, six large vessels were laid down but not completed during the war. Two more were begun and never launched. Two twin-turreted, wooden-hulled monitors were built, one of which was never completed.

At present, the Portsmouth yard includes in its confines some of the oldest extant shipbuilding facilities in the country. The copper and tinsmiths shop dates from 1826; the mast, boat and riggers shop from 1837. In 1975, the complex was named a National Historic Mechanical Engineering Landmark by the American Society of Mechanical Engineers.

# Boston Navy Yard

Boston, a city prominent in the maritime culture of the nation, was an obvious location for a navy shipbuilding facility. It should be borne in mind that, in the pre-Civil War and pre-transcontinental railroad American economy, this Massachusetts city was the second largest port in the United States. New York was by far the largest, with New Orleans third in size, as measured by import and export tonnage, and, in the 1860s, San Francisco fell a distant fourth.[13]

In 1800, the Navy Department purchased 35 acres near the confluence of the Mystic and Charles Rivers on the Charlestown Peninsula, across the Charles from Boston proper. (It should be noted that the yard was often referred to as the Charlestown Navy Yard, causing some confusion with the naval facility at Charleston, South Carolina.) The area was known as Moulton's Point and had been the disembarkation spot for the British regu-

Boston (Charlestown) Navy Yard, 1876 (panorama combining two photographs). The building to the left with the shorter chimney is the smithery. The low colonnade, with a flag staff behind, masks the saluting battery. Twin brick and granite stuctures house machine shop, foundry, and smithery. There are three vessels in ordinary: outboard is the steam frigate *Wabash*, next (housed over) is *Niagara*, and third is the steam sloop *Iowa* (with four funnels). One ship can be seen on the stocks behind the masting shears. Bunker Hill battle monument is seen on left in the background. (US Navy)

lars ordered to dislodge the Yankees dug-in atop Bunker Hill (actually Breed's Hill) in June, 1775.

By 1869, the yard covered 83.5 acres, not including the 86-acre naval hospital grounds nearby. The navy yard was third in size behind those at New York and Norfolk. Boston yard's first vessel came down the ways in 1813, and the largest by 1863 had been the steam frigate *Merrimack*. A total of twenty-three ships had been constructed there before the Civil War. It should be noted that the most famous Boston-built naval vessel was the frigate *Constitution* of 1797. She was constructed in a government-leased private yard in Boston itself, three years before the navy possessed their own shipyards.

Ship docking and building capabilities at Boston were extensive. There were three ship houses, three building slips and one dry dock. The latter, referred to as the 'Constitution' dock after the first vessel to enter the facility, was the oldest navy yard dry dock,

having been commenced in 1827 and completed in 1834. Originally it was 305 feet long and capable of handling the largest naval vessels; in 1857 it was lengthened to 370 feet. It cost about $700,000 to build – a not inconsiderable amount in those days – but certainly a bargain given the many decades it was in use.

It was constructed of the best hammered granite, laid on pilings driven down to bedrock. A floating gate rested in a groove in the sides and bottom of the entrance to the dock, retaining the water until the ship within was properly shored and stabilized. It is interesting to note that this gate, which measured 60 feet wide by 30 feet high and 16 in breadth, was built much as a ship, with an oak keel and stems which projected into the grooves, and planking of yellow pine, covered with copper sheathing. Atop the upper deck were four ship-pumps, operated by fire-engine type 'brakes' (levers) and twelve men each, which could evacuate the water in the gate in an hour and a half, allowing the removal of the gate from its grooves to admit a vessel to the dock. A granite three-story structure housed a steam engine with three boilers to operate the pumps for the dock itself, as well as power a sawmill and machine shop.[14] This dry dock still exists, and was used to dock the frigate *Constitution* for her bicentennial refit.

The three ship houses ranged from 260 to 307 feet in length, and each was 142 feet wide. There were 2645 yards available in wharfage – slips and waterfront – a third in length to Portsmouth and New York in this regard. There were two masting shears and two cranes listed at Boston in 1869.

Among the Bureau of Construction's shops, Boston's joinery

**R**ope walk, Boston Navy Yard, *c.* 1890. Built in 1836, this structure was the navy's only such facility. The building still exists today. (US Navy)

and sawmill were by far the largest of those types on the east coast. The mast shop was second in size to Norfolk's, making it the largest available after the latter was taken by the rebels.

Boston's Bureau of Steam Engineering department was the largest in the east, having the most square footage devoted to boiler shops, iron and brass founding, and machine shops. Washington's pattern shop was larger in square footage but it appears that Boston had a wider range of tools of all types necessary for engine work, both repair and construction. Some 1300 workers found employment here, 350 of whom were machinists.

Workshops for the Ordnance department were the largest short of Washington's, capable of employing 190 workers. Storage for Provisions and Clothing was equal to that at New York, both of which fell short of that formerly available at Norfolk.

Under the Department of Equipment and Recruiting, Boston boasted the navy's only full fledged rope walk. This facility occupied almost 100,000 square feet and was built in 1836. At the height of the war effort, working day and night, it produced 1400 tons of cordage for the fleet (though it was estimated that the navy purchased twice that much on the open market). This despite the predominance of steam vessels in service, and the increased use of wire rope. The ropewalk employed 350 ropemakers.

Overall, Boston Navy Yard, though far from the largest in area, was in many ways the best equipped. In addition to the ropewalk, it had the largest number of both iron and woodworking tools as well as engines and boilers to power this machinery. These, together with the three ship houses and equal number of building slips, and the large dry dock, gave it the largest capacity for new construction of all the yards.[15]

During the war years, nineteen warships were built or begun at Boston. Of these, three, including one wooden-hulled monitor, were never completed, and six of the total were commissioned after the war ended. One additional vessel, the hull of the ship of the line *Virginia* had been on the stocks in the yard since 1818 and was finally broken up in 1874.

# New York (Brooklyn) Navy Yard

New York City was potentially the largest port in the world, and, by far the busiest in the United States during the Civil War era. Government statistics show that in 1855, over 1.3 million tons was registered in foreign trade in New York, and 6883 vessels – over 3.1 million tons – entered or cleared this port involved in that pursuit. On average, without the vicissitudes of weather and other factors, this amounted to about twenty vessels daily. This figure does not include the coasting (and California) trade, fishing or whaling vessels, or various other categories of government or private shipping.

The city's dominance of the American maritime scene is reflected by the fact that of a total of over $260 million in imports to the United States in 1855, nearly $165 million entered through New York. The export figures were similar: $113 million of a total of $275 million exited the port. The second largest district was Massachusetts, primarily Boston, of course, which counted some $45 million in imports and $28 million in exports.[16] In this milieu, the navy yard in New York was amidst the largest maritime community in the United States and, given the fact that the American merchant marine of the 1850s was second only to Britain's, one of the most important in the world.

New York Navy Yard was located due east from Manhattan across the East River on Brooklyn's Wallabout Bay. Before the founding of the yard in 1800, the navy's presence in the port was limited to two wharves. The yard itself was originally 43 acres on the site of a commercial shipyard and eventually became the largest on the east coast, consisting of 150 acres, plus 33 in what was known as the Cob Dock. The latter began as the site where vessels dumped their cobblestone ballast, and which, about the

**P**ost-war view of Brooklyn Navy Yard. In the background is the Cob Dock, an island formed from cobblestone ballast dumped there over the years. It was eventually broken up at the turn of the century to make room for larger vessels. (US Navy)

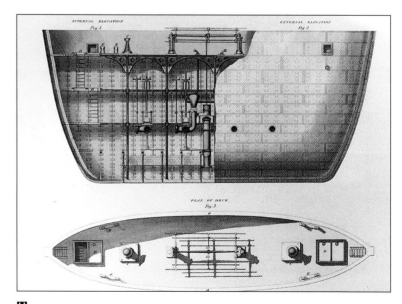

**T**he floating gate, New York dry dock; a ship-like structure of 217 tons. From Stuart's *The Naval Drydocks of the United States*.

**B**rooklyn Navy Yard, June 1861. This yard was the prime site for conversion of purchased vessels to naval use. Nearly 200 such vessels entered service at New York. The large vessel on right is the steam frigate *Wabash*; in the center is the ship of the line *North Carolina*. (*Harper's Weekly*)

time of the Civil War, was cribbed to provide an area for vessels to tie up. Cob Dock was demolished around the turn of the century.

Shipbuilding and out-of-water repair sites totalled five: two ship houses, one dry dock, one floating dock, and one launching slip. The ship houses were 360 and 350 feet long and 128 and 140 feet wide respectively. The stone dry dock measured 320 feet by 70 feet. It was begun in 1841 and completed (after some interruption in the work) in 1851.[17]

The dry dock was considered a significant engineering achievement of that era and cost some $2 million. Its floating gate weighed 217 tons and was built of wrought iron, the first and largest of its kind in the country. The turning gates weighed

187 tons, but could be operated by four men on each leaf. In all 80,000 tons of stone were used in the construction of the dock and the average vessel could be docked in less than three hours.[18]

In terms of other facilities for ship repair, New York had the second largest waterfront – nearly a mile and a half – and the largest timber shed and sail loft of the east coast yards. Its boat shop and smithery were second largest. As appropriate to such a maritime community, its storage facilities were particularly commodious, especially in the areas of ordnance, and wet provisions, the latter under the Bureau of Provisions and Clothing. The general storage building was unique in having steam-driven machinery for making coffee, mustard and other small stores.[19]

In the 1830s one of the educational movements in the navy was the 'Lyceum', a society dedicated to 'promote the diffusion of useful knowledge...in the service and cement the links...' of the naval officers' profession. Several were begun in the various yards, but the largest was at New York, established in 1833. In order to accomplish these goals, a library and reading room was established, along with a museum. Papers on various naval subjects were read and discussed and the *Naval Magazine* was published in 1836 and 1837. Contributors and members included author James Fenimore Cooper, Alexander Slidell MacKenzie, and Matthew C Perry.

The museum and library had significant collections, and in one year (after the Civil War) boasted a visitorship of over 10,000. The institution was dissolved about 1888 and apparently most of the collections were accessioned by the US Naval Academy. The organization was the precursor of the US Naval Institute which was founded in 1873.[20]

The Lyceum was housed in Building No. 1 on the yard, a fine example of Greek Revival architecture. This structure later housed the yard commandant and the headquarters of the naval district.

During the Civil War, the navy built or began twenty-one warships at Brooklyn, of which nine were completed for war service. Nine more vessels were begun in 1862 through 1864 and completed after the war. (One of these, the *Algonquin*, was completed but was unsatisfactory and not commissioned.) Three more were never finished, including one wooden-hulled monitor. In an additional category was the *Roanoke*, the steam frigate converted to a triple-turret ironclad.[21]

It appears that New York became the primary yard for the conversion of merchant or captured vessels for blockade service. Of about 380 vessels purchased or absorbed into the service during the war, about 190 were brought in at New York or Brooklyn. It is assumed that the majority of these were converted at New York, though research to confirm this is not available. (The only available source in which this total is given puts it at 416, which is wildly erroneous.[22]

As one writer has put it, New York Navy Yard 'worked at capacity during the entire war', and a substantial percentage of this work was the repairing of blockading vessels. In one year 158 vessels were repaired there. Of the blockading squadrons (North Atlantic, South Atlantic, East Gulf and West Gulf squadrons) the North Atlantic squadron rarely sent vessels as far as New York, preferring to spread them between Washington, Philadelphia and smaller facilities at Baltimore, Norfolk, and Hampton Roads. According to statistics recently developed by Dr Robert Browning on the North Atlantic squadron, New York received only 6 per cent of that squadron's repairs throughout the war.[23] Comparable statistics are not available for the other squadrons. However, logic has it that New York would have been the preferred choice over Boston or Portsmouth, due to distance, and over Philadelphia and Washington, due to their limited waterfront areas. To do the work

required, employment in the yard expanded from a daily average of 1650 in 1861 to nearly triple that number. It nearly doubled in 1862 and by 1864 the daily average was 5390. At various times in the latter year, over 6000 men were working in the yard. Expenses for labor rose from $679,000 in 1861 to $3.95 million in 1865.[24]

# Philadelphia Navy Yard

The Philadelphia naval shipyard had been originally leased by the government before its purchase in 1800 for $38,636. At the outset it was 11 acres, but by the Civil War it covered 21.36 acres. It was by far the navy's smallest yard and its urban location prevented further expansion. By the mid-point of the Civil War, actions were taken to move the facility to another local site, a larger tract, known as League Island where construction began in 1871.[25]

VIEWS IN NORTH AMERICA, *Taken from nature, July 1850, by the patent Talbotype process, by W. & F. Langenheim 216 Chestnut St Phila & 247 Broadway N. York. Series 1 Penns?* Nº 2.

THE U. S. STEAMSHIP "SUSQUEHANA." *Building at the Navy Yard Phil?*

**P**hiladelphia ship yard was the smallest on the east coast, and had the least waterfront area. By the mid-point of the Civil War the department had begun plans to move the facility elsewhere. This rare view shows the steam frigate *Susquehanna* fitting out in 1850; her paddle boxes can be seen to the right center and her bow is near the building to the left. (Library of Congress)

Sectional dry dock, Philadelphia. The nine sections were semi-independent and could be divided into as many as four smaller docks, each with its own steam pumping engine. From Stuart's *The Naval Drydocks of the United States*.

The old yard had had an important history, having built one of the nation's first ships of the line, the *Franklin*, in 1815, and the service's first successful steamer, the *Mississippi*, in the 1840s. John Ericsson's *Princeton* – arguably the first screw warship – also went down the ways at Philadelphia. During the Mexican War, when the navy required boats for the amphibious landings on the enemy coast, three hundred 50-foot long 'surfboats' were produced here.[26]

Philadelphia had only 387 yards of waterfront, roughly two-thirds of that of the navy's second smallest yard at Washington. There were two ship houses and two floating dry docks (one built during the Civil War) for vessel repair.

The pre-war dock was a patented Sectional Floating Dry Dock, begun in 1849 and completed in 1851. This type of dock was designed in what could be termed modules: each of the nine sections was 30 or 32 feet long and 175 feet wide. When all were joined (at the 175-foot sides) the dock was 282 feet long with a floor measuring 105 feet in width and capable of handling a 5000-ton vessel. The dock was of white oak and pine and of about 4000 tons displacement.

The advantage of the sectional design was its capability of connecting only the number of sections necessary to support the length of the vessel to be taken out of the water. Within certain limitations, the unused sections of the dock could be used for other ships. There were four steam engines in the complex, arranged with coupling shafts to the pumps of each section. It should also be noted that as much as 6 feet could be maintained between each section, thus extending the vessel length capacity of the entire dock.

As with the balance dock at Portsmouth, a granite basin and marine railway was associated with the sectional dock. A steam-powered hydraulic cylinder, hauled the vessel out of the dock on to bedways on the yard. In theory, as many vessels as available marine railways could be serviced by this dock, but Philadelphia's space constraints limited it to two railways.[27]

A detailed description of the facilities at this yard is not necessary. Suffice it to say that, in general, all the requirements for a yard were in place; they were simply proportionally small. It is also noteworthy that use of this yard was also hampered by the frequent icing over of the river.

Despite these disadvantages, Philadelphia was extremely active during the Civil War. Fifteen vessels were laid down here, with eight actually commissioned during the conflict. One, an ironclad monitor, was broken up before completion. A record of sorts accompanied the construction of the steam sloop *Tuscarora*. She was laid down on 26 June and launched 24 August 1861; just fifty-eight days.[28]

The loss of Norfolk made Philadelphia an important repair facility, particularly for the North Atlantic Blockading Squadron. At least in 1861, Philadelphia accomplished about a third of their repair work.[29]

The transition to an ironclad, steam-powered navy seriously influenced the navy's decision to move the Philadelphia yard to League Island. Secretary Welles believed a new yard, specifically adapted to the needs of steam engineering and iron vessels was needed. The new site would have access to fresh water anchorages as well as supplies of iron and coal. Nine hundred-acre League Island, donated by the city of Philadelphia, met these criteria, and eventually was chosen over other proposed sites at New London, Connecticut and Narragansett Bay, Rhode Island. The last warship to be completed at the old Philadelphia Navy Yard was the steam sloop *Quinnebaug*, commissioned in 1875. The yard was sold at auction later that year.[30]

# Washington Navy Yard

For many years after its founding, Washington Navy Yard had a reputation as the nation's most favored naval establishment. Its location in the new capital city, for good or ill, placed it under close scrutiny by the legislators who funded it and the executive branch which commanded it. As President, Thomas Jefferson at once deprecated the value of 'admiralty' and yet was fascinated by the naval applications of science and technolgy. The upshot was the favoring of the yard with new improvements, while keeping a close eye on the activities of the navalists there.

The Washington yard, while founded at the same time as the other east coast facilities, was the only one built contemporaneously with the city in which it was located – as it were, out of bare ground. Thus, Jefferson was allowed to take a hand in the architecture of the place, calling in his friend, architect Benjamin Latrobe for the purpose.

**W**ashington Navy Yard in the mid 1800s. Due to the shallowness of the river, by the 1830s larger vessels were not being constructed at this yard. (US Navy)

Tingey House, Washington Navy Yard. Benjamin Latrobe designed the original yard, most of which was destroyed by the British in 1814. This building, now quarters for the chief of naval operations, and part of the gate and guardhouse are all that remain of his Federal style structures. (Photograph by the author, 1996.)

An adjunct to the yard was an ordnance gunnery range. In this instance, guns are being tested against various types of iron armor cladding. (USAMHI)

Latrobe, who had designed a classically inspired waterworks for Philadelphia and dome for the Capitol, was appointed Engineer of the Navy Department, and laid out the first plan for the navy yard. Jefferson, fascinated by the idea of long term shore preservation of the navy's vessels, had Latrobe draw up a dry dock some 800 feet long, with capacity for almost the entire navy. With a vaulted ceiling and Doric columns, Jefferson proposed it as an 'economy measure': able to preserve the fleet for years on dry ground and under cover while dispensing with an expensive corps of anti-democratic (according to Jefferson) naval officers.[31]

The dock was never built, but Latrobe contributed some twenty structures in the yard itself, ranging from anchor and timber sheds to two shipbuilding slips. Unfortunately, the British torching of Washington took most of Latrobe's buildings. Still remaining are the Tingey (Flag Quarters) House and the Gate and Guardhouse, both dating back to 1804.

The Washington yard during the Civil War covered 42 acres on the Anacostia, also known as the eastern branch of the Potomac River. It had one ship house, 612 yards of waterfront and slips, but was without a dry dock. In general, the yard was lacking in extensive infrastructure for the wood-and-rope facets of naval endeavours, with minimal timber and oakum storage, and small masting shop, mold loft, and sail shops. Prior to the Civil War only twelve sailing ships and two steamers had been constructed at this yard.

In contrast, the yard was noted for metal work of all kinds, including ordnance, steam engines and anchors and chain. Before the war, John Dahlgren had headed the ordnance department and saw to it that the yard became the navy's leader in that area. The yard's ordnance factory turned out significant numbers of Dahlgren's boat howitzers, plus gun carriages, fuses, primers, ammunition, and signal flares. Dahlgren set up practice and testing batteries for weapons and projectiles, to determine such things as a weapon's service life, maximum powder charges for various shells, and to evaluate experimental guns. During the war, the yard had the largest brass and iron foundry in the Ordnance bureau, employing 115 foundrymen. Overall the Ordnance department employed over 600 men during the height of wartime production.[32]

The Department of Steam Engineering also had a substantial establishment here, with the capacity for employing over 900 in its shops. In addition to a machine shop of over 50,000 square feet, Washington had 14,000 square feet of foundry space, and, most important for the manufacture of steam engines, a 20,000 square foot pattern shop. In all, about eight steam engines were built at Washington's engine works.

Finally, the navy's only anchor and chain shops were at Washington under the Bureau of Equipment and Recruiting. These covered over 50,000 square feet and could employ some two hundred men when at full capacity. Under the same cognizance was a 5000 square foot facility for manufacturing ships' galleys.[33]

During the war, the Washington yard was primarily devoted to ordnance and machinery, and secondarily to ship repair and refit. No ships were built at the yard and the major engine project was the erection of the machinery of the steam sloop *Pensacola* in 1861. (The last vessel built at the yard was the sloop *Nipsic* in 1873.) The same year saw the North Atlantic Blockading Squadron send about 33 per cent of its repairs to this yard; the following year the percentage dropped to 15. It is not clear why no ships were built at the yard during the conflict, but it may well have been to keep the yard free for the unending stream of repair jobs from the blockading squadrons.[34]

# Norfolk Navy Yard

The site of Norfolk Navy Yard had been selected by the Royal Navy shortly before the outbreak of the American Revolution, and tradition has it that it had been used previously by that service for careening their vessels. In any event, the area – the Elizabeth River in the Gosport section of Portsmouth, Virginia – was then taken by that state for their Revolutionary War naval service. After the war, the Virginia navy was disbanded and the yard then fell into disuse.

When the Federal navy was begun in the 1790s, Gosport yard (as it was officially named until 1862) was selected as the site for constructing one of the navy's new frigates, and the yard was lent by the state for that purpose. By 1800 when a permanent naval establishment was being provided, the Norfolk yard, though only 16 acres, was already a major equipping, victualling and recruiting station, particularly for operations in the West Indies. Therefore the purchase of the yard was an obvious step to a nation whose southern frontier was the northern border of Spanish Florida.[35]

By the outbreak of the Civil War, the yard was the third largest in acreage after Portsmouth and New York, covering 108 acres, and was considered by many as the premier naval facility in the country, particularly as an arms and munitions depot. Three building slips with their ship houses, a magnificent granite dry

Before the war, Norfolk – or Gosport – Navy Yard was 'the premier yard' of the nation. Its loss to the Confederates was a major catastrophe for the Union and the navy: some 1200 guns were stored there as well as several warships, including the steam frigate *Merrimack*. (US Navy)

The Confederates abandoned the yard in May 1862 and proceeded to wreak more destruction than the Union had done when they had torched the yard the previous year. (US Navy)

dock completed in 1834, machine shops, foundry, ordnance building and shop comprised some of the major structures of the base. In the years before the war, seven steam warships had been built there, including two of the *Merrimack* class frigates.[36]

In 1861, despite obvious signs of impending conflict and the yard's vulnerable setting in a slave-holding state, work at the yard, including capital improvements, continued apace. After the change in Administration in March 1861, Lincoln wished to avoid offending the states still in the Union, including Virginia, and thus little was done to defend the yard or move the vessels to safer environs.

War erupted on 12 April, Virginia seceded five days later, and time had run out to do anything other than attempt to destroy what could not be removed from the yard. Of the twelve

vessels there, only the 24-gun *Cumberland* was towed to safety. Among those left was the steam frigate *Merrimack*, which, though burned to the waterline, would reappear in less than a year as an ironclad. The effort to destroy the yard was botched and much of it, including the shops, escaped serious damage. Equally destructive to the Union cause was the loss of ordnance: some 1200 guns, including at least 50 Dahlgren guns fell into Confederate hands. The loss of this yard and its property and ships has been estimated at over $9.6 million and has been likened to a Civil War 'Pearl Harbor'.[37] One significant parallel was the fact that many of the vessels lost in both incidents were essentially obsolescent: wooden sailing ships – except *Merrimack* – at Norfolk; battleships at Pearl Harbor.

The yard only remained in Confederate hands until May 1862, when they were forced out, also attempting to destroy all that was left behind. They were more efficient than the Yankees had been, leaving only eight structures uninjured, with significant damage to the dry dock and other docks, and hulks blocking the channel.

Though the machine shops were soon back in operation, it would be over a year before the dry dock was operable, and the yard itself was capable only of minor repairs throughout 1863. However, in 1864 the North Atlantic squadron was using the yard for the largest percentage of its work. (It should be noted that there was an army ship repair facility at Norfolk which handled some navy work during this period.) It would be many years before the Norfolk yard would retreive its pre-war prominence.[38]

## Pensacola Navy Yard

The original navy yards were all in the first thirteen states, but the expansion of the Union soon required a naval presence on the Gulf coast. The purchase of Louisiana in 1803 drew attention to New Orleans as a possible site for such a yard. However, the acquisition of the territory of Florida presented alternatives at Key West and Pensacola. The latter was chosen and Congress appropriated moneys for that purpose in 1825.

In the next two decades, the yard was given low priority, though it saw some use during the Seminole Indian wars and the suppression of piracy on the southern coasts. It was not until after the Mexican War that signficant funding came its way, including moneys for a floating dry dock in 1847. By the Civil War, there was also a building slip, and two ships had been built at the yard, the steam sloops *Pensacola* and *Seminole*.[39]

The Confederate seizure of the yard was excruciatingly easy: four days after Florida seceded from the Union, a regiment of armed Floridians appeared at the gates and demanded the surrender of the place. The commandant struck his flag without a murmur. It is noteworthy that the yard had been established long before the state was formed and admitted to the Union. Consequently the yard had never been held by the state of Florida, and therefore the state still had no right to 're-take' it. Such niceties had no bearing though, obviously.

The loss of the yard was not such a severe blow as that of Norfolk some months later, though the yard was taken intact. There were about fifty buildings on the yard, a dozen of which were officer quarters, and the floating dry dock. The only vessel on hand was the old steamer *Fulton* which was out of the water and stripped for repairs.

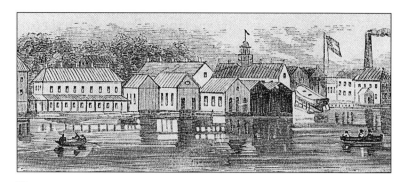

**P**ensacola Navy Yard was the navy's only facility on the Gulf coast. The Confederates captured it simply by marching up to the front gate. Fortunately, it was not nearly as important or well equipped as Norfolk had been. From Benson Lossing's *Pictorial History of the Civil War*, 1866.

The yard remained in Confederate hands until May 1862, when they evacuated it and burned as much property as possible in the process. 'The Yard is a ruin,' was the succinct report on its condition after the Federal forces re-took it. However, what remained was sufficient to encourage David G Farragut to select it as the naval depot for the West Gulf Blockading Squadron.[40]

The first ships of Farragut's squadron arrived for repairs in early 1863 and thereafter came in a regular stream, interrupted for a few months by a yellow fever epidemic in the summer of that year. Though Farragut boasted of the renewed capacity of the yard in 1864, in truth, its repair capabilities were hampered by lack of heavy machinery, skilled machinists, and a dry dock (the old floating dock had been sunk by the Confederates). To give some perspective to the conditions in the re-captured yard, one can read much into Secretary Welles' post-war (1866) report that most of the wartime arrangements at the yard were of a temporary nature. The officers, for instance, were living in 'old kitchens and stables', and far too little 'of a permanent character' had been done. With small post-war appropriations, it would be years before the yard was truly restored.[41]

## Mare Island Navy Yard

The acquisition of California from Mexico for the first time fulfilled the national ambition of reaching the Pacific coast; the astounding discovery of gold less than a year later sparked a migration to that seemingly promised land. The population of the territory spiked from 15,000 to 100,000 in a year, and admission as a state followed in 1850. The nation now needed a naval base on a new ocean, and the obvious location was San Francisco.

Mare Island Navy Yard, California, 1855: the navy's first yard on the west coast. David G Farragut was the yard's first commandant and oversaw the first construction there. (US Navy)

The sectional dry dock, Mare Island Navy Yard. This structure was nearly identical to the dry dock built for Philadelphia yard. Its parts were manufactured in New York and were shipped to California for assembly. The ship shown is the steam sloop *Hartford*. (US Navy)

Mare Island, comprising 1066 acres on San Francisco Bay, was selected and purchased in January 1853. Soon the small naval presence expanded to a respectable working yard, complete with dry dock and a workforce monthly payroll of over $50,000.[42]

The dry dock was a story in itself. A somewhat modified version of the sectional dock built at Philadelphia, its modular construction made it an appropriate candidate for transshipment – in pieces – from its manufacturer in New York. It was contracted in May 1851, and was in operation a year later, antedating even the selection of the specific yard site on the bay.[43]

By the outbreak of the Civil War, the yard had produced the first naval ship built on the west coast, the paddle steamer *Saginaw*, and had become the base for the navy's Pacific squadron. During the course of the conflict, the yard had nothing to fear from the secessionists beyond wild rumors of plots to take possession of the place or of raids by Confederate commerce destroyers such as *Alabama*.

These rumblings, however vague, vibrated down the wires of the new transcontinental telegraph and convinced Congress that a modern ironclad, preferably a monitor, would soothe the fears of the locals. As with the dry dock, however, the USS *Camanche* turned out to be a do-it-yourself project. Accepting the impossibility of such a craft safely rounding Cape Horn, the navy sent her in pieces on a transport, to be assembled on arrival. Completed after the war, she remained a local fixture into the 1890s.

In summary, the California yard heard not a shot fired in anger during the Civil War. Occasionally a steam sloop would put in for provisions, coal, or repairs, then depart across the Pacific pursuing ephemeral Confederate cruisers. Such was the extent of Mare Island's contribution to the naval war.

# Wartime naval stations

As the war unfolded, crushing the rebellion required an offensive war strategy on the part of the Union. One natural consequence of this strategy was increasingly extended lines of supply and communications. In the naval effort, maintaining the blockade was dependent on continuous supplies of provisions, water and coal, as well as maintenance and repair of vessels and equipment. In the war on the rivers, the same needs applied, but in support of virtually continuous waterborne and land offensives. These factors resulted in the establishment of new naval supply and repair facilities as conveniently positioned as possible for the various blockad-

Anchor shop, Hilton Head Island. (USAMHI)

ing squadrons as well as to the ever moving front lines down the heartland of the country. Before the war ended there were bases for the river operations at Cairo and Mound City, Illinois, and Memphis, Tennessee. On the coasts were facilities at Baltimore, Maryland, Beaufort, and Port Royal, South Carolina, Ship Island, and New Orleans, Louisiana and Key West, Florida. In addition to the above, there were numerous smaller sites where storage or repairs were made on an ad hoc basis – usually until more appropriate facilities were either captured or constructed.

On the east coast, one of the largest facilities outside the navy yards was at Baltimore. It was limited in facilities and wharf space, having only one dock, and one set of ways for hauling out vessels. The dock was so narrow that sidewheelers in many instances were required to remove their wheels to clear its sides. The wharf was also overcrowded and much work was therefore contracted out.[44]

Farther south, in the Hampton Roads area, Old Port Comfort and Fortress Monroe became temporary sites for both repairs and supply. Stationed there was the storeship *Brandywine* which served as floating carpentry shop was well as an engine parts depot. Until moved to the re-captured Norfolk yard, there was a foundry, smith, and machine and carpentry shops, totalling over 7000 square feet of building space, at Old Point Comfort. Additionally, part of Fortress Monroe, an army installation, served as a navy gunpowder magazine.[45]

The North Atlantic Blockading Squadron had several small facilities at New Berne, Roanoke Island, Washington, and Beaufort, North Carolina. The only hauling out ways were at Washington, however, and repairs at New Berne were at an army facility. Beaufort had both repair shops and a storage warehouse.[46]

Port Royal, South Carolina provided the Union with a sheltered harbor. In one part of the naval facility there was a machine shop built out of two whalers. Relatively small repair jobs could be accomplished there, but major engine repairs required a trip to a northern yard. (USAMHI)

The South Atlantic Blockading Squadron had early access to the enemy coast after the Battle of Port Royal in late 1861. As a result, both Hilton Head and Port Royal Islands fell into Union hands. Taking advantage of the harbor at Port Royal, Admiral DuPont commandeered two whalers, attached them broadside to broadside and made one a machine shop, the other a storage hulk. (A similar arrangement had been used by the French at the Crimea.) Later, the ship of the line *Vermont* was set up as a store-ship, and an ordnance hulk was brought in.[47]

At the far south of Florida, Key West — which never fell into Confederate hands — became an important rendezvous for vessels in and out of the Gulf of Mexico. In addition to an ordnance storeship, there was a coaling station and provisions warehouse there, as well as a much-used admiralty prize court. This station remained in use at least through the Spanish American War.

On the Gulf, before the capture of New Orleans in 1862, the blockading squadrons set up a station at Ship Island at the mouth of the Mississippi. After New Orleans was safely in hand, a station was opened in that city, including ordnance and provisions storage.

On the western rivers, the navy at first was subordinate to the army, only supplying expertise and officers for an army-built and supplied flotilla, headquartered at Cairo, Illinois, at the confluence of the Mississippi and Ohio Rivers. Slightly to the north on the Ohio was Mound City, the building site of several of the ironclad gunboats. Both these stations were sites of repair and supply facilities, including, at Cairo, ways for hauling out vessels. At Cairo was a receiving ship and a wharf boat, large enough to house ordnance, equipment, commissary stores, shops, and officer quarters.

Navy yard, Memphis, Tennessee. During the 1840s a move was afoot to encourage the cultivation of hemp in the US. Memphis was chosen as a site for a navy yard and, in particular, a rope walk. The yard was abandoned before the Civil War, then re-captured by Union forces in 1862. (US Navy)

In 1862, after the battle of the same name, Memphis, Tennessee was taken by Union forces, landing a fully equipped navy yard on the Mississippi River in the process. The facility had been built by the US Navy in the 1840s but was abandoned before the war. The Confederates re-activated it and the re-conquerors found it as large as the yard at Kittery and complete with shops and storage facilities.

Late in the war, there was much discussion about setting up a permanent navy yard on the Mississippi, with Memphis and Cairo as major contenders for the site. In the event, only a small station (and hospital) was retained after the war, and that at Mound City, mainly as a site for the laid-up ironclads. For obvious reasons, no mid-American navy yard was deemed necessary.

## Sackets Harbor

The northern maritime border of the United States is at present the longest undefended boundary in the world; but during the Civil War, it was not so. The Confederates used Canada as a base for various – and futile – plots against the Union, and throughout the war, the only treaty-allowed US Naval vessel, the paddle-wheeler *Michigan*, was armed blatantly to the teeth – far beyond her treaty limit. (Indeed, one of the botched rebel plots was aimed at taking the vessel and turning her against Lakes shipping.) Her

base of operations was Erie, Pennsylvania, on the lake of the same name. Due to ice on the lakes, she was regularly laid up during the winters.

The only permanent naval presence on the Lakes was at Sackets Harbor, on Lake Ontario, New York. The raison d'être for this yard was the long-standing, incomplete hull of a ship of the line, *New Orleans*. She had been laid down as a 120-gun ship in 1814 as part of the arms build-up of the War of 1812 and left undone with the coming of peace. She was broken up in 1883, probably setting some kind of record for years on the stocks. The yard itself included a ship house, wharves, and small buildings, all of which were maintained with less than $10,000 annually, including pay for two officers (as of 1860). Post-war, expenses were often less than $1000. This yard was discontinued with the break-up of the *New Orleans*.[48]

## Overseas facilities

An American colonial empire was far in the future. On one hand, this meant that the United States Navy's overseas responsibilities were significantly less than those of the European powers. The negative consequence of this was a lack of wholly owned real estate on which to place overseas coaling or provisioning stations. To fill this void, a string of leased sites had been accumulated at strategic spots in the cruising areas of the respective squadrons.

In 1860, there were eight overseas stations. The European squadron provisioned at Spezia, Italy, and vessels on the Pacific had sites at Hong Kong, Valparaiso, Chile, and Panama City, in what was then known as New Granada. On the Atlantic side of the isthmus of Panama was a facility at Aspinwall, now known as Colon. The Brazil squadron supplied at Rio de Janiero. The African squadron was supplied at St Paul de Loando, Angola. (This site replaced Porto Praya, Cape Verde Islands in 1860). Each of these had a naval storekeeper to maintain the needed levels of provisions, clothing and small stores (buttons, combs, razors, scissors, and the like). The largest depositories were at Hong Kong and Rio de Janiero, holding inventories of over $60,000 each in 1860.[49]

The overall impact of the navy yards and other naval repair facilities on the naval war itself has never been thoroughly explored. The only statistical study to date is in Dr Robert Browning's book on the North Atlantic Blockade Squadron. He points out: 'The repair problem for the squadron was severe. A gunboat averaged over twenty per cent of the war in a repair facility.' Further: 'The navy never solved its repair problems, because as the facilities improved, the numbers of vessels increased.' Some of Brownings tables show that during 1863 and 1864, nineteen per cent of the ships in the squadron were away for repairs – some 19 out of 102 vessels. One of the lowest points in the war was September 1864 where 39 per cent of the vessels were away at various repair sites – two-fifths of the squadron.[50]

Though comparable statistics are not available for the South Atlantic, East and West Gulf squadrons, it seems reasonable that the percentages would be, if anything, significantly worse for those units. First, the North Atlantic squadron was the nearest of all the squadrons to both the yards and the northern port cities. (Washington and Baltimore were a mere half day steaming from the Chesapeake, for instance.) Second, the most extensive repair facilities were located farther north, at Boston and New York, placing the most southern and western squadrons at yet another geographical disadvantage. Of course, the extreme example was the West Gulf squadron: the closest full-fledged yard was Washington, over 2000 miles distant. At 10 knots, this would place a blockader from Galveston about six days out and six back, significantly increasing her time off station.

The implications of these statistics are serious ones for the study of the effectiveness of the entire blockade effort. Certainly the number of vessels employed by the navy was huge, but these out-for-repair statistics make it possible to estimate that at any given time, a full one fifth of the fleet was off station or under repair. (One should also take into consideration the fact that Browning's numbers do not include days the vessels were off coaling or victualling, or were on station but in need of repairs.) In this light, recent scholarship indicating the apparent ease with which runners broke the gauntlet is somewhat more comprehensible.

These high percentages of vessels out for repair lead to obvious questions concerning causes. Some obvious factors were: the numbers of machinery breakdowns, the lack of local (on station) repair facilities, and the size and capacities of both navy yards and leased civilian yards and docks. Contributing to the breakdown problem were factors such as the relatively primitive state of steam engineering, the fact that neither naval nor merchant ship machinery was built for blockade conditions, long, uninterrupted days and weeks at sea, under way, and the large percentage of inexperienced engineers in naval service during the emergency.

To deal with the situation, on-station shops were set up and handled minor repairs, but with Pensacola and Norfolk at reduced capacity, major work was of necessity sent north. And, as has been pointed out, the remaining yards were built according to peacetime requirements – to service less than 75 vessels, rather than over 500. It is difficult to see how the Navy Department could have done other than they did, without a major restructuring of priorities. There was no massive effort to expand the yards and their capacities, indeed, the two most southern yards were the most circumscribed in territory and therefore the least appropriate for expansion. Rather, much of the work was contracted to civilian yards and shops.

It should also be remembered that the majority of the work was steam engineering related, not traditional wooden hull and rope-rigging repairs, most of which could be handled on station. This meant that expansion of repair capacity involved significant capital expense for specialized machinery, as well as both buildings and significant lead time. Though the department did begin to enhance their engine shop facilities during the war, it appears that much of the new machinery did not come on line until very late in the conflict or afterwards. Meanwhile, civilian machine shop owners continued to be the beneficiaries of the department's repair funds, and the navy continued to compete with others, including the army, in this sellers market.

## Chapter Four

# THE SHIPS OF LINCOLN'S NAVY

The war vessels of the United States Navy in the Civil War era can be broken down into two broad categories: those built at the behest of the navy, whether in navy yards or by contract, and those acquired by capture, purchase, or transfer from other government agencies. The former comprised the bulk of the pre-war fleet and again regained primacy after the termination of the conflict. The latter, though far outnumbering the purpose-built vessels while the war continued, were quickly discarded afterwards.

**Imaginary illustration of the Union fleet's ironclads, 1862. It is riddled with inaccuracies. Some of these vessels were yet to be completed:** *Keokuk* **(front, left),** *Dictator* **(far left),** *Roanoke* **(center), Stevens Battery (forward right),** *New Ironsides* **(behind Stevens Battery),** *Monitor* **(far right). A ninety-day gunboat and the steam sloop** *Brooklyn* **are in the background on the left and right respectively. Probably the most accurate rendition is of the little Stevens Battery, also known as** *Naugatuck.* **(US Navy)**

Within these two modes of acquisition, the vessels can be further subdivided by their intended areas of operation. For obvious reasons, vessels intended for river work were distinct from those built for the high seas. However, a third category – coastal vessels – could be applied to lighter draft oceangoing ships as well as the monitor-type ships.

The purpose-built naval ships can be divided into the conventional wooden-hulled hybrid steam-and-sail vessels, and the ironclads. The former ranged from ninety-day gunboats, at about 160 feet in length, to steam frigates such as the *Merrimack* and *Colorado*, with weaponry ranging from 5 to over 40 guns. In the latter group of conventional vessels were the wartime designed sidewheel double-ended gunboats, specifically intended for riverine operation.

The Union's ironclads were for the most part variations on John Ericsson's original *Monitor*, or at least retaining the pattern of low freeboard and turret-mounted guns. The strangest of these were built for river service, drawing as little as 4 feet and propelled

by stern paddle wheels. Casemated vessels were more common on the rivers, where the concentrated weight of the turret and machinery militated against retaining the light draft necessary for such waters. (It should be noted that many river ironclads were technically converted from commercial vessels. However, the extent of these rebuilds throws them into the 'purpose-built' category.) Two broadside ironclads, *Galena* and *New Ironsides*, saw service in coastal operations, and were the only such vessels in American service. It would not be until the 1880s that the navy would enter the world naval armament race and begin the process of creating a blue-water, battleship navy.

A sub-category among the purpose-built ships held the remaining units of the sailing navy, dating mostly from the 1840s and 50s, with broadside armament ranging up to 50 guns. Less than a dozen were in commission or available at the outset of the war, but they proved useful in blue-water operations, particularly in searching out the Confederate cruisers. Also available but not put into service were several ships of the line, such as *New Hampshire* and *Vermont*, and the venerated frigate *Constitution*. The first two had long since been relegated to receiving or station ships; the latter was a training vessel at the Naval Academy. The conflagration at the Norfolk Navy Yard in 1861 put paid to a great number of the older sailing vessels, including the huge 120-gun *Pennsylvania*, and certainly hastened the end of the old sailing fleet.

The vessels acquired by the navy for the emergency, were, as could be expected, an extremely motley group. The majority were intended for the blockade and therefore were neither very deep nor very large. In most cases, presence was emphasized rather than speed or armament: an internationally recognized blockade was determined not by the efficiency of the vessels, but by their existence on station. For these reasons only a few substantial ocean steamers were brought in, though these proved useful in deep-water anti-cruiser operations. The Navy Department caught considerable public sarcasm when it appeared that they would purchase anything that would float, including New York Harbor ferry boats. And indeed, some of the purchased vessels proved ill-suited to navy usage. The ferries, however, made good gun platforms for joint army operations on the rivers.

Conversion of merchant vessels for naval use was usually relatively simple, rarely resulting in irreversible change in the ship's character. It typically involved strengthening decks below newly installed weaponry, removal of superfluous deck cabins, installation of ammunition storage spaces, and, often, adding protective sheet iron over pilot houses and other vulnerable spaces.

Propulsion systems in the steam vessels also produced significant differences in usage. The sidewheel ships utilized steam machinery which was markedly simpler and significantly more reliable than that of the screw steamers. They were, generally, speedier than the screw vessels and proved their worth on the blockade, where the typical runner was also propelled by sidewheels. From the naval standpoint, however, paddle wheels were anathema, with their highly vulnerable paddle boxes and highly placed machinery. Hence, the typical Union navy screw sloop, though quite well armed, was significantly slower than the converted sidewheel merchantman, a situation not ignored by the adversary. Riverboats were as a rule, side- or stern wheel vessels, as screws were easily fouled and damaged by river obstructions and debris.

Finally there were miscellaneous vessels in less defined categories. These include the ships on the ways or nearing completion at war's end, various auxiliary and supply vessels, torpedo vessels (launches and boats), and experimental submersibles.

What follows is a description of the major classes or categories of Union naval vessels of the war. Historically significant or unusual individual vessels will be presented in some detail throughout.

# Conventional steam warships

The mid nineteenth-century steam sloop formed the bulk of the vessels of the US Navy at the outbreak of hostilities, and, again became the mainstay of the fleet in the post-war decades. The majority of the wartime navy-yard built ships were based on pre-war designs ranging from the ninety-day gunboats upward. The typical steam sloop or gunboat had a single gundeck with weaponry built around one or two large smoothbore pivot guns and two or more broadside carriage guns. Their rig ranged from two-masted schooners to full-rigged ships, and the machinery was usually a two-cylinder simple-expansion unit typically yielding 7 knots cruising speed, though some of the larger sloops bettered this with larger engines and the advantage of length.

Due to the shallow water emphasis of this conflict, the larger steamers were not repeated in wartime construction. Specifically, the frigate *Merrimack* and sisters, though powerfully armed, at 22 feet or more in draft, were unable to enter key southern ports. Generally, the southern coast dictated a maximum of 16 feet draft for any vessel's optimum usefulness in this war.

## Unadilla Class

The so-called ninety-day gunboats were built for the blockade and their origin can be traced to within a month of Lincoln's proclamation of this policy. Their general arrangement, size (158 feet between perpendiculars, 28 feet breadth, 10 feet draft, 671 tons) and armament (single large pivot gun and two broadside guns) was based on an early gunboat, the *Pocahontas*, of the 1850s. Twenty-three were built, all under contract to civilian shipbuilders. The number built was said to have been based on the number of available yards and the ninety-day appellation came about from a delivery date contract stipulation for four of the vessels. In fact, the shortest time from contract to commission was the *Unadilla*, at ninety-three days.

Their hulls were wood, usually white oak framing and yellow pine plank, with diagonal iron strapping for increased longitudinal strength. Engines were simple expansion two-cylinder units of the back-acting (return connecting rod in British parlance) variety with cylinders of 30 inches diameter and two boilers, yielding 400 horsepower and 10 knots maximum speed. They were provided with forced draft fans, surface condensers, and bunkers for 112 tons of coal. The 9-foot screw could be disconnected to reduce drag when under sail alone. Though designed as schooners with gaff topsails and a single fore topsail, operations in ports and on rivers often resulted in dispensing with the sails entirely. The complement of these vessels ranged from 65 to 100 men.

Armament for these ships centered around the midships pivot gun, usually an 11-inch Dahlgren smoothbore or 100-pounder Parrott rifle. Circular pivot rails allowed its use on either side, with a 16-foot segment of each bulwark built to unship and allow considerable field of fire. Two 24-pounder carriage guns, plus a 20-pounder boat howitzer completed their armament.

The performance of these vessels was not spectacular, but cer-

**N**inety-day gunboat (*Unadilla* class), *Huron*. **The twenty-three contract-built gunboats proved sturdy and competent, but not fast. Usual ordnance was a single 11-inch smoothbore on pivot between fore mast and funnel, two 32-pounders in broadside and a rifled gun on the forecastle. Their primary assignment was on the blockade. (USAMHI)**

tainly was more than adequate, considering their hasty genesis and construction. They were initially able to make 10 knots or more under steam but the constant steaming required on the blockade detracted materially from this capability. They were not considered capable of extended cruising at sea, but were quite suited to blockade work.

The ninety-day gunboats were all in commission by 8 March 1862, with four participating in the attack on Port Royal in November 1861. All save one were in commission at the close of the war and many had acquired enviable reputations in combat. Only one, the *Sciota*, had been sunk, and twice at that. The first time she was involved in a collision, and the second time she fell victim to a mine in 1865. Ten had been with Farragut at New Orleans. *Cayuga* had been the vulnerable lead ship in that operation and came away with forty-two hits. All save the *Kineo* racked up captures on the blockade, totalling 146. *Sagamore* led with fifteen schooners and four sloops; *Kennebec* led in capture value at $1.5 million. Several lasted beyond the war, with the last (*Unadilla*) sold in November 1869, in Hong Kong.

**K**ansas **class gunboat,** *Nipsic*. **Twenty feet was added to the ninety-day gunboat design, plus another pair of broadside guns, to create this class. The first did not see service until 1863. From Charles Boynton's** *History of the Navy During the Rebellion* **of 1868.**

### NINETY-DAY GUNBOATS: UNADILLA CLASS

| | | |
|---|---|---|
| *Aroostook* | *Cayuga* | *Chippewa* |
| *Chocura* | *Huron* | *Itasca* |
| *Kanawha* | *Katahdin* | *Kennebec* |
| *Kineo* | *Marblehead* | *Ottawa* |
| *Owasco* | *Pembina* | *Penobscot* |
| *Pinola* | *Sagamore* | *Sciota* |
| *Seneca* | *Tahoma* | *Unadilla* |
| *Winona* | *Wissahickon* | |

## *Kansas class sloops*

These eight vessels were designed to rectify some of the ninety-day ships' shortcomings. Additional length and larger engines were introduced to enhance speed and added breadth to provide a steadier gun platform, resulting in measurements of 171 to 179 feet by 30-feet beam. A variety of engines was tried, and some yielded good speed, but the unusual machinery generally created maintenance problems. All retained two-masted rigs until the post-war years when the remaining ships received a third stick. All were armed with single pivot guns amidships plus four broadside weapons, usually 32-pounders or 9-inch Dahlgrens.

These vessels proved to be significantly faster than the ninety-day ships, and a 10-knot cruising speed is probably a fair general-

ization for the group. Their wartime careers were significantly shorter than the earlier class (only two were in commission as early as 1863). Five participated in the operations against Fort Fisher in late 1864-early 1865. Two, *Maumee* and *Pequot*, were decommissioned at the war's end. All but *Yantic* were out of service by 1883, and *Yantic* remained in various auxiliary roles until disintegrating from age as recently as 1929.

## KANSAS CLASS:

| | | |
|---|---|---|
| *Kansas* | *Maumee* | *Nipsic* |
| *Nyack* | *Pequot* | *Saco* |
| *Shawmut* | *Yantic* | |

## *Mohican and class*

These screw sloops came to be among the most useful and long lasting vessels of this era. Of ten included in the class, six saw over twenty years service each, and three, over thirty years. Though all received the requisite periodic refits and modifications, they generally ended their careers without major changes. Of course the exemplar of the group was the *Kearsarge*, which made herself a legend with the defeat of the Confederate cruiser *Alabama* off Cherbourg in 1864.

Two groups are included in this class: six built in 1859 and four added, using the same designs, as a wartime measure in 1861. Another screw sloop, *Pawnee*, was authorized with the 1859 group, but was of a totally different character, both in hull design and armament, and therefore is not considered part of this class. *Pawnee* is presented on page 67.

The ten were built to six plans, two at 188 feet and the remainder at 198 feet in length. Listed below are their names arranged according to their respective designs (with building dates):

*Mohican* ('59) *Kearsarge* ('61)

*Tuscarora* ('59) *Wyoming* ('61)

*Iroquois* ('59) *Oneida* and *Wachusett* ('61)

*Dacotah* ('59)

*Seminole* ('59)

*Narragansett* ('59)

Congress authorized these ships in 1858, after the Secretary of the Navy indicated the need for steamers capable of coastal work both in home waters and in response to the continuing trou-

bles in China (the T'ai P'ing Rebellion). Operations in the Far East implied oceangoing capabilities as well. The new ships would replace sailing vessels and a few obsolete paddle-wheel ships in such roles. Ostensibly the new sloops were to be 'full power' steamers, as opposed to the earlier frigates such as *Merrimack* which were officially auxiliary steamers.

These vessels represented more than a mere incremental application of the screw steam principle to another segment of the American navy, however. In terms of weaponry and its relation to hull design, these ships were a significant break from the past.

The *Mohican* and class represents the first time major war vessels were designed without emphasis on broadside guns. By 1855 John Dahlgren's 11-inch gun (capable of throwing shell as well as shot) had successfully completed trials, making it theoretically possible to replace no less than four 32-pounders with a single weapon throwing a 132-pound projectile. The extension of that logic, along with Dahlgren's advocacy of minimizing the variety of weapons in a given battery, was the genesis of these vessels: ships for which no precedent has been found.

The upshot of this was a class wherein a 200-foot gundeck supported as few as six cannon. For comparison, the 1854 *Constellation* (as well as the *Hartford* and class) had a battery of 20 to 24 guns. Of course, the size and weight (10 tons including carriage) of the 11-incher precluded broadside use as well as conventional carriages. Adaptation of pivot rails (racers) on deck enabled use of the guns on either broadside. The ultimate extension of these principles would be seen in the 1863 *Monongahela*, which joined Admiral Farragut with a battery of three pivot guns.

There were two major varieties in this group. *Narragansett* and *Seminole* were shorter by 10 feet, narrower by 2 feet, and, at 1043 and 1230 tons respectively, significantly smaller than their companions. Each carried a single 11-inch pivot gun while the others were designed to mount two 11-inchers. All carried four 32-pounders in broadside. All the 1859 vessels began their careers with such batteries. However, in the 1861 vessels and in later refits of the 1859 ships, there was considerable variety. Rifled 100-pounder Parrotts were often substituted for the Dahlgrens (*Mohican* carried one on her forecastle pivot rails), and an additional pair of broadside guns was sometimes fitted. Several, including *Kearsarge*, had topgallant forecastle mounted rifles, usually 30- or 50-pounders.

The vessels were designed to draw 13 feet or less (*Narragansett* and *Seminole* were to draw 10 feet) and their hull construction was

Steam sloop *Wyoming* or *Tuscarora* (*Mohican* class). One of the few wartime views of these ten significant vessels. Six differing designs were used but all had a similar armament – two large pivot guns and four 32-pounders or 9-inchers in broadside, plus a rifle forward. The grey hull was standard for blockade duty. Note the open aft pivot port. (US Navy)

unremarkable. However, the concentration of fewer weapons towards midships allowed the use of quite sharp hull lines in the pursuit of speed. Decks and internal arrangements were simple, with a long unbroken gundeck but with the berth deck interrupted by machinery spaces. It is unclear whether all were fitted originally with topgallant forecastles; photos or plans show this feature on *Kearsarge*, *Tuscarora*, and *Iroquois*. Short quarterdecks were incorporated in a few of these sloops. In the post-war era, forecastle and quarterdecks proliferated, with the former sometimes extending to the fore mast.

The emphasis on steam power is quite evident in early plans and wartime photographs. The original rig for these ships was unsubstantial; topmasts and topsails only and no square sails on the mizzen. One, *Oneida*, may have been schooner rigged. In post-war years, economy moves brought re-emphasis on sailing rig and resulted in much greater sail area being provided for these sloops.

All were engined with two-cylinder machinery, usually back-

or direct-acting, with two or three boilers, producing around 700 to 873 indicated horsepower. One, *Dacotah*, had geared engines. All managed 11 to 12 knots early in their service lives. *Dacotah* recorded 13.2 knots on trials. It appears that *Iroquois* and *Narragansett* were built with hoisting screws; the other vessels' propellers simply uncoupled for sail-only cruising.

The careers of these screw sloops involved more extended cruising at sea than any other class of wartime steamers. All save *Narragansett* and *Seminole* made cruises in search of various Confederate raiders. The former was on the Pacific for the war's duration; the latter was a fixture on the blockade. *Wyoming*, *Tuscarora* and *Kearsarge* were at sea through most of the conflict with *Tuscarora* instrumental in forcing the abandonment of CSS *Sumter* in 1862. *Wyoming* was upholding trading privileges in Japan, and sank a Japanese warship in the process. She circumnavigated the globe in the course of her first cruise, returning yet again to the Far East in 1865. *Kearsarge*'s war record was uneventful cruising until her victorious encounter with *Alabama* in 1864. The commanding officer of *Wachusett* 'accidentally' rammed and captured the Confederate cruiser *Florida* in neutral waters. *Tuscarora*, *Mohican*, *Oneida*, *Iroquois*, and *Seminole* saw action in various coastal campaigns, from Northern Virginia to Mobile Bay.

The shortest post-war career belonged to *Oneida*, which was sunk in a collision in 1870. *Seminole* was sold the same year. Next

**P**ost-war view of *Iroquois* (*Mohican* class). This view shows the class's typical appearance in peacetime. Note the substantial ship rig. Quarter galleries were not usual in this class. (USAMHI)

to be discarded was *Mohican*, in 1872 at Mare Island, California. Taking her place was another *Mohican*, in 1885, built as a 'repair' of the original, hence some confusion as to the duration of the career of the 1859 vessel. *Kearsarge* was lost in the Caribbean in 1894, though the guns with which she downed *Alabama* had long since been enshrined ashore. The last of this noteworthy class was *Iroquois*, sold in 1910.

## Ossipee and Sacramento classes

These ten vessels were essentially enlargements of the *Mohicans*, with increased beam for steadiness and length for speed. They retained the big pivot gun battery as applied to the *Mohicans* but in the *Sacramentos* a third 11-inch smoothbore or 150-pounder

Parrott was mounted forward. As noted previously, *Monongahela* became the apotheosis of Dahlgren's 'all big gun' ideas, arriving for duty on the Mississippi River with only the three big pivot guns. Farragut, concerned with rate of fire and vulnerability in the river campaigns, immediately added six broadside guns. Typically, therefore, they were armed with two 11-inch, one 150-pounder rifle and four 32-pounders or four 9-inch smoothbores.

---

### OSSIPEE CLASS
205'x 38'x 16'9" (1934t)
*Ossipee Juniata Adirondack Housatonic*

### SACRAMENTO CLASS
225'-232' x 37'6"-38' x 16'10"-17'7" (2030 - 2526t)
*Sacramento Shenandoah Ticonderoga Monongahela Lackawanna Canandaigua*

---

All were powered by back-acting machinery designed by chief engineer B F Isherwood and had telescoping stacks and disconnecting propellers. They typically cruised at 11 to 12 knots. Early on all had rather sparse barque rigs, and in some cases, neither

Steam sloop *Lackawanna*: a post-war view of a *Sacramento* class vessel. Ship rig, knee bow and bowsprit were typical post-war additions. (US Navy)

bowsprits nor cutwater knees. With post-war rebuildings came loftier masting, additional yards, cutwater knees and bowsprits. Some were ship rigged. Extensive quarterdecks and fore decks were also added for peacetime cruising. Incidentally, *Monongahela* and *Lackawanna* had improvised iron plating on their cutwaters for use in ramming the Confederate ironclad *Tennessee* at the Battle of Mobile Bay.

All went into service between August 1862 and June 1863. Three – *Lackawanna*, *Monongahela* and *Ossipee* – were at Mobile Bay and three others – *Juniata*, *Shenandoah* and *Ticonderoga* – were at the Fort Fisher operations. All participated in the blockade, with the exception of *Adirondack*, which was wrecked on her first cruise in August 1862. *Housatonic* made history as a victim: the first warship to be sunk by an enemy submersible (the *H L Hunley*), off Charleston in 1864.

Their post-war careers were generally long, with the exception of *Sacramento*, which was lost in the Far East in 1867. Five of the ships were active into the 1880s. *Monongahela* was particularly note-worthy after the war: a storm washed her ashore at St Croix in 1867, after which she was refloated. Her machinery was later removed and she finished her career as a sail-training ship, finally succumbing to fire at Guantanamo Bay in 1908. Her remains can still be seen there.

## Hartford class steam sloops

These five sloops were essentially replacements for the obsolete sailing sloops such as the 1854 *Constellation* (the last such sailing vessel launched by the navy), which mounted some 20 guns on a single open gundeck with pivot guns on forecastle and poop. The new ships were comparable to the British corvettes *Cadmus* and *Pearl* of 1856, and were to have a maximum draft of about 18 feet, enabling them to operate in southern ports. The five were authorized in March 1857, with four constructed at navy yards and the fifth, *Brooklyn*, contracted to Jacob Westervelt, a prominent builder of clipper ships.

The five were built to different designs, with relatively similar dimensions and armament; hence the denomination as a class.

### HARTFORD CLASS
*Hartford*: 225'x 44' x 23'3" (2550t)
*Richmond*: 225'x 42' x 20'8" (2604t)
*Brooklyn*: 223'x 43' x 22'8" (2532t)
*Pensacola*: 230'8" x 44'6" x ? (3000t)
*Lancaster*: 235'8" x 46' x 22'3" (3290t)

The unique vessel of the group was *Lancaster*, with significantly greater dimensions and displacement than the rest. She mounted 24 broadside 9-inch guns, plus two pivots, and was the only vessel to have a complete spar deck throughout her career. The broadside battery of *Richmond* and *Brooklyn* was 16 guns; the remaining pair, 20 each – all with some variations through their careers. In the

Farragut's flagship, the steam sloop *Hartford*, 1864. This class carried 18 to 22 guns in broadside, plus forecastle rifles. *Hartford* shows her rig as reduced for the Battle of Mobile Bay, and a grey hull. Besides being workhorses during the war, these vessels had long post-war careers. (US Navy)

Outboard and sail plan of *Hartford*, 1864 (modern reconstruction). (Smithsonian Institute)

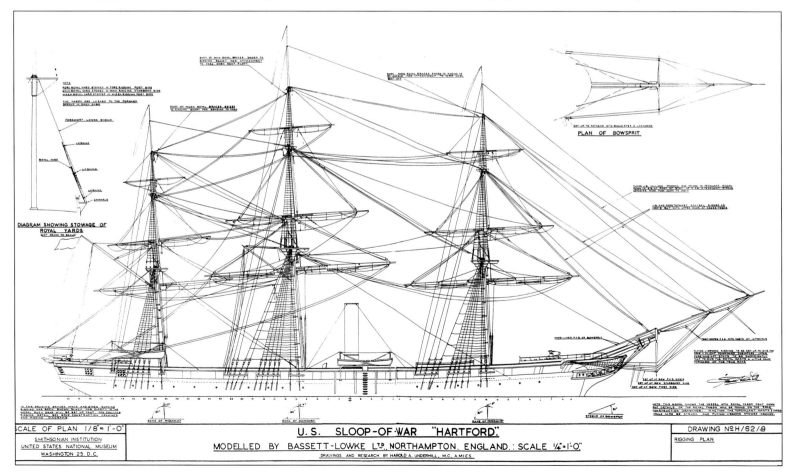

post-war years several had 8-inch rifles (conversions from Dahlgren smoothbores) mounted abaft the fore mast on pivot rails to fire on either beam.

All had two-cylinder back-acting or direct-acting machinery. Only *Brooklyn* and *Lancaster* had identical engines. However, *Lancaster* was given significantly greater boiler capacity. *Pensacola's* machinery was an experiment in the steam expansion controversy of this era and proved an unmitigated failure, weighing in at twice that of the *Lancaster*, for instance, and significantly less efficient. Conventional engines were installed in her late in the war. She was reboiled in 1878 and became the only one of the class with twin funnels. The class was not particularly noted for speed. With sail, *Hartford*, for instance, could attain 11 knots, and most cruised under steam at 8 to 9 knots.

Hull construction and design was conventional. Significant use was made of live oak and iron diagonal strapping, certainly contributing to the long careers of all these ships. *Brooklyn* was said have had four watertight bulkheads, though these were simply substantial wooden partitions. All were ship rigged and *Hartford* made use of rigging screws (turnbuckles) rather than deadeyes (as early as 1864). *Lancaster* gained a ram bow during a rebuild in the 1870s, along with a heroic eagle figurehead, which survived and is on display at the Mariner's Museum in Virginia.

All went into commission in 1859 or 1860, though *Pensacola's* machinery problems delayed her actual service until 1861. The wartime careers of these ships were action filled (excepting *Lancaster*, stationed on the Pacific coast for the duration), with their significant firepower and moderate draft making them a natural choice for operations against coastal fortifications. *Hartford*, *Richmond*, *Brooklyn*, and *Pensacola* were at New Orleans and all but the latter were also at Mobile Bay in 1864.

All exceeded thirty years of active service, with *Brooklyn* first to go in 1891. The other four served into the following century, with *Hartford*, having become a venerated icon as Farragut's flagship, surviving until 1956.

## Merrimack class steam frigates

Six frigates were authorized in 1854, the first screw-propelled class in the US Navy. In the tradition set down so vividly by *Constitution* of 1797, these ships were to be larger than their counterparts in other navies, and faster than more heavily armed enemies. Five of these were 'double banked' frigates with a main gundeck carrying from 24 to 28 of the new 9-inch Dahlgren smoothbore shell guns,

**S**team frigate *Wabash*. The *Merrimack* class ships were far too deep for many southern ports but their 40- to 50-gun batteries were formidable when the range and depth allowed. This view was taken when she was a receiving ship at Boston after the war. Note the elaborate stern decoration. (US Navy)

and the upper deck originally armed with 8-inch shell guns in broadside and a 10-inch Dahlgren on the forecastle. The sixth ship, *Niagara*, was unique and is discussed on page 67.

### MERRIMACK CLASS STEAM FRIGATES
*Merrimack* 256'10½" x 50'2" x 26'2½" (4635t)
*Wabash* 262'4" x 50'2" x 26'2" (4774t)
*Minnesota* 264'8½" x 50'2" x 26'2" (4833t)
*Roanoke & Colorado:* 263'8 1/4" x 51'4" x 26'2" (4772t)

As shown here, there were four hull designs, and only two identical vessels in the group. The hull design was an enlargement of a conventional frigate configuration, with longer port spacing

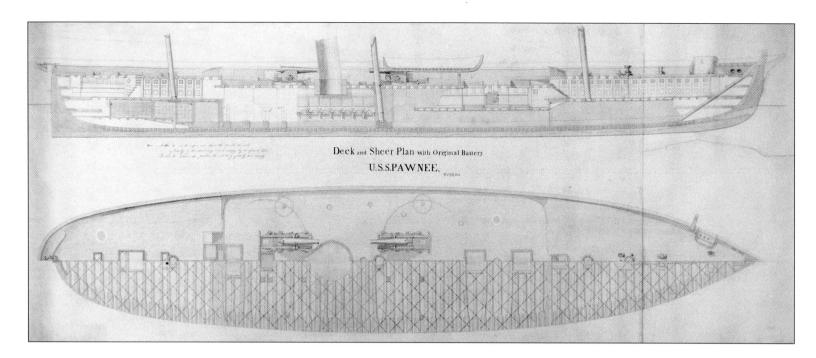

Deck and Sheer Plan with Original Battery
U.S.S.PAWNEE.

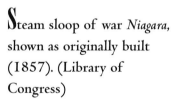

*Pawnee* with her original battery: four 11-inch guns on pivots. The plan shows iron diagonal support strapping under her deck. (National archives; photograph by the author)

*Steam sloop of war *Niagara*, shown as originally built (1857). (Library of Congress)

to accommodate the newly developed Dahlgren shell guns. (It should be noted here that another vessel was built to this design: the *Franklin*, completed after the Civil War). Hull construction was principally oak and two sets of diagonal iron strapping imparted longitudinal strength.

Engines for these vessels were two-cylinder installations, with 72-inch cylinders on *Merrimack* and *Wabash*. *Minnesota, Roanoake* and *Colorado* had trunk engines, with larger diameters but similar cubic capacity to the other vessels. All had telescoping funnels and hoisting screws.

In service, the ships drew considerable attention, particularly overseas, where their battery was considered quite formidable.

Unfortunately, they proved to be quite slow ships, unlikely to exceed 8 knots under steam. In any case, the Royal Navy built two classes of screw frigates (eleven vessels) in response.

These vessels, as built, had limited use in the War Between the States. Drawing some 23 feet, they could not enter the majority of the southern ports. *Wabash* participated in the Port Royal expedition in 1862; she and *Minnesota* and *Colorado* were in the bombardment of Fort Fisher late in the war. *Merrimack* of course was burned at Gosport in 1861 and reappeared with iron casemate in 1862 as the Confederate *Virginia*, destroying USS *Cumberland* and *Congress*, and harrying sister-ship *Minnesota*. *Roanoke* was cut down and saddled with three Ericsson turrets and armored sides. She sat out the war as a guard ship, being too deep for close-in work.

*Colorado* participated in the 1871 Korean punitive expedition and was sold in 1885. *Minnesota* became a stationary training ship and was sold in 1901. *Wabash* served in Europe, then was sold in 1912.

The preceding classes comprised the majority of the navy-built screw-propelled unarmored war vessels during the war. Three other pre-war ships round out the total: *San Jacinto, Pawnee* and *Niagara*.

The first of these was built in 1851 and was the navy's second screw steamer. She was armed with six 8-inch shell guns and measured 210 feet and 2200 tons. Her claim to fame was in stopping the steamer *Trent* and taking the Confederate diplomats, Mason and Slidell.

*Pawnee* was built contemporaneously with the *Mohican* class, but by contract with John Griffiths of New York. To achieve a 10-foot draft he designed a beamy hull with concavity at the stern and twin screws. She was first given four 11-inch Dahlgrens, all on pivot rails, but was rearmed with broadside 9-inchers, eventually carrying twelve of these, plus two large rifles. She was exceedingly useful in river fire support operations throughout the war. She proved excessively leewardly at sea and had a short post-war career.

*Niagara* was contracted to George Steers, famous for his yacht *America* and other fast vessels. He attempted to combine sharp clipper hull lines with a frigate's weaponry, apparently intending to have *Niagara* carry a battery comparable to her navy-built sisters (*Merrimack* and class). This was only possible by making her significantly larger than the other five – 328 feet between perpendiculars and 5540 tons. When launched,

she was the largest vessel built in the US to that time.

Despite her commodious gundeck, she was only given spar deck weapons: twelve 11-inch Dahlgrens, all on pivot rails. She proved to be fast – 10 to 11 knots under steam – and was known to exceed 16 knots under sail. Before the war, she laid the first Atlantic Cable (with HMS *Agamemnon*). During a mid-war refit she was given a full complement of twenty 11-inchers on the gundeck, along with the dozen spar deck guns. This enormous battery brought her ports dangerously low and she reverted to her dozen guns shortly thereafter. Later, in European waters, she captured the former cruiser *Georgia*. Her commander refused combat with the rebel ironclad ram *Stonewall* in 1865, and she was laid up and sold in the 1880s.

Finally there were six screw steamers which had been purchased in the late 1850s: *Mohawk, Crusader, Pocahontas, Mystic, Sumter,* and *Wyandotte*. These were 157 feet to 169 feet long and displaced 450 to 750 tons and carried 4 to 7 broadside guns. *Sumter* was sunk in 1863 and *Mohawk* was sold the next year; the rest served throughout the war.

## Paddle-wheel vessels

The last major American paddle-wheel warships were the *Susquehanna* and *Powhatan*, of the early 1850s. At 3824 and 3865 tons respectively, and carrying no less than fourteen 9-inch or larger guns on their long open decks, both these veterans of Commodore Perry's Japan expedition continued to be useful during the civil conflict, particularly in the coastal campaigns. Both survived many years after the war. The third major sidewheeler was

Paddle steamer *Powhatan,* sister-ship to *Susquehanna,* shown in an 1850s illustration from Charles Stuart's *Naval and Mail Steamers of the United States.* Both vessels carried at least 14 guns throughout the war and generally operated with the Atlantic blockading squadrons. (Photograph by the author)

**M**ississippi, the 1840s paddle steamer and veteran of Perry's Japan expedition. She carried 20 guns – note the open forward pivot port – and was a powerful element of Farragut's New Orleans fleet until lost under fire in 1863. This photograph shows topmasts taken down for river operations. (USAMHI)

**S**assacus class double ender *Mendota*, shown on the James River with topmasts stowed. These vessels had mid-ship paddlewheels and rudders at each end. Shallow draft, maneuverability and speed – 14 knots – made them excellent for river operations. (USAMHI)

the *Mississippi* of 1841. At 3220 tons and able to mount 20 guns of 9-inch or larger, this reliable vessel was with Farragut on the Mississippi River until lost at the Battle of Port Hudson in 1863. Smaller pre-war sidewheelers were the *Water Witch* (255 tons), *Saranac* and *Saginaw*. The latter remained on the west coast throughout the war. Another, the ex-Revenue Cutter *Harriet Lane* (600 tons, 4 guns) was a useful addition to the fleet until captured in 1863. The iron-hulled *Michigan* of 1841 was stationed on the Great Lakes throughout the war.

The double-ended gunboats complete the inventory of navy-built conventional steamers. Thirty-nine of these, in three classes, saw wartime service. These were specifically for river service, with light draft – 6 to 7 feet – and rudders at each end. Paddle wheels

were less likely to foul river obstructions than submerged screws and provided for reliable, speedy operation: the machinery was invariably a single cylinder directly connected to the paddle-wheel shaft. Their batteries featured a large pivot gun at each end, plus, on later classes, 4 broadside guns. Most of the vessels were built in civilian yards, by contract.

The *Octorara* and class numbered twelve, built to nine distinct designs, ranging from 730 to 1120 tons, and 207 to 232 feet in length. All went into service in early 1862. The *Sassacus* class, numbering twenty-eight vessels, were all 1173 tons and 236 feet long. Twenty-seven of these entered service during the war. One of them, *Wateree*, was iron hulled. The *Mohongo* class eventually numbered seven, but only the *Muscoota* and *Suwannee* were commissioned before Appomattox. These were iron hulled (255 feet long, 1173 tons) versions of the *Sassacus* class. All were contract-built and were the first American class of iron-hulled ships (excepting the ironclads themselves). It is noteworthy that many of the double enders were soon given light iron sheathing around pilot houses and other vulnerable areas, to protect crews from small-arms fire.

# Ironclad vessels

The ironclad navy can be subdivided into monitors (revolving turret, low freeboard vessels) and casemated ships, with the preponderance going heavily to the former. Sixty monitor type vessels were begun during the war, with thirty-seven completed by the end of 1865. There were nineteen non-turret vessels, of which fifteen were for river service. Only two oceangoing broadside armored vessels saw wartime service: *Galena* and *New Ironsides*.

Ericsson's ironclad *Monitor*, showing modifications made after the Battle of Hampton Roads, including angled glacis around the pilot house (forward), extended funnels and awning over the turret. No broadside photographs of the vessel exist. *Monitor* changed the entire face of the navy during the war. *Monitor* and *Virginia* (ex-*Merrimack*) fought the first battle between ironclad vessels, and Ericsson's turret was the first to see combat. (US Navy)

John Ericsson's original *Monitor* was less a ship than a motorized floating gun platform. She was built to combat the Confederate ironclads; not to decimate fortifications or fight at sea. Her two 11-inch smoothbore Dahlgrens sat behind eight layers of 1-inch iron, bent into a turret 20 feet in diameter. Two layers of ½-inch plates covered horizontal oak beams forming the upper deck of the ship, which in itself was protected by vertical side armoring: 5 inches of iron over 25 inches of oak. At the time of her encounter with *Virginia* (ex-*Merrimack*), the turret and a pilot house were the only parts of the ship higher than her 18-inch freeboard.

Her machinery was also Ericsson-designed: two pistons in a single cylinder operated 'vibrating levers' which connected to the propeller shaft. She attained 6 knots and had independent auxiliary engines which were able to rotate the turret (at 2½ turns per minute) and ventilation blowers.

Finally, the iron hull itself was unique. She was flat bottomed with bilges at 35° from the horizontal, angling up to the shelf which held her vertical iron and wood side armor. Ericsson made no attempt to give her more than a simple curve fore and aft, rather than ship like lines. Shallow draft was one of the government's requirements and she drew only 10 feet 5 inches when complete and ready for sea.

Completed, the ship was 179 feet by 41 feet 6 inches and displaced 987 tons. Her complement was forty-nine. She had been

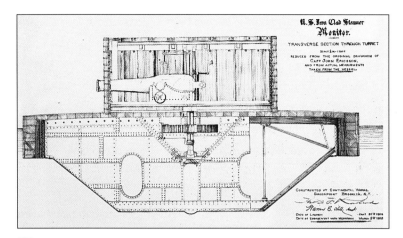

**M**idship cross-section of *Monitor*. Ericsson simplified the design for quick construction dispensing with as many curved elements as possible, including the hull curves. Side armor was 30 inches: five layers of 1-inch iron over 25 inches of oak; the turret was made up of eight 1-inch plates, bolted together. Twin 11-inch Dahlgrens could be run out by one man at the hand wheel. (US Navy)

laid down on 25 October 1861 and commissioned on 25 February the following year, some twelve days before ending the unfaltering rampage of the CSS *Virginia* at Hampton Roads. The *Monitor*'s later career was relatively uneventful, though a few modifications were made, including increased protection for the pilot house and a more conventional funnel. She sank in a gale while under tow off Cape Hatteras on 31 December 1862.

The *Monitor* was not the first ironclad; the Crimean War batteries at Kinburn have this distinction. *Monitor*'s turret was the first to be operational, and her clash with *Virginia* (ex-*Merrimack*) was the first battle between ironclad vessels.

## PASSAIC CLASS MONITORS

*Camanche Catskill Lehigh Montauk Nahant Nantucket Passaic Patapsco Sangamon Weehawken*

Ten *Passaic* class monitors were built, with their authorization coming less than a week after the Battle at Hampton Roads. Major improvements were the mounting of the pilot house above the turret, giving the hull faired ship-like lines (and a sheer), 11-inch turret armor, and providing for two 15-inch smoothbore Dahlgrens (though a shortage of these limited the wartime batteries to one 15-inch and 11-inch gun each). The 15-inch gun was the largest available during the war, firing a 440 pound projectile. The number and type of changes over the original *Monitor* essen-

**V**iew of the turret on the *Passaic* class monitor *Catskill*. The ten ships of this class were significantly different from the original monitor: they had ship-like hull lines and a pilot house mounted above the turret. Each carried one 11-inch (or 150-pounder rifle) and one 15-inch Dahlgren. Note that the 11-inch gun barrel, in the right of the photograph, protrudes through the turret, and the 15-inch bored gun does not. *Catskill* was the lead ship in the April 1863 attack on Charleston. (USAMHI)

tially made the *Passaic*s vastly different vessels, only retaining the general configuration of the *Monitor*.

All were built by contract. *Passaic* was commissioned in December 1862, eight others by April 1863, and *Camanche*, assembled on the west coast in May 1865.

All were 200 feet by 45 feet and 1335 tons displacement. They drew 11 feet 6 inches: somewhat deeper than the original *Monitor*. Seven were involved in the 7 April 1862 attack on Charleston, which proved a debacle for the Union Navy. They proved unwieldy and slow (maximum speed about 7 knots, 4 knots in a current), and they were vulnerable to hits at the turret's juncture with the deck, jamming the turret's rotation. Their rate of fire was slow — five to seven minutes per round for the 15-incher — and aiming the turret was somewhat haphazard. Later, a protective ring was placed around the turret base, and extra protection was given to the vulnerable pilot house.

Though these ships were inappropriate against fortifications, their value against enemy ironclads was soon manifest. *Weehawken* encountered the ironclad *Atlanta* in 1863. Her 15-inch shot penetrated 4 inches of iron and 18 inches of wood, and brought *Atlanta*'s surrender with five shots.

*Patapsco* was mined in January 1865 and *Weehawken* sank in a storm in 1863. The remainder had major post-war rebuilds, replacing their wood deck beams with iron, and remained in the inventory for decades, though infrequently in full commission. Several were commissioned during the Spanish American War. The last of the class were sold in 1904.

## CANONICUS CLASS

*Canonicus Catawba Mahopac Manayunk Manhattan Oneota Saugus Tecumseh Tippecanoe*

The *Canonicus* class numbered nine vessels, built incorporating the improvements added to the *Passaics* after the assault on Charleston in April 1863. Externally the most obvious change was increased length and sharper bows, features which, along with larger engines and more boiler power, were to add speed to the vessels. Furthermore, all had twin 15-inch guns in the turrets, with their barrels machined down to allow them to protrude through the gunports.

Canonicus in 1907, as part of the Jamestown Exhibition Naval Review. Note the modern monitor in the right background and battleship on the far left horizon. *Canonicus* was the last Civil War monitor; she was sold in 1908. (US Naval Institute)

They measured about 225 feet by 43 feet and displaced 2100 tons. Sponsons were added to lessen the drag produced by the armored overhang, and they attained 8 knots.

*Saugus* was first in commission (7 April 1864), and two (*Catawba* and *Oneota*) were sold to Peru before commissioning. *Tippecanoe* was completed after hostilities ended. *Tecumseh* was the most famous of this class: she was mined at Mobile Bay in August 1864, sinking with most of her crew where she remains to this day. The first to be sold was *Saugus*, in 1891; the last, *Canonicus*, in 1908.

Other than the original *Monitor*, plus members of the *Passaic* and *Canonicus* classes, the *Dictator* was the only other single turret Ericsson-designed coastal monitor to see service during the war. (The Light Draft Monitors, reviewed below, were not entirely Ericsson designed.)

John Ericsson intended the *Dictator* and a never-completed companion, *Puritan*, to be oceangoing craft attaining 16 knots. At 314 feet by 50 feet and 4438 tons, *Dictator* was one of the largest iron vessels built in the US up to that date. Her side armor measured 6 inches of iron over wood backing, and the turret plating was 15 inches. She was armed with two 15-inch Dahlgren smoothbores on specially designed carriages, and was powered by 100-inch diameter cylinders. Though commissioned before the war's end, problems with her machinery and boilers prevented her participation in combat. She eventually was capable of 10 knots. She was decommissioned in 1877. *Puritan*, which was to have 20-inch guns and was over 340 feet long, was never completed; a new vessel took the name in the 1870s.

Light Draft Monitor *Casco*, 1864. The result of a botched design based on a preliminary Ericsson sketch, these twenty-three vessels were to draw 6 feet and have a *Passaic* type turret. The first launched had less than 3-inches freeboard, without stores. Attempts to rectify the situation resulted in the conversion of some to 'torpedo boats', as shown here, with one exposed gun. The remainder had nearly 2 feet added to their hulls. The effort proved fruitless, and all were disposed of quietly. (USAMHI)

*Onondaga*, twin turret monitor, with two 15-inch smoothbores and two 150-pounder (8-inch) rifles. Her 15-inchers heavily damaged the Confederate ironclad *Virginia II* in January 1865 at Trent's Reach. Photograph taken on the James River in 1864. (US Navy)

## Casco class: Light Draft Monitors

The original Ericsson design for these twenty-three vessels was significantly re-worked by Alban Stimers of the navy's ironclad office, with ballast tanks worked into their hulls to allow reducing their profile in combat. This and other added weights resulted in a 3-inch freeboard, without stores and ammunition, on the first ships launched. Major modifications, including deletion of the Ericsson turret, and addition of a spar torpedo, did little to rectify their inherent problems. They had been intended for very light draft river work but in the end did well to remain afloat at all. All were broken up or sold by 1875.

## Double turret monitors

Five twin-turret monitors were completed in 1864-65: *Onondaga*, *Monadnock*, *Miantonomoh*, *Tonawanda*, and *Agamenticus*. Only the first two saw wartime service. *Onondaga* was designed by G W Quintard with Ericsson turrets, carrying two 15-inch smoothbores and two

8-inch rifles. She was iron hulled (226 feet by 49 feet 3 inches, 2592 tons) and had 11¾-inch armor on her turrets and 5½ inches on her sides. With twin screws she made 7 knots. She was commissioned in March 1864, and was active on the James River flotilla. Her 15-inch projectiles easily penetrated the 6-inch iron of the Confederate *Virginia II* at Trent's Reach in early 1865. She was sold to France after the war and broken up in 1903.

*Monadnock* was wooden hulled, enabling her construction at Portsmouth Navy Yard, New Hampshire. She carried four 15-inch guns in Ericsson turrets with 10 inches of plating; side plating was five inches at the sheer. Twin screws drove the vessel, powered by Ericsson engines. She measured 250 feet by 53 feet 8 inches and 3295 tons. She made 7 to 8 knots and participated in the attacks on Fort Fisher late in the war. In 1865 she rounded the Horn to San Francisco, taking heavy weather in her stride, though fitted with a substantial breakwater to protect the forward turret. She was broken up in 1874 and a new iron-hulled vessel obtained her name. The other three double-turret monitors were variations on *Monadnock*.

Additionally, at the war's end, four *Kalamazoo* class monitors were under construction, each to carry four 15-inch guns and 15-inch armored turrets. These were never completed.

## Roanoke: triple turret monitor

*Roanoke* was more a product of 'monitor fever' than a calculated plan. The 1854 steam frigate was cut down and saddled with three Ericsson turrets with 11-inch armor, along with 4½ inches of side armor and a ram bow. She carried two 15-inchers, two 11-inchers and two 150-pounder rifles on her 278-foot wooden hull. She may have been of more use as a steam frigate: she was too deep for river work; she rolled too dangerously to be safe at sea. She remained on 'guard' duty on the James River from June 1863 to the end of the war and was broken up in 1883.

*Roanoke*, the navy's first triple turret warship. Converted from the steam frigate sister of *Merrimack*, the vessel had 4½-inch forged iron side armor and a ram. The weight of three turrets made her top heavy and useless at sea; deep draft limited her usefulness close in. She remained a 'guard ship' at Hampton Roads during her active service. (US Navy)

## Casemate ironclads: Galena, New Ironsides, Keokuk

The first two were contemporaries of *Monitor*, intended as possible alternatives to that vessel. *Galena* (180 feet, 738 tons) employed interlocking iron armor (about 3 inches thick) over 18 inches of wood on an otherwise conventional wooden hull. She carried four 9-inch Dahlgrens and two 100-pounder rifles. With Ericsson engines she made 8 knots and rolled heavily at sea. Her armor proved totally inadequate against Drewry's Bluff in 1862: she was penetrated repeatedly with significant losses. She was later disarmored and served until 1869.

The *New Ironsides'* casemate was given 4½ inches of forged iron over some 15 inches of wood. She was 232 feet between perpendiculars, over 57 feet beam and 3486 tons; with armor only extending the length of the battery of fourteen 11-inchers and two 150-pounder rifles. Athwartships iron and wood bulkheads completed the battery 'box'. She was built by Merrick and Cramp and bark rigged. Though underpowered and leewardly at sea she proved nearly impregnable to shot, particularly in the protracted actions at Charleston in 1864. Had it not been for 'monitor fever', *New Ironsides* might have become the pattern for later Union ironclads. She was accidentally destroyed shortly after the war.

*Keokuk* used another experimental armor scheme: iron and wood sandwiched vertically under ⅞₆-inch boiler iron. She was 159 feet and 677 tons with two stationary 'turrets' each carrying an 11-inch Dahlgren. She was delivered in February 1863, and was sunk at Charleston in the April, completely riddled by enemy shot.

The ironclad *Galena*. Built simultaneously with *Monitor*, *Galena* carried four 9-inchers and two 100-pounder rifles. Experimental 'rail and plate' cladding failed to prevent shot from passing completely through the ship at Drewry's Bluff in 1862. She finished the war stripped of most of her armor. (USAMHI)

*Keokuk* utilized weak iron-interspersed-with-wood plating and mounted two 11-inch guns in non-rotating casemates with side and fore and aft gunports. (US Navy)

## Sailing vessels

The US Navy had seven ships of the line at the war's beginning. Two, including the 120-gun *Pennsylvania*, were lost by fire at the Norfolk Navy Yard. None of the remainder were in active roles. Of thirteen frigates, seven were in active service. There were fourteen active sloops including the 1854, 20-gun *Constellation*. Two brigs rounded out the sailing fleet.

*Sloop* of war *Cumberland*, 24 guns. One of the last sailing warships built by the navy (1852), she was sunk by the ironclad *Virginia* at Hampton Roads ten years later, with heavy loss of life. Photographed at Portsmouth Navy Yard. (Portsmouth Navy Yard Historical Society)

## Acquired vessels

Rather than individually detailing the acquired wartime vessels, the following is a survey of these vessels, by size, propulsion, mode of acquisition and, in some instances, specialization. These are approximate numbers, based primarily on Paul Silverstone's *Warships of the Civil War Navies*. Note that the Mississippi River squadron is dealt with separately.

About 345 vessels of all types were acquired by purchase and/or capture by the navy during the conflict, including 251 steamers and 93 sailing ships. Of the total, eighty-four were captured, fifty-five of them steamers. Seven were brought from other government agencies, namely the Revenue Service and US Coast Survey. Note that the total number of captured vessels is much larger than the number actually taken over for navy use.

Some thirty-four large (over 200 feet) steam paddle-wheel vessels were acquired for combat roles, sixteen by purchase and

*Commodore Perry*, one of several New York ferryboats purchased early in the war, all named 'Commodore...' by the navy. They carried up to 5 guns on their wide decks and proved useful for gunfire support on the rivers. (US Navy)

*Vanderbilt*: a former trans-Atlantic steamer donated by magnate Cornelius Vanderbilt and one of the largest and fastest of the converted steamers. She mounted twelve 9-inchers and two 100-pounder rifles and could attain 14 knots. She spent much of the war on the high seas or in the West Indies in search of Confederate cruisers. (USAMHI)

eighteen by capture. (Note that captured merchant vessels were technically purchased via prize courts.) The largest was the *Vanderbilt*, at 340 feet and 3360 tons, donated for $1 by Cornelius Vanderbilt. Eleven large screw steamers were purchased and four captured. Of the purchased screw steamers five were sister-ships acquired before their completion, and armed with 8 to 10 heavy guns: *Proteus*, *Nereus*, *Neptune*, *Glaucus*, and *Galatea*. Medium sized steamers (over 100 feet) numbered sixty, forty of them screw vessels. Nineteen of the total were captures, plus *Harriet Lane* from the Revenue Service and *Hetzel* from the Coast Survey. Small steamers, less than 100 feet, numbered thirty-two, four of them captured. Additionally, eighteen harbor ferries were purchased.

Auxiliary vessels — not armed for combat — numbered twenty-seven, of which eight were captures. Eighty-one tugs were

USS *Fort Donelson*, formerly the blockade runner *R E Lee*. Originally an Irish sea ferry, she ran the blockade twenty-two times before capture in 1863. She was commissioned in June 1864 and made one capture as a blockader.

River gunboat *Conestoga*. Originally a merchant steamer, conversion to war purposes involved strengthening her decks to support her 6 guns, cladding her sides with 5 inches of oak, and lowering boilers into the hold. She was lost in 1864. (US Navy)

acquired, including two by capture and one from another agency. Additionally, the navy had four tugs built.

Of the sailing vessels, there were thirteen full-rigged ships, eighteen barks, two brigs, and thirty-eight schooners and sloops, in addition to twenty-two purchased mortar schooners. Of the total, three were from other agencies, and twenty-eight were captures. One was found: the yacht *America* was raised from a river bed in Florida. None of these figures include the Stone Fleet: sailing vessels purchased and sunk at the entrances of various Southern ports in an attempt to block access to these ports.

# The Mississippi River Fleet

This flotilla was originally under the War Department, but was transferred to the navy in August 1862, with other vessels transferred as completed. Twenty-four ironclads were built, with two of

these incomplete by the war's end. The first three vessels of the fleet were 'timberclads', and nine were turreted. Eight ironclads were massive rebuildings of merchant steamboats. There were twelve rams – structurally strengthened conventional steamers with little ordnance – intended for close combat, specifically, *Vindicator* and *Avenger*, which attained over 15 miles per hour.

There were some seventy-six 'tinclads' – converted merchant steamers with light iron plating. Other modifications included lowering of machinery into the holds, strengthening the decks for ordnance, and removing passenger accomodations. Forty-nine were stern-wheelers and twenty-three were sidewheel vessels. The largest of the latter were *Black Hawk* and *Oachita*, at over 230 feet each, carrying 10 and 23 guns respectively. Stern-wheel vessels were of particular use in narrow waterways, and sidewheelers were more manoeuverable. The tinclads typically measured 150 feet to 175 feet and carried 6 to 8 guns.

The three timberclads were converted in 1861 by direction of

Tinclad *Ouachita*, 1864. Captured from the Confederates in 1863, she was 230 feet long, and carried 23 guns in US service – one of the heaviest armed of the converted riverboats. (US Navy)

Proposed plan for a river ironclad by James B Eads. Width of river allowed vessels to be designed with significant forward firepower, as shown here. *Benton*, which was based on this plan, had 16 guns, with 4 across the bows. (National Archives; photograph by the author)

Ironclad river gunboat *Cairo*, 1862. The seven City class gunboats were only armored on the pilot house, the fore casemate and past the second gunport (note the line of demarcation in the photograph). With 13 guns, from 32-pounders up to 100-pounders, they were powerfully armed. Their plating (2½ inches), plus wood backing, was not impenetrable, however. *Cairo* was sunk by torpedo in December 1862. (USAMHI)

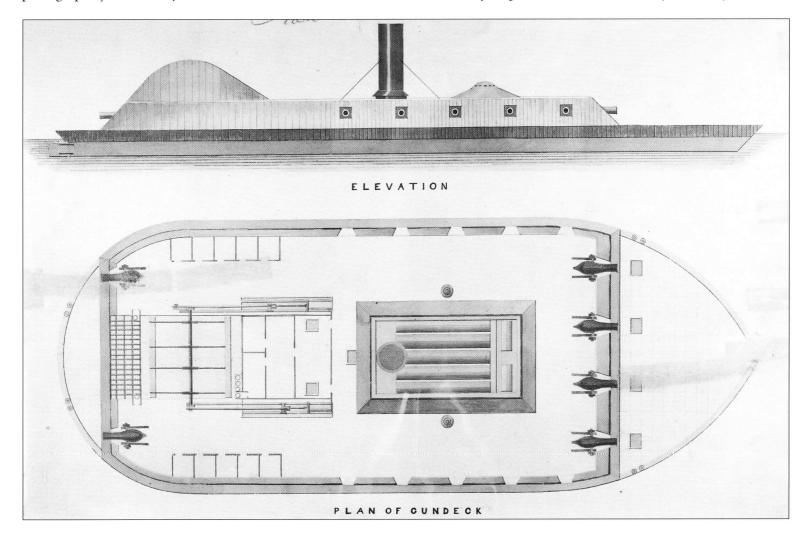

ELEVATION

PLAN OF GUNDECK

Captain John Rodgers of the navy – detailed to the army to assist in river operations. *Conestoga*, *Lexington* and *Tyler* had their cabins removed and 5-inch oak planking installed. Timber strengthening was added and their boilers lowered into the holds. The first carried six guns, *Lexington* nine, and *Tyler* thirteen. Though of 'exceedingly rough' construction, they served well through the war. *Conestoga* was lost in 1864.

The first ironclads were the City class: seven vessels built by James B Eads, a well known civil engineer, and designed by S M Pook, naval constructor also on loan to the army for the purpose. These 'Pook Turtles' were 175 feet by 50 feet with paddle wheels recessed in the stern, and 2½ inches of iron on the forward casemate and 60 feet down the sides and pilot house. The oak backing measured 24 inches thick forward and 12 inches on the sides. They carried 13 guns each, usually a mix of 32-pounders, 8-inch (64-pounders) and 30- to 100-pounder rifles: three across the bow, four on each broadside and two at the stern. Their hulls were basic scows: flat bottoms with angled bilges. Their two cylinders and five boilers yielded a tentative 5½ knots – at the mercy of the river currents. Note that vessels for river operations emphasized fore and aft firepower.

They were the first ironclads in US service (the *Carondelet* was commissioned January 1862) and all were active through the western river campaigns. Their armor was not impenetrable and was often supplemented by their commanders. Three, *Cairo*, *Baron de Kalb* and *Cincinnati*, were sunk (two by mines) but the latter was raised for further service. *Cairo* was recovered from the Yazoo River in 1962 and her partially reconstructed remains are at

Vicksburg Military Park, Mississippi. Other class vessels were *Mound City*, *Cincinnati*, *Louisville* and *Pittsburgh*.

Other early casemate vessels were *Essex* and *Benton*, both radical conversions, the former from a stern-wheel ferry; the latter from a catamaran boat originally built for removing snags and other river obstructions. *Essex* had a huge two-deck casemate and was 205 feet by 60 feet, carrying 8 heavy guns. Her armor was 1¾-inch iron and 30 inches of wood. In adverse currents, she was towed. *Benton* was 187 feet by 75 feet and carried 16 heavy guns – four of them across her wide bow – making her the most powerful of the 'riverclads'. Her plating was 2½-inches forward and ⅜-inch aft with 20- to 30-inch wood backing. She also was a stern-wheel ship and was as underpowered as others of her type, making 2½ knots against the current, 5 in slack water. Both vessels served successfully throughout the war.

*Chillicothe*, *Tuscumbia*, and *Indianola* were purpose-built casemate vessels, commissioned between September 1862 and early 1863. The first had side paddle wheels, mounted on her quarters, with a forward casemate housing two 11-inch Dahlgrens. Her forward plating was 3 inches, with 2 inches on her hull sides. Temporary cabins were built between the casemate and stern-wheel housings. She made 9 miles per hour upstream – one of the few such steamers to exceed expectations. Her longitudinal strength was lacking, however, and she required added iron strapping to prevent her hull from hogging, but she served throughout the war.

*Tuscumbia* was a broader version (72 feet) of *Chillicothe*, with three 11-inch guns in the athwartship forward casemate. She was 176 feet long and was powered by four cylinders, two for the

**T**uscumbia: a crudely built gunboat with massive forward firepower. Three 11-inch Dahlgrens loomed behind her forward casemate, plus two 9-inch guns aft. Note the absence of broadside guns. (US Navy)

paddle wheels and two for a pair of screw propellers. A stern case-mate was given two 9-inch guns and her great width required crosswise in addition to lengthwise hog chains. She was exceedingly poorly constructed and spent much time in refit.

*Indianola* was identical in power plant to *Tuscumbia*, but carried two forward 11-inch smoothbores plus two stern 9-inchers. She was 175 feet by 52 feet and had a checkered career: she was forced aground and captured; blown up by the Confederates; then re-possessed by the Union and plans were made to re-build her.

*Lafayette*, *Choctaw*, and *Eastport* all were based on merchant steamer hulls and machinery. They were huge but carried relatively little ordnance, though *Lafayette* and *Choctaw* had substantial rams. *Lafayette* was 292 feet by 66 feet, carried a pair of 11-inchers, two 100-pounder rifles, and, for a short time, two 9-inch smoothbores. *Choctaw*, at 270 feet by 69 feet, had three 9-inchers, one 100-pounder, two 30-pounders, and two 24-pounders. *Eastport* which was 280 feet by about 57 feet, carried four 9-inch smoothbores, and a pair each of 50- and 100-pounders. The *Lafayette* could make 4 knots and the *Choctaw*, half of that. *Lafayette's* armor was 2½ inches, plus a layer of rubber, then wood backing. The

*Choctaw* was a massive conversion of a river steamer 270 feet long and 69 feet across. She carried only 5 guns and mounted a ram on her bow. Thin armor was backed by india rubber: a fruitless experiment. (US Navy)

Light draft river monitor *Osage*. (US Navy)

Milwaukee class river monitor. Their hulls were iron with watertight subdivisions. (Poe Collection, US Military Academy, West Point)

Cross section of an Eads gun turret of the *Milwaukee* class ironclads. The large steam cylinder in the center of the turret was attached to the gun platform, and allowed the guns to be lowered into the hull for loading. The guns were also run out, elevated, and trained by steam power – probably the most advanced technology of the war. (National Archives)

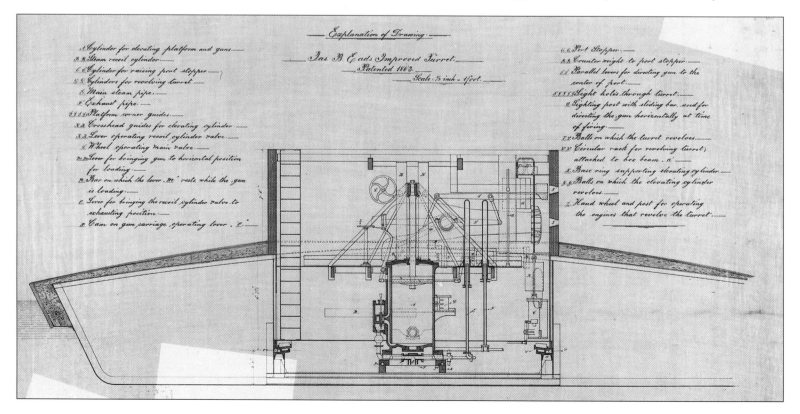

rubber merely rotted away, a useless experiment in protection. *Choctaw* had 1 inch iron on the casemate plus 30 inches of wood, and a layer of rubber between. Their sluggishness made their rams of little use. However, in an instance which demonstrated the power of the river currents, the tug *Lily* drifted down on *Choctaw*'s ram and was impaled and sank immediately. The big ironclad was anchored at the time.

*Eastport* was captured from the Confederates while under construction. It is not known whether she was completed to the rebel plans and little documentation remains to give specifics on the vessel.

The armor of these boats was inadequate, but their very size was an asset: they could take many hits in non-critical areas. *Eastport* was blown up to prevent capture during the Red River (Louisiana) Expedition in 1864.

Seven turreted vessels were completed for river warfare. *Osage* and *Neosho* were an unusual combination of stern paddle wheels and turret; *Ozark* and the *Milwaukee* class had quadruple screws.

*Osage* and *Neosho* carried a single Ericsson turret each with two 11-inch Dahlgrens and 6-inch plating, and 1½-inch plating on the steeply crowned decks. Only this crown allowed habitation of the hull as they drew not more than 4 feet of water (26 inches at launch). They were credited with 12 miles per hour, but cruised at 7½ and measured 160 feet by 45 feet. *Osage* was attacked by Confederate cavalry in 1864 – one of the more bizarre episodes of the war – and she was mined in March 1865.

*Ozark* had a single Ericsson turret, identical to *Osage* and *Neosho*, and measured 160 feet by 50 feet with a 4½-foot draft. Though criticized for 'structural weakness' she had three 9-inchers and one 10-incher added – exposed – on her deck. Her plating was about 2 inches on the sides and 1 inch on deck. Four cylinders operated her four 7-foot propellers, yielding 6 miles per hour and devouring more fuel than a steam frigate. She participated in the Red River Expedition of 1864.

James B Eads, bridge builder, designed the *Milwaukee* class, each with two turrets, four 11-inch guns and four propellers. Three received an Eads-designed forward turret which incorporated Coles-type ball bearings around the perimeter, and a steam mechanism to lower the gun platforms into the hold for loading. Their turret armor was 8 inches and their side armor was 3 inches with wood backing; the deck plating was ¾-inch on *Chickasaw* and *Kickapoo*, twice that on *Milwaukee* and *Winnebago*. Their machinery

was similar to *Ozark*'s and yielded a maximum of 9 miles per hour. Their iron hulls were 220 feet by 56 feet, drew 6 feet and had both transverse and longitudinal bulkheads. *Winnebago* and *Chickasaw* were at Mobile Bay, and *Milwaukee* was mined in 1865 – her bulkheads significantly delaying her sinking. *Chickasaw* existed until 1944 as a river ferry.

The preceding has enumerated the major part of the Union navy in commission during the war. Miscellaneous other vessels included captured warships, such as Confederate ironclads *Atlanta* and *Tennessee*, an unsuccessful submersible (*Alligator*), an experimental spar torpedo boat, small boats such as Lieutenant Cushing's torpedo launch which sank the ram *Albemarle*, and the Stone Fleet, which numbered forty-five vessels.

Finally, the vessels under construction should be mentioned. Some forty-five wooden steam sloops and frigates, ranging from 1100 to 4200 tons were begun in 1863 to counter any possible foreign intervention. These included vessels such as the 17-knot *Wampanoag*, aimed at raiding enemy commerce, and completed in 1867. Also unfinished was the monitor *Puritan*, the *Kalamazoo* class of twin-turret monitors (four vessels), two river monitors (*Marietta* and *Sandusky*) and the 15-knot casemate ironclad *Dunderberg*. The latter, at over 7000 tons, was one of the largest wooden ships ever built. She was sold to France in 1867. Of course, the ironclad Stevens Battery, – begun in 1842 – remained undone: she was broken up in the 1880s.

In summary, the US Navy of the Civil War was a massive undertaking. By the war's end some 690 vessels had been in service, compared to the 50 available in 1861. Of the total, about 160 were navy-built vessels. There were around 140 in the Mississippi River fleet. These figures must all be taken as approximates: many vessels were in support roles and were not officially commissioned and no small boats are included (nor the Stone Fleet). Furthermore, this is an aggregate number; a running total of all vessels utilized during the war, rather than a single total at one particular time. Also, no other government agencies are represented; for instance the army's own transport and gunboat fleet and Revenue Service vessels.

The US Navy of the Civil War was the largest it would be until the Second World War, and, at least in raw numbers, was among the largest in the world. Both in terms of ships and the administrative and personnel aspects, it was a prodigious effort.

## Chapter Five

# SHIPBUILDING IN IRON AND WOOD

By the sixth decade of the nineteenth century, the heyday of the wooden ship of war was drawing to a close. The Royal Navy's *Warrior* and the American *Monitor* set the stage for the modern iron-hulled and armored warship. The transition of course was hardly begun in the American navy, the *Monitor* was only the third iron ship in an otherwise conventionally wooden-hulled service. As such, several types of construction must be examined here: conventional wooden shipbuilding, iron-hull construction, and both iron-and wooden-hulled ironclads.

It should be noted that many Civil War ironclads were one-off experiments, and often unsuccessful ones at that. Rather than attempting to study each (as I did in my volume on ironclads in *The Old Steam Navy*), I have selected ships which were both historically significant and for which a considerable amount of documentation exists for their design and construction. These examples should be sufficient to give the reader a wide overview of United States naval shipbuilding techniques and processes during this critical period. What follows are *Monitor* to show the construction of an iron-hulled armored vessel, the steam frigate *Merrimack* to represent the wooden shipbuilding of the 1850s, and *Merrimack*'s sister-ship *Roanoke* to illustrate the conversion of a wooden steam frigate to a turret ironclad.

**J**ohn Ericsson's ironclad *Monitor* was unlike anything that had gone before, and was less a ship than a floating engine-powered gun platform. This is one of the few photographs of the vessel. (US Navy)

## The ironclad *Monitor*

This little vessel, from concept through construction was a tour de force for John Ericsson. Certainly this ship marked the boundary of the possible in the technological milieu of the day, and only a monumental ego such as Ericsson's could have pulled it off.

The design itself was, to say the least, unusual. Even to modern eyes it is eccentric: to eyes accustomed to towering square-riggers and formidable bulwarks, this 'flatiron' must have bordered on the ludicrous. Without belaboring what countless others have described, we must review the actual structure.

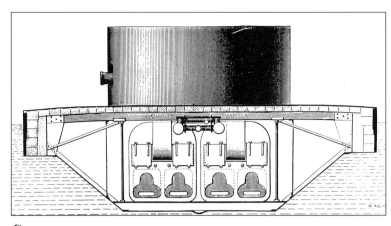

Cross section of the *Monitor* showing her dead flat bottom and angular bilges. Ericsson designed her to be built as much as possible from readily available components of flat and angle iron. (The Century Company)

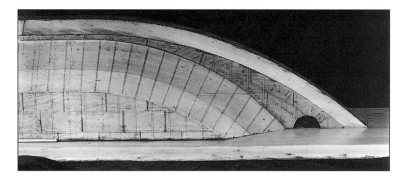

Close up of forward portion of half-hull model reveals that it is marked to show every iron plate and seam – many with their actual dimensions. This model would have been a reference on site at T F Rowland's Continental Ironworks in New York where the vessel was under construction, or, more accurately, assembled. (US Navy)

The iron hull itself was flat bottomed, with parallel sides curving on simple arcs to meet at stem and stern. The bilges angled upward at 35°, again with regular curves fore and aft. (Ericsson avoided any curve or complication, including sheer, which might slow her construction). A shelf surrounded the hull, on which the oak and 5-inch iron side armor was laid. Stretching across the top of this armor and forming the base of the lightly armored weather deck, were square timbers. In the center of this 'raft' deck was the twin-gun turret on its spindle. Afloat, the vessel had about 18 inches of freeboard.

In the hull was a single deck with quarters located forward and turret machinery amidships. Aft was the Ericsson-designed engine, which was in itself a rather eccentric mechanical oddity, plus the boilers and coal bunkers. Far forward, a small square pilot house protruded above the deck, and both the rudder and anchor were protected by the armored overhangs at her ends.

The *Monitor*'s iron hull, though decidedly un-'shipshape', was built with conventional techniques of the era. The hull plating was iron, 7/16- to 1/2-inch thick, arranged in longitudinal strakes. The longitudinal edges overlapped, with strakes alternating in-and-out. Transverse 'ribs' of 3-inch by 6-inch angle iron every 36 inches

Original half-hull model of *Monitor* re-emphasizes her rectilinear hull. (US Navy)

formed the framework of the hull, with 3-inch by 3-inch angle iron midway between each frame. The ends of the longitudinal plates were secured together with flat butt plates. To support the main interior deck – which in a conventional ship would be called the berth deck – 12-inch deep iron floor 'timbers' were employed. Amidships, two iron bulkheads supported the weight of the turret, and two parallel rows of stanchions, running fore and aft, attached the hull frames to the upper deck structure.[1]

The hull was fastened with rivets, while bolts and spikes were used for the iron and wood side armor. Through bolts connected the 1-inch layers of iron turret armor plate.

Unlike wooden construction which allowed for trial and error on site, simply because hand tools sufficed for working the material, iron shipbuilding relied on precise fitting before assembly. Thus Mr Ericsson ordered iron plates cut to size at the manufacturer and pre-drilled or punched for the rivets. Each plate was marked by letter (indicating the strake) and number, to correspond with the plates drawn and numbered on a scale model of the vessel. At the shipyard, once the plates and angle iron were delivered, it was a matter of systematically assembling them. If the previous work was accurately done, only minor fitting was required.

Before describing the construction process, it would be appropriate to describe the contemporary methods of producing both hull and armor plates.

There were two basic methods of manufacturing plate iron: rolling and forging. In the former process, the puddled molten iron was sent between a series of upper and lower rollers which forced it into flat sheets. The distance between the upper and lower tiers of

Planer for armor and turret plates, as used at the Continental Ironworks in 1862 – though probably after *Monitor* was completed. (*Scientific American*, **25** October 1862)

**H**ydraulic ram for bending turret plates. **One-inch plates were placed on a curved bed and subjected to 1400 tons of pressure to assume the required shape.** (*Harper's New Monthly Magazine*, September 1862)

rollers decreased gradually to produce the requisite thickness of the metal. This was the quickest and least expensive method available, as it used the least manual labor. However, in the USA, the maximum thickness possible with the rolling machinery available was 2½ inches. Armor thicker than this was usually laminated in 1-inch layers. On the monitors and other vessels, rolled iron was used extensively by layering 1-inch rolled sheets.[2]

To avoid the weakness inherent in layered armor, forged or hammered plates were used, for which theoretically the only thickness limitation was the capacity of the steam hammer and the lifting apparatus at the foundry. This process began with piles of scrap iron, heated white hot and melted into 'blooms' usually 4 feet long and 6 inches square, which were piled and heated to ductility. The resulting hot raw slabs were placed under a steam-powered hammer – the mechanical equivalent of the smith's sledge – and pounded unmercifully into the required shape. By the Civil War there were steam hammers in the United States weighing 7½ tons, enabling the making of the armor for such vessels as *New Ironsides* and *Roanoke*.

Once the plates were of the proper dimensions, holes were made for the rivets or bolts. The thinner material such as hull and 1-inch armor, could be punched. More substantial plates were drilled using a drill mounted over a roller bed on which the plate was moved from one hole to the next. As with the majority of this type of shop machinery, the drill was steam powered, that is, a stationary steam engine operated a series of shafts and pulleys mounted on the overhead, with appropriate belts and gearing designed to transfer the power to the individual machines being operated in the facility.

The working of iron was no simple thing, and, as can be judged from the above description, hammered iron was more

expensive to manufacture than the rolled variety, in the main because of the need for significantly more laborers and time. Consequently, with the two vessels mentioned above, the armor-making process seriously delayed their completion and their entry into the war, whereas the rolled-iron armored monitors appeared nearly as quickly as the plates could be assembled.[3]

The actual assembly of the *Monitor* took place in the shipyard of T F Rowland at Continental Iron Works in New York. The engine and other mechanical components were built at Delamater Iron Works and the turret and its machinery at Novelty Works, also of New York City.

The vessel's keel was laid on 25 October 1861 in a ship house specially constructed for the vessel. The keel was a series of plates 90½ inches in length, each with a 4-inch deep U-shaped water limber down the center. This trough, combined with a deliberate trimming of the vessel by the stern, would carry water aft in the hull. Following the laying of the keel, the major longitudinal bottom plates, each 132-inches by 36-inches and weighing about 600 pounds were laid in strakes on each side of the keel.[4]

The vessel's assembly at the shipyard involved between 140 and 200 workmen. Portable furnaces were set up at locations around the stocks on which the hull was built, in which the rivets were heated. Boys then carried the hot rivets to the workers on the hull. On the outside of the hull, a worker thrust the rivet through its pre-punched holes and held it with an iron bar; on the inside of the hull, the exposed rivet end was hammered by a second worker

The turret was completely assembled around a wooden framework in the shop. Locations for rivet holes were determined and the gunports were drilled at this stage. The turret would be re-assembled on board the ship. (*Harper's New Monthly Magazine*, September 1862)

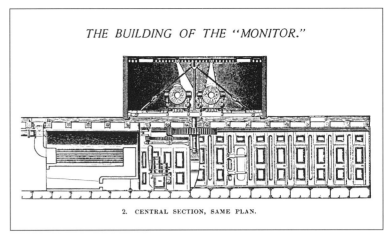

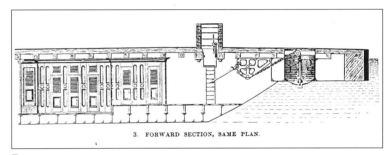

Longitudinal section of the *Monitor* showing interior joinery and simplicity of design. From *Battles and Leaders of the Civil War*, Vol. I.

to form the head. As the rivet cooled the joint was tightened.

Rivetting was the only skill necessary in iron ship construction, and only repetition was required to complete the hull — frame and skin. On *Monitor* as well as later versions of the ironclad, the hull was surrounded, about 5 feet from its top, by a 4-foot wide shelf. Triangular pieces braced the shelf to the hull side, and the armor was laid upon this shelf.

At the intersection of the hull and shelf were vertical oak blocks, 1-foot square, completely surrounding the hull. Outside these were horizontal strakes of pine, forming the backing for the iron. Five thicknesses of 1-inch iron were bolted on the ouside of the wood strakes, completing the hull side armor.

The deck beams were of 10-inch square oak. The ends of these were bolted to vertical plates which in turn were riveted to the side of the upper portion of the hull. Diagonal bracing also supported the beams and connected them to the hull framing. Pine planking covered by two layers of ½-inch iron armor completed the upper deck and thus the hull structure itself.

The major variations in the cross-sections of the hull were fore and aft. Aft, transverse truss frames supported the deck beams and the side armor, and they also formed the 'tunnel' for the shaft and propeller. Cantilevered forward, under the deck beams, was the anchor and its machinery.

Turret construction again made use of 1-inch iron, eight layers thick. The raw, flat, rolled iron 'boards' 9 feet long and about 33 inches wide had to be bent and accurately drilled for assembly. The turret was pre-assembled at the ironworks, dismantled, then re-assembled on the ship after the vessel's launch.

Bending the iron to the curvature of the turret was by a specially prepared hydraulic 'ram'. The straight plate was laid upon a curved bed, 1400 tons pressure was applied, without heating, and the plate assumed the correct curvature.

The plates were then set up around a wooden framework mockup of the turret and locations for the bolt holes were determined. The layers were staggered in such a way as to prevent the joints in each layer from coinciding and thus weakening the iron bulwark. Any minor hole mis-alignments were rectified by a two-edged reamer. After the initial assembly, the gunport holes were drilled, through all eight layers at once.

On the vessel, the turret was re-built, with the inner two layers riveted to the iron beam which formed the turret base. Long through bolts attached the six other iron tiers to the interior two, and additional vertical plates were bolted over the interior butt joints. Slightly below the top of the turret interior, an angle-iron shelf was installed, on which the turret top rested. The top was a combination of railroad and perforated plate iron, and was secured by its own weight.

Once launched, the more mundane and conventional aspects of the vessel were undertaken. The living spaces were fine examples of the joiners art, with nicely finished black walnut partitions. In fact rather exotic hardwoods were not unusual in warship officers' living areas of this era. Unlike other small warships, however, the *Monitor* had more than adequate height between decks – over 7 feet. This extra space facilitated ventilation of the interior by leaving open space above the bulkheads between the officers' cabins. (It might be noted also that the turret interior was nearly 9 feet in height – a dimension chosen by Ericsson to alleviate the concussive effect of the guns' discharge on their crews.)[5]

The contract for the vessel was signed 4 October 1861 and she was commissioned the next February, on the 25th. Less than two weeks later she met and checked the destructive reign of the CSS *Virginia* in Hampton Roads. Rarely in the history of warfare have innovative technology and military necessity been so appropriately and propitiously coordinated.

# USS *Roanoke:* wooden steam frigate converted to ironclad

The Confederate ironclad *Virginia* had originally been the Union steam frigate *Merrimack*, captured, cut down, and rebuilt with a formidable iron casemate. Not two weeks after the battles at Hampton Roads, the Bureau of Construction and Repair proposed to 'razee' her sister-ship, *Roanoke* and fit her with iron cladding. Given the success of the *Monitor*, and the resulting politi-

cal power of Ericsson's coterie, there was no question of a slanted iron casemate for her, or of any turrets other than Ericsson's. (The bureau's original proposal was to use Cole's-type turrets with their rollers on the turret's circumference.)

The only serious question was the number of turrets *Roanoke's* wooden hull would support. Strictly on the basis of her dimensions (252 feet between perpendiculars and a beam of 53 feet), John Lenthall, chief constructor, and chief engineer Benjamin F Isherwood intended her to have four, each with two 12- or 15-inch guns. She was to be cut to her gundeck, have 6-inch armor on her sides, somewhat less on her ends, a substantial ram, and be ready in three and a half months. Much of this proved overly optimistic.

The bureau's original specifications called for a 22 feet 9 inches draft – not a great variance from that which she had had as a steam frigate. This makes it appear that she may have been intended as a seagoing vessel, a rather unnecessary item for this war. Even before the final order went out to undertake the conversion, Assistant Secretary Fox noted: 'I am afraid she will be useless.' In any event, work was begun late in March 1862.[6]

Once *Roanoke* was decommissioned, she was stripped of the glory that was the sailing frigate – her masts and rig. Next went her spar deck and bulwarks down to the gundeck. With the exception of the actual armoring, the only major modification in the ship's structure were the supports for the turrets. A circle of ten stanchions carried the weight of each turret through the lower decks to the ship's bottom. Power for their rotation was supplied

**S**team frigate converted to monitor, *Roanoke*, photographed after her decommissioning in 1865. Her turrets have been roofed over. Unlike *Monitor*, *Roanoke's* side plating was forged, rather than rolled iron. (US Navy)

by small oscillating steam engines. As with other Ericsson turrets, a center 'step' was incorporated on which each turret's spindle rested. When rotation was required a wrought iron 'key' was driven between the step and the spindle, raising the turret up and off its ways on deck. When raised, the turret's weight was entirely on the spindle, and in turn, on the *Roanoke*'s keelsons.

We have seen above the methods by which Ericsson's turrets were built, as well as the forging process for the side armor. The fitting and forming of the *Roanoke*'s side plating must now be decribed.

The 4½-inch-thick plates (reduced from the original plan's 6 inches), left the forge measuring 12 to 15 feet long and 3 feet wide. Each weighed 4000 to 7000 pounds. All were dead flat, and would require bending to conform to the curvature of the ship's hull sides, as well as drilling to accept the attaching bolts.

First, plate-mounting holes were drilled in the hull's sides. Then, a thin board the size and shape of an armor plate was positioned onto a pre-drawn location on the hull, and the bolt holes were marked. This template was numbered to identify its exact position on the ship, then delivered to the shop to be laid on the plate prepared for that location. The markings were then transferred to the plate for drilling.

A crane and manpower transferred the plate to a roller bed for drilling. At the same time the holes were countersunk — inletted to accept the head of the tightened bolt, thus making the surface of the plate and the top of the bolt even. (Leaving the bolt head exposed would allow it to be broken off when struck by shot, loosening the plate.)

The plate was placed, again using manpower and a crane, into a furnace with a moveable iron cover in preparation for bending. Once at the proper temperature it was transferred to a press, the bed of which consisted of a series of bars across its width. The individual bars rested on stout adjustment screws — one at each end — allowing each to be raised or lowered to match the required curvature of the plate. A die with corresponding adjusting bars composed the upper part of the press. A thin template matching the curve of the vessel side was placed on the bed and the bars were adjusted to conform to its shape.

While these preparations were being made, the plate in question was heating to a cherry red, resting on a three fingered iron 'hand' or sling. A portable crane was then brought and a chain attached to the 'hand' to move the plate to the press. The upper die was dropped upon the plate, which almost immediately assumed the pre-set shape. The screws could then be manually

**F**orging a bloom. Piles of scrap metal were heated and beaten into slabs 4 feet long and 6 inches square, using steam-powered hammers such as this one. Long handled protrusion from the bloom allowed the worker to turn and align it under the hammer. The blooms would then be re-heated and hammered into *Roanoke*'s side plating, 4½ inches thick. This was blacksmithing on an industrial scale. (*Harper's New Monthly Magazine*)

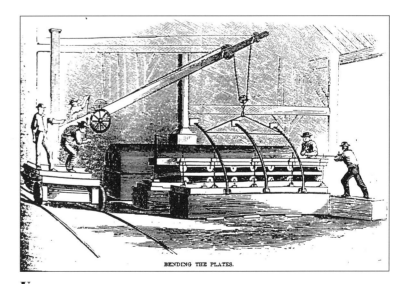

BENDING THE PLATES.

**U**sing a thin template from the ship's side, this bending machine would be set up to match the curvature required. After heating, the plate — weighing sometimes as much as 7000 pounds — was moved onto the bed of this machine and the top die was lowered to force the plate into its new configuration. (*Harper's New Monthly Magazine*)

**T**rucking plates. Forging iron plates was labor intensive and time consuming. Only *Roanoke* and *New Ironsides* had forged armor plating: all the monitors used 1-inch laminated iron plating, which was rolled rather than forged. (*Harper's New Monthly Magazine*)

**O**nce the iron plate was aligned and rammed into place on the ship's side, bolts were run through and secured by 3½-inch nuts. This shows the four-man wrench made for this operation. (*Harper's New Monthly Magazine*)

operated (two men were required) to make minor adjustments in the shape. Needless to say this was exceedingly hot work, though the bending took less than ten minutes. The portable crane was then employed to remove the plate and place it on a four-wheel dolly to be wheeled away and cooled.

The plate was then delivered to Brooklyn Navy Yard, where the *Roanoke* was in dry dock, held up by shores and blocks. The plate was let down by guys to the scaffold, where a crew manipulated it into position using handspikes, levers and rams. Once

aligned with the pre-drilled holes in the hull, bolts were driven through, one every 14 to 18 inches, along the length of the plate. The bolts were galvanized, 1⅝ to 1¾ inches in diameter. A nut, 3½ inches square and 2 inches thick was tightened on each, on the inside of the hull, using a particularly long handled wrench, wielded by several men.

On the ship, the lower strakes of plating were extended forward beyond the stem to form a ram. The gap between the extensions of the side plating was filled with iron and wood. The whole was bolted solidly together making a formidable forward protrusion. An iron 'hood' was placed over the rudder and screw for their protection, and two layers of thin iron were laid on the upper deck.

As Secretary Fox had predicted, the *Roanoke* was useless. The weight of the turrets made her center of gravity uncomfortably high and her draft was too deep for close-in coastal work. Furthermore, when the turrets were keyed up and all their weight was on the keelsons, their combined weight threatened to force out the ship's bottom.[7]

## *Merrimack:* wooden-hulled steam frigate

The following is a composite of general naval construction methods in use in the 1850s and 1860s with the dimensions and description of the US steam frigate *Merrimack* of 1855. *Merrimack* was a 40-gun vessel officially described as an 'auxiliary steam' ship, listed at 4600 tons and measuring 256 feet 10 inches between perpendiculars and 50 feet moulded beam. She was a square-rigged vessel with a two-cylinder horizontal steam engine, two boilers, and screw designed to be hoisted for sailing. (Note that when the vessel was built, the accepted spelling for her name included the final 'k', though post-war writers have tended to drop it.)

The general principles of constructing a wooden-hulled warship had been in place for centuries. The majority of the changes through the decades had been incremental and evolutionary, rather than revolutionary. Indeed, even the introduction of an alien propulsion into the confines of the hull seriously affected only the actual sites of the engine and its propeller (or paddle wheels) leaving the balance of the hull, at least in terms of construction materials and techniques, nearly untouched.

The hull design process made use of both half models and

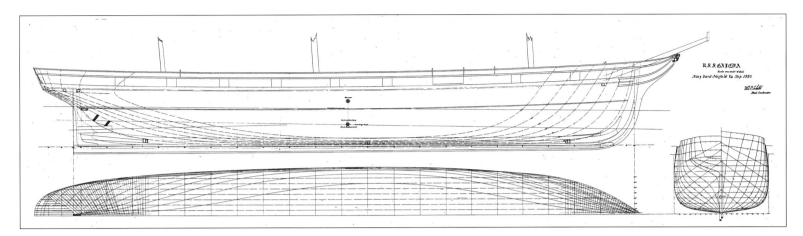

Hull design plans (draughts) for the wooden sloop of war USS *Galena*. Top is the sheer plan showing the gunports and general appearance of the vessel, plus curved lines representing the width of the hull at 2-foot intervals. Right is the body plan showing the shape of the hull at regular intervals, bow and stern on the right and left portions of the drawing respectively. Finally, the half-breadth gave the viewer the shape of the hull as seen from below, with topographic-type lines indicating the width and curvature of the hull every 2 feet up from the keel. (National Archives)

drawings (draughts). The half-hull model consisted of a layered sandwich of 'lifts' each representing a longitudinal horizontal section of the hull. It was the pattern for the curves of the hull, and measurements from it were transferred to the three types of draughts employed: sheer, body and half-breadth. These were all much like topographical maps, showing contours of the hull from differing viewpoints.

The sheer plan sliced the hull longitudinally at the centerline, and showed the locations of decks, gunports, and hull curvature cut along vertical sections. The body plan divided the hull at the midship section, with one side of the drawing delineating the stages of the widening hull from stem to midships; the other half showing the stern portion.

The half-breadth was probably the best portrait of the sharpness (or bluff-ness) of the vessel's entrance and stern lines, and showed the hull as it would appear from beneath, looking upward. It showed the shape of the hull, usually in 2-foot slices, from the keel up. If the vessel had a 10-foot draft, for instance, there would be five lines on the half-breadth drawing showing the shape of the hull at each 2-foot level above the keel.

These plans, plus a sail plan, were all that were usually made when a ship was in the proposal stage. Often a half-model was presented as a visual aid to the department by a builder soliciting a construction contract. Detail plans of decks, hold, planking, joinery, etc., would be formulated after the vessel was under construction (though in many instances, detail plans were not necessary for the completion of the ship).

Once the three basic plans were complete, and/or the half model in hand, the actual dimensions and shape of each segment of the wooden fabric of the vessel's framework could be determined simply by scaling up from the draughts or model. The complete set of dimensions of all frames was termed the mold (or mould) loft dimensions. To illustrate: a frame located at station X (a point a certain distance from midships) might be 2 feet wide at 2 feet above the base line, and 4 feet wide at 6 feet above the base, and so forth at 2-foot intervals to the top of the frames. These statistics were set down in tabular form and, theoretically, a graphic plan of the vessel could be drawn using these figures alone.

The dimensions were then taken to the mold loft at the shipyard where each frame was chalked out, full size on the floor of the loft. Thin board patterns (called molds) of each section of each frame, as well as the other hull timbers were made, as templates for cutting the wood itself.

In the timber yard, men would then begin selecting wood appropriate for the various shapes necessary, matching as closely as possible the natural curve and grain with the hand-drawn one. All varieties could be used from the straight and true to the crotch piece where the branch met the tree trunk. When the wood was selected, the sawyers cut it to the rough size and shape necessary, often with a two-man saw, with one of the two in a purpose-dug pit — needed for the larger timbers. Steam-powered saws came into use prior to the Civil War, as well as machines for bending timber to the required shapes. Bringing the timbers into their exact configuration after the sawyer's job was done was the work of a skilled adze-man.

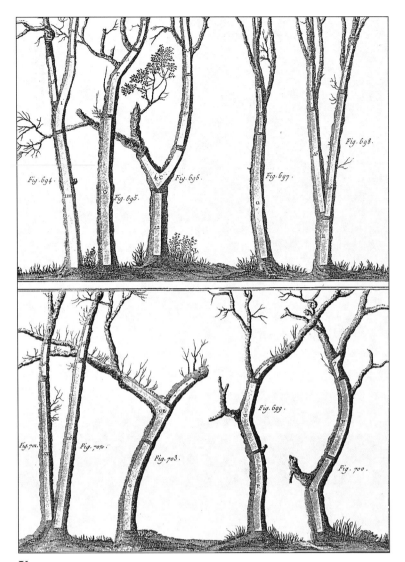

**V**arious shapes of ship timbers as cut from trees. Note that even crotch-pieces were useful, particularly for bottom timbers which crossed the keel. From *Encyclopedia Methodique Marine*, 1789, and reprinted in the *Nautical Research Journal*.

The timber cutting was done in a sequence designed to match the steps of construction. The keel was first, followed by the stem and stern posts. Framing began at the midship dead flat point and worked forward and aft simultaneously. Deck framing followed, then planking.

Before the building process was begun, the slip was prepared, The preparation of the slip was an exacting process. If it was improperly constructed, there could be dire results on launching, ranging from the hull stopping partway down the ways, to actually breaking the ship's back. The larger the vessel, the greater the danger of mishaps at launching.

The ship's keel rested on a series of stacked wooden blocks set 4 to 6 feet apart the length of the vessel, with the top cap block of each stack declining at a predetermined angle to the water's edge. The increments in height ranged from ½ to 1½ inches per foot of the length of the vessel. Larger vessels were given smaller declinations, to prevent excessive friction-heat build-up at launch. The declivity also determined the speed of the hull at launch and the angle it 'tipped' into the water. The lowest block of each stack was long enough athwartship to support shoring for the ship's bilges and bottom. For long term support, the blocks were on pilings, which in turn rested on bed rock. For launching, a temporary cradle was erected to stabilize the hull as it moved down the ways.[8]

The false keel was the first part of the hull to be laid down in the building slip. This was in effect an extension of the main keel, the same width, but of less depth, designed simply to protect the keel in case of grounding or other mishap. As with the keel proper, its length precluded its fashioning from a single timber, and several segments of timber were joined to form it. On *Merrimack*, the plans indicate this keel was no more than 4 inches thick.

The keel, the most massive unit of the hull, was actually in two layers, each composed of seven sections, ranging from 32 to 45 feet long, and 18½ inches wide. The sections were connected by joints known as scarphs; the ends of the timbers were cut diagonally to form an overlapping union. The scarph joints themselves were over 9 feet long, and were both bolted and 'coaked'. Coaking involved inletting short vertical pieces into the overlapping ends of the timber segments, preventing their side and fore and aft movement. Atop the keel and running its length on each side was a rabbet: a groove some 4 inches deep, intended to take the edges of the hull planking.

The actual process of uniting the keel sections involved painting the scarphs, and laying felt on the joint and around the coaks. After aligning the coaks, the pieces were joined using clampscrews. No less than six copper bolts were driven through each joint, and clinched on rings on the underside of the keel.

Once complete, the keel assembly was 250 feet long and about 3 feet high. On *Merrimack*, it was of white oak, and weighed something in excess of 65,000 pounds. (One cubic foot of white oak weighs 58 pounds.)

The completed keel was then centered on the blocks and fastened with cleats. Its centerline was marked, as well as the location of each frame, with frame numbers painted on the side.

The stem (also of white oak) was next to be raised. It was composed of at least two major timbers. Again, these were attached using scarph joints; in this instance with hooked or nibbed scarphs, which added more strength than simple diagonal joints. As with the keel, rabbets were cut into the stem to take the forward ends of the planking. The stem was raised with a derrick, scarphed and bolted, then supported with forward and side shoring timbers.

The sternpost followed the stem in erection. It was a single straight timber, with rabbets for the aft planking ends. Though equal in width to the keel where they joined, on *Merrimack* the sternpost was a full 2 feet in thickness at the centerline of the propeller shaft aperture. It was attached to the keel by tenons and bolts. In the angle formed by keel and sternpost a knee was positioned, bolted and coaked to each of those timbers.

With these three elements – keel, stem and stern – in place, the framing of the hull could begin. The frames were far from simple 'ribs'. Each frame was in fact double – two complete wooden semi-circles, each consisting of segments known as floor timbers and futtocks. The floors were the sections which crossed the keel, and futtocks made up the balance of the structure. Each of the two floor timbers (one per half-frame) had a 'long arm' and a 'short arm', and were placed on the keel with the long arm of one timber on the same side of the keel as the short arm of the other. Then the first futtock would necessarily be attached to the short arm, the 'second futtock' would be attached to the long arm on the same side of the keel, the third would be attached to the first, the fourth to the second, and so forth, overlapping each other up to the rail. The final segments were called the top timbers. This overlapping construction technique was designed to prevent any two joints on the assembly from coinciding, and all the parts of the frame would be mutually supportive.

The actual process of constructing and raising the first frame – which was always the midships or 'dead flat frame' – required working platforms on either side of the keel. On this, the various pieces of one course of the frame were laid out, and their butts coaked together, yielding one complete course of the frame. Next, the second course was laid atop the first and marked for the location of the joints and coaks in the lower frame. The second course was taken back off and bored for coaking. When the coaks were in place (usually round coaks of oak, locust or lignum vitae), the second course was re-placed on the first and driven down upon it. Bolts were driven in to secure the assembly, usually three to a scarph. Now the actual frame, both courses, was complete, laying on the platform.

In preparing for raising the frame, straight timbers called cross-palls were attached across the frame, one at the level of each of the vessel's decks. These served as temporary supports during the erection process. A plumb bob was attached to the center of the cross-pall and then the frame was ready to be put in place. Two pairs of shears were employed, one on each side, to lift the frame. Utilizing the plumb bob and the centerline of the keel (marked previously), the frame was aligned fore and aft and athwartships, then shoring secured it from below, at the height of the wales and at the heads. The dead flat frame was the most crucial, as all the others, forward and aft, were aligned or 'regulated' from it.

At this point the shipbuilding measurement terms must be dealt with. Many of the ship's timbers were of wood of a specific thickness, on which a mold or pattern was laid. The 'sided' dimension was the 'thickness'; the 'molded' dimensions were those across the

**C**ross section of a steam frigate. Each frame was composed of sections, beginning at the bottom with floor timbers which crossed the keel. Several sections, called futtocks, completed the frame up to the rail. For strength, each frame actually consisted of two complete 'sets' of floors and futtocks. Note the hull planking, interior ceiling, deck clamps, and knees supporting the deck beams. The dotted lines indicate the location of through bolts. (Wilson, *An Outline of Shipbuilding, Theoretical and Practical*)

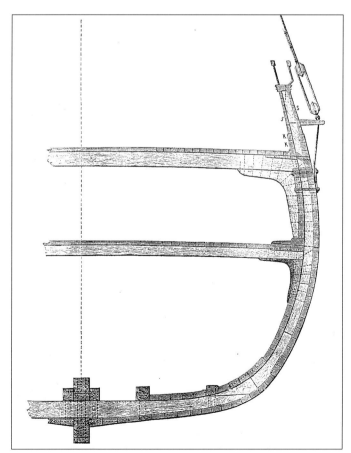

timber at various points, perpendicular to the sided dimension. On frames, the sided dimensions ran parallel to the keel. Molded dimensions were taken across the timber, usually at the keel, then the wales, then at the rail, with the timbers gradually decreasing in moulded size, and usually retaining the same sided dimension.

On the frigate *Merrimack*, the frames were of live oak, sided 14 inches in the lower timbers where they met the keel, and 13 inches in the top timbers (at the rails). Thus each (double) frame was 28 inches across at the keel and 26 inches in the upper works. The molded dimensions ranged from 17 inches at the keel, tapering to about 8 at the lower port sill, and 6 inches at the rail. Naval vessels were notorious for their heavy scantlings — and American naval vessels in particular — hence the legendary ability of 'Old Ironsides' to bounce cannon balls off her sides. The use of live oak was part of this 'secret', as well as substantial framing (molded as well as sided dimensions), thick planking, and, finally, use of small 'room and space' or 'timber and space' dimensions. The latter is the distance measured from the front of one frame to the front of the next frame. (On a frame house, a somewhat comparable dimension would be 'centers': frames on 18-inch centers etc.) On *Merrimack*, the room and space was 34¼ inches. Given the 'sided' (fore and aft) dimension of each pair of frames (28 inches), we find that only 6 inches of every 34¼ inches along the majority of her hull was unoccupied by a frame. (And, as we will see, the fore and aft 'cant frames' were even more crowded.) These framing dimensions, in addition to other side timbers — planking, ceiling, deck clamps, etc., made for a massive bulwark against foreign matter in this vessel.

With the dead flat frame in place, work proceeded both forward and aft from it simultaneously, until all of the perpendicular frames were in place, forming what was called the 'square body' of the vessel. Forward and aft of the square body the curvature of the hull precluded use of frames mounted perpendicularly to the keel. In lieu of these were the cant frames which filled the areas between the end of the square frames and the stem and stern posts. These frames were canted forward or aft at increasing angles until they filled in their respective areas. Viewed from above, these frames spread fan-like from the square frames to the stem and stern posts. At the stem, the more forward cant frames would seat on the stem rather than the keel.

Supporting timbers, called ribbands and harpins, were attached to the outside of the frames for their support until framing was complete. The ribbands were on the square frames; the harpins on the cant frames. These timbers were attached both for support and to mark where bevelling was required on the timbers. Three tiers of shoring timbers supported the frames, and scaffolding was erected around the vessel during this phase of construction.

To further strengthen the bottom of the vessel, filling frames were added in that 6 inches of space between each of the frames. These timbers ran from the keel to the turn of the bilge on the *Merrimack* and, when thoroughly caulked, made her bottom uniformly solid for most of her length. Such filling frames were a peculiarly naval practice, with merchant hulls limiting the fill frames to one in each frame interval, or, on small vessels, eliminating them altogether. The purposes of these filling frames were to strengthen the bottom against grounding and other accidents, create a watertight bottom, and eliminate the openings in the bottom which otherwise would attract unhealthy detritus.

Two other major hull structures were the forward and aft deadwood. These were both seemingly random assemblages of timbers that formed the increasingly narrow V-shaped areas which finally terminated at the stem and stern posts. Nature did not supply timbers with such radical angles, rendering normal framing practices impossible, and the necessary expedient was simply to build up a solid mass of wood to form the contours of the hull and provide the foundation for normal framing higher in the structure. Another function of the after deadwood was as part of the support for the propeller shaft alley.

Also at the ship's extremities were the breast and stern hooks, which united the sides of the hull together. These timbers were V-shaped, with the angle resting on the stem or another timber of the forward deadwood, and each arm of the 'V' was attached to the cant frames on its respective side. On *Merrimack*, there were

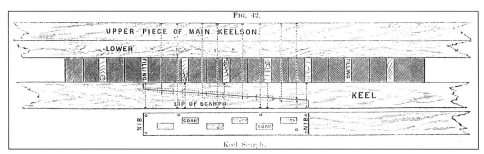

Side view of the keel and keelsons, with frames sandwiched between. Note the coaks let into the scarph joint to prevent slippage. On the steam frigate *Merrimack*, which was some 250 feet on the keel, the keel/frame/keelson assembly was nearly 7 feet high. (Wilson, *An Outline of Shipbuilding, Theoretical and Practical*)

Diagonal iron strapping for a wooden-hulled steam frigate. As wooden vessels became longer to accommodate engines and larger guns, the tendency of the hull to droop at the ends increased. These iron straps, 4½ inches wide, were installed basket-fashion from the keel upward. Some vessels had two sets, one in side the frames, another outside. (Wilson, *An Outline of Shipbuilding, Theoretical and Practical*)

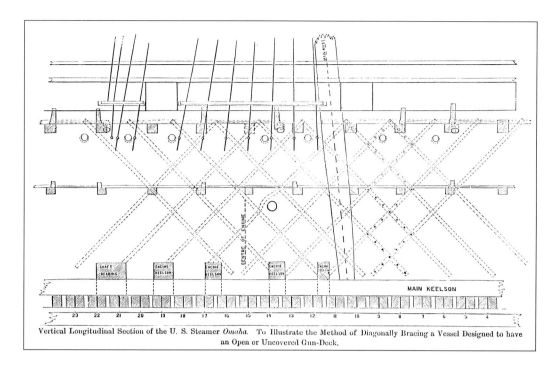

Vertical Longitudinal Section of the U. S. Steamer *Omaha*. To Illustrate the Method of Diagonally Bracing a Vessel Designed to have an Open or Uncovered Gun-Deck.

seven breast hooks, all live oak, with the highest at the spar deck level, and lowest at the crotch of the stemson (the latter being the most interior timber of the forward deadwood). There were three stern hooks, all located on the after deadwood, above the level of the propeller shaft.

At this juncture the hull had obtained its general profile, with all frames — both square and cant — in place, whether on the keel, the fore and aft deadwood, or stem and stern posts. Little of a permanent nature had been done to consolidate the structure longitudinally, however. As will be seen, the longitudinal integrity of wooden ships was always in question, and in fact became increasingly problematic as hulls were lengthened to accommodate steam machinery. The key longitudinal structural components, other than the keel itself, which, without support was insufficient in any case, were the keelsons.

The main keelson was laid directly upon the floor and filling timbers. On *Merrimack*, this keelson was at least 18 inches wide and was composed of five layers of live oak, each 6 inches thick, to a height of 30 inches. All were coaked to the floor and filling timbers at 15-inch intervals, with two rows of coaks. Copper bolts ran vertically through the layers of timber.

On either side of the main keelson were the sister keelsons. These timbers were 15 inches deep on the *Merrimack* and were coaked to the floor and filling timbers. As with the keel proper, the timbers comprising the sister keelsons were scarphed together. They were sometimes bolted athwartships through the lower part of the main keelson.

On steam vessels, other fore and aft members were necessary to support the engine and boilers. These paralleled the main keelsons and were of the same height. Between these were athwartship timbers to complete this foundation assembly.

The keel and keelson assembly, which, on *Merrimack*, was nearly 7 feet from top to bottom, consolidated the lower portion of the ship. However, no comparable structure was possible in the higher reaches of the hull. Any keel-like structure of substantial strength placed high in the ship would add unacceptable top weight and disturb the stability of the ship. Thus the upper reaches of the wooden ship's hull were given longitudinal strength only by the planking. Consequently, it is of no surprise that the major problem in long wooden hulls was hogging: the 'drooping' of the ends of the vessel in relation to the middle.

To counteract this weakness, there had been efforts to introduce diagonal bracing into wooden warship hulls. Joshua Humphreys had installed wooden diagonal 'riders' for the *Constitution* and her sister-ships. Later, in Britain, naval constructor Sir Robert Seppings developed a system of wooden diagonals for larger warship hulls.

A direct outgrowth of Seppings' work was the use of iron diagonal strapping, a system which was lighter, stronger, and more comprehensive than that of using relatively short timbers in the hull. On the *Merrimack*, the iron straps were 4½ inches wide by ¾ inches in section and were let into the inside of the frames. Two sets crossed each other at right angles and ran from below the turn of the bilge to the spar deck clamps. Bolts 1⅛ inch in diameter fas-

Deck framing, showing beams (athwartship), carlings (longitudinal) elements, as well as knees and mast partners. Note that the keel and keelsons were the only continuous (though scarphed) longitudinal timbers in the wooden ship. (Wilson, *An Outline of Shipbuilding, Theoretical and Practical*)

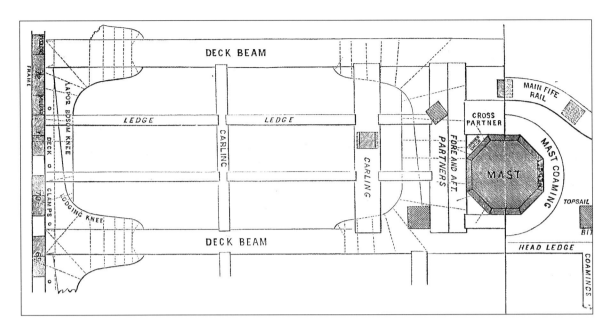

tened the bars at their intersections as well as to the timbers. Iron braces were also employed on the outside of the stern. (Plans of a sister-ship show six parallel straps running diagonally over the stern deadwood and bolted thereon.) When complete, the main hull strapping formed a basket-like support system, which seems to have been particularly effective, especially in conjunction with live oak framing, as the sister-ships of *Merrimack* survived over thirty years, and one (*Wabash*) was not sold until 1912.

With the strapping let into the inside of the frames, and the fore and aft structures in place, the hull was prepared for planking. Inside the frames, the fore and aft strakes of planking intended to support the ends of the deck beams were designated deck clamps. On *Merrimack* there were three of these strakes beneath each deck, all of white oak. Both gun and berth deck clamps were 7 inches thick; spar deck clamps were 6 inches. Care was taken that the butt ends of inside planking did not end on the same frame as the ends of the outside planking.

Planking that was laid over the floor heads and first futtock heads were the bilge strakes. On *Merrimack* these were 6½ inches thick. 'Ceiling' consisted of the planking strakes completing the interior of the frames (between or among the above listed thick strakes), and was 4½ inches thick, also of white oak. The projecting edges of the thicker plank strakes were chamfered to smoothness.

Some of the interior strakes were only fastened temporarily at this stage. As will be seen, through bolts were to be used to attach the outside planking. These bolts would also form the permanent bond of the interior planking to the frames.

The outer hull planking was composed of garboard strakes,

bottom plank, main wales, channel wales and sheer strakes. The garboard strakes were those next to the keel, and were the thickest of the planking – 10 inches on the *Merrimack*. Main wales were thicker (at 7 inches) than the sheer strakes and bottom planking (5 inches) and formed one of the main longitudinal ties in the hull. Channel wales were between the main and spar deck gunports. They were to take the bolts for the chain plates and provide support for the upper works.

Preparation for planking began with a half model, painted white. On this all gunports, air ports, scuppers, valves and other apertures in the hull were marked. On this was drawn the exact planking plan, and measurements were scaled off this to the timber.

On the framed hull itself, long battens were nailed around the frames at the height of the sheer. A line was cut in the timbers to mark the location of the sheer (topmost) strakes. As the planking progressed, the temporary ribbands were removed and planks which were to have extreme bends were steamed beforehand in preparation for bending.

On naval vessels the fastening of the planking was much more substantial that that on merchant ships. The latter generally – even in the twentieth century – made almost exclusive use of treenails – cylindrical oak pins – driven through the plank into the frames. In naval practice, bolts were used. In general, the planks were 'square fastened' in naval construction: in each frame the planks were attached by two through bolts and two short fastenings (bolts). The through bolts were rivetted on rings on the inside of the ceiling. The short fastenings were over two times the thickness of the plank. Heads of the bolts were punched in a ½ inch from the plank face.

ENGLIS.

POILLON.

WESTERVELT.

Five ninety-day gunboats in various stages of construction, mid 1861. Planking has begun on most of these, with the vessel on the top left nearly complete. Note the crude scaffolding and absence of machinery. Unlike iron shipbuilding, wooden vessels could be constructed without specialized tools or large capital investment. From *Harper's Weekly*. (US Navy)

Planks ranged from 35 to 50 feet in length, with the shorter pieces on the bottom. In width, strakes from the port sill to the light water line were 8 inches; increasing gradually to not over 12 for the bottom planks. In general, the planks were also thinned fore and aft, as well as planed smooth and fair. Of course, the plank seams required caulking before taking to the water.

Completing the hollow girder which was the hull were the decks. The major deck framing components were the beams: the principal cross members; knees securing the beams to the ship's sides; and carlings — longitudinal members between the beams. Other timbers formed the receptacles for the masts, beds for bitts and capstans, and framed the hatches. The whole, for each deck, was planked and caulked.

*Merrimack*'s beams were yellow pine, ranging from 16 inches by 12½ inches for the spar deck, to 16 inches by 13½ inches (berth deck), to 17 inches by 14½ inches for the main or gun deck. The length of some of these — nearly 50 feet — made it necessary for them to be made of two pieces. The portions were scarphed together and solidly coaked and bolted.

Caulking. Tarred hemp was driven into the crevices between planks to prevent leakage. (*Harper's New Monthly Magazine*)

The importance of the fastenings at the ends of the beams cannot be over-emphasized. The beams were the members which held the sides of the ship in place and therefore were subject to immense stress from several sources: the natural working and twisting of the hull in heavy weather and seas, the weight of the guns and the shocks of their firing, and from the stresses on the masts when under sail.

The length of the beams was determined first, after their location was marked on the clamps. A specialized rule with sliding arms was employed, and the arms were extended until they met the inside of the frame timbers. Both the length and bevelling were determined at this time, with the measurements transferred to the rough beams for cutting.

The initial fastening between beams and clamps was a dovetail joint. The beam was driven down onto the joint and two bolts secured it into the clamp strake. This was only the beginning of a very impressive complement of beam fastenings.

Four types of knees were used on the *Merrimack*: hanging, lodge, lap, and dagger. The first hung vertically from the lower side of the beam, and its body (the vertical component) was secured to the ship's side. The horizontal portion was about 4½ feet long; the vertical, 6 feet for the berth deck and the entire distance between the decks for the others.

Lodging knees were entirely horizontal: one arm lay along the forward side of the beam; the other along the deck clamp. Lap knees were similar, but lay on the aft side of the beams. When a gunport or other object prevented use of a hanging knee, the body of the knee was angled diagonally down from the beam and called a dagger knee. Coaks and bolts held the knees to the beams and frames of the vessel. Hanging knees often had seven bolts into and through the side timbers; lap and lodge knees, five into their respective beams.

Carlings and ledges were the secondary timbers between the beams. Carlings were the fore and aft timbers between the beams, with large vessels such as *Merrimack* having two on each side of the centerline. Ledges ran athwartships from the sides to the carlings, and from carling to carling.

The final major timbers in the decks were the mast partners. Cross partners and fore and aft partners enclosed the mast openings. The fore and aft pair were supported by lap and lodge knees comparable to those on the side of the deck frame and corner chocks completed the mast's framing.

The planking of the deck would seem to be a simple proposition, but in fact was not as straightforward as it appears. First, the three outside strakes of planking, nearest the sides, called the thick strakes, were about 2 inches thicker than the planking proper, with the extra thickness let into recesses in the tops of the beams. Second, there were deck stringers: two or three strakes on either side of the centerline hatches, which were 1 inch thicker than the rest of the planking. These were jogged over the beams to make them even with the other planking. Third, the centerline plank strake was generally half an inch thicker than the rest of the deck. Finally, of course, the seams were thoroughly caulked.

The planks were secured with a pair of spikes into each beam, plus one in each ledge the plank crossed. All the fastenings, bolts or spikes, were inset about ¾-inch below the top of the plank and wooden plugs were driven in to achieve a smooth surface.[9]

The preceding has set forth the construction of the major elements of a steam frigate's hull. Many of the nautical minutiae — bitts, stanchions, bulkheads, hammock nettings, scuppers, air ports and so on — have been left out, as they were incidental to the main hull structure.

The typical steam sailing vessel of the era was launched without engines and boilers, and provisions were made during the hull construction for sections of the deck to be removed for their installation. As mentioned above, the hull was prepared with the installation of engine and boiler keelsons and cross members on

Once launched, usually with only lower masts in place, the vessel was often put into dry dock for coppering. USS *Vandalia* is shown well into fitting out (1874). Note the staging on her side, wire rigging and zinc paint. (US Navy)

the bottom, and the sternpost was of sufficient width to accept the aperture for the propeller shaft. With the exception of providing coal bunkers, a place for the funnel, and a framework for the hoisting screw mechanism, the basic hull structure was that of a sailing vessel. In fact, in Britain in the 1840s and 1850s, it was common to convert sailing warships, particularly ships of the line, to steam, by the simple expedient of adding the appropriate number of frames to the center portion of the hull. (A similar plan was broached in the US, but rejected as ships of the line – sail or steam – were too expensive to operate and were unnecessary for the navy's cruising mission.)[10]

A ship was also launched without much of its masting and rigging. Usually only the lower masts were stepped at this time. Coppering of the hull was reserved for after the launch, in some instances simply to get the vessel off the ways in preparation for laying down another keel.

The launching itself was a complicated procedure. It involved building a temporary cradle for the hull, with vertical timbers extending from the hull's bilges to long timbers known as sliding ways. Shortly before launch, wedges were driven in to elevate the hull sufficiently to knock away its supporting timbers, leaving the hull on the sliding ways, restrained by strategically positioned shoring. On signal, the temporary shores were knocked away, releasing the hull to slide down the greased ways.

The floating hull then was the scene of months of fitting out, with swarms of workmen moving in and out of her hatches and up and down the rigging. The *Merrimack* was laid down in July 1854, launched June 1855 and completed and commissioned 20 February 1856. For comparison, one of the faster wartime keel to completion times was eight months for the steam sloop *Canandaigua* in 1862.[11]

It is noteworthy that wooden warship construction was a labor-intensive procedure and one in which large workforces could accomplish much in a short time. Often during the Civil War, work slow downs were due to material shortages on the part of the steam engine manufacturers, as material shortages on the hull could be rectified by substitution of other species of timbers (though the substituted timbers were usually of inferior grade and thus detrimental to the longevity of the ship).

Furthermore, in contrast to the construction of iron ships, the building of wooden vessels did not require specialized or complex tools or expensive infrastructure. The only large mechanical device involved, other than the building ways, was a crane or shear legs, which could be contrived out of raw timbers. It was possible to construct an entire wooden sailing war vessel, from raw timber upward, within the confines of a navy yard. The contrast with iron vessels was stark, as exemplified by Ericsson's *Monitor*. Each and every iron component of that vessel was made and cut to specifications elsewhere, usually at an ironworks or foundry. The shipyard had become simply a location where assembly took place. Thus the entire character of shipbuilding in the mid nineteenth century, in particular the transition from wood to iron and steel, was being changed in its very essence by the Industrial Revolution, with steam propulsion only the initial phase of the trend.

# Chapter Six

# NAVY UNIFORMS, EQUIPMENT AND SMALL ARMS

Surgeon Undress    Lieutenant White Service    Boatswain's Mate    Captain Full Dress    Chief Engineer Service Dress

UNITED STATES NAVY, 1852

The uniforms of the US Navy during the Civil War era were subjected to the effects of sometimes contradictory factors. Among these were the vast and sudden expansion of the personnel force and the increasing importance of the steam engineering corps and other staff positions. There was at the same time a move to de-emphasize the anti-egalitarian character of the officer corps by limiting the more ostentatious uniform elements. Over against this was the necessity to create additional ranks, including those commensurate with operational units far larger than any previously seen in the American navy. These factors resulted in three distinct groupings of uniforms: those based on the 1852 regulations, which were seen in 1861 and 1862; major alterations which came into being in mid 1862; and newly reworked regulations of 1864.

At the war's outset, navy uniforms were under the regulations of 1852. The three rows of cuff lace indicated a captain – the highest permanent rank in the navy at the time. The full dress uniform had the broad gold seam stripe on the trousers and gold edged high collar. Note the broad gold lace around the service cap also. At this juncture staff officers (surgeons and engineers seen here) had not reached high 'assimilated rank'. Note the traditional enlisted garb, which changed little through the nineteenth century, though the 'sennet' cap shown here was soon replaced by the flat cap nicknamed Donald Duck in the twentieth century. (US Navy)

Officers of the *Monitor*, 1862. Still under the 1852 regulations, all are wearing the service dress rolling collar frock coat, except the officer standing to the far right, with the popular five-button sack coat. Note also his straw hat, authorized for wear in warm weather. Seated on the right is Charles Dana Green, executive officer, with lieutenant's cuff lace. The row of cuff buttons indicating masters was eliminated in the July 1862 uniform regulations. (US Navy)

At the war's beginning, uniforms were governed by regulations promulgated in 1852 and modified spasmodically since then. Commissioned officers were authorized full dress, undress, and service uniforms. The full dress attire consisted of the blue double-breasted 'body coat' with tails and a standing collar and two rows of nine buttons each. Epaulets, cocked hat and a sword with knot were to be worn, with a white vest, black silk stock, and pantaloons with gold lace stripe on the outside seam. A double-breasted frock coat with rolling collar and plain trousers was the basic undress

combination with either cocked hat or a service cap. A white or blue vest could be worn according to the season and shoulder straps could be substituted for epaulets. The service dress substituted the service cap for the cocked hat and made epaulets and sword optional. White trousers were authorized with all uniforms in the tropics and according to season elsewhere. Finally, straw hats were allowed on shipboard in tropical climates and in summer. These were low crowned, with a wide brim and black ribbon.

There were two other officer's uniform jackets in use during the war. One was a short shell jacket — essentially the frock coat without skirts. This was primarily seen at the Naval Academy and and on younger officers who had retained it from their academy days. The second was the sack coat, a naval version of a popular style of the times. It was considered service dress and was single breasted with five buttons. It could be worn with sleeve lace and shoulder straps or without. When worn without lace and straps, rank was shown by insignia on the collars.

The American naval officer corps was composed of three

commissioned ranks: lieutenant, commander, and captain. A fourth designation, that of master, consisted of both warrant and commissioned officers, and a fifth, flag officer, had been instituted in 1857. The last, however, was for the commander of a squadron, rather than a permanent rank. The use of 'flag officer' rather than 'admiral' again reflected the American distaste for aristocratic 'admiralty'.

In this era, rank was shown in a variety of manners on the uniform. (It had not been many years since that rank had been shown by major variations in the uniforms themselves, such as the wearing of – or absence of – epaulets.) In 1861, on the full dress, rank was shown by the number of rows of lace on the cuffs, and presence of buttons rather than lace, width of the lace on the standing collar, trouser legs and cap, devices on the epaulets and shoulder straps, decorative lace on the cocked hat, and variations in cap devices.

Generally speaking, the silver eagle designated captains and flag officers. Crossed silver fouled anchors were for commanders, and single anchors indicated lieutenants and below. On shoulder insignia, captains wore single stars with the eagle; flag officers, two stars. Trouser seam lace ranged upwards from the master's ⅜-inch width to 1½-inches for the captain. Lace on the standing collars matched the width of that on the trousers. Three-quarter-inch strips of lace indicated the rank on the cuffs: three for captains, two for commanders, one for lieutenants. Masters wore three navy buttons in lieu of lace strips.

Caps also had the eagle and fouled anchor devices for their respective ranks. A wreath of oak and olive branches surrounded each of the devices, and a gold lace band circled the service cap below the wreath. Width of this lace was equal to that worn on collar and trousers.

The black cocked hat was worn with two variations. Captains and commanders wore six rows (three loops) of bullion on the side with the inner pair entwined. All others wore four rows (two loops) of bullion with a single button at the lower end of the loops.

Midshipmen and passed midshipmen both wore the officer's pattern uniform. The latter wore no lace on the collar bottom and had neither lace nor buttons on the cuffs. The midshipman's collar distinction was a fouled anchor, with no lace whatever. In the service uniform, the cap device was the fouled anchor without the band of lace below. Neither were authorized to wear epaulets. Passed midshipmen wore a ½-inch by 4-inch gold strap as a shoulder distinction and ¼-inch lace on the trouser seam.

Three of the four 'civil officers' of the navy – paymasters, sur-

geons, and engineers – had only recently been accorded ranks comparable to line officers. This action regularized the uniforms of all officers except the chaplains, who were required to wear a black single-breasted rolling collar coat with black covered buttons and no other insignia. Meanwhile, chief engineers, surgeons, and paymasters with over twelve years service were authorized the two sleeve stripes of a commander; those with less than twelve years, a single sleeve stripe, In full dress, no lace was authorized on the trousers, and no distinctive insignia were allowed on the epaulets. On the service cap, collar, and shoulder straps, crossed oak leaves marked the engineers, wide oak sprigs indicated surgeons, and oak sprigs, paymasters. The exception to this was on the engineer's standing collar, which was given ½-inch gold edging.

The final pre-war addition to the officer's uniform was the addition of an embroidered five-pointed star above the lieutenant's sleeve stripes, to indicate duty as an executive officer. This star eventually became the standard emblem of all line officers.

The master's mate rating of this period included warranted and enlisted personnel. The former were authorized single breasted frock coats with nine buttons and rolling collar, worn with a cap with vertical anchor device and two gold bands. The latter wore a double-breasted jacket, with six buttons on each breast, and a cap with only the anchor device.

The enlisted sailor's uniform had long been more a matter of tradition than of regulations. It was first described in a directive of 1841. The familiar frock, in blue, was woollen. In those days, when sailors often made their own uniforms, the result was a variety of yoke patterns, as well as often elaborate embroidery thereon. The white frock was of linen or duck, with the collar and cuffs sometimes covered with blue dungaree or nankeen. Again, colorful embroidery was encouraged on these garments. The trousers – blue wool or white duck – were worn with either color frock with two rows of buttons. Fly front trousers were also in use during the war.

There was in short a blue cloth shell jacket for seamen and petty officers, originally authorized in the 1830s. Two rows of nine small buttons each decorated its front. These could be buttoned or the jacket could be fastened using a loop around two buttons at the base of the lapels.

The enlisted man's hat was either straw or blue cloth. The white straw 'sennit' hat had a low crown and broad brim, with a black ribbon. It was for dress occasions in warm weather. The cloth cap was a long naval tradition, and its ribbon was decorated with the name of the wearer's vessel, in gold. The top of these caps were commonly given a decorative sunburst or other designs, again in embroidery. A white cover could be worn over this cap during warm weather.

Other garments in use were working suits consisting of a loose jumper, without the narrow cuffs, overalls, and foul weather coats. The latter were varieties of the pea coat – double-breasted, medium length, made of coarse navy blue wool. These items, along with low shoes and underwear were not mentioned or described in the regulations of the period.

Petty officers were to wear an eagle and anchor device on the sleeve between elbow and shoulder. Boatswains, gunners, carpenters, masters-at-arms, stewards, and cooks wore this on the right; all others (quarter masters, quarter gunners, captains of forecastle, top, afterguard, and hold, armorers, coopers and corporals) wore it on the left. The only distinguishing mark seen on the average seaman was a white chevron on the upper sleeve. This was a watch mark, worn on the left sleeve for the port watch and vice versa. (See next chapter on enlisted life on shipboard.)[1]

With the firing on Fort Sumter and President Lincoln's declaration of a blockade of the States in Rebellion on 19 April 1861, the navy suddenly required personnel far beyond the previous statutory limit – some 7600 enlisted, plus approximately 500 line officers. By the war's end there were 6759 officers (volunteer and regular), and 51,537 enlisted personnel. On 16 July 1862, Congress passed legislation creating new grades for this rapidly expanding officer corps, and the navy shortly thereafter (31 July) issued appropriate changes to the uniform.

In fact, the mass influx of volunteer officers had already brought a modification to uniform requirements. As of 6 September 1861, the volunteer officers were not required to purchase full dress uniforms, only the undress combination.

The new regulations confirmed the directive to volunteer officers by abolishing the hoary full dress coat with tails and standing collar and eliminating the lace-trimmed trousers. The full dress was now the frock coat worn with epaulets, cocked hat and sword with knot. (The tail coat would be reintroduced after the war.) The undress combination was the frock coat with cap and shoulder straps or epaulets, with or without the sword. The service dress called for shoulder straps and cap, again with or without the sword.

The navy now had five new ranks to be reflected in the uniform: rear admiral, commodore, lieutenant commander, master, and ensign. The sleeve decoration was now combinations of two different widths of lace strips, ¾- and ¼-inch, much like that of today's service. The ensign was to wear a single narrow band, the master, a wide band, and the lieutenant, a combination of each. Lieutenant commanders wore two wide bands and an additional narrow band between the two designated a commander. The captain had three wide bands and the commodore added narrow bands between them. The rear admiral had added a single narrow band above those of the commodore.

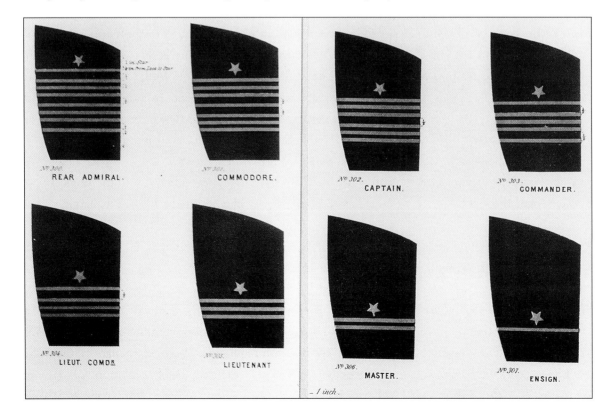

REAR ADMIRAL.    COMMODORE.    CAPTAIN.    COMMANDER.

LIEUT. COMDR.    LIEUTENANT.    MASTER.    ENSIGN.

Cuff lace, 1864 regulations. The majority of Civil War photographs reflect this regulation as it was in effect when the greatest growth occurred in the ranks. From *Illustrated Catalogue of Arms and Military Goods,* Schuyler, Hartley & Graham Co., 1864.

Officers of USS *Kearsarge*, mid 1864. Though the regulations had changed twice since the war began, Captain John A Winslow, third from left in the front row, retains the 1852 cap with wide lace as well as that regulation's captain's cuff lace (three stripes). The remainder of the officers have 1863-64 regulation uniforms: four lieutenant commanders (or staff equivalents) can be seen with four rows of lace, and two masters wearing two stripes each. (US Navy)

Epaulet devices were modified as well, with the rear admiral obtaining the old flag officer emblems – eagle, anchor and two silver stars. The commodore's devices was as the admiral's minus one star. The fouled anchor became the center element for the captain and below, with an eagle for the captain, silver oak leaves for the commander, and gold oak leaves for the lieutenant commander. Two gold bars designated lieutenants and one gold bar, masters. A simple anchor sufficed for the ensign. Note that these devices – excepting the anchor – were similar in concept and order as those of the army, and are the core of the rank insignia of today.

The shoulder straps were generally similar to the epaulets, with the anchor as the center element. The eagle, however, was not used on the admiral or commodore's straps, only the anchor and one or two stars. The cap device had the anchor as the centerpiece for those up to lieutenant, the eagle for the remaining ranks up to rear admiral, who wore a centered single star. A standard wreath surrounded all the other elements.[2]

The next major uniform change was instituted in either 1863 or 1864. The uncertainty of the date is due to the fact that the changes are not reflected in regulations until 28 January 1864, but were published earlier in commercial catalogs, dated 23 May 1863. The new regulations were apparently an attempt to 'simplify' the sleeve lace by replacing the narrow and wide lace combinations with equal-width (¼-inch) stripes, one per grade level. The maximum – eight – indicated a rear admiral, and the single line of lace denoted an ensign. Spacing was to be ¼-inch between each row, with specific exceptions which were to have ½-inch spacing. This created the uniform most often seen in wartime photographs.[3]

It should be kept in mind when dealing with the subject of uniforms that photographs of the period can be confusing. It is not unusual to see officers wearing combinations of elements from different uniform regulations, particularly hats of the 1852 style together with frock coats with 1864 regulation cuff lace, or other such combinations. Officers at sea for long periods of time

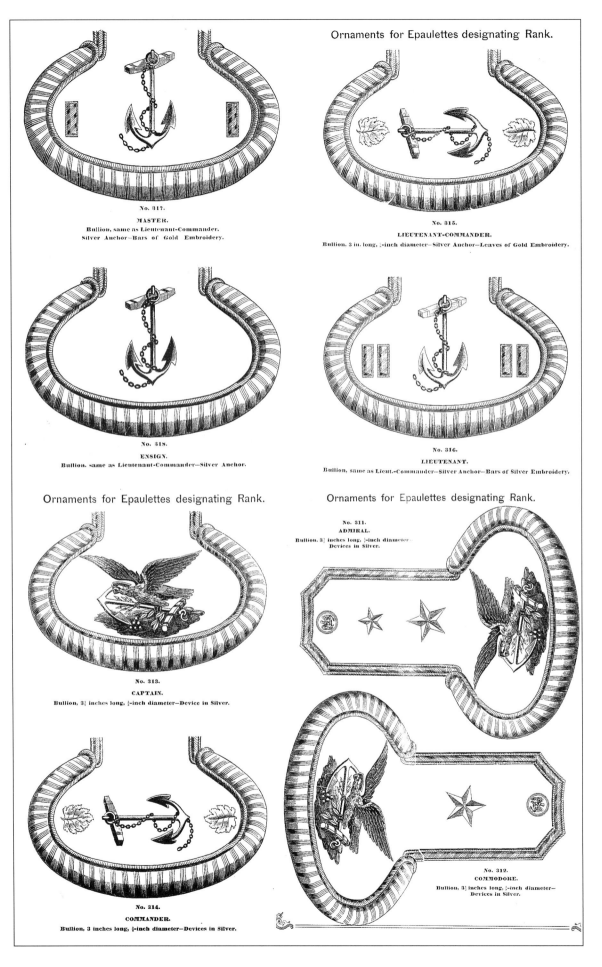

Ornaments for Epaulettes designating Rank.

No. 317.
MASTER.
Bullion, same as Lieutenant-Commander.
Silver Anchor—Bars of Gold Embroidery.

No. 315.
LIEUTENANT-COMMANDER.
Bullion, 3 in. long, ½-inch diameter—Silver Anchor—Leaves of Gold Embroidery.

No. 318.
ENSIGN.
Bullion, same as Lieutenant-Commander—Silver Anchor.

No. 316.
LIEUTENANT.
Bullion, same as Lieut.-Commander—Silver Anchor—Bars of Silver Embroidery.

Ornaments for Epaulettes designating Rank.

Ornaments for Epaulettes designating Rank.

No. 313.
CAPTAIN.
Bullion, 3½ inches long, ½-inch diameter—Device in Silver.

No. 311.
ADMIRAL.
Bullion, 3½ inches long, ½-inch diameter—Devices in Silver.

No. 314.
COMMANDER.
Bullion, 3 inches long, ½-inch diameter—Devices in Silver.

No. 312.
COMMODORE.
Bullion, 3½ inches long, ½-inch diameter—Devices in Silver.

Epaulet devices, 1864 uniforms. Epaulets were authorized for full dress only. Shoulder straps utilized the same rank devices: stars, eagle, oak leaves, bars and finally, the single fouled anchor. From *Illustrated Catalogue of Arms and Military Goods*, Schuyler, Hartley & Graham Co., 1864.

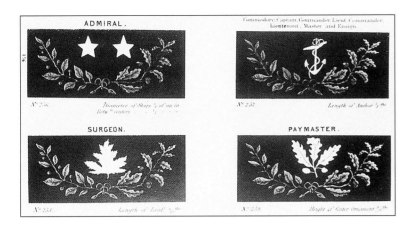

Service cap devices, regulations of 1863-64. Not shown are chaplain, with cross device and engineer, with crossed oak leaves, representing a propeller. From *Illustrated Catalogue of Arms and Military Goods*, Schuyler, Hartley & Graham Co., 1864.

might have retained the older style uniform, or simply were loath to lay out money for the new.

The 1864 instruction included a full dress uniform, with cocked hats, epaulets and sword. However, it was a combination to remain in storage for the duration of the war.

The same uniform instruction also introduced an embroidered 1-inch star to be worn ¼-inch above the top row of sleeve lace. The star denoted a line officer and has remained so to the present day. In January 1864, the star was authorized for warrant officers, midshipmen, boatswains, gunners, and master's mates receiving $40 per month.

Later in 1863, further changes were authorized, in this instance to the uniform cap. To correspond with the reduced amount of lace on the sleeves, the cap also lost it's wide gold band. At the same time the overhang of the top was reduced to ¼-inch larger than the band. Furthermore, all line officers except for the admiral were to wear a silver fouled anchor in the center of the cap's wreath. Two stars replaced the anchor for the rear admiral. Staff officers wore corps devices in place of the anchor. These were: medical corps, oak leaves; paymasters, an oak sprig; engineers, crossed oak leaves; professors of mathematics, the old English letter 'P'; naval constructors, a sprig of two oak leaves and two acorns; chaplains, an oblique cross; secretaries, the old English letter 'S'.

In December 1863, a circular was issued requiring that rank be shown on the points of the overcoat collar. These were to be the same devices as those on the shoulder straps, except the lieutenant and master bars were to be silver rather than gold.

Uniform of 1864. An Old English 'C' designated a carpenter. (National Archives)

The 1864 instructions continued some rank distinctions indicated by the uniform itself. The standard nine button double-breasted frock coat was to be worn by warrant officers, midshipmen, third assistant engineers, and clerks, but with medium rather than large navy buttons. The large button variety of the frock coat was authorized for boatswains, gunners, carpenters, and sailmakers.

Leading petty officers — masters-at-arms, yeoman, stewards, paymaster's stewards — were now authorized a coat rather than the enlisted jumper. This was the jacket with two rows of six medium buttons, originally in the 1862 regulations for shipped or rated master's mates.

Shoulder straps were authorized for forward warrant officers. An old English style 'B' indicated the boatswain; a 'C' for the carpenter. Gunners and sailmakers had no center device.

The creation of the vice admiral rank (for D G Farragut) required a new uniform circular. Three stars designated this rank on the uniform cap, shoulder straps, and collar points. One row of 2-inch lace, plus two rows of 1-inch lace above the wide lace showed the rank on the sleeves. The rear admiral's sleeve lace had one less narrow row. This narrow-wide combination would continue to this day to designate flag ranks.

The 1863-4 uniform regulations were short-lived, being superceded in December 1866. As noted before, the full dress body coat was reinstated, along with cocked hat and epaulets. The standing collar reappeared, with its variations in lace widths indicating rank. In 1869, the narrow-wide sleeve lace combinations reappeared, much as they had been in the pre-war years. All in all, the officer's uniform had shed the wartime practicality enforced by the austere hand of Gideon Welles and now reflected the gold-laced decor of peacetime operations.[4]

# Naval small arms

The naval small arms of the mid nineteenth century reflected the technological flux of that age: an era when advanced ideas were often stymied by inappropriate materials and primitive techniques. It was also an age when the mystique of technological change generated an optimism out of proportion to the actual results; an optimism which saw little need for intensive testing and evaluation and sometimes brought disaster in the field.

Two areas of change which revolutionized small arms of the era were breech-loading and multiple shot weapons. Accompanying these was the development of the self-contained metallic cartridge. All three of these were in existence by the beginning of the Civil War, often with less than satisfactory results. The progress made in these areas can be judged by the fact that the standard infantry long arm was a muzzle-loading, single-shot rifle. The handgun of choice was the revolver — multiple-fire to be sure — but still using the percussion system with its distinct operations for loading powder, shot and igniting cap for each chamber of the cylinder. Though metallic cartridge weapons were extant during the war years the technology of cartridge design was primitive, as well as that involved in ejecting the spent round from the chamber. Consequently, relatively few were adopted for military use until the post-war era.

The weapons adopted by the US Navy of course reflected a different combat milieu than those of the sister service. Boardings and landing parties required small arms, in addition to snipers in the tops. Otherwise, the typical bluejacket had little use for long range weapons. In fact, the opposite was true: close range and rapid fire were optimum characteristics of the favored weapons. Further, sustained long term use of weapons in battlefield conditions was unheard of in naval combat. These factors made it possible for the navy to adopt guns which might have been rejected by the army as unsuitable for combat conditions.

# Pistols and revolvers

In December 1866, the navy inventoried its small arms held in various storage facilities. Even at this late date, some quarter century after the first revolvers entered the inventory, there were 3434 single-shot percussion pistols on hand. Indeed, in the wartime requirements for weaponry of all sorts, 5153 such handguns were purchased on the open market or transferred from army stocks. Thus the old — and very obsolete — single-shot percussion pistol was the third largest wartime acquisition, after Remington (5960) and Whitney (6276) revolvers - and outnumbered the Colts by some 500.[5]

The navy had been the first government agency to adopt the percussion system for pistols. In November 1843, three hundred .54 caliber cap-and-ball weapons were ordered from N P Ames of Springfield, Massachusetts. By September 1845 there were 3832 of these 'Model 1842' pistols in navy hands.

The weapon itself was 11⅝ inches in length and weighed 2 pounds. The barrel was browned and furniture, brass. The only unusual feature was the 'boxlock': the hammer was located inside the lockplate, a characteristic which may have appealed to the navy due to their constant concern with avoiding rigging and other entanglements. The pistols initially cost $5 each, though the final group was obtained at $4.75 per gun. The initial 300 of these can be distinguished by a convex lock plate; on the later variety, the plate was flat — a difference which probably contributed to the lower cost of the later guns.[6]

A second group of single-shot percussion pistols in navy inventories was made by Henry Aston of Middletown, Connecticut. Three thousand of these were obtained through the US Army Ordnance department in 1850. These pistols were of the Army Model 1842 — .54 caliber, 14 inches long with an 8-inch barrel. They had brass furnishings but had the hammer mounted outside the lockplate in the accepted manner. The navy also procured nearly identical versions of this pistol made by A Waters and Ira Johnson.

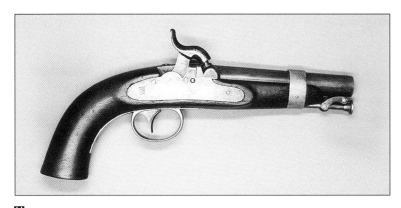

The Ames 'boxlock' pistol of 1842. Unlike conventional percussion arms, it's hammer was recessed behind the side plate. (Steve Selenfriend; photograph by the author)

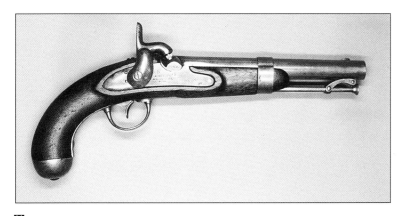

The navy also purchased army-model percussion pistols such as this one, made by A Waters. These, including varieties made by H Aston and Ira Johnson were .54 caliber and 14 inches long. Note the conventional configuration of hammer. (Steve Selenfriend; photograph by the author)

An anomaly which has not yet been explained is the existence of US Navy marked pistols made by Henry Deringer of Philadelphia. A contract for boxlock pistols was executed with Deringer in 1845, but records indicate none were ever delivered to the service. The original buyer of these pistols is not known.

It is also noteworthy that the navy as late as the 1850s was converting their old flintlock single-shot weapons to the percussion system. Some 6000 such conversions – pistols, muskets and rifles – were done at the army's Watertown Arsenal (New York) up to 1853. The conversion was done by cutting off the flintlock's breech and attaching another with the percussion cap nipple built in. These were the last single-shot percussion pistols obtained by the navy before the Civil War.[7]

The percussion system applied to the revolving cylinder was patented by Samuel Colt and applied to the Paterson model pistol in 1837. The first government to order these weapons was the short-lived Republic of Texas, which issued a .36 caliber version to their naval forces in 1839. The US Navy obtained 100 Patersons in 1841 and a batch of 50 in 1845, at $25 each.

No new revolving pistols were purchased by the navy until June 1852, when Commodore Matthew Calbraith Perry was outfitting his expedition to Japan. A special order for 100 Colt revolvers resulted: twenty-five .44 caliber Dragoons, fifty 'plated' Model 1851 Navies, and the balance, Pocket Model 1849s (.31 caliber). At least twenty of the Army Model Dragoons were gifts for the Japanese.

The Colt 1851 Navy was the next revolver purchased in quantity by the service. This six-shot weapon weighed 2 pounds 10 ounces and had a 7½-inch barrel. Its .36 caliber ball could penetrate six 1-inch boards at 16 yards. The 'Navy' appellation is somewhat misleading: in fact the first quantity orders for the gun were from the army, and before the introduction of the .44 caliber Colt in 1860, it was nearly the standard cavalry handgun. The 'Navy' terminology of the day referred to any .36 caliber belt pistol. The 1851 Navy was purchased in quantity by the navy in 1856, with a total of 2750 being procured before the onset of the Civil War. It has been suggested that the navy obtained some 5000 additional 1851 Navies through the army in 1861 and 1862. No documentary evidence of this has been found. It should be noted also that, in contrast to other military issue Colt Navies, the navy contract guns had steel rather than brass backstraps and trigger guards.

Shortly after the firing on Fort Sumter, the navy's first order for new Colts arrived – 500 at $25 a piece, with accessories. This group, however, was the Model 1860 Army .44 caliber 'holster pistol'. Developed from the 1851 frame, this gun weighed 2 pounds 11 ounces and had an 8-inch barrel with ratchet-type loading lever. The early numbers of this group had fluted cylinders. A total of 1150 of these were received by the navy between May and September 1861. Many, if not all, of these guns were issued to the Mississippi squadron. This was appropriate considering the role of the army in forming the squadron, and its primary function being the assistance of the army in the river campaigns.

The last group of Colt revolvers purchased during the war was the New Model (1861) Navy pistol. This was the .36 caliber version of the Army pistol, with 'streamlined' loading lever housing and round barrel. A total of 3370 New Models were delivered between late 1861 and September 1862 at $23 each.

The navy ceased ordering Colts in September 1862, when Remington revolvers became available at $12 each – virtually half

The Colt 1851 Navy was the first percussion revolver purchased in quantity by the service, with 2750 obtained before the Civil War. The .36-caliber 1851 Navy was one of the most popular handguns of the war – very common on both sides, particularly in cavalry units. It was lighter and smaller than its army counterpart and thus handier to use. (Steve Selenfriend; photograph by the author)

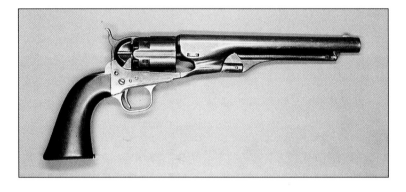

Colt 1860 Army. This .44 caliber weapon was commonly found in naval service on the western rivers, where army-navy cooperation was more continuous and pronounced than on the coasts. The earlier serial numbers such as this one had fluted cylinders. (Steve Selenfriend; photograph by the author)

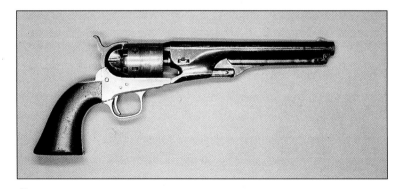

Colt 1861 Navy. These reverted to the 'standard' .36 naval caliber. (Steve Selenfriend; photograph by the author)

the price of the Colt. The only other Colts purchased during the conflict were a small number of .31 caliber Model 1849 pocket pistols. These were obtained on the open market from the Union Defense Committee of New York, and were all six-shot weapons with 5-inch barrels. All were marked 'UDC' and given navy inspection markings.

An inventory of weapons in 1866 showed almost 3000 Colts on hand in various navy yards, and by 1873 all non-Colts had been disposed of. Around 2000 of the Colts were modified to fire .38 caliber rim-fire cartridges between 1873 and 1876.[8]

Between 1861 and the war's end the navy purchased five varieties of revolvers in addition to the Colts. The earliest was the Savage or North Savage, first tested by the navy in January 1858, and manufactured in Middletown, Connecticut by the Savage Repeating Firearms Company. This weapon, patented by Henry North, was unique in its action, having a circular finger-hole lever (or toggle) below the trigger. Pulling this lever back allowed the cylinder to slide away from the barrel, advanced it to the next chamber and cocked the hammer. Releasing the lever reseated and sealed the cylinder to the barrel. (As might be expected, operating this lever required a substantial effort on the part of the operator's fingers.) Once this operation was complete, the trigger could be pulled, firing the weapon.

The first model of the Savage, purchased by the army, was known as the 'figure 8' Savage. A later version was distinguished by a guard strap around the trigger and cocking lever, adding yet more bulk to this awkward weapon. The later model was the only type obtained by the navy.

The upshot of successful trials was an order for 300 of the .36 caliber pistols at $20 each. Though ordered in 1858, deliveries were delayed until April 1860. The delay was due to a reorganization of the company as well as the incorporation of minor improvements in the weapon. In May 1861, eight hundred Savages were ordered, making a total of 1100 delivered to the navy by 14 September 1861. An additional twenty-six were obtained through the Union Defense Committee of New York City in 1861, rounding out the navy's inventory of Savage revolvers.

At 3 pounds 6 ounces, the Savage was by far the heaviest navy revolver used during the war. This and the distinctly awkward cocking/rotating toggle action – which required three fingers to operate – no doubt made it less popular than the others used by the service. On the positive side, it's solid frame (completely surrounding the cylinder), as opposed to the Colt's open frame, made it a very strong weapon.[9]

The year 1861 brought two small orders for revolvers to meet the emergency needs of the service. The first was on 1 July, when 100 pistols were ordered from Benjamin Joslyn of Worcester, Massachusetts.

Joslyn's revolver was unique in having a side mounted hammer. The method of turning the cylinder was also unique to Joslyn's patent, and apparently the source of weakness in this design. Other than these distinctions, the pistol was similar to the Remington, in having a solid frame around the cylinder. It should also be noted that this was a five-shot, .44 caliber pistol – both unusual for navy handguns.

The army had tested the gun successfully in 1858 but had not purchased, and the navy tested it in June 1861, again with satisfactory results. Of the one hundred received by the navy, however, several of the first lot of fifty and seven of the second half of the order were defective. Most of the problems were in revolving the cylinder. The army, which ordered 1100 of the pistols, purchased no more after April 1862. One user complained that 'one half of the time [it] will neither cock nor revolve'.

The only other small order for revolvers was in December 1861 when 100 Starr pistols were purchased at $20 each. These guns, patented by Ebenezer Starr of New York, were probably the most unusual pistols in the navy inventory. Not only did the gun's frame 'break open' for access to the cylinder, but the gun was one of the earliest double action revolvers – that is, a single trigger pull both cocked and fired the gun.

The order for these .36 caliber guns was in two parts: forty were sent to Washington Navy Yard, the rest to New York. Though the latter apparently entered the active inventory, all forty sent to Washington were rejected. It was found on testing that the percussion caps obstructed the rotation of the cylinders. This ended the navy's interest in the Starr pistol.[10]

As has been stated, Remington and Whitney were the two largest suppliers of revolvers for the wartime navy. The latter firm, located in Whitneyville, Connecticut, had been founded by Eli Whitney Sr, whose same inventive mind had introduced interchangeable parts to gun manufacturing and produced the cotton gin.

By the late 1850s, Eli Whitney had patented a revolving pistol, the production model of which was first purchased by the US Army in October 1861. Some 11,000 were in army use by the end of the war. The first naval purchase of the pistol was in February 1863, with sporadic increments until 15 March 1865, totalling 6268.

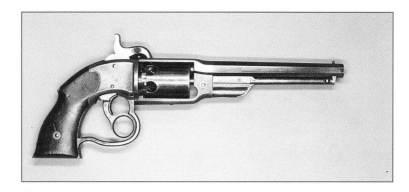

One of many Colt competitors was the North Savage, a heavy weapon wherein the finger-operated lever rotated the cylinder and cocked the gun (an operation otherwise accomplished by pulling the hammer back in most other revolvers of the time). (Steve Selenfriend; photograph by the author)

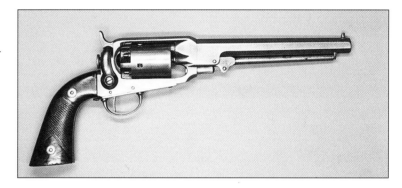

The Joslyn revolver featured a side-mounted hammer and proved to be defective in its method of revolving the cylinder. It was also .44 caliber and five-shot, as opposed to .36 and six-shot navy standards. (Steve Selenfriend; photograph by the author)

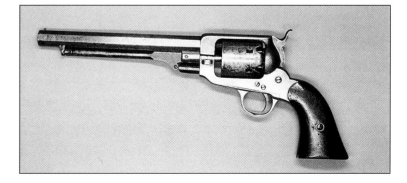

The Whitney, seen here, and the Remington were the most successful Colt competitors – and they were significantly cheaper. Both had the advantage of a solid frame surrounding the cylinder, compared to the Colt's open-top frame. (Steve Selenfriend; photograph by the author)

The weapon itself was .36 caliber, weighed 2 pounds 7 ounces, and had a 7⅝-inch barrel. Unlike the Colt, it had a solid frame, as well as a simpler method of removing the cylinder. In army service there were complaints about parts breakage under heavy use, but it appears that the navy got good service from the Whitneys.

The last handgun purchased in quantity was made by E Remington & Sons of Ilion, New York. The Remington firm had been in the firearms business since 1816 and had had their first army and navy contracts in 1845.

There were three distinct Remington models purchased by the navy. The first was the Remington-Beals, patented in 1858. These were six-shot, .36 caliber weapons with 7½-inch barrels. The Beals models can be distinguished by a small loading lever and frame cut in a straight line in front of the top of the cylinder. The Model 1861, also known as the Old Model, was fitted with a larger loading lever, channelled to allow the removal of the cylinder pin without lowering the lever. This modification was less than satisfactory, as it was found that the recoil sometimes forced the cylinder pin forward and jammed the cylinder.

The New Model retained the larger loading lever but reverted to lowering the loading lever to allow removal of the cylinder pin. Externally, the New Model frame was cut in a curve forward of the upper part of the cylinder, exposing some of the barrel threads.

The navy first tested the Beals revolver in August 1862, comparing it to the Colt weapon. It was found to be more accurate and much easier to dismantle. (The Colt's cylinder could not be removed without detaching the barrel — the latter operation requiring loosening one screw and punching out the barrel lug through the cylinder pin). A total of 5960 Remingtons were obtained at prices from $12 to $15 each.

Remington's first wartime contract was received on 15 September 1862, for 100 revolvers. The 1862 and early 1863 orders were for the Remington-Beals patent gun or the Model 1861, for a total of 1616 weapons. The late 1863 and 1864 orders (4344 guns) were for the Remington New Model. About 1400 of the total went to the Mississippi squadron.

It is noteworthy that the navy reverted to single-shot pistols after the war. Remington had introduced the simple and strong

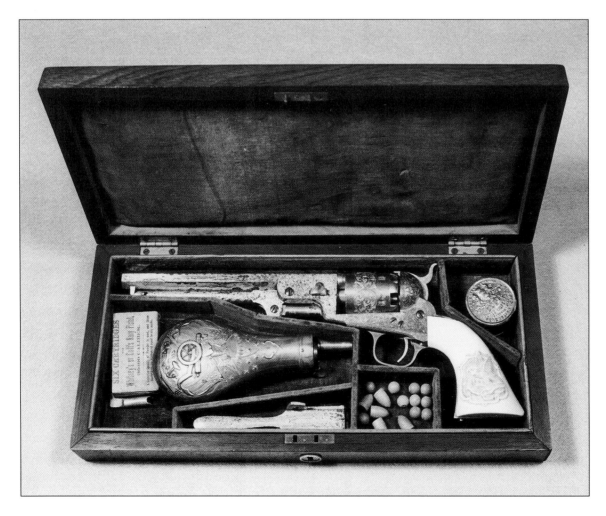

All the weapons illustrated on previous pages are shown in their standard finish — usually blued barrel and cylinder, case hardened frame and brass or steel backstrap and trigger guard, with wood grips. Special finishes, including nickel and silver plating, elaborate engraving and ivory grips were available both from the manufacturers and other craftsmen, at significantly higher prices. Shown here is an example of a presentation Colt Navy, complete with padded case and accessories (powder flask, bullet mold, etc.). (Steve Selenfriend; photograph by the author)

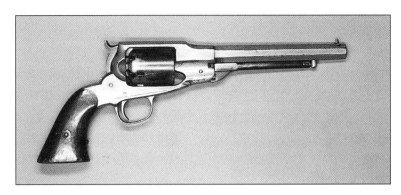

**R**emington-Beals .36 caliber revolver was the first variety of the Remington purchased by the navy in 1862. (Steve Selenfriend; photograph by the author)

rolling block mechanism and combined it with a .50 caliber rim-fire metallic cartridge. The navy first purchased this weapon in 1866. The revolver was re-introduced in the 1870s.[11]

There were, of course, numerous presentation pistols from the Civil War era. These were often elaborately engraved and plated, and presented in cushioned and inlaid cases. Many were non-standard arms and as such are not part of this study.

# Long arms

The navy's long arms were a mixed lot during the Civil War. They ranged from twenty-year-old Jenks carbines, to new but obsolescent .69 caliber muzzle-loading rifles, to the most modern Spencer repeating cartridge guns. As with pistols, firepower and compactness were the navy's primary criteria. (It should be noted here that the marines did not follow the navy in choice of weapons, and in fact tended to rely on army pattern weapons. See next chapter.)

The navy's adoption of breech-loading long arms dated back to the Hall flintlock rifle, Model 1819. Only a few of these saw navy service, but in 1839 the navy made the rather astounding jump to a breech-loading, percussion gun with the acquisition of the Jenks carbine.

This weapon, invented by William Jenks of South Carolina and manufactured by N P Ames, was unusual in having a hammer which operated laterally rather than in the normal vertical arc. This made for fewer protrusions above the top of the barrel, making the weapon less liable to tangling in rigging or clothing. The .54 caliber rifle was 52½ inches long and was loaded by means of a lever on top of the breech. This opened the chamber, allowing

the charge to be inserted. Folding the lever back into the stock closed the breech block. A carbine version of the weapon was also issued.

Two further varieties of the Jenks were acquired. Remington arms manufactured the gun with the addition of Maynard's tape primer. This device, resembling in general the child's roll of caps, eliminated manually attaching a percussion cap to the nipple for each discharge.

In 1861 J H Merrill converted Jenks guns to use paper cartridges in lieu of the loose powder and ball system. At the same time, the unique 'mule ear' hammer arrangement was dispensed with and replaced by a standard 'overhead' hammer. Two-hundred-and-forty of these were obtained by the navy, through the army's Ordnance department in 1861.

Though over twenty years in service the Jenks was still in the navy's inventory at the outbreak of the war. In May 1861, thirty thousand carbine balls for the Jenks were ordered for New York Navy Yard, and 15,000 were sent to the Portsmouth yard. In June of that year, authority was given to replace the Jenks guns on the *St Lawrence* with Sharps rifles. It is not known when the last of the weapons was phased out.

The next percussion breechloader obtained by the navy was the rifle version of Colt's revolver. Sixty Colt Paterson revolving carbines were delivered to the navy in 1841, and, four years later, another 100 were ordered. The guns were used during the Second Seminole War, on the Pacific during the Mexican War, and were on hand with Perry during the Japan Expedition.

These guns were essentially larger versions of Colt's pistols, which, theoretically, would have made them good weapons.

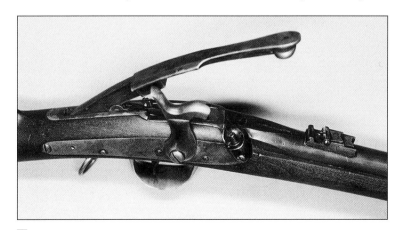

**T**he Merrill version of the Jenks, which dispensed with the 'mule ear' hammer and substituted a standard hammer. These were purchased by the navy in 1861. (Steve Selenfriend; photograph by the author)

Four breech-loading long arm systems: (from top) Joslyn, Perry, Sharps and Hankins, and Sharps. All are shown with the action open or partially open. The long lever atop the stock opened the action on the Joslyn. Lowering the trigger guard pivotted the breech open on the Perry. The same action moved the barrel forward on the Sharps and Hankins, and dropped the breech block downward on the Sharps. All were single-shot percussion excepting the Sharps and Hankins, which took a .56-52 caliber metallic cartridge. (Steve Selenfriend; photograph by the author)

However, when firing the long arm, the cylinder was in close proximity to the user's face – and the escape of hot gases between the cylinder and the rear of the barrel was not a pleasant experience. Further, there was a danger of several, or all the cylinders detonating simultaneously due to stray powder or flashover from the chamber being fired. On the rifle, the hand supporting the forestock was likely to sustain major injury if this occurred.[12]

The navy and marines used .44, .52, .56, and .64 caliber versions of the Colt, the last pre-war purchases being the 1855 model. It is noteworthy that the Colt rifle was issued to the Navy of the Republic of Texas in the early 1840s. Some may have been acquired by the US Navy when that small service was subsumed on annexation in 1845.[13]

The only Colt rifles obtained during the war was an order for 500 of the Model 1858 late in the conflict. Other than that, the number of other Colts still in the inventory during the Civil War is unknown, but their quirks certainly made them unpopular weapons.

The next breechloader tried by the navy was the Perry percussion carbine, a .54 caliber gun recommended by John Dahlgren, one of the service's pre-eminent ordnance experts. As with some other designs, this gun used a pivoting breech, in this case opened by lowering the trigger guard. The weapon also employed a tube which fed percussion caps onto the nipple.

Benjamin F Joslyn of Worcester, Massachusetts patented a breech-loading mechanism in 1855. The navy purchased 500 Joslyns in that year, manufactured by A H Waters of Millbury, Massachusetts. These were percussion weapons, using a lever atop the breech and buttstock. This lever was hinged with a pin above the chamber, and operated somewhat in the opposite manner from

Two versions of the Sharps and Hankins: top shows the early model with leather covering for the barrel, intended to prevent corrosion. Some 6500 were purchased by the navy. (Steve Selenfriend; photograph by the author)

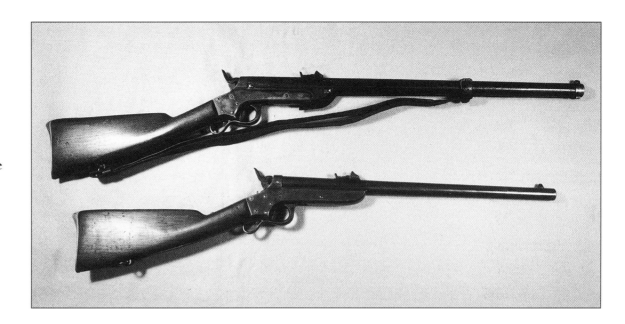

that of the Jenks, i.e. the lever lifted from the rear, rather than from the front. In any event, the weapon was not without defects.

In 1862 a new Joslyn was introduced, this time using a rimfire .52 caliber Spencer round. The breech system now incorporated a swinging breechblock, loaded by lifting a hook-type friction latch on the right and throwing the breechblock over to the left. It does not appear that the navy used these guns, and an improved breech latch mechanism was introduced in 1864.[14]

Despite the increasing number and types of breech-loading weapons available in the late pre-war period, the navy reverted to a traditional muzzleloader with the so-called Plymouth rifle. This weapon was concocted by John A Dahlgren and named for the US sloop *Plymouth*, a vessel Dahlgren had fitted out for ordnance testing (in particular for the Dahlgren smoothbore shell gun).

The impetus for this gun was apparently the army's adoption of .58 caliber for its standard rifle-musket in 1855. Dahlgren, conversely, opted for retaining the previous standard size .69 caliber and indeed used much of the hardware from the .69 caliber 1842 pattern army weapon for the Plymouth. The larger bore was intended to capitalize on its shock effect, both for boarding parties and shore operations.

The original Plymouth pattern rifle was dated 1858. One hundred of these were manufactured, most with brass barrel bands, trigger guard, etc. Shortly after the outbreak of war, the Bureau of Ordnance requested estimates for the cost of producing '.75 caliber' weapons in a short amount of time. The result was the manufacture of 10,000 on the Plymouth pattern, by Eli Whitney at Whitneyville, Connecticut. On these production weapons, steel replaced the brass furniture.[15]

The next major breechloader purchased in the late 1850s and used during the war was the Sharps. This weapon's mechanism, patented by Christian Sharps, was built around a sliding breechblock, which dropped away from the end of the barrel when the lever/trigger guard was lowered. Raising the trigger guard levered the breechblock upward and it's upper edge sliced off the end of the paper cartridge, exposing the powder for firing.

Two hundred and one Sharps rifles and one hundred carbines were purchased by the navy in 1856-57, all in .52 caliber. In the period 1859 through 1861 another 2450 rifles were obtained, all in .56 caliber. The rifle was 53 inches long; the carbine, 37½ inches. The navy considered the Sharps the best breechloader available, and at one point early in the war would have paid up to $47 each for the gun – an extraordinary price for the times.

As has been stated, the self-contained metallic cartridge had been invented before the war. However, for the use of masses of infantry, the availability of simple powder and lead ball far exceeded that of manufactured cartridges. Indeed, the army rejected the Spencer repeating cartridge rifle because it feared the gun's capacity would encourage the soldier to shoot too often. There appears to have been some truth to that speculation. In any case, the navy made use of four cartridge-type long arms during the war, only one of which was a repeater.

The Sharps and Hankins was a single-shot, .52 caliber weapon obtained by the navy in both rifle and carbine lengths. They were manufactured in Philadelphia to a patented design by Christian Sharps. Lowering the trigger guard/loading lever allowed the gun barrel to slide forward, opening the breech. Inserted was a Sharps .56-.52 rim-fire cartridge – that is a .56 caliber shell turned down to accept .52 caliber bullets. Returning the trigger guard slid the barrel back to the breechblock for firing.

These weapons were noteworthy for three advanced features. Their firing pin, rather than being simply a solid extension of the hammer, was, in the 'New Improved' model, within the receiver itself. The gun also had a hammer safety mechanism and a cartridge extractor system.

Those carbines made for the navy had a leather covering for the barrel, intended to prevent salt water corrosion. In practice, the leather was yet another element to deteriorate in the elements. About 6000 carbines and 500 Sharps and Hankins rifles were purchased for navy use. Later examples dispensed with the leather covering.

Similar in appearance was the Maynard system, invented by Edward Maynard, a Washington DC dentist, and manufactured by Massachusetts Arms Company of Chicopee Falls, Massachusetts. This carbine's barrel tilted upward at the breech for loading, and used a brass cartridge ignited by a percussion cap. The cartridge had a hole through the center for ignition and was re-usable. The navy tested the gun in 1859 with outstanding results: one Maynard was fired 562 times before being cleaned, with little powder build-up.

Both .35 and .50 caliber Maynards were manufactured, with the main complaint concerning the larger bore gun: the recoil was excessive due to the light weight of the gun (about 6 pounds). The navy used the .50 caliber weapon.

The Spencer rifle was invented by Christopher Spencer and manufactured in Boston, Massachusetts and Providence, Rhode Island. It was a seven-shot weapon loading brass rim-fire cartridges by way of a tubular magazine through the stock. The rounds were forced into the chamber by a compressed spring in the tube. Pulling the trigger guard down opened the breech and extracted the spent round. Returning the guard to the up position closed the breech on the new round.

The Spencer was tested extensively by the navy and in one instance fired all seven rounds in ten seconds. John Dahlgren reported one rifle was fired over 500 times with only one misfire, and that due to a faulty cartridge. Eventually 1000 were in the hands of navy or marine corps, with the first order placed in July 1861.[16]

There were, of course, in addition to the above, weapons acquired by the navy for testing or small purchases, such as the Gallagher carbine. As there was a constant stream of experimental and specialized weapons being evaluated during the war, a study covering these would be a volume unto itself.

The Plymouth rifle, a .69 caliber weapon designed by John Dahlgren shortly before the war. Though an obsolescent design, 10,000 were used during the conflict. Also shown are the bowie-type bayonet designed for the gun, and the Whitney Plymouth pattern sword-bayonet of 1861. (Steve Selenfriend; photograph by the author)

# Sword bayonets

The sword bayonet was designed for two purposes – use as a hand held weapon or attached to the rifle. Their patterns were similar to short swords or cutlasses and had cast brass hilt and grips. A ring and a slot in the grip allowed its attachment to the barrel, using a stud brazed to its side. It measured 20 to 30 inches long and were carried in a scabbard on the left side.

There are six varieties of sword bayonets known for naval rifles. They were made for: the Whitney 'Plymouth' Model 1861, Joslyn Model 1855, Sharps Models 1855 and 1859, Spencer rifle, and Sharps and Hankins rifle. Additionally, there are in existence Colt revolving rifle bayonets which may have been naval issue.

Another bayonet variety was specifically for the Plymouth rifle and was patterned on the famous bowie knife. This weapon had a spear-point blade 12⅛ inches long, a brass one-piece pommel, guard and backstrap, and a walnut grip with four finger grooves. One-thousand-eight-hundred were purchased from N P Ames company between August 1861 and October 1864.[17]

It appears that the bowie knife bayonet was not accurately made and did not fit the Plymouth barrel without modification. Therefore, their primary use was as a hand weapon, rather than as a bayonet.

# Swords, cutlasses and dirks

Regulation naval edged weapons were the officer's sword and the cutlass. The former was required and was part of the uniform. The latter was part of the equipage of the naval vessel and was stored in easily accessible racks on deck. A third was the officer's dirk, which was often worn, but not mentioned in regulations until 1869.

There were two sword types in use during the Civil War – the patterns set forth in regulations of 1841 and 1852. The older design was distinguished by an eagle-head pommel, P-shaped knuckle bow and small oval guards with oak leaves and acorns in relief. The scabbard was decorated with oak leaves and acorns at the tip and a floral design at the throat. As these swords were purchased by individuals from assorted manufacturers, there exist significant varieties in decoration and design.

The 1852 model sword was distinguished by a wide counter guard with oak leaves, acorns and 'USN' in its design. The pommel flared outward in Phrygian helmet style with stars and eagle in

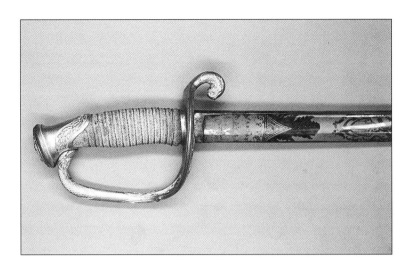

Officer's dress sword, 1852 pattern (two views). This pattern remains the navy standard, although the modern version has a lighter hilt and narrower blade. (Steve Selenfriend; photograph by the author)

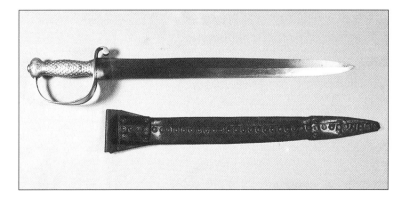

Model 1841 cutlass. This had a solid brass hilt and a 22-inch blade. About 6600 were purchased before the war and some continued to be used during the conflict. (Steve Selenfriend; photograph by the author)

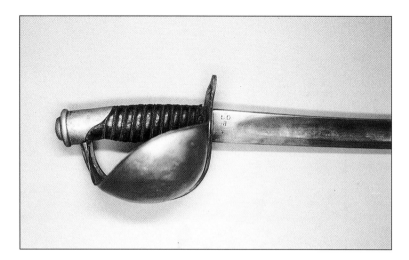

The 1861 pattern cutlass, of which 22,000 were made. (Steve Selenfriend; photograph by the author)

Battle-axe, used mainly for cutting away rigging, etc. during battle. (Steve Selenfriend; photograph by the author)

relief; the knuckle bow was a simple curve in place of the P-shape. The scabbard had carrying rings at the throat and middle, with a dolphin-shaped tip. Five hundred of these were purchased by the Navy from N P Ames company, but the majority were obtained by the individual officers.

The 1852 sword is, with two obvious changes, still the standard naval officer's sword. The two significant differences are a narrower blade and a lighter hilt. Of course, there are highly decorative, and rare, presentation varieties of both, but these are beyond the scope of this book.

The first standard Civil War navy cutlass was the model of 1841, a straight-edged weapon with heavy solid brass hilt. It was similar to the army's foot artillery sword of 1832, was 26¼ inches long, with a 22-inch blade. These were manufactured by N P Ames of Springfield, Massachusetts, and were known to have been used in the western rivers campaigns during the war. A total of 6600 were purchased by the navy from 1842 through September 1846.

The more familiar 1861 design cutlass was 32 inches long, with a curved blade and solid half-basket guard, again made by N P Ames. Twenty-two thousand of these were made for the navy, with the last order dated September 1864. One variation of this weapon had an embossed swirl pattern with 'USN' cut out in the guard, and gilt instead of brass wire around the grips. Though termed the 'officer's' cutlass, this weapon is of uncertain affinity.

The most primitive hand weapons of the war were the pike and battle axe. The former was specifically for resisting boarders and was a simple hardwood staff, 8 to 9 feet long with an iron point, which was about half the length of the land variety pike. The battle-axe was iron with a hickory haft, measuring 20 inches overall. It was required by members of fire-fighting parties on board ship to cut away rigging and wreckage, but certainly found more lethal use in hand to hand situations.[18] Both of these weapons were rendered obsolete by long range ordnance which brought an end to the swashbuckling era when enemy vessels were captured by boarding.

# Chapter Seven
# THE ENLISTED SAILOR

"DON'T GIVE UP THE SHIP."

"Ships our cradles, decks our pillows,
Lulled by winds and rocked by billows;
Gaily bound we o'er the tide,
Hope our anchor, Heaven our guide."

The sailor in the US Navy of the Civil War inherited the colors of the tars of time immemorial. Even the intrusion of the steam engine brought no great alteration to the life of a sailor at sea. It merely gave the majority of them yet another source of dirt and grime to be holystoned off or polished out. The customs and traditions of sea life – the watches, superstitions and salty comraderie – varied surprisingly little. Those 'webbed feet' of the inland river forces and on sail-less ironclads no longer handled the sails, but the remainder of the typical routines continued to be applied by conscientious officers and mates.

## Manpower and recruiting

Amongst the traditions was that of the volunteer service. Though the draft had been instituted to achieve the numbers needed for the land forces, the navy relied on old fashioned recruiting. Only when shortages became acute were conscriptees employed – and those very late in the war.

In 1861, the enlisted force numbered no more than 7600 men. By the war's end there were over 51,000 in service. The actual number of men who served during the war is not known, but there were over 118,000 enlistments, with some sources suggesting

Illustration from *The Kedge Anchor or Young Sailor's Assistant* (1847 edition), capturing the patriotic and religious overtones common to the popular conception of life in the navy in the mid nineteenth century.

as many as 132,000. Despite the large numbers, the recruiting methods were exceedingly simple.[1]

First, the basic standards for acceptance as a recruit were far from exclusive. Minimum height was 4 feet 8 inches. Minimum age was eighteen, and, with parental consent, thirteen (by regulations of 1863). No inexperienced men over thirty-three were accepted and none over thirty-eight, unless approved by the department. Two years at sea qualified the applicant as an ordinary seaman; four years and an examination enabled him to ship as a seaman. Otherwise, the enlistee was shipped as a landsman. Statutes on the books since the War of 1812 forbade enlisting foreigners and there was a prohibition against enlisting the incompetent and 'idiots', but these prohibitions tended to slide as the war progressed. Of course, vessels on foreign station were more likely to ship foreign nationals in the course of their cruises. Special dispensation was necessary to enlist ex-slaves, a subject which will be dealt with later in the chapter.[2]

The system became even less exclusive as the wartime demands grew. Though monthly enlistments numbered from 1500 upward in 1862 and 1863, they continually fell short of the service's needs. The shortfalls were for the most part due to the effects of army recruiting. First was the commonly available bounties to new recruits, amounting sometimes to $300 per enlistee (over two years pay). Second were the draft quotas set for each state. Those enlisted in the navy did not apply toward meeting those numbers.[3]

A three-year enlistment was normal practice early in the war. This, however, did not produce sufficient numbers due to the general belief that the war would be over quickly. Consequently, the term was reduced for a short time to one year, with an eye to tempting fishery and coastal seaman into naval service. An unexpected consequence was an influx of new immigrants poorly adapted to naval requirements, and this short enlistment was soon discontinued. However, in times of critical need, terms as short as one to three months were utilized. The latter occurred at the time of the Roanoke Island Expedition in early 1862. Later in the war, enlistments for the duration were instituted.

The supply of enlistees was encouraged by cash incentives. Three dollars a head was paid to anyone who supplied seamen, ordinary seaman and firemen; ten per head was paid for landsmen and coal heavers. The premium for the latter categories was to counteract the army's substantial bounty payments for raw recruits. Unfortunately, some practitioners in this trade used methods hardly distinguishable from the classic 'shanghai', sometimes involving drugs and drink.[4]

The manpower shortage was exacerbated by the desertion rate. Unfortunately, no overall figures are available to reveal the extent of this problem. However, it was so great that at one point the department hired detectives and offered rewards to stem the tide. Included in the deserting ranks were the bounty jumpers: those who accepted their enlistment bonus, then at the first opportunity, jumped ship, often to repeat the process elsewhere. It appears that blacks deserted less frequently, no doubt in view of the fact that

Powder boy, US Navy. Regulations allowed thirteen-year olds to enlist, with parental approval. At least two were awarded the congressional Medal of Honor during the war. Note the embroidery on the uniform jumper. (USAMHI)

Recruiting, possibly 1862. Note the emphasis on pay and prize money. One-year enlistments — and sometimes shorter terms — were thought necessary to fill the ranks. (US Navy)

# THE CONSCRIPT BILL!
## HOW TO AVOID IT!!

# U. S. NAVY.

# 1,000 MEN WANTED, FOR 12 MONTHS!

| | |
|---|---|
| Seamen's Pay, - - - - - - | $18.00 per month. |
| Ordinary Seamen's Pay, . . . . | 14.00 " " |
| Landsmen's Pay, . . . . . . | 12.00 " " |

### $1.50 extra per month to all, Grog Money.

# $50,000,000 PRIZES!

Already captured, a large share of which is awarded to Ships Crews. The laws for the distributing of Prize money carefully protects the rights of all the captors.

PETTY OFFICERS,—PROMOTION.—Seamen have a chance for promotion to the offices of Master at Arms, Boatswain's Mates, Quarter Gunners, Captain of Tops, Forecastle, Holds, After-Guard, &c.

Landsmen may be advanced to Armorers, Armorers' Mates, Carpenter's Mates, Sailmakers' Mates, Painters, Coopers, &c.

PAY OF PETTY OFFICERS,—From $20.00 to $45.00 per month.

CHANCES FOR WARRANTS, BOUNTIES AND MEDALS OF HONOR.—All those who distinguish themselves in battle or by extraordinary heroism, may be promoted to forward Warrant Officers or Acting Masters' Mates,—and upon their promotion receive a guaranty of $100, with a medal of honor from their country.

All who wish may leave HALF PAY with their families, to commence from date of enlistment.

Minors must have a written consent, sworn to before a Justice of the Peace.

### For further information apply to U. S. NAVAL RENDEZVOUS,

## E. Y. BUTLER, U. S. N. Recruiting Officer,
### No. 14 FRONT STREET, SALEM, MASS.

FROM WRIGHT & POTTER'S BOSTON PRINTING ESTABLISHMENT, No. 4 SPRING LANE, CORNER OF DEVONSHIRE STREET.

Recruiting in May 1861, New York City. After the initial rush to the colors, and the reality of a long bloody war set in, crowd scenes such as this one became rarities. Insufficient personnel was one of the most besetting problems in the navy throughout the war. From Frank Leslie's *Illustrated Newspaper*. (US Navy)

they were in hostile territory whether slave, free, or navy. The rate was higher for the foreign-born sailor, whose enlisting was possibly a ploy to travel at navy expense. Desertion rates were likely to have been significantly higher in the Mississippi squadron where access to the shore was relatively easy.

At last, in 1864, Congress approved enlistment bounties for the navy. These were $100, $200, and $300, payable for one-, two-, and three-year terms, respectively. These amounts were substantial sums for the time — several months pay for a typical day laborer. Despite this concession, naval enlistments never met overall personnel needs during the war.

It should also be noted that those who re-enlisted within three months of their previous discharge were entitled to three months' pay at their former rate. This applied even if the man re-enlisted immediately after his separation from the service.[5]

Naval recruiting was done at a 'rendezvous'. These were at the navy yards and in any municipality likely to supply sailors. New York City supported several, for instance. A junior officer, accompanied by a medical officer, would simply open an office, let the purpose be known, and examine and sign up qualified applicants. There was a minimal physical examination on site. The applicant was required to sign the shipping articles as well as an oath of allegiance approved by Congress in 1861. Those with previous service were required to produce their discharge as proof they had not departed the navy under less than honorable conditions. Those accepted were forwarded to a receiving ship at one of the navy yards, accompanied by two forms: a transcript list enumerating previous service, rating, and bounty information, and a descriptive list setting forth age, occupation and physical characteristics.

The only speciality that required a skill examination was that of fireman. In addition to the usual health requirements, he had to prove to an engineering officer his ability to 'manage fires properly with different kinds of fuel' and to use blacksmith's tools in steam machinery repair. Of course, this era was long before there were civilian agencies for certification of various maritime specialities.[6]

Given the simplicity of this system and its obvious shortcomings, it is amazing that any sort of efficient enlisted force resulted. There were indeed many abuses of the system; some deliberate; most well meaning but misdirected. The pressure on recruiting officers to meet quotas led to an increasing number of undesireables passing successfully through the initial rendezvous proceedings. If the substandard recruit remained at the receiving ship for any length of time, he was likely to be found out and mustered back to civilian life. If, on the other hand, the demand for sailors was immediate, he might pass quickly through the receiving ship to a active vessel, passing on to that commanding officer the onerous task of weeding out the unacceptable – after the fact.

The applicable regulation reminded the recruiters that none 'convicted of an infamous crime' need be enrolled. But of course the lack of any kind of systematic personal identification or background check left wide the door to the criminal and hard cases – as well as the ex-army deserters and bounty-jumpers. The meeting of minimal physical and mental criteria certainly had its obvious down side. This, in addition to the competition with the army already mentioned, served to make the shortage of personnel a continuing problem throughout the conflict, often resulting in vessels with incomplete complements. More seriously, otherwise combat-ready ships sometimes remained at their berths for lack of manpower. In one instance, the frigate *Niagara* lay off Gloucester for several weeks in late 1863 attempting to complete her crew. In the end, she sailed with a significant shortage. Later, in 1864, the Secretary of the Navy reported thirty-five vessels waiting to complete their complements, with an aggregate need of over 10,000 sailors. Thus, achieving numbers sufficient for the task was, as one authority put it: 'a problem that became so severe...that it made insignificant, by comparison the problems of getting the ships constructed and outfitted' and it 'became one of the most debilitating factors that weakened the navy during the war.'[7]

# Pay and incentives

The old line sailor was a man whose entire existence was marked out by the navy and the wooden hull in which he hung his hammock. His needs were few: the navy provided room and board and regular pay. It would not be until the twentieth century that marriage and a family were considered normative for a sailor.

In 1862, enlisted men's pay rates ranged downward from $45 per month for a yeoman in a ship of the line, to $8 or $9 per month for a boy. A seaman earned $18, the ordinary seaman, $14, and the landsman, $12. These rates had varied little over the previous decades; in 1830, a seaman had drawn $12 and the ordinary seaman, $10. In terms of purchasing power, the dollar also had fluctuated little over the years. Inflation was not a significant factor until the mid point of the war itself, eroding about half the value of the dollar by the war's end. There was no concomitant adjustment in naval pay.

The pay itself of course was low, even by the standards of the time. Typical wages for civilian jobs during the war years can be judged by a few examples: carpenters made from $1.75 to $2.25 per day; blacksmiths, $1.50 to $2.25; ordinary day laborers, about $1.50 per day. Of course, prices were proportionately lower: a bushel of corn brought 68 cents and $10 could often purchase an acre of land. Among petty officers, pay was for some rates based on the rate of the vessel on which they served; for others, on the level of skill or responsibility involved. For the yeoman the levels were for ships of the line ($45 per month), frigates ($40), sloops ($30) and smaller vessels ($24). Master's mates were the highest paid in that category, receiving $40 per month, while the armorer's mate made $20. Firemen, first and second class, made $30 and $25 per month respectively.[8]

The only other regular cash payment available to the sailor was that in lieu of the spirit ration. 'Grog' in the US Navy had long been a fact of life, but a rising tide of temperance and reform had eventually ended it. Beginning in 1831, the sailor was allowed to refuse his ration and receive a payment in its stead. In September 1862, Congress abolished the spirit ration altogether and mandated a 5 cent per day payment to all entitled to it.[9]

Another source of income was prize money. Though the possibilities were the stuff of dreams, the reality was much more mundane. First, luck had to provide the prize itself, and these came more often to the fast blockading vessels. Second, the prize had to be of considerable value in terms of vessel and cargo. Once taken, a prize court adjudicated the case. Court costs, ranging from 5 to 15 per cent were deducted from its value, then, by law, one half of the proceeds was designated for the naval pension fund. Finally, the amount each crew member received was proportional to his pay. That said, a valuable prize taken by a vessel with a small crew could still net a small fortune even for the cabin boys. For example, the tug *Eolus* captured the runner *Hope* in 1864, and netted the cabin boy $432 – something over four years' pay. This was not a common occurence. A slower or unlucky blockader might bring in less than $100 in a 'season'.[10]

The receiving ship *Independence*, Mare Island, San Francisco. She was typical of the 'guardo' vessels which served to house recruits until they were assigned a permanent ship. The old ship of the line remained on duty until sold in 1914. (US Navy)

The pension fund mentioned above was the only cash benefit available to naval personnel. It had been instituted as far back as the War of 1812, but had varied in application and amount since then. By the end of the Civil War the fund had accrued over $14 million in prize money. Payments were awarded to those disabled in the line of duty and the survivors of those killed, including widows, children and other dependents. Petty officers, seamen and dependents received $8 per month if entitled to these payments.[11]

Other than medical care while in the navy, the only non-monetary benefit was the Naval Asylum. This was a retirement home for, as the regulation read, 'disabled and decrepit naval officers, seamen and marines'. Twenty years service was the basic eligibility requirement, and those with naval pensions commuted that payment in return for room and board. Residents received a clothing allowance of $3 monthly as well as a 'good conduct' allowance of $1 and were required to contribute work appropriate to their condition and age. The asylum was located at Philadelphia and housed some 150 inmates in 1868.[12]

## The receiving ships

As with the army, there was as yet no formalized basic training for enlistees in the navy. In the army, however, unless an emergency threw the raw recruits immediately into the fighting, the men drilled and practiced with their weapons while awaiting combat. There were no training ships per se for the naval recruits; in their stead were the 'guardos' as the old receiving ships were nicknamed. These were generally obsolete but not necessarily decrepit ships of the line, serving out their hull's service life moored at one of the

yards. Their longevity was legend. *Vermont* was finally sold in 1902; *Alabama* in 1901. The record may have been *Independence*, launched in 1814 and sold a century later.[13]

Aboard the receiving ships were both raw recruits and experienced men, in each instance awaiting a billet, on a newly commissioned vessel, one out of refit, or on ship with battle or other personnel losses. Therefore, the seaman's stint on the guardo was of uncertain duration. In his time there, he was given rudimentary instruction on military courtesy and, as the vessel was a fully rigged ship, practice on handling sails, rigging, and boats. Cutlass practice was, of course, part of the regime, as well as repelling boarders, fire-fighting, etc. Time not spent in these pursuits was occupied by holystoning the decks and polishing the brass. Even so, all this was done on a stationary ship, giving it an air of unreality.[14]

The experience of life at sea provided sufficient training for all. Once on his assigned ship, the new sailor was introduced to both a system and an organization much of which had been formulated in its essentials literally centuries before. The antecedents were found in the British navy harking back to the days of Samuel Pepys, and, with the exception of the adjustments due to the adoption of steam, little had changed on the wooden-hulled man-of-war.

## Shipboard organization

The green recruit, once on his assigned vessel, found himself in a world apart, as distinct from life ashore as the very sea was from the dark earth. Life was regulated to an extent incomprehensible to the uninitiated, and was based on both the exigencies of life at

"ABANDONED SHIP"
U.S.S. Ossipee.

Deck of the steam sloop *Ossipee*, in possibly a staged photograph. A poorly managed ship might look like this: note dirty and stained deck, unstowed grating and other items lying on deck and elsewhere, and haphazardly coiled lines. Hammocks have been stowed poorly in the hammock rails. On a tight ship the canvas covers would have been even fore and aft rather than undulating as these are. (US Navy)

sea and possible presence of an armed adversary. Additionally, all aspects of the duties and requirements of the men were necessarily designed to be understood by the lowliest of men – a substantial proportion of which were of the type that one might wish to avoid on dark nights in port cities. As Herman Wouk wryly observed in *The Caine Mutiny*, the navy was 'a master plan designed by geniuses for execution by idiots'.

Under sail or steam at sea, there was no relief from maintenance of certain basic and critical functions, not the least of which were manning the helm and standing watch. The crew worked 'watch and watch': they were bisected into starboard and larboard (port) watches, in alternating four-hour segments, putting, theoretically, about half the crew on duty at any one time.

The ship's day began at noon with the afternoon watch (until 4pm), followed by the two dog watches – 4 to 6pm and 6 to 8pm. These two short segments were designed to allow dinner for each half of the crew, but were not necessarily the routine on all vessels. The 8pm to midnight was the 'first watch', the midnight to 4am was the mid watch and the 4 to 8am was the morning watch. The fore-noon watch filled out the twenty-four hour period. Once the sailor was assigned to a watch, he would be alternatively 'on' or 'off' in four-hour shifts (or two on the dog watches.)

Although there had been some instances as far back as Napoleonic times in which three eight-hour shifts were instituted, the four-hour remained orthodox throughout this era, and after. Most commanding officers preferred the two-watch system because it kept a larger number of men available at any given time. Another variation on the watches was subdividing the four-hour shifts into two two-hour segments, each covered by half of the men on that watch.

Each watch was further divided into divisions, each of which covered a major portion of the vessel. The workforce divisions were forecastlemen, fore, main and mizzen topmen, and the afterguard. Each division provided men for particular guns, sails, and ship's boats.

The document which assigned the sailors to individual tasks was the Watch Bill, which was the responsibility of the executive officer, and was made out at the beginning of each commission. It was essentially a blank form listing, by number, the job assignments within each division. Since manning guns, sails and small boats did not usually occur simultaneously, it was possible for each sailor to be assigned one of each. And, of course, all the tasks and divisions were listed twice: once for the starboard and once for the port watch.

A contemporary Watch Bill for the steam sloop USS *Richmond* can serve to illustrate this system. The ship's Forecastle Division, when at full complement, consisted of forty men, twenty each on port and starboard watches.[15] The tasks were numbered one through forty, with odd numbers on starboard, even on port watches. Number 1 was the Captain of the Starboard Forecastle Division; Number 2 held the comparable title on the port watch. In this instance, Number 1 was assigned to the vessel's Parrott rifle, but had no sail or boat to man. Number 2 was, in battle, assigned to the Master's Division (see Quarter Bill below).

The sailor assigned Number 3 was to work the fore yard and be one of the sixteen to man the rifle; he had no boat assignment. Number 4 (port watch) manned gun number four, a broadside 9-inch Dahlgren, crewed the First Cutter, and was also on the fore yard.

Men in the Forecastle Division had assignments on the rifled gun, and guns number one, three, five and seven. Men from this division formed part of the crew of the ship's launch, gig, first, third and fifth cutter. Their positions aloft were on the foresail, jib, flying jib, and fore trysail. Other duties included rigging the bowsprit, setting up the fore rigging, fishing and catting the anchor, and keeping the deck clean from head to fore mast.

The thirty-three men of the Fore Top Division were divided aloft among the topsail, topgallant, royal and fore trysail. They were spread between six broadside guns and the rifle, and four different ship's boats. There were thirty-six men in the Main Top Division, with comparable duties on the main mast. The smallest division was that of the Mizzen Top, with twenty-eight positions, including those on the spanker and peak. Each of the divisions also had specific parts of the upper deck and channels to clean.

The largest division was the Afterguard, which, on *Richmond* numbered forty-three on each watch. This large number was in part due to their assignment to the main sail and yard. The division was also the home for the majority of the ship's boys, carpenters and two nurses.

The Watch Bill was composed of the majority of the ship's enlisted crew. On the *Richmond*, the total of all divisions would have been, at full complement, 223 men, plus messenger boys. Of course, all the divisions were not manned completely, though *Richmond* was apparently reasonably well off in that regard. None of the divisions except the Afterguard was short more than two men. The Afterguard, however, was thirteen men short on each watch.

Not included on the Watch Bill were the firemen and coal heavers, marines, and the so-called 'idlers'. On *Richmond* there were twelve firemen, nine coalheavers, and twenty-five marines per watch. The idlers were the sailors whose duties required them to be day workers: bakers, cooks, servants, and yeomen. Though not part of a watch, they were assigned duties when 'all hands' was called. There were sixteen idlers on *Richmond*.

The entire enlisted complement of the *Richmond*, marines included, was 364. In fact, in early 1865, she was forty-eight men short.

Of course, it should be pointed out that the sailor's particular assignment, whether to a specific yard, gun or boat, was one which involved specific duties depending on the evolution being carried out by the vessel. Aloft, a main top man, for instance, would loose, furl, reef or bend the topsail, rig the topsail yard and topgallant yardarm, lash the upper (jeer) block for raising or lowering the yards, man the braces when tacking and wearing, and send down light spars when clearing for action.

In some instances, his specific duties, along with his particular division and numbers, were printed in billet form kept in the sailor's hat, though it is somewhat ludicrous to imagine the typical, and often illiterate, bluejacket puzzling over a scrap of paper amid the mad rush of the crew up the ratlines. The reality, of course, was traditional on-the-job training; literally 'learning the ropes' by repetition upon repetition of the duties required.

After the Watch Bill set the general rule of the sailor's daily

Crew members on the deck of the *Monitor*. Each watch was divided into messes, and the men in each were issued rations and were responsible for preparing their own meals. Note the pots and pans on the left; the low box on the right may be their table. (The tall rectangular structures are the vessels funnels.) (US Navy)

existence, the Quarter Bill delineated his duties in action. In addition to setting down the sailors' specific positions at the guns, it included the Master (also called the Navigator) and Powder Divisions. The latter listed the chain of men handling powder and ammunition from the magazine to the guns; the former included miscellaneous personnel required in battle such as wreck clearers, messengers, helmsman, and pump and signal men.

Nine-inch broadside guns were, by regulation, to be fully manned with seventeen men, though as few as half that many would suffice in a personnel shortage. On *Richmond*, no gun had less than fourteen assigned. Of course, the vessel had 18 of these Dahlgrens, thus allowing complete manning of either but not both broadsides. The rifle, a 100-pounder Parrott, had fifteen men on its crew, three short of its complement.[16]

The gun crews were divided into loaders, tacklemen, handspikemen, spongers, gun captains, and powder boys, and all had secondary duties. Some were boarders, some manned pumps or fought fires, and some trimmed sails. Each crew on *Richmond* included one or two petty officers and a balance of sailors, ordinary sailors, and landsmen.

The guns themselves were divided into divisions: First Division included the rifle and the 3 forward broadside weapons,

Second Division included the next 3 Dahlgrens, and the third was composed of the aft 3 broadside guns. On the *Richmond*, in 1865, each division was commanded by an ensign.

In addition to the Watch and Quarter Bills, the sailor's life was further regulated by the Mess and Fire Bills. The latter was simply a list of men and their duties in case of fire on board. The Mess Bill divided the men into groups of twelve to fourteen each. Though not a formal unit, the sailor's mess became his 'home' while on a naval vessel, comparable to the platoon in the modern army. On some vessels, each gun crew comprised a mess, but this was not universal.

Each mess selected a cook who was responsible for drawing the provisions, taking care of the messing gear and policing their area of the berth deck. This 'cook' was more properly an orderly who held the key to the group's mess chest, containing utensils, coffee pot, canisters of coffee, sugar, and 'table' of sail-cloth, and who carried out the group's decisions concerning disposition of their issued rations and any supplements acquired by purchase or other means. The mess cook was allowed an extra ration, and was exempt from certain other duties.[17]

Each mess was assigned an area on the berth deck, generally compatible with the location of their watch duties, with the forecastle watches farthest forward, and so on. Starboard aft were the separate messes for petty officers, mechanics and appointed officers. The latter included masters-at-arms, yeomen, orderly sergeants, and apothecary. Firemen and marines were traditionally messed on the port side aft.

In addition to forming the meal-time organization, the mess served as the conduit for mail delivery and for the issuance of small stuff, such as tobacco, cap-ribbons and the like, and other mundane organizational tasks. Beyond these semi-official aspects, the mess of course became a basic element of the social structure of the ship, for good or ill.

# The sailor's life: deportment, discipline, duties and rights

By any standards one might apply, life aboard a mid nineteenth-century man-of-war was harsh, in terms of the rigorous physical environment, the duties and expectations placed on the sailors, as well as the disciplinary system employed to maintain order on board ship. One familiar comparison is to liken the sailor's milieu to that of other contemporary low paying employment, with the conclusion that the sailor at least had his basic needs met by the navy and a permanent place to live. Whether these homely attributes amounted to sufficient compensation for calling a hammock and sea-chest a home, for manning a swinging yardarm 70 feet above a cold violent sea, for an absolute absence of privacy, for a diet commonly infested by vermin, for a home always in motion and not infrequently deluged without and within can be judged by the reader.

The life of a seaman, if judged by the text devoted to them in the US Naval Regulations of 1865, was exceedingly simple. After disposing of all the duties of the various officers, warrants and petty officers in some 106 pages, it reads: 'All other persons composing the crew are hereby enjoined to yield, on all occasions, a willing, cheerful, and prompt obedience to those placed over them; to be especially attentive to their stations and the instructions they may receive; to avoid difficulties with each other, and departures from regulations; to be always tidy about their persons and effects; and, in a word, to contribute all in their power to promote order and harmony.' Patronizing — or at least paternalistic — optimistic and idealistic are the words that come to mind in reading these phras-

es. The officer's ideal seaman was to be obedient, tidy, and harmless — nothing more.[18]

Discipline in the US Navy during the Civil War was based on the Articles of War, which were updated in 1862. The Articles were as familiar to the sailor as the navy could make them: they were read religiously at general muster, on the first Sunday of each month. Commonly nicknamed the 'rocks and shoals' — at least in the twentieth-century navy — these grim paragraphs starkly listed both the crimes and other mis-deeds and their possible consequences in the naval disciplinary system.

The trespasses ranged from mere 'gestures, or menaces' directed at another 'person in the navy', to murder and, of course, desertion. Crimes of omission were not neglected: an officer, for instance did not 'fail to encourage' his subordinates to the 'utmost exertions to join in battle'. General morality was regulated by such directives as requiring divine services to be read on Sunday, though attendance was only 'earnestly recommended' rather than mandatory. In this connection, any 'irreverent or unbecoming behavior' was punishable by court martial. Further, 'profane swearing, falsehood, drunkenness, gambling, fraud, theft or any other scandalous conduct tending to the destruction of good morals' was not to be condoned.

The majority of the articles were, of course, aimed at maintaining the rule of law, buttressing the standing heirarchy on board ship, and protecting government property. Punishable were various evidences of insubordination, from sleeping on watch to striking an officer, as well as disobedience to orders, desertion and mutiny. The sobriquet 'rocks and shoals' probably referred to the injunction against any who 'intentionally or willfully suffers any vessel of the navy to be stranded, or run upon rocks and shoals, or improperly hazarded...'.[19]

The penalties which were countenanced ranged from death, to 'such other punishment as a court-martial may direct'. Corporal punishment, other than death, was no longer found in the navy. Flogging, that age-old and often mis-used penalty, had been the object of decades of criticism, much of it from non-naval sources. Agitation for its prohibition had reached Congress as early as 1820, and the practice had been abolished in the army in 1812. The 1840 publication of Richard Henry Dana's book *Two Years before the Mast* with its horrific description of the practice, as well as Herman Melville's *White Jacket* of the same era, gave increased momentum to the popular movement. In 1850, the practice was outlawed by congressional mandate. This, despite vocal opposition on the part of many, including both naval officers and seamen. The former objected on several grounds, not the least of which being that flogging was a very visible method of intimidating would-be miscreants. The veteran sailors, in some instances, were disgusted that the service should forego this 'manly' form of punishment. Indeed, the British navy did not eliminate the lash until the 1870s.

In its stead was a system of summary court martials for minor offenses, the introduction of the honorable discharge as an incentive for good behavior, and re-enlistment bonuses for those honorably discharged. Additionally, all punishments were to be recorded in the ship's log. By the Civil War, the day of arbitrary punishment was at an end.

In the Secretary of the Navy's Annual Report of December, 1855, it was reported that in the six months after the passage of the honorable discharge legislation, enlistments in the navy tripled from 896 to 2891. Though the Secretary admitted that 'other favorable circumstances' might have contributed to this increase, he noted that the period (the heyday of the clipper ship) was one in which the US merchant marine was offering higher wages and shorter cruises. In all, he expected great results 'notwithstanding painful apprehensions and gloomy forebodings of disastrous consequences' from critics of the abolition of flogging.[20]

The unruly sailor, spared the humiliation of flogging, was to be given one or a combination of any of the following penalties: reduction in rate or pay; confinement, with or without irons, single or double; solitary confinement; solitary with bread and water; deprivation of liberty; additional duties; dismissal from the service with a bad conduct discharge. The death penalty, or long term imprisonment with hard labor, was warranted but not mandatory for mutiny, striking an officer, murder, espionage, desertion, sleeping on watch, and leaving his station before being relieved. Equally destructive to an officer's career were such actions as causing a naval vessel to be stranded or 'improperly hazarded', destroying public property, 'treacherously' striking the flag to an enemy, displaying cowardice, shirking duty in combat, neglecting to prepare the vessel properly when entering an action, failing to 'do his utmost to overtake and capture or destroy' an enemy vessel, and not affording 'all practicable relief...to American or allied vessels engaged in battle'.[21]

To allow for quick resolution of disciplinary problems, usually while at sea, the Articles allowed for the calling of summary court martials for cases involving enlisted men, petty officers and below. The summary court consisted of three officers and a recorder, and the penalties issued thereby were subject to remission by the officer who ordered the court martial.

Any punishment involving loss of pay was subject to review by the Secretary of the Navy.

The general court martial, by contrast, could only be convened by order of the President, Secretary of the Navy, or the commander of a fleet or squadron. It was composed of five to thirteen officers and had powers similar to civilian judiciaries, including penalties for witnesses who refused to testify. It is obvious that the general court martial was not of particular utility on a small man-of-war, and thus the summary court became a necessity, particularly in a wartime situation and on small vessels with a limited number of officers available to serve.

The displacement of flogging – which had no strictures or regulations on its application – with a true disciplinary system based on non-corporal punishment was a step with far-reaching implications for the service. Harold Langley, historian of nineteenth-century social reform in the navy, linked this sea change in both the type and character of discipline to the 'foundations of a real career enlisted service.'[22] In terms of the internecine conflict at hand, it is probably worth noting that after 1862 no United States navy man, white or black, was subject to the capricious or arbitrary crack of the lash. In fact, it is possible that by that date, officially sanctioned flogging was to be found only in the slave-holding south.

Within the subject of naval law and order falls that of mutiny. Fortunately, it appears that naval insurrection was rare during this war. As with the subject of desertion, however, very little has been written thereon. In any event, there was only one serious case of mutiny during the course of the war.

The merchant steamer *Ocean Queen* was in transit from New York in May 1862, with 220 former army draftees who had recently volunteered for the navy. They were in the charge of Lieutenant Daniel Ammen and a boatswain. Also aboard were 1040 passengers, including women and children. A small coterie – about a dozen – of the draftees, which Ammen suspected had been rejected by the army, quickly voiced dissatisfaction with their berthing arrangements and food. Verbal threats and disrespect flowed and resulted in an attempt by these men to force their way into the cabin and spirit room. Ammen, and others of the ship's officers, fired on them, and two were killed. This ended the insurrection. Ammen was court martialed, but exonerated of any wrong doing in their deaths.[23]

It was an unusual example of a mutiny. Though under navy discipline, the men were on a merchant vessel. The mutineers' complaints were far from serious ones, judging from descriptions of the event, and in fact appear to have been trumped up simply as an excuse for revolt. In any event, this appears to have been the only serious naval rebellion of the war.

# Petty officers and specialities

Landsmen, ordinary seamen and seamen made up the bulk of the enlisted grades, with coal heavers and firemen becoming increasingly important as the fleet developed into steam. There were elites within the enlisted grades and special skills which set them apart, both in pay and level of responsibility. The following is a survey of some of the duties of the more important petty officers.

The boatswain's mates were the leading heads of the ship's company and were responsible for passing all orders given by the officer of the deck. They signalled – by pipe – veering, hauling, etc. Their routine duties were centered around the ship's rigging and spars. Twice daily they surveyed from truck to main chains, as well as storage areas, noting conditions of yards, blocks, halliards, braces, and all such, reporting to the executive officer and recommending repairs or changes. An authority of the era considered the bo'sun 'an indispensable part' of the vessel, both for his expertise in seamanship and his leadership of the crew.[24]

Gunner's mate was second in precedence among the petty officers. He was overseer of the ship's ordnance and ordnance stores. The battery itself – condition of carriages, tackle and furniture – was under his purview, and he maintained the magazines and shell rooms, accounting for the expenditure of all powder and projectiles. When large guns were moved or handled, he acted as the resident expert on the proper methods.

Also near the apex of the enlisted ranks was the quartermaster. His primary duties related to conning the ship and signals. He both read hoists from other vessels and had signals made. He steered or supervised the helmsmen, and dealt with the sounding lead and log.[25]

The above were the senior petty officers of the line; the enlisted equivalents of deck officers, who held warrants and had leadership responsibilities. Other line petty officers were: coxswains, quarter gunners, and captains of the main, fore, mizzen top and the afterguard.

Non-line petty officers included yeomen, carpenter's mates, armorers, sailmakers, machinists, apothecaries, band masters, and other specialities. These ratings and other 'day men' were termed 'idlers' when it came to their schedules: they were not regular watch standers, but had stations assigned in all ship evolutions.

Boatswain's Mate (Bo'sun), on the gunboat *Cayuga*. The bo'sun was the senior petty officer on board. Their pipe communicated orders from the officer of the deck; their eyes surveyed the vessel daily from truck to stowage. William Young, shown here, was awarded the Medal of Honor for his conduct at the passage of the forts below New Orleans. (USAMHI)

The sailmaker had charge of all sails, awnings, wind-sails, and every piece of canvas on board the vessel. Their condition was under his eye, as well as their availability and stowage conditions.

The carpenter oversaw the rudder, capstan, tiller, bilge and force pumps, lightning rods, ship's boats, and such things as gratings and air ports. In general, he was to care for the hull and spars of the ship, with the above list merely the appurtenances to his main responsibilities. He reported on all damage, both normal wear and tear or battle-related, and supervised all the needed restoration and repair. At sea, it was the carpenter who was called when the naval constructor failed. In one Civil War instance, a new sidewheel steamer was found incapable of steering within sixteen points of its intended course. The carpenter re-built the entire steering apparatus and rectified the problem. In other words, the carpenter – and that was a mis-nomer – was an indispensable part of the crew.[26]

The chief appointed petty officer of any vessel was the master-at-arms. This man executed the police duty on the ship: assisted by the marine guard and ship's corporals. They enforced all regulations from light's out to dealing with mutiny, had charge of offenders and saw to it that their punishments were carried out.

Appointments to these ratings were based on performance and demonstrated expertise in the required areas. Only the boatswain had a specific length of service requirement: seven years, of which one year was to have been as a petty officer.[27]

## Firemen and coal heavers

These men were not petty officers, but had a speciality of sorts. No experience was necessary to enlist as a coal heaver. They were to receive and store the coal (though the lower ranks shared the work of coaling during the war). Once the coal was in the bunkers, the heavers had the onerous and gritty duty of moving it

within the bunkers if necessary, as well as delivering it to the boiler rooms. This was by far the dirtiest job on the steamer.[28]

Fireman was the next rung up in the engineering department. This involved firing the boilers as well as oiling the machinery. Firing was in its own way, an art, and an examination was required for promotion to, or enlistment in, this category. The quantity and location of the coal on the grates in part determined the efficiency and economy of the machinery, and therefore was of much importance to the commanding officer. Additionally, poor firing could burn out the boilers entirely.

## Daily shipboard routine

As with all military entities, the ship's crew lived by the clock. Regularity of schedules and their associated activities gave structure to the day and was an aid to both the men who were the subject of the schedules as well as to the officers who saw to it that the tasks were carried out accordingly. The following detailed description applies to the conventional sail-and-steam warship,

**Holystoning the weather deck – a daily ritual accomplished before breakfast. The holystones removed grit, ashes, and a layer of the wood deck in the process. (US Navy)**

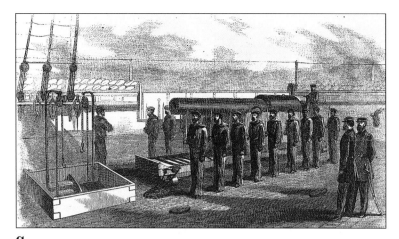

Sunday morning inspection on the gunboat *Metacomet*, 1864. Shipboard routine included the inevitable inspections. This appears to be the entire 10-inch pivot gun crew. Note also the neat line of stowed hammocks, seen atop bulwarks on either side of the pivot port. From *Harper's Weekly*. (US Navy)

and most of the practices varied little from the days of sail.[29]

At sea, the typical day began on the 4 to 8am watch, though the specific times varied with the vessel and the circumstances. Reveille was sounded by the marine bugler and the day began with the rousing shouts of 'Show a leg!' as the men were not too gently roused from their hammocks. In a spate of hurried activity, the hammocks were rolled and lashed with seven turns of manila rope – with each turn spaced equi-distant from the others. To guarantee uniformity the diameter of the hammocks was sometimes measured by a properly sized hoop. They were then carried to the spar deck and stored in the hammock rails atop the main bulwarks, with the sailor's crew number 'up and out' for quick identification later. Often a gauge was used to 'preserve a symmetrical line' of hammocks with respect to the height of the rail. Nettings covered the line of hammocks and the whole became additional protection from splinters and small arms fire. In theory, from reveille to hammock stowage was to take a mere seven minutes.[30]

Timing aside, the next daily convention was washing down the decks – an increasingly onerous job with the introduction of ash-producing steam engines. This process, particularly on the weather decks, was more akin to sanding or grinding the wood – usually pine or oak – than simply washing it down. Indeed, both sand and salt water were sluiced generously on the unpainted planking, then 4-foot long holystones were repeatedly dragged across by crews of four men each, supervised by the boatswain's mate. The holystones, which also came in smaller sizes – called bibles or testaments – were blocks of soft sandstone with enough grit to take a layer of

wood off with their repeated use. It is said the term holystone originated from its use to clean the decks before Sunday divine services. On some vessels, methods of cleaning the decks were alternated; with or without sand and with or without holystones.[31]

The morning cleaning included washing clothes and polishing the brass and other metal brightwork, such as railings, binnacle, door hardware, etc. In the process, the guns received their share of attention. Photos of the era show the gloss shine on the hulking black barrels of the Dahlgren smoothbores, and their equally spotless pivot carriages.

The morning continued with a general check of the rigging – blocks, halyards, etc. This involved necessary maintenance such as eliminating Irish pennants (dangling lines) and tightening loose lines, and often the use of fancy Flemish coils to clean up tangles of line on deck. Such touches marked the difference between an ordinary ship and one truly 'shipshape – Bristol fashion' in sailor parlance.

At 7.15 the first of many inspections began with the ship's boys and servants. The master-at-arms checked the boys for tidiness and then ran them up to the masthead, and back – an exercise which no doubt dispersed any morning sluggishness and inattention.

Some two-and-a-half hours into the day, after the decks were dried and cleaning gear stowed, came breakfast. The menu consisted of black coffee and salt 'junk' or hard salted beef. The men ate in their messes, and kept their utensils, cookware and food allotment in the group's mess chest.

Once the mess chest was resecured and breakfast cleared away, and after a smoke break, the crew turned to for inspection at quarters. Both men and guns were scrutinized for readiness in the event of enemy activity or the appearance of a blockade runner.

After inspection the day was taken up with drills and exercises or work details. The various drills might claim the entire day, only interrupted by lunch. Often the routine was to exercise with the big guns in the morning; small arms in the afternoon. With the former, target practice might mean shooting at old flour barrels at 1200 to 2000 yards, and competition for accuracy was encouraged among gun crews.

The crew was drilled for any eventuality. In this instance the crew of the *Hartford* practice repelling boarders and manning the 11-inch Dahlgren. This and image on page 132 are dated 1877, but little had changed in the exercise or the equipment since the Civil War (though the 11-inch gun was a post-war addition to *Hartford*). (US Navy)

Cutlass and small arms exercises, *Hartford*, 1877. A wide variety of drills and exercises, plus the duties intendant on maintaining a sail-and-steam vessel at sea filled the time in otherwise uneventful days on the wartime blockade. (US Navy)

Then there were the never-ending exercises and practices in preparation for every foreseeable emergency and combat situation. There were collision drills, abandon ship drills, explosion drills fore and aft, and fire drills. There were the battle exercises: repelling boarders and boarding an enemy vessel, for attacks starboard and port, for night attacks, and for any other contingency for which a training routine could be devised. The executive officer varied the sequence daily, depending on the needs of the crew, and in light of an impending engagement, or according to his whim, as the case might be.

Given the fact that the battle scenarios required the appropriate weaponry, there was definitely an element of 'playing soldier' involved, with swords, axes, pistols and cutlasses, and even hoary pikes being wielded by a bunch of boys, most of whom were not far beyond puberty. In fact a full fledged battle was sometimes enacted, complete with blanks in the broadside guns, 'killed dead' and 'wounded' sailors scattered about, the marine bugler ripping out 'boarders away', and the commanding officer, brandishing his sword, leading the boarding party over the bulwarks (or, in this case, to the bulwarks).[32]

Significantly more mundane were the work details and other seemingly unending tasks endemic to a wooden ship. Somewhere – always – on board was a place which needed paint. The blockade with it's incessant station-keeping offshore quickly weathered and tore at the ship's exterior. As such, when weather permitted, one could usually discern sailors with bucket and brushes adding a coat to the black or grey hulls.

Indeed, painting was often a great deal more than the twentieth-century equivalent of opening a can of commercial enamel. Paint was often made aboard ship, usually with some combination of lampblack, varnish, linseed oil, turpentine and litharge (white lead). Painting the barrels of the Dahlgren smoothbores, for instance, required boiling and stirring the ingredients and the lacquer had to be applied hot in two coats, but only after scraping off the old finish.[33]

One of the most unpopular tasks was coaling ship. Refueling could well take an entire day, as well as require the majority of the crew. Once the collier was along side, the process began and continued without let up until it was complete. Often, boards

were run between the ships – the state of the sea permitting – and the coal was carried on in bags, buckets or wheelbarrows. Though some might remain in bags for stowage, most was shovelled into the bunkers through the deck scuttles. The end of the task found all hands exhausted and insidious coal dust infiltrating every crevice, requiring the next day's clean-up to be a particularly thorough one.

Noon brought lunch, and again the messes organized themselves, and their sail-cloth 'table cloths' went down on the berth deck. Staples of the navy were salt beef ('salt horse') and pork, with coffee and vegetables. One of the latter was nicknamed 'dog's bodies': peas boiled in a cloth. If available, local purchases might supplement the navy's menu. Specifics on naval rations are discussed later in the chapter.

After the post-lunch drills or work details, a light meal was served at 4pm, followed by the smoking lamp. At 5.30 the men were called to quarters and guns and stations were inspected again. This pre-darkness inspection was not mere ritual: on the blockade, night was often the cover for the blockade runners.

Inspection complete, the men were allowed to retrieve their hammocks and prepare to sleep. The hours of dusk afforded the only true relaxation time on board the vessel, ending at 8 or 9pm with tattoo.

This was the time for whatever leisure activities the sailors might enjoy in the limited confines of the ship's decks. Sedentary activities ranged from reading – often encouraged by the library which regulations required be kept on board – to carving, elaborate decorative knot-tying ('marlinespikework'), embroidering uniforms, and writing letters home. Some sailors were more creative: they trained cockroaches, danced the quadrille on the fantail, played musical instruments, and placed and answered personal ads in northern newspapers. Of course, this was the time when the older salts wove many a yarn and the younger men were apt to a bout of spontaneous skylarking. If there was a religious group active on board, this was the time for meetings. At tattoo, lights were out and all was quiet until reveille began the sequence again.

There were, of course, significant regular exceptions to this daily routine. On Sunday, 'divine service' was read by the chaplain or ship's commanding officer. Attendance was not mandatory, but was encouraged. On the first Sunday of each month a general muster was held and the crew was read the Articles of War. On many ships, regular days were set aside for such things as clothing and bedding inspection, clothing and small stores issue, scrubbing hammocks, airing bedding, scraping masts, and overhauling cables.

The preceding account has not included the activities inherent in actually operating the vessel. All of the above were secondary to the requirements imposed by nature's elements on a sailing vessel intent on making a passage. Regardless of routine, time, temperature, sea conditions or day of the week, the helm was to be manned and watches kept. On the sailing vessel or the steamer with sailing rig, the inconstancy of the wind and currents made it necessary that other activities be relegated to second place behind maintaining the spread of sail appropriate to the wind and sea conditions. For the sailor, of course, this meant a constant state of readiness and possibly suspense, particularly in dirty weather or confined seas. The call for 'all hands' overrode sleep, watch schedules, and all else in dire situations.

Similar, but more unremitting, were the constraints of the engine and boiler rooms. On the monitors and other exclusively engine-powered vessels, engineers, fire crew and coal heavers labored without cessation, seeing to it that the engine maintained the desired revolutions per minute, and the boilers supplied the needed steam with the minimum expenditure of precious coal, and without breakdown. In both battle and storm, that propulsion system was a vital element in the very survival of the vessel and its crew.

Above and beyond the maintenance of the propulsive machinery of the vessel and the safety of its crew in all weathers, an unexpected encounter with an enemy would throw all other considerations and routines to the winds. Then it was expected

Leisure time on the after deck. Note the black sailors to the right background. It is estimated that over 16,000 blacks served in the Union navy. Unlike the army their pay was equal to that of the white sailors. (USAMHI)

Newspapers were read voraciously, particularly after major actions, with sailors poring the lines for mentions of their own vessel's part in the battle. *Harper's Weekly* and others were the national papers of the day. From *Harper's Weekly*. (US Navy)

that training and all the trumped up drills and exercises would pay off with a crew ready to fight for their lives unhindered by mere interruption of sleep or routine.

# Quality of life

We have discussed the nuts and bolts of the sailor's life: his basic job requirements, his daily schedule, his pay, training and the disciplinary system. However, something should be said about the general conditions on board the ships of the navy: almost literally the atmosphere in which all of this occurred. The title of a recent article on the subject: 'Men, Monotony and Mouldy Beans...' reflects a little of this aspect of the men's lives.[34]

One of the men's most frequent complaints was the heat. The blockade, after all, was of the southern coast, none of which was above the 37th parallel and which, farther south, edged the Tropic of Cancer. Particularly on the Gulf Coast, as well as in the waters of South Carolina and below, summer was a tropical nightmare of heat and humidity, with temperatures commonly beyond the 90°F mark. On the wooden ships, ventilation was minimal and men below decks sweltered in the suffocating heat. The presence of the steam engines, constantly turning to maintain readiness for action or chase, simply multiplied the sources of heat on board. One fire-room sailor compared his situation to that of a 'crab' in a 'pot of hot water'.[35]

On the ironclads, the situation was not improved. The monitors, with their accommodations below the waterline, were particularly unpopular. The iron sweated, and the men wrote of condensed moisture running 'in streams from their bulkheads'. Going out on deck to escape the heat was a futile exercise. When steam was up it was nearly impossible to walk on the hot iron armor deck plating. A layer of planking added later in the ships' development did little to alleviate the problem.[36]

Winter on a naval vessel at sea was not necessarily an improvement. Though the southern winters, particularly from Virginia south to north Florida, were mild in terms of temperature extremes, the cold was accompanied by bone chilling rain and humidity. One can imagine the atmosphere on board unheated ships at sea in these conditions. At least on the steam vessels warmth could be found near the engine and boilers. On the monitors, one sailor reported that it was like 'living in a well'.[37]

Next to the weather, a favorite object of complaint among the sailors was the menu. The navy provided bread, salt beef or pork, dried apples, dessicated potatoes and vegetables, sugar, tea, vinegar, molasses, rice and butter, cheese when available, and coffee, costing the government about 25 cents per sailor per day.

In theory this was a sufficient and, by the standards of the time, healthy diet. However, between theory and practice lay such factors as unsafe canning techniques, under-scrupulous government provision contractors, poor storage and logistical snags. Supplies might be regularly received if the vessel was close to a naval station or depot and, conversely, the more remote one's blockade station, the less predictable the arrival of foodstuffs. Long delays in the delivery process, and improper handling and storage might add less than welcome occupants to the food as well as unhealthy 'aging'. One sailor wrote of worms in the hardtack, cockroaches in the coffee, and cheese 'hard as flint'. Flour was reported hard enough to throw across the deck and not break – even after boiling.[38]

Fortunately, there were opportunities to supplement this repetitious regimen. Whenever the vessel put in for supplies or repairs, the men were usually able to purchase comparative delicacies on the open market. This might be as close as Ship Island, New Orleans, or Pensacola on the Gulf, or Key West, Port Royal, or Beaufort on the Atlantic. All were in Union hands by late 1862. Major repairs or refit might bring the vessel to a northern port with yet wider varieties of food at hand.

The unofficial sources of supplements were often as close as the waters off the side. In Virginia shores, crabbing was common; off Cape Fear, there were 'shad and herring by the barrel'. Oyster beds yielded their treasure and local fishermen often sold their catch. Then there were the products of foraging on the enemy's coast or river valleys. Landing parties might relieve the hostile populace of turkeys, cattle, eggs, fruit, sweet potatoes, or whatever happened to be ripe for the picking. Of course, the sailors on the western rivers were the fortunate ones in this regard, as they normally had close access to the shores.

One other source was particularly welcome, and that was packages from home. The holidays would bring armloads of parcels, many with sweets, pies, fruit cakes, and plums sent by loved ones determined to contribute to the season's festivities. These, with the extras procured specifically by the crew beforehand would alleviate the humdrum life for the few days of relaxation from routine that marked the extent of the crew's celebration of Christmas and New Year's Day.

The coming of Thanksgiving and Christmas also gave impetus to the on-board spiritual efforts which usually were less overt

Mariner's Church, New York. This was one of many established in the ante-bellum years when a spiritual revival of sorts broke out in the navy. A Christian sailor on liberty might find fellow believers and a 'church' here. From C C Jones' *From the Forecastle to the Pulpit*, 1884.

through the balance of the year. Prior to the war, culminating in the mid 1850s, there had been an extraordinary spiritual movement among the American sailors. Revival meetings and daily 'divine service' became staples on many vessels. One, the huge *Niagara*, had such a religious contingent that pews for hundreds were set up on her commodious decks and she came to be called 'The Gospel Ship'. Additionally, there were shore equivalents organized to support the evangelistic efforts going on at sea, resulting in seamen's 'churches' in many ports. Thus, when the seaman had liberty, he had the choice of the world's vices, or fellowship with other sailor-believers.[39]

The war's massive personnel influx diluted these religious convocations, though it is noteworthy that many of the pre-war ships retained a large number of their older sailors well into the war, with the new volunteers usually assigned to equally new ships. In any event, the spiritual infrastructure subsided significantly during the conflict.

However, in addition to the official divine services, the sailors often had access to periodical literature which originated in the pre-war religious fervor. These included *The Sailor's Magazine*, *The Seaman's Friend*, and *The Lifeboat*. The latter was placed by the American Seamen's Friend Society, which also placed thousands of books in the ship's libraries during the war.

It is also noteworthy that among the navy's leadership were

those whose religious devotion was marked and who were concerned with their men's spiritual health. A man who at one time in his life chose the navy over the evangelistic ministry was Rear Admiral Andrew H Foote, who preached 'hellfire and brimstone' on Sundays and fervently delivered the same to the rebels whenever possible. His repute as a fighter was such that, had he not died from an accident early in the war, he may well have rivalled Farragut in his accomplishments. He is famous for the fights at Forts Henry and Donelson, and allegedly delivered that famous deliberate mis-quote of Christ: 'Believe ye in me, believe ye also in gunboat.' Others with less overt, but firm and unflinching faith were Farragut, John Rodgers, Dupont and John Winslow of *Kearsarge* and *Alabama* fame.[40]

Routine, humdrum and monotony were probably the words most appropriate for the sailor's life on the blockade. On board, as has been seen, there was precious little leisure time, and the ship's captain, if he was wise, encouraged as many 'safe' activities as possible on his vessel. On large ships there might be entire bands or theatrical ensembles. On the steam frigate *Minnesota* was a group of escaped 'plantation darkeys' whose song, dance and comedy routines regularly entertained in the evenings. The officers of the *Vanderbilt* bought a full set of musical instruments and organized a minstrel band. The crew of the bark *Brazileira* set up a quarterdeck faux theatre, complete with flag-decorated stage and printed programs. Their offerings, including 'The Laughable, Burlesque Operetta of Bombashes Furioso' were elaborate and – at least in the opinion of their captive audience – 'really very funny'.

The contrived entertainments, whether group efforts or the individual's were, of course, in the best sense, diversions. They deflected the sailor's thoughts from that which he was missing: home, family, and 'his best girl'. Nothing could truly replace the first two of these. Women, however, unlike one's 'best girl', were sought out at every opportunity. Whenever 'real-alive young ladies' appeared, whether passing on ferries, arriving as officers' guests, or employed at the social agencies organized for the blacks in the occupied Carolinas, a 'state of mild phrenzy' prevailed on board.[41] (The latter group, which included teachers and social workers, were probably the only 'permanent' females to be found in the navy's precincts, other than a group of nuns who provided nursing services during the western rivers campaign.)

In any event, the lack of female companionship was essentially unsolveable, at least legally. And it should be pointed out, whether for good or ill, that the majority of the navy's men were not 'sailors' in the true sense: they were civilian volunteers whose attitudes towards lack of females was less hardened than that of the old line seafarer.

Finally we have reached the subject of 'liberty'. On the surface, the monotony and separation from home-like comforts was far from fatal. However, it was a morale defeater with results which were often manifested in the men's behavior – or lack of it – when shore liberty was finally achieved. Though the Civil War sailor seems to have gained a rather innocent reputation, at least from the modern standpoint, he was as capable of mischief and troublemaking as the twentieth-century seaman. It is probably fortunate that there were not a great number of 'wide-open' towns available to offer the footloose sailor the depravity – or at least the good times – which he might be seeking.

On the eastern seaboard, there were two prominent 'liberty ports' – Port Royal, South Carolina, and Beaufort, North Carolina – both occupied by federals early in the war. The former, called the 'Southern Federal Capital', encompassed both the town and a large army presence, resulting in 'a good deal of society'. Generally, this was 'polite' society, with few sources of strong drink or other illicit activities. Popular activities were on the pedestrian side – merchants, photographers, and relatively low-key saloons. There were churches available for Sunday services, of course.

Beaufort was apparently even less exciting, described by one sailor as 'a string of houses, a number of churches, and lots of sand'. Billiards, bowling, and 'poor beer' marked the extent of the wild activities thereat.[42]

Only when the ship was due for re-fit or major repairs did the men see the lights of a genuine city. New York, Philadelphia,

**V**ariety show, USS *Wabash*, on the Atlantic blockade. Note 'Hatteras' painted on the backdrop to the left of the ship's name. The circles on deck are rails for the pivot gun. In large crews, more elaborate entertainment was often concocted, including amateur theatrics.
(USAMHI)

Baltimore, Washington, and Boston, had navy yards or substantial repair facilities. There the sailor could indulge his tastes, whether illicit or otherwise. It is not necessary to delineate the former here, as it usually involved women, drink and the Civil War version of the shore patrol. On the other hand, the sailor with spiritual, religious leanings, could usually find a place to worship or fellowship at the American Seamen's Friend Society or the Seaman's Church in the major port cities.

# Black sailors in the Civil War navy

Even as this is being written there are major efforts being made to chronicle in detail the contributions of black sailors to the Union naval effort. Though the results will probably not reach the popular level of the film *Glory* which celebrated the heroism of blacks in the army's Charleston campaign, they will be equally significant to the understanding of the war and race relations.

The number of blacks in the US Navy has been estimated as high as 29,000, though the currently accepted number is over 16,000. This uncertainty is due to the same anomalies at work in determining the overall numbers of enlistees (or enlistments of individuals) during the war, as discussed earlier in this chapter. If the total number of enlistments is taken at 118,000, then approximately 15 per cent of the sailors were black.[43]

On individual vessels the percentages could be much more substantial. Some examples, taken from original crew muster lists, are in order here. On the western river ironclad *Tuscumbia*, when commissioned in 1863, there were 10 blacks of a crew of 127. By late 1864, the number had ballooned to 44 (out of 144 total crew). This was 30 per cent. In fact, almost every vacancy, whether due to battle or other causes, had been filled by former slaves.

The river timberclad gunboat *Tyler*, in January 1863, had fourteen blacks of a crew of forty-one. Later on there were 31 blacks in her enlarged crew of 106.

On the sidewheel river gunboat *Meteor* the number of blacks ranged from thirteen to sixteen in a crew of forty-two to forty-seven at various times during 1864.

On the blockade was the steamer *Hunchback*. The largest number of black crewmembers was thirty-five, in April 1865, when her total crew was 151.[44]

On some of the small, transport or auxiliary vessels, the percentages were higher. One such vessel reportedly had an all-black crew with white officers – a pattern often seen in Union infantry regiments.

The origin of black recruiting had come as early as July 1861, when Flag Officer Silas Stringham asked the Navy Department what to do with the large numbers of blacks escaping to the Federal blockading squadron. They were still a political problem, as the emancipation proclamation was another two years away. Welles replied that Stringham ought to use them, and in September official orders to that effect were issued. The term used was anomalous: 'contrabands', which implied that they had been the property of the secessionist masters, seized as an act of war by Union forces.

By December 1862 the blacks were being allowed to enlist and began serving alongside whites on Union vessels. Unlike the army, which paid them less than their white counterparts, the navy gave them equal pay. They were enlisted as landsmen, and allowed to advance to the position of ordinary seaman, then seaman. It is unclear whether any attained the rank of petty officer, and it appears that they were given the dirtiest jobs available: many were coal heavers or firemen.

In July 1863, D D Porter wrote General Order Number 76, which outlined the Mississippi squadron's policy on the matter. Part of this read:

'Owing to the increasing sickness in the squadron, and the scarcity of men, it becomes necessary for the efficiency of the vessels to use the contrabands to a greater extent than before. The white men can not stand the southern sun, and exposure to which invariably brings on the disease of this climate, remittant fever. But while employed only on the ordinary duties of the vessels, I find that little or no disease exists. The blacks must therefore be used altogether as boats' crews, or for duty requiring exposure to the sun, every precaution being taken to keep them from being sick. The blacks must also be used to defend the vessels where there is a deficiency in the crew. This policy is dictated by necessity, and it is believed that in cases of emergency the blacks will make efficient men...they must be kept distinct from the rest of the crew. They can be stationed at the guns...to pass shot and powder, handle handspikes, at train-tackles and side-tackles, pumps, and fire buckets; and can be exercised separately at great guns and small arms.... The policy...is to use the blacks, and every officer should do his utmost to carry this policy out.'[45]

Robert Smalls took the CSS *Planter* from Charleston harbor and steamed her out to the Union blockaders. His masters accused him of theft; the Union called it a prize of war and awarded him $1500. He was later employed as a pilot by the South Atlantic squadron. (National Park Service)

This unique document probably summarizes the attitude of the navy towards the black sailor. Note that the idea of keeping the blacks separate from the remainder of the crew is mentioned twice. It would be interesting to inquire how it would be possible for the blacks to exercise at the great guns 'separately' if they were to be part of their crews.

Separately or together, the blacks fought and died for the Union cause and ultimately for their freedom. The number of casualties and other statistics are at this point in time uncertain. It is known that at least two blacks were awarded the Congressional Medal of Honor. (See below.)

No description of the contributions of blacks in the Civil War is complete without the story of Robert Smalls of South Carolina. Smalls, a young slave, had been trained as a pilot in the shallow waters around Charleston. On a dark night in mid June

1862, he waited until his masters were ashore and took the vessel on which he was employed out to sea, coolly dispensing the proper recognition signals as he passed the Confederates at Fort Sumter. He steamed straight for the astonished Union blockaders, narrowly avoiding becoming their target. On board with him were three men, two women, and a baby boy. Smalls immediately became a hero in the North, especially among his fellow blacks, and was paid $1500 as part of the prize money for the steamer — which became the USS *Planter*. Smalls remained in the area as a pilot, obtaining employment with the Union blockading fleet. Later in the war, his repute was such that he met with President Lincoln as a spokesman for former slaves. Generations later, his memory is still revered by blacks in that area of South Carolina.[46]

## The Medal of Honor

Until 1862 the United States had no medals for military heroism. The only medal previously awarded had been the Purple Heart, given to those wounded in battle. In late December 1961, Congress authorized the navy Medal of Honor, followed shortly by the army version of the award. It was, and is, the highest award the nation can bestow.

The first navy Medal of Honor was dated 3 April 1863, and 307 were awarded to seamen or marines during the Civil War. Of these, five went to boys. The youngest with ages listed on the citation were Oscar F Peck, aged fifteen, and James Machon, sixteen. Of the five, one was Robert Blake, a 'contraband' (an escaped slave). Two of the boys were on the same vessel (*Varuna*) at Farragut's passage of the forts below New Orleans. The boys in all likelihood were the youngest to ever receive the Medal of Honor. A second black honoree, Joachim Peck, was on the *Kearsarge* when she sank the *Alabama*.

On the negative side, another nine medals were awarded to those who forfeited it by misconduct or desertion.[47]

## Chapter Eight
# THE NAVAL OFFICER CORPS

The American navy's officer corps, at the outset of the Civil War, was an exclusive aristocracy with hereditary leanings. It drew its strength and reputation from that band of intrepid heroes of the Quasi-War with France, the Tripolitan wars, and, most importantly, the War of 1812. Bainbridge, Hull, Preble, Decatur, Porter, Stewart, Perry, Rodgers...the lot of them had the mantle of victory about them almost from the day the navy put to sea against France. With few exceptions, it seemed that the only prerequisite for American victory in the War of 1812 was to meet the enemy on relatively equal terms.

It is appropriate to note here the number of those prominent family names which had carried through from those august founders to the Civil War. There were descendants or collateral descendants of nearly all those listed above serving in the Civil War officer ranks, and a significant number were highly placed. Most notable were the Porter and Rodgers families. Both David Dixon Porter and William D Porter were sons of the Commodore D D Porter of *Essex* fame. Additionally, David G Farragut was the adopted son of the famous commodore.

The Rodgers family members were descendants of Commodore John Rodgers, who was one of the first officers on the frigate *Constellation* in 1798 and who commanded the *President* when she demolished the *Little Belt* in 1811. Four direct Rodgers descendants served in the Civil War – John and Frederick (brothers), Christopher Raymond Perry Rodgers and George Washington Rodgers (cousins). Their naval influence was widened by the family connection to the Perrys (descendants of Oliver Hazard Perry) by way of John Rodgers's aunt, Ann Maria (Perry)

Rodgers. Coincidentally, the Perry and Rodgers family were related to both the Meigs and the Blairs. The former included the Quartermaster General of the Army (Montgomery Meigs) and the latter included Lincoln's Postmaster General, Montgomery Blair, and the influential Congressman from Missouri, Francis Preston Blair.

This heady aura was unmatched in the American army. That service had the 'scourge' of volunteerism. Professional soldiers were the exception during the Revolution, and professionals had, with few exceptions, made the land War of 1812 a disaster. It is fortunate for the nation that the army had – by its own straps – generated an incomparable core of officers by the efforts of the Military Academy at West Point – a group which conquered Mexico and would shine on both sides during the Civil War.

The small size of the American fleet prior to the war had served to limit the number of naval officers as well as promote their exclusivity. However, the establishment of the Naval Academy in 1845 was a step towards democratization, and the Civil War itself would serve to purge some of the less productive of the old guard, and somewhat dilute the remainder with volunteers of all stripes and backgrounds.

As the war began, two contradictory trends had to be reconciled within the officer ranks. First was the massive defection to the South; second was the need to enlarge, as well as tailor, the officer corps to meet wartime needs.

The number of officers who abandoned the Union navy, presumably to join the Confederacy, has not been exactly determined. Gideon Welles gave the number as 322, though another document, which covers the period from December 1860 to December 1863, listed 422 names, ranking from acting midshipmen to captain. The latter list, however, includes many who hailed from the North and who may have resigned for non-political reasons. Either way, this was about half of the entire officer corps.[1]

The losses were not inconsiderable, in numbers or quality of men. Fifteen captains – the highest rank of that time – 'went south'. More ominously, the majority of the officers of the new Confederate Navy were ex-Union men – a ready-made core of experience for the infant service.

Despite these losses, the navy's officer ranks had to be pruned yet more, to yield, as Charles O Paullin put it, a group suited to 'the sterner requirements of war'. To yet be eliminated were the aged and infirm, such as those commanders still remaining at age sixty, and lieutenants at fifty. Thus, the authorization for a naval retired list was passed by Congress in August 1861. Further retirement legislation followed, including setting the mandatory age at sixty-two, and maximum years in service at forty-five. Shore duty was allowed for those on the retired list.[2]

Even as the ranks were being depleted, Lincoln called for the blockade of the southern coasts and the appropriate number of vessels – and men – to maintain it. Secretary Welles immediately, taking the responsibility upon himself, began accepting volunteer officers, chiefly from the merchant service. His actions were validated on 24 July 1861, when Congress authorized the temporary increase of the navy, establishing a naval volunteer officer corps. This group included deck officers, engineers, paymasters, and surgeons, all limited to the rank of lieutenant commander, and deliberately kept separate from the career officers in terms of entry qualifications, and promotion and separation requirements.

Around 7500 men were in the volunteer officer ranks during the war – about the same number as had been in the entire service previously. Toward the end of the war, volunteers numbered as follows: 2060 line officers, 1805 engineers, 370 paymasters and 245 surgeons. Thus, the volunteers shouldered the majority of the responsibilities of the Civil War navy, and on many vessels, particularly those obtained specifically for the blockade, there were only volunteer officers.[3]

For the line officers, legislation of 16 July 1862 was to be one of the most important since the founding of the navy. For the first time, Congress specified the number of grades as well as the number authorized in each rank; two ranks above captain were authorized, those of commodore and rear admiral. (Prior to this, 'commodore', as well as 'flag officer', was only a position held temporarily, rather

than a pay grade.) Of course, the higher grades were an absolute necessity with the enlargement of the fleet and with the forming of squadrons each of which could be larger than the entire peacetime navy. In the pre-war service, the various squadrons had rarely numbered more than eight vessels, and had been commanded by captains designated 'commodore' for the purpose.

A total of nine grades were authorized, four more than previously. These new grades, in addition to the two listed above, were ensign and lieutenant commander. Nine rear admirals were authorized; eighteen commodores, thirty-six captains, seventy-two commanders and 144 each of the lower ranks, down to midshipmen, of which no specific number was set. A board was formed to recommend those they considered worthy of elevation, and, from those, seniority determined their order of precedence. During the war, the rear admirals were selected by their personal merit, courage, and accomplishments; in peace, the system reverted to that used for the other ranks.[4]

This legislation established the relative ranks of army and navy as well as authorized a new pay scale, setting the maximum at $5000 for rear admirals at sea. (For purposes of comparison, heads of departments received $3500 and the Secretary of the Navy was paid $8000 per year.) Shore duty, of course, netted significantly less remuneration, and those on the retired list received a figure near half-pay. Ensigns received $1200 while at sea and midshipmen, a stipend of $500. Surgeons' pay ranged from $3000 downward, depending on length of service. This was equivalent to that received by commanders and captains. Paymasters could earn as much as $2200, about the level of lieutenant commanders; assistant paymasters (as well as chaplains) were equivalent to lieutenants in pay. Engineers with over fifteen years service made $2600 per year, about the same as commanders on shore duty. The pay decreased for first, second and third assistant engineers, with the latter only drawing $750 per annum. This pay scale applied equally to the volunteer officers.[5]

The Promotion Board met in mid 1862 and made its recommendations, which were roundly criticized – by those who were passed over. In 1864, an examining board was instituted and all officers below commodore were required to pass mental and physical standards as a prerequisite to promotion. Furthermore, strict seniority was to be supplemented by an officer's distinguished record or heroism, which could allow advancement within his grade level.

In the same year, the rank structure gained yet another rung, with the creation of vice admiral. One position was authorized by

Congress and David G Farragut was immediately promoted thereto, earning $7000 per year. (The final step was to be created in 1867, when Farragut became America's first full admiral.)[6]

# Officer education and training

By the Civil War the United States Naval Academy had become the primary source of officers for the service. The academy had been organized in 1845 as the Naval School at Philadelphia, a development encouraged by such men as Matthew Calbraith Perry. It replaced the rather irregular system which consisted of midshipmen's schools at the various navy yards for the academic aspects of the training and on-board stints on operational vessels for the practical portions of the curriculum. In this system, consistency and quality of content was as varied as the individual instructors and there was no common course syllabus or standard course duration.[7]

In 1850, the school was renamed the Naval Academy and was moved to its present location at Annapolis, Maryland. The cadets' curriculum was divided between four years of academics and summers aboard a training ship. Examinations ranged from written tests to practical skills exhibitions before the examiners. The latter included practice with broadside guns, fleet tactics with boats, infantry exercises, field battery exercises and embarking and disembarking field guns from boats, and use of broad and small swords. Academics included such staples as chemistry and 'natural philosophy', but did not embrace steam engineering until 1864.[8]

Secretary of the Navy George Bancroft was instrumental in establishing the US Naval Academy. For the first time, the education of naval officers was centralized, first at Philadelphia, then at Annapolis, Maryland. (US Navy)

US Naval Academy grounds on the Severn River at Annapolis, photographed shortly after the Civil War. The training vessels include the famous schooner yacht *America*, and double turret monitor, *Tonawanda*. The monument to the naval heroes of the War of 1812 is left of center. (USAMHI)

Post-war view of the academy shows 'Old Ironsides' (the frigate *Constitution*), on the right, and *Santee*, both by then training vessels for midshipmen. *Constitution* had been assigned to the academy in 1860 and sailed to Newport, Rhode Island where the academy was re-located for the duration of the Civil War. (USAMHI)

By the Civil War the academy had some 250 cadets enrolled. Of these, the upper three classes were detached from their safe haven and assigned to active service. The academy itself was moved from Maryland to temporary quarters at Newport, Rhode Island for the duration of the conflict.

In the rapid build-up of the fleet, from less than 50 to over 500, there was little time to put a program into place to train officers. And, once the upper three classes of the academy had been swept into active service, there was no other source of potential officers available except the merchant service, plus the odd former officers re-applying for the emergency.

Those who applied for acting volunteer commissions as deck officers had to meet basic requirements of previous service at sea and pass examinations on seamanship, navigation and gunnery. According to published regulations, acting master's mates were to be between the ages of twenty and thirty, and have been at sea, before the mast or as an officer, for five years. Acting ensigns were to be between twenty-five and thirty-five and to have twelve years

Atlantic House, at Newport, which became home to the academy during the war, while the Annapolis campus was being used as an army hospital. (USAMHI)

Eight members of the Naval Academy class of 1861. The immediate need for hundreds of new officers for the war effort put these young gentlemen into active service immediately. The academic life of the three upper classes was pre-empted by the nation's pressing needs. (US Navy)

Midshipmen learning the surveyors transit, 1860s. (US Navy)

Practice with the field howitzer, 1860s. Academy requirements included gun handling as well as boat drills, in addition to the academic curricula. (US Navy)

sea experience. Acting masters and acting lieutenants were to have at least three months service as acting ensign or acting master's mate, and be recommended by their commanding officer. Acting lieutenants, similarly, were to have six months' minimum previous naval service in the next lower grade, and to have been mentioned in dispatches for 'highly meritorious conduct in battle.'[9]

Late in 1864, a department circular set forth parallel prerequisites for volunteer officers in the Mississippi squadron. Acting master's mates were to have three years before the mast, if they hailed from the Atlantic states; only one year, if on service on the lakes on rivers, or with the army. Similarly, acting ensigns were to have eight years sea service if from the seaboard states, or three if from inland states, or as an officer on board steamers. Promotions above ensign were to be recommended to the department by the commander of the squadron, and not without 'evidence of his citizenship, place of nativity, fair English education, proof of loyalty and sobriety, and have passed a physical examination.'[10]

The line officer candidate's written examination material included knowledge of rigging ship, stowing the hold, bending and handling sails and the deep-sea lead line, working anchors and cables, tacking, wearing, and the 'ordinary evolutions'. Navigation skills required were the use of the log-line, compass, sextant and quadrant, dead reckoning, and determining longitude by the chronometer. In gunnery he was required to station men at the guns and know the exercises, including use of tangent sight and fuzes. Ability to conduct small arm and broad sword drills was also expected.

All the above were part of the examination for prospective acting volunteer ensigns. (Acting mates, which only required three years previous sea experience, were only expected to display general intelligence and an 'aptitude for the duties'.) Acting volunteer masters were required to demonstrate significantly more skills with the sextant and chronometer, and had to show an ability to use charts. Gunnery requirements included use of the boat howitzer and broadside rifles, skill at mounting and dismounting of broadside guns, and stowage in the magazine and shell room. Furthermore, the candidate was to be proficient in the 'ordinary branches of English education – reading, writing, arithmetic, and geography...'.

Beyond all the above, the acting volunteer lieutenants were to demonstrate the ability to manage the vessel under sail and steam and be able to station crews for all evolutions. Those wishing to stand for promotion to acting volunteer lieutenant commander were to be examined on all the above areas, but with 'more precision'. Their ability to make reports was scrutinized and in general they were examined with an eye to determining their qualifications for independent command.

The boards formed to select men for promotion to the various grades were composed of three or four officers. The higher the rank being dispensed, the higher the rank and larger the proportion of regular officers on the board.[11]

The above examination subjects and board requirements were found in a Navy Department circular dated 9 August 1864.

Despite the prerequisites and testing, the quality of the volunteer officers apparently varied wildly. One chronicler compared the average 'acting officer' to 'hotel hallboys', only less 'intelligent and agreeable'. It would be inappropriate to judge the group as a whole, however, and some of the negative opinions expressed at the time must be weighed in light of a bit of professional jealousy existing with the regular officers.[12]

There were, however, a sufficient number of efficient volunteer officers to inspire the department to open the ranks for a limited number to be given regular commissions. Although this idea surfaced in 1863, it was not implemented until 25 July 1866, when a total of 150 officer positions were created for meritorious wartime volunteers who had had at least two years service.[13]

# Duties and privileges of line officers

Whether regular or volunteer, the line officer inherited a substantial weight of responsibilities, graduated, of course, according to his rank and position. The accompanying privileges were as stringent, in their own manner, as the officer's prescribed duties.

The commanding officer of any given naval vessel was the sole arbiter, within the regulations, of every aspect of that command, both animate and inanimate. On taking command, he was to first familiarize himself, in exhaustive detail, with the vessel — her construction, building materials, sailing characteristics in every conceivable kind of sea and weather conditions, and strengths and weaknesses. The addition of a steam engine simply widened the scope of his required knowledge. The regulations encouraged experimentation with the ship and her engines to allow the commander to have intimate knowledge of the capabilities of the machinery, particularly at high speed or in manoeuvers. He was aided in his self-education by reports received from previous commanders. If the ship was new, the commander may well have seen her under construction or at least discussed her with the naval constructor at the yard. Indeed, on a sailing ship, the commanding officer was given much latitude in the final outfitting and rigging of the vessel for sea. This leeway was such that naval architects sometimes found themselves overruled by commanding officers who actually took their creations to sea. The results were not uniformly positive, but the vessel's commanding officer was very much within his rights to do so.

As far as possible, the commanding officer was also to know his officers and their capabilities. Most important was the executive officer, on whom much of the day-to-day routine devolved. As one writer observed, the captain who failed to delegate a large portion of the work to his executive officer would 'soon succumb

to fatigue, or to nervous imbecility'. Though the captain was in the end responsible for such things as designing the Watch, Station, Quarter and Fire Bills, for instance, in practice these relatively mechanical tasks were almost uniformly devolved on the executive officer. The same can be said for the organization of the various exercises, drills and other crew-training issues, as well as keeping conduct and liberty books.

The commanding officer was solely responsible for the ends to which the executive and other officers provided the means. Only he determined the vessel's course, authorized clearing for action, determined the ship's response to actual or suspected adversaries, and was authorized to surrender a United States ship. The commanding officer could be brought up on charges for grounding and loss of the vessel, failure to properly prepare the ship for battle, failure to engage an enemy to the fullest extent, and neglecting to assist another US vessel engaging an enemy.

Finally, there were reports. The commanding officer reported to his squadron commander, the commander-in-chief of the fleet, any of the bureau chiefs, or directly to the Secretary of the Navy, depending on the nature of the report.

Groundings and extensive damage required a report to the Bureau of Construction and Repair at the termination of the cruise. Preparations to take the ship to sea were the subject of communications with the Secretary of the Navy, who would inform the commander of his squadron assignment. Quarterly reports were also to be sent to the Secretary, as well as a remark book or journal, describing, from an operational standpoint, all ports of call entered, with their salient features, including anchorages, currents, availability of supplies and provisions, etc. After action reports went to the Secretary of the Navy if the ship was acting singly, or to the fleet or squadron commander, if appropriate. These reports included evaluations of the men in combat, along with recommendations for awards and promotions. If the vessel was lost in battle, the captain was finally responsible for seeing to it that the signal books and other sensitive documents were suitably weighted and committed to the sea.[14]

The executive officer was the 'organizer and law-giver on board' and the one responsible for the 'trimness and general tidiness of the ship herself; for the external appearance of her crew; for the general drill and exercises, as well as the condition of a single mess or a single store room'. He was the man between: an intermediary and interpreter of the captain to both crew and officers, and, conversely, the one through which all approached that isolated officer.

When the commanding officer was not on deck, the executive officer supervised the working of the ship; when the captain appeared, and all hands were called, he relayed all orders to the crew.

The reports he received were those of the daily minutiae, by which he could judge the various departments aboard and translate specifics into a general report for the captain. Among those who reported directly to him were the boatswains, gunner's mates, carpenters, sailmakers, paymasters, and division chiefs.

His knowledge of the ship and crew was to be as broad as the commanding officer's, but with a depth that came from intimate contact with both. He was to examine the ship daily and report his findings; he was to literally keep the keys to every locked storeroom. In modern parlance, he was the safety officer on board, tasked with ensuring proper precautions were taken when the magazine was opened for disbursing or receiving powder. As the man who organized the crew into its constituent parts, he was to constantly monitor its operation and make personnel changes as necessary, particularly in the wake of action with the enemy and the resulting casualties. Finally, he was in charge of the ship's discipline: all misconduct was reported to him, for transmission to the commanding officer, who determined, with the executive officer's advice, the appropriate punishment, short of a court martial.

Next downward in the chain of command were the watch and division officers, who were, depending on the size of the ship, lieutenants, masters, or ensigns. On taking watch, that officer, with sidearm, was to immediately acquaint himself with the position of the ship at sea and in relation to shore points and the location of any vessels in the vicinity. He was to supervise lookouts, steering, trimming of sails, and, if necessary, running lights and fog signals. At the approach of a strange sail at night, he was to notify the commanding officer. No changes in course were to be made without orders from the captain. However, he was responsible to see to it that collisions were avoided. During the night watches, the marine guard was to make rounds and report to him any violations, whether smoking, unlawful lights, or other misconduct.

The watch officer was to control all access to the vessel during his tenure. He was to see to it that any boats leaving the side were properly manned and suitably clothed, and that those coming alongside, carrying provisions or stores, were expeditiously unloaded. He was to keep an accurate account of all items coming aboard during his watch, and check for prohibited articles. Finally, he was to ensure that the proper marks of respect were made for officers arriving aboard or leaving the ship.

Division officers were responsible 'in all respects' for the efficiency of that division. This was a broad mandate, incorporating keeping the guns in constant condition for action and training of the gun crews. Above and beyond this, he was to give his personal attention to 'the cleanliness and good appearance of the men', including examination and inspections of bedding and uniforms, and having necessary items issued and kept in good order. In action, he directed the preparations and firing; afterwards, the cleanup and stowage of the weapons.

At the lowest rung of the officer ranks was the midshipman, who was in training for a commission. Before the advent of the Naval Academy, midshipmen were assigned to cruising ships, to be under the general supervision of the commanding officer. The 'young gentlemen' were to have an octant or sextant, 'an approved treatise on navigation' and one on marine surveying, plus blank journals. They were to ascertain the position of the ship daily, by observation or dead reckoning, attend classes and instruction provided for them, and keep journals as directed. In the pre-war navy much of their shipboard academic instruction was undertaken by the chaplain. As noted elsewhere, midshipman's schools of rather uneven quality had been instituted at the navy yards as an attempt to regularize the midshipmen's academic curriculum. These had been replaced by a single naval school in 1845, which became the US Naval Academy shortly thereafter. This ended the long and useful tradition of seaborne midshipmen in the navy.

Two other positions will complete this survey of the officer corps: squadron and fleet commanders. The former had been the highest position possible in the navy prior to the creation of the ranks of rear and vice admiral, and was held by captains with the temporary title of commodore. The latter came about during the Civil War and its holder was denominated the commander-in-chief.

These senior positions require little explanation as to the duties of their incumbents. They were obviously required to see that their vessels were fitted out appropriately for the assigned tasks, oversee the relations between the fleet or squadron's vessels and the various bureaux, regularly inspect ships of their command, direct fleet or squadron exercises, provide leadership, direction and facilitate coordination for all the activities and campaigns of the unit, report and communicate directly with the Secretary of the Navy, and, when on foreign station, communicate with the American diplomats in that place. These were the ultimate uniformed administrative positions in the navy. The prestige of these men and their position was such that their roles overlapped signifi-

Wardroom on the US monitor *Montauk*. Louvered doors gave entrance to the officers' accommodations. Seating at table reflected rank status on board. The high ceiling is not artistic licence: monitors with only one deck below the weather deck often had 9-foot ceilings. From *Soldier in the Civil War*. (US Navy)

cantly into the areas of general policy usually reserved to the bureau chiefs and the Secretary of the Navy himself. Certainly the accumulated experience of these men, in peace and war, was not to be taken lightly by any Secretary of the Navy who, as a political appointee, may well have had no maritime or naval background whatsoever. An extreme example of this occurred in 1869, when Admiral D D Porter was de facto Secretary of the Navy 'under' Adolph Borie, who freely admitted his ignorance in practical naval matters. Fortunately for the principle of civilian control over the military, this state of affairs in the Navy Department was short-lived.

As one climbed the officer hierarchy, increases in rank and accession to higher positions were accompanied by concomitant prerequisites, along with the accumulation of ornaments for the uniform. (See Chapter Six for descriptions of the latter.)

At the apex of the rank pyramid, the rear admirals and commodores (in 1865) were those who were entitled to the whole panoply – guns, band, marine guard, and flag of his rank. On assuming command, the rear admiral was to be received by all officers, in full dress, with the crew arranged on the side opposite his entrance way. The commanding officer was to meet him at the gangway and a full marine guard plus band was in attendance. Drums gave two ruffles and the band played a march, then he ordered his flag hoisted – a plain blue rectangle flown at the mizzen. At this, thirteen guns were fired. On visiting any vessel of his fleet the same ceremonies were to be observed, with the salute immediately after he gained the deck. If he was departing the vessel for a short time, an officer's guard replaced the marine guard, only two ruffles were permitted and the salute was dispensed with. At his return, the same cast and roles pertained. Ceremonies for a commodore were identical but he rated only eleven guns, and his flag was the broad pendant – a swallow-tailed blue flag with a single star thereon.[15]

Officers of all grades were allotted accommodations by rank, with the most senior, the commander-in-chief down to commander, in cabins. Lieutenant commanders to ensigns, plus most of the staff officers, had rooms opening to the wardroom, with the senior officer given the most forward stateroom. Line officers occupied the starboard side staterooms; staff, including chief engineers, surgeons, paymasters and the like, the port side. On vessels such as monitors, where officer country was forward on the berth deck and the commanding officer's cabin was just aft the anchor windlass room, the precedence was reversed with the highest ranks in the aft-most cabins. In the wardroom itself, the protocol of rank held true at the table with the highest rank presiding and junior officers trailing down the sides.

The lowest echelons, such as assistant engineers, mishipmen, master's mates, officer's clerk, and others, were steerage officers. They occupied common rooms located forward of the ward-

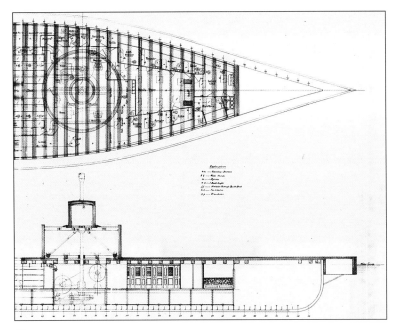

Officers' privileges included, of course, individual cabins on board. This plan of the monitor *Tippecanoe* shows accommodations forward of the turret. Far forward on the port side was the commanding officer's stateroom with a sofa on the left bulkhead. Also on the port side were cabins for ensign, paymaster and chief engineer. On the starboard side were cabins for another ensign, navigator, and, farthest aft, the executive officer. The cabins opened into the officers' wardroom, which measured about 18 feet wide by 24 feet long. The captain's cabin was a commodius 12 by 14 feet. (National Archives)

The commanding officer's stateroom on a monitor. In this instance, the bow of the ship is to the left, with the watertight door opening to the anchor well. Note the bed on the far (starboard) side, structural stanchions in the center of the room, and typical Victorian Eastlake domestic interior detailing. (Photograph is possibly from the 1890s.) (US Navy)

room, with assistant engineers to port and others to starboard.

The size and layout of the ship determined the spaciousness of all the accommodations. A wardroom officer, even in something as large as the steam frigate *Minnesota*, had only a 6-foot by 8-foot cabin. The assistant engineers (eight to twelve of them) on the same vessel shared a 10-foot by 16-foot living space. By contrast, the captain's cabin might be the breadth of the ship. Even in a small gunboat such as *Pocahontas* the commanding officer had an 8-foot by 12-foot cabin, plus two personal storerooms – not palatial by shore standards, but substantial for a seafarer. As naval constructors tended to use quality woods – walnut and mahogany were not unusual – the fit and finish of the officers' areas, and particularly the captain's stateroom, was impressive. Even the officers' quarters on the monitors were similarly finished, and usually had the added luxury of 7-foot, or higher, ceilings. The only discordant note on some of the conventional steam sloops and sailing ships was the presence of long stern chasers – though highly polished ones – amidst the panelling and brass furnishings.[16]

Attainment of higher rank and the privileges alluded to above was regulated according to time in grade, and experience. In the 1865 regulations, at least two years of sea service (exclusive of Coast Survey service) was required in each grade from midshipman to lieutenant commander, before nomination for the next higher level. Also, the grade of lieutenant was not to be conferred until the officer had served at least one year each as a master, ensign and as a midshipman out of the Naval Academy. Ranks of captain and above required presidential nomination, and each grade had its seniority list.[17]

In the regulations the requirements for sea service were prefaced by the phrase 'as a general rule', and during the war, swift promotion was the rule rather than the exception. Of course there were extreme examples: the heroic William B Cushing began the war as an acting master's mate and was a lieutenant commander by Appomattox. In peacetime, by contrast, he did not reach comman-

**O**fficers' leisure time activities during the war included hunting. Note the dogs and master seated in the center of the photograph with fowling piece and game bag. (US Navy)

der until 1872. Skipping grades also occurred. In the upper ranks, an excellent example was D D Porter, who leapt from commander to rear admiral in 1863.

Line officers, whether volunteer or regular, were the upper strata of the officer corps. The other necessary professionals – surgeons, engineers, paymasters and chaplains – occupied distinctly anomalous positions in the navy. Particularly in the case of surgeons, they found themselves, despite often superior academic backgrounds, fighting to maintain their official status vis-à-vis the deck officer corps, who jealously guarded their time-honored perquisites. This line-versus-staff controversy burbled along for the better part of the nineteenth century, and surfaced with particular vehemence in the war years, when the mix was further complicated by the rapid expansion of the officer corps.

Surgeons and assistant (or passed assistant) surgeons were brought into the navy through the Bureau of Medicine and

Surgery, and their number before the war was limited to sixty-nine of the former and eighty of the latter. Even in 1860, there was significant discontent with these limitations, particularly in light of the lack of a retired list, and the number of aging members who were incapable of sea duty. Another contentious point was the constant sea-duty required of them, due to their small numbers, unlike the deck officers of which there were sufficient numbers to allow them shore duty after a cruise. The surgeons balked at the department's tendency to place priority on sea-duty over service in the naval hospitals. The surgeons contended that hospital service was necessary for the health of shore personnel as well as to provide physicians with opportunities for acquiring vital experience in a relatively stable environment. Thus the small surgeon force was spread over all the commissioned vessels of the fleet, plus five hospitals, and the navy yards and receiving ships.

The wartime demand forced the navy to authorize an increase in the numbers in the medical corps. By 1862 there were 198 – eighty surgeons and 118 assistants in the ranks, and a small retired list had been added. Ninety-three additional were volunteer acting assistant surgeons. By the end of the war there were 245 of the latter.

Appointments and promotions of surgeons were entrusted to a board of three of their peers, which met annually. Assistant surgeons with five years naval service, two of them on shipboard, were eligible to apply for promotion, and were to provide testimonials by surgeons for whom they had served and a personal case-book or journal of practice to the examining board. Note that in the mid nineteenth century, there was no accepted, universal standard of professional practice, or institutions to provide such, and this was of course true in most professions, leaving the navy little choice but to rely on their own resources to determine the qualifications of the individual applying for the position.

By 1864, the navy's surgeons and assistants had finally won the coveted right of 'equivalent' or 'assimilated' rank. This principle had been promulgated in 1846 and gave surgeons and assistants rank equal to commanders or lower, depending on their length of service. This development had come despite vehement opposition from the line officers, who argued that 'rank' and the accompanying privileges was cheapened by the admission of non-military personnel. Rank indeed determined such things as the location and size of the holder's apartment on board ship, his position and presence at the wardroom table, and his relative position on entering or leaving the ship. Before rank was conferred officially, officer-like privileges were available to the individual medical person only at the behest or sufferance of the ship's captain. Surgeons were the first staff officers to break the line officers' stranglehold on military rank in the navy, and by the Civil War, they had reached a significant plateau: surgeons with fifteen years service held rank equivalent to captains.

The duties of the surgeon on the naval vessel were both managerial and medical. He was in charge of sick bays and medical store rooms and appointed attendants and nurses, with the number of the latter two determined by the complement of the vessel. He examined each member of the crew before a cruise and made daily reports thereafter on the condition of the sick on board. When provisions were obtained, he inspected both food and water for quality. When the vessel was readying for battle, he was to prepare, or supervise the steward, a place to receive and treat the wounded. During the battle, he provided immediate care for the casualties; in its aftermath, he prepared a casualty report and determined their long term needs. Finally, he evaluated the wounded who applied for pensions and arranged for sick or seriously wounded sailors to be transferred to the naval hospitals. Assistant surgeons were to perform the same duties if the surgeon was absent, and were to superintend the weighing and mixing of medicines.[18]

The paymaster, formerly called the purser, was the staff offi-

Assistant surgeon, 1862. Surgeons, as well as paymasters, engineers and chaplains, were long denied the rank commensurate with their profession. By the end of the Civil War the problem of 'assimilated rank' for staff officers was close to resolution. (The row of cuff buttons indicates an equivalent rank of master in the 1852 uniform regulations.) (US Navy)

cer in whose charge fell the entire fiscal operation of the naval vessel. His duties revolved around both money and the objects which it purchased. In addition to disbursing the men's pay, he controlled the purse when it came to supplies and provisions. Not only did he disburse payment, the paymaster inspected the goods, particularly provisions, as well as issued clothing and small stores to the seamen. Finally, he inspected store rooms, bread room and issue rooms for suitability and security. The assistant paymaster shared these duties and substituted for the senior officer when necessary.

Paymasters had received the privilege of assimilated rank shortly after the surgeons in the 1840s. By 1864, they were equivalent to lieutenant commanders, commanders or captains, depending, in five year increments, on their length of service. A board of three paymasters was required to promote an assistant paymaster to the higher rank.[19]

The advent of the steam engine added another category to the list of non-military staff on the warship. Unfortunately for their cause, the steam engineers were 'mere mechanics', men who worked with their hands and often looked the part, appearing on deck with oil and grease-sodden clothes and leaving a greasy trail on holystoned decks. And they were not necessarily the most genteel or educated of men, given the fact that most were indeed, self taught in the mysteries of the primitive steam engine and its boilers and appurtenances.

Assimilated rank came to the engineer corps in January, 1859, with chief engineers of more than twelve years service attaining the level of commanders and downwards to third asistant engineers who were equivalent to midshipmen. It should be noted that staff officers had no right to exercise command. While on duty, for instance, the commanding officer and executive officer, regardless of their rank, took precedence over the staff officer.[20]

While four new ranks were added to the service hierarchy during the war, the engineers were for a time left behind, until equivalents were re-established in 1863. At the same time the post of fleet engineer was established, with rank equivalent to a captain.[21]

The line-versus-staff controversy was not over by the end of the war, as far as the engineers were concerned. Other aspects still remained unsolved. Assistant engineers, for instance, held commissions more akin to warrants than to the line officer's and consequently were denied many of the privileges their nominal rank would have merited. Further, the post-war move to offer a limited number of regular commissions to exemplary volunteer line officers was not repeated for the benefit of staff officers. These and cutbacks in the use of steam in the peacetime navy tended to force the engineering staff into a defensive mode for much of the post-war decade.

In any event, the engineering corps saw a massive increase during the war, and well it should have, as all the navy's purpose built vessels and the vast majority of its wartime acquisitions were steam powered. The corps of engineers numbered 192 in 1861, in accordance with the mandated composition of the engineering staff of each steamer: one chief engineer, two first assistants, two second assistants, and three third assistants.

Fortunately, only twenty-two engineers departed with the seceding states — a small percentage compared to that of the line officers. A mass of volunteer engineers began to flood in to man the vessels of the blockade and those on the rivers. By the end of 1861 there were 404 engineers in the navy; by the end of the war, there were 2277. Of the latter, 474 were regulars and the remainder, volunteers.

The quality of these men was not on a par with their quantity. In fact, the engineering corps maintained high standards and stringent testing for its regular officers throughout the war, while requiring little of those who applied for volunteer service. One authority stated that 'almost anyone who could show a letter of recommendation' from an engineer or person of prominence could obtain an appointment as an acting assistant engineer.

Along with the merely competent and the outstanding new engineers were those for whom an appointment as 'acting third' with its $750 stipend was seen only as a suitable means to avoid the ranks of the marching army. Fortunately, the wartime regulations required from four to ten engineers on each steamer, thus minimizing the danger inherent in employing one of these unqualified men in an engine room. It was only when several of these incompetents were 'shuffled together' in one place that disaster struck.

Probably the most egregious example of official engineering incompetence occurred in a war steamer coming out of New York, apparently with a newly minted engineering crew aboard. After a few hours at sea, the engine stopped, then reversed of its own accord. No amount of cogitation amongst the engineers could determine the cause, and the commanding officer was obliged to sidle her back to the harbor stern first. At the yard the chief engineer was consulted and the problem solved in less than two minutes. In steam engineering terms, the 'eccentric had slipped'. Simply put, in a modern automotive context, the gear shift was in reverse.[22]

Navy regulations set forth the duties of both chief and assistant engineers. The former, of course, was the senior engineering officer on a steam vessel, and was responsible for all aspects, both mechanical and personnel related, of the engine and boiler room and related areas, such as paddle wheels, screw propeller, smoke pipe, hatches, etc.

The chief engineer set up schedules for his assistants: Watch, Quarter, Fire and Cleaning Bills, and saw to it they were posted prominently. He was to evaluate and institute training for the assistant engineers and firemen, supervise them on a daily basis, and submit a fitness report on each when he left the vessel or at the end of a cruise.

Of course, the chief was to familiarize himself with the intricacies and characteristics of the vessel's machinery. This would include knowledge of its capabilities under any conditions, with any type of coal or under adverse circumstances. In this connection, he was to evaluate the stores and quantity and quality of coal available for any given cruise and plan accordingly.

Reports made up a great part of his duties. When under way, he was expected to carry out the orders from the commanding officer on deck, and, if given an order which he felt would unduly strain the engine or cause a breakdown, inform the senior officer immediately, with reasons for his opinion. (Because few deck officers were trained in steam engineering, this aspect of the engineer's duty was particularly important during the Civil War era.) On a daily basis he was to give a report on the machinery to the commanding officer; on a quarterly basis, he was to make a more general report to accompany the quarterly synopsis of the steam log. This was to include, among other things, the number of revolutions turned, rate of coal consumption, maximum speed under steam in smooth water, horsepower attained, and the number of assistants, firemen and coal heavers aboard. He was encouraged to include in the latter any suggestions for bettering the efficiency of the vessel's machinery and appurtenances.

The welfare of his crew was under his purview, and was particularly critical in warm climates when the fires were up or at least banked continually. He was to check the temperature in the coal bunkers twice during each watch and report this to the officer of the deck. In extreme situations, under way, the firemen and coal heavers might be relieved at intervals shorter than their normal watch would require. As temperatures over 100°C were not unusual in the internals of the engine and boiler room, it was only humane to allow regular relief for the men.

In connection with this there was a rather unusual requirement: to provide oatmeal 'without charge, at such times and in such quantities as the Commanding Officer may direct' to coal heavers and firemen. This peculiar provision, found in the 1865 navy regulations, is of course not explained therein. It appears that there were two possible uses for oatmeal in this context. It was a long standing European custom to serve oatmeal with water to overheated men – a mixture thought to aid in keeping body temperature down. Second, a mixture of oatmeal and water could be added to the boiler water, and the meal would find its way to any leaks in the tubes, and the bloated mass would temporarily stanch the flow.

The assistant engineers were expected to step in if the senior engineer was absent. However, their normal duties were more intimately involved with the actual operation of the engine, and less managerial in character. The assistants' tasks ranged from lubricating the journals to keeping the actual steam log, which they had to update hourly.

Promotion in the engineering, at least in the regular, non-acting ranks was contingent on sea service, plus performance on examinations. The test material for promotion to second assistant engineer was the basis for tests for the higher grades and covered familiarity with various types of valve gear, the principles of expansive use of steam, the construction and peculiarities of various types of boilers and condensers in naval use, and the rudiments of mechanics, along with practical application of skills in the operation and repair of engines, boilers and appurtenances. Two years at sea as a third assistant were a prerequisite to promotion to second assistant engineer; three years as a second to go on to first assistant. The test for first assistant added sections on the theory of the steam engine, the use of logarithms and algebra, Euclidean geometry, trigonometry, the ability to draw any given part of a steam engine and superintend its construction, and general knowledge of the principles and use of paddle wheels and screw propellers.

The chief engineering position required at least two years experience at sea at the previous grade, plus testimonials by other senior engineers and officers, and an examination upgraded from those for the lower grades. This was to include mechanical philosophy, physical laws of steam, types of steam engines and their advantages and drawbacks, and be able to erect a steam engine in a given vessel. Chemistry and metallurgy and the laws of combustion and corrosion were also in the examination materials. As can be seen, the chief engineer was expected to be a professional in every sense of the word.[23]

The position of chaplain was equivalent to a commander or lieutenant commander, with the dividing line between the grades at twelve years in the service. Applicants were to be no more than thirty-five years old or less than twenty-one, be ordained in 'some religious denomination' and be 'of unimpeached character'. A physical examination was required but not a professional one. It is noteworthy that there was, in the mid nineteenth-century United States, no question of non-Christians in the chaplaincy; it was an era when Americans even looked askance at 'Romish' Catholics.

In addition to officiating at divine service and funerals, they were to give 'Christian instruction' to the ship's boys and supervise their education. With the permission of the medical officer they were to visit the sick and 'afford consolation'.

The lot of the chaplain at sea was not to be envied. Doing the work of an evangelist among men long enured to hardships and thoroughly self-sufficient – and usually derisive of religion – would have been daunting to all but those certain of their own calling and spiritual strength. In any case, there were very few in the service, and they were mainly on larger vessels or at the yards. In 1862, sixteen were on the active list, only two of which were at sea. Only twenty-one were active at the close of the war.[24]

# Chapter Nine

# THE CIVIL WAR MARINE CORPS

**M**arines in formation, USS *Hartford*, 1877. The marines' primary function has always been ship-board police. Only in the twentieth century have they gained major military roles ashore. As shown here, the marine guard has always been a perquisite of the senior naval officer on board. (US Navy)

The popularly assigned and cultivated image of the United States Marine Corps is largely constructed around this storied service's activities since the turn of the twentieth century. Probably the most notable early example of the 'Marines have landed...' to catch the national eye was the defense and relief of the Peking legations during the Boxer 'rebellion' in 1900. The Marine Corps today basks in an elitist reputation burnished by two World Wars and innumerable small expeditions to rescue beleaguered Americans in hostile lands. Certainly the 'John Wayne' image was a product of the Pacific operations in the Second World War.

The contrast between the self-perpetuating legend of the modern marines and that of their Civil War predecessors is stark. There seem to be but two common elements. First is their small numbers, though of course the present service is significantly larger in proportion to the other branches than it was in the nineteenth century. Second is their original and continuing role; providing guards and security on board ships of the navy.

There were marines on US naval vessels as early as 1775 – before the Declaration of Independence – and those units were in turn patterned on the British marines, which were permanently established in the mid seventeenth century. The marines as a type appeared the century before, and were simply men trained for infantry combat, under the complete control of the admiralty.

The first marines under the re-constituted US Navy followed the examples and roles of their colonial and royal naval predecessors. First, in an age when the naval crews were often made up of the least acceptable stata of society, a force was necessary to literally protect the officers from the crew. Second, in battle the

Ashore, the marines have traditionally guarded US naval installations. In this instance, two uniformed marines man the gates at Boston Navy Yard in 1874. (US Navy)

marines manned the fighting tops, assigned to pick off the adversary's officers. Third, when needed, the marines provided extra bodies to man the broadside guns. This last probably provided the basis for the size of the marine contingent on a given vessel — roughly one marine per gun.

The original act establishing the unit called for thirty-three officers and 880 enlisted men. The enlisted men included drummers and fifers, thirty-two of each. The corps was designed to provide contingents for thirty-two vessels, as well as detachments to guard public property, including navy yards.

The governance of the corps was somewhat ambiguous. Ashore, they fell under the army's Articles of War; at sea, they obeyed navy regulations. This situation was corrected in the 1830s when shore marines were put under naval jurisdiction. Throughout this era, marine officers were always subordinated to naval officers at sea. The marines were paid significantly less than the sailors, and marginally less than their army counterparts.

The duties of the marine guard on board early naval vessels were set by the individual commanding officers, with Captain Thomas Truxtun on the *Constellation* issuing the most detailed instructions. The marines were to muster with the crew at general quarters, drill under arms twice daily, practice musketry and tac-

tics, and keep their arms, uniforms and equipment clean, with daily inspections. With the master-at-arms, they were to patrol the vessel and prevent unauthorized fires and movement among the crew. They were expected to go ashore on 'certain Enterprizes during an Expedition or Cruize [sic]' where their military training would be utilized, and, of course, they were to man the fighting tops and form a defense against boarding in battle.

The early years of the corps were not the stuff of their later legend. The low pay and lack of enlistment bounties kept their numbers down and their uncertain role in relation to the sailors led to their misuse by commanders at sea. These factors led to tensions between both officer and enlisted ranks of each branch on board ship, as well as serious attempts, particularly in peacetime, to disband the corps and to train sailors in their stead.

The survival of the US Marine Corps can be attributed to both tenacious leadership and the presence of marines in critical and high profile events in the ensuing decades. The latter events, both in peace and war, served to bolster the arguments for the utility of the corps in either milieu.

The fame of the corps was not, of course, found in their primary assigned duties as ship guards and shipboard infantry. The role of ship guard was mere routine — necessary but un-remarkable. As to the importance of musketry in ship-to-ship engagements, on American naval vessels the emphasis was on overwhelming broadside firepower, resulting in relatively few extended point blank slugging matches. Rather than marines picking off the enemy's leadership on the quarterdeck, the 32-pounders demolished the gundeck. Grappling and boarding were, consequently, less common in these circumstances. When it did occur, particularly in actions with the Barbary powers, the marines were quite effective.

In any event, the corps found its niche on shore — in war or peace. As early as 1804, and with increasing regularity, foreign and domestic shores provided them with theatres on which to perform their ship-borne infantry role.

During the wars with the Barbary powers a contingent went ashore in North Africa in one of the earliest, and most unusual, actions in all of the American foreign military operations. Marines formed a small part of an informal army of mercenaries and North Africans which marched 600 miles across the desert to overthrow the troublesome Bashaw of Tripoli. With naval gunfire support, a Tripolitan fort was subdued and a marine ran up the American flag. John Greenleaf Whittier immortalized the action in verse and the marines received plaudits in the press.

The 'shores of Tripoli' gave way to marines-as-infantry participation in battles from the War of 1812 through the Mexican War. Often, the 'glory' they imbibed exceeded their actual accomplishments, which had little impact on the overall course of the campaign or engagement itself.

The Battle of Bladensburg in 1814 was an example of the latter. A marine and naval force, along with local militia, attempted to stem the British advance towards Washington in what is now a northeastern suburb of the capital city. Though greatly outnumbered, the marines and sailors held their ground and in fact beat off British attacks until the militia dispersed and left them without support. This was the only substantial resistance to the British advance on the city and the subsequent burning of the public buildings there. It was not until afterwards that the marines and sailors found themselves hailed as heroes of the hour in a city hard pressed for good news.

In the 1830s and 1840s marine battalions were offered to the War Department for Indian campaigns in the southeast – Georgia and Florida. This marked a new phenomenon for the service: these units, often 300 to 400 hundred men, were raised from the marine barracks in the various navy yards, rather than from naval vessels, and operated independently of naval command.

An equally independent marine battalion was attached to the army as it invaded the interior of Mexico in 1847. Though originally in a support role, the unit, in the confusion of battle, found itself among those taking the gates of the castle of Chapultepec, Mexico City. After the conquest, marines were detailed to provost duty in the city, based, some say, on the fact that their uniforms, with their crossed white belts, were less soiled and more impressive than the army's.

Though the actual sequence of events in the assaults, and the question of whether the marines took the gates before the army arrived, remain shrouded in the battle's confusion, the legend of the marines and 'the halls of Montezuma' was given another stanza.

On the domestic front, the marines also gained a reputation as a force in being, quickly available for emergency duty. As early as 1824, a detachment of thirty was called to put down a Massachusetts prison riot and did so without firing a shot. In the next decades they were called out to put down a riot in Washington DC, end a slave revolt in Virginia, and patrol a fire-ravaged New York City. These and other incidents placed the marines in a favorable light with the general public, which in turn served to justify the existence of a marine presence on shore as well as aboard naval vessels.[1]

The Civil War ultimately produced little of lasting effect on the marine corps. Beyond the significant increase in force levels little changed during the conflict. Marine missions remained limited to ship and yard guards and battalion sized augmentations to army or navy land contingents. Though a significant part of the Union war effort involved amphibious-type assaults, there was never any serious consideration of expanding the marine mission to such roles. On the contrary, some felt that utilizing marines in this way would detract from the marines' seagoing character and, as one authority stated: 'risk amalgamation with the Army.'

As with the navy, the marines' single most serious non-combat difficulty was obtaining the number of recruits for the duties they were required to perform. As the numbers of naval vessels skyrocketed, the need for shipboard marines grew in proportion.

Congress authorized increases in marine strength in 1861 and 1863. In the former instance, ninety-three officers and 3074 enlisted were the upper limits – about twice the pre-war strength. By war's end, the numbers were eighty-seven officers and 3774 men.

Attaining these goals proved exceedingly problematic. First, until 1864, the marines had no enlistment bounty program like that of the army. Second, marine recruits were not credited to local draft quotas. The result of these factors was reflected in the numbers: though authorized a total of 3074 in 1861, marines numbered only 2355 in June 1862. A year later, with their authorized strength at 3600, there were less than 3000 in the ranks, despite lowering the minimum age.[2]

Only the February 1864 conscription act ameliorated the recruiting dilemma by counting marine enlistments toward local quotas. Several large cities also began offering bounties to marine enlistees about this time. Furthermore, given the massive casualty lists of the army's 1864 Virginia campaigns, it may well have been considered safer to be a marine. In any event, these factors finally placed the marine and navy recruiting programs somewhat on a par with the army's.

In the officer ranks, the leanest times were at the war's outbreak. Of a total of sixty-three in October 1860, twenty defected to the Confederacy, nineteen of which were company grade officers. By early the next year, thirty-eight new second lieutenants were in service. This filled the numerical – though not the experiential – gaps in the ranks.[3]

The upper echelon of marine officers had nearly the opposite problem of advanced age. Most of the leadership were in their sixties. The Colonel Commandant at the outbreak of the war was

John Harris, in his early sixties, who was commissioned during the War of 1812 and had last seen combat in the Seminole wars. In itself this tendency towards a higher average age was not a fatal deficiency. However, of the senior officers, only two had served as battalion commanders in the field; the remainder saw themselves as administrators only and contributed little else to the corps during the conflict. (When Harris died in 1864, he was replaced by Jacob Zeilin, aged fifty-nine, who had at least seen battalion service in the Mexican conflict.)[4]

At sea and in the field were the two facets of Marine Corps' participation in the war. As ship guards the marines had a continuous but obviously limited role, with small numbers participating in most, if not all, the naval actions of the conflict. Ashore, marine battalions were organized on an as-needed basis and usually operated in concert with army or navy units, or both. Few were involved in the major pitched battles, and there were no independent marine battalion operations. Between these extremes were the typical landing parties which punctuated normal operations both on the coasts and on the rivers. These usually consisted of both marines and seamen and had no major strategic significance or results.

Battalion operations for the corps began and ended with conspicuous failure. In between, their accomplishments were of little consequence in the overall wartime picture.

Bull Run, the first major battle – and Union loss – of the war had no laurels for the marine battalion involved. Some 336 were in the unit, none of which were over three weeks into their enlistment. Only six officers had seen combat at all. Only the naivety of the times – the common expectation that the Rebels would run at the first sight of an artillery piece – can explain the high expectations implicit when Secretary Welles volunteered this group.

The outcome of First Bull Run was of course an ignominious rout of the Union force, most of which were as inexpert as the marine contingent. It would have been auspicious if the leathernecks had 'held the line' in their inimitable fashion, but that was not to be. Placed in line with artillery and New York regiments, they found themselves under heavy fire at short range, then fell out – with the New Yorkers – under a Confederate light cavalry charge. The marine retreat preceded the general debacle by three hours. Their losses numbered forty-one killed, wounded or missing.[5]

The battalion had little opportunity to recoup its reputation in the following months. Refitted and retrained, Flag Officer Samuel Dupont had them attached to the South Atlantic

The Civil War saw the marines increase in number and participate in relatively large units in cooperation with the army. In some instances the marine guard contingents at the yards – the group at Washington Navy Yard is shown here – were called together to form a brigade. There was a brigade at First Bull Run, though they were new recruits and did not give a good account of themselves. (USAMHI)

Blockading Squadron as a source of infantry under direct navy control. In the six months of their existence, from October 1861 to March 1862, they had little to do. Confederate resistance in coastal forts melted after a naval cannonade, and the marines only role was as caretakers until the army arrived in force.

Later brigade- and battalion-sized combat operations occurred at Fort Sumter (1863), Fort Fisher (1864) and in the South Carolina lowlands. Only the latter could be considered a success, and that a limited one.

At Fort Sumter, a battalion of one hundred men and six officers was amalgamated with ships' guards and sailors, totalling some 450, in a night-time boat attack on the fort. Nothing, it seems, went right in this assault. Twenty boats were towed by steamer to the jumping off point; only seven actually found their way to the beach. The remainder – half of which were to land in a second location – either remained unengaged or were driven off by the fire of an enemy steamer. Those who landed found, instead of the expected upward slope to the fort, a well defended vertical wall. They found themselves targets of guns, grenades, and an occasional brick. The enfilading fire of the Confederate ironclad *Chicora* soon added to the above hazards. All this while the men were illuminated by a well-directed locomotive headlight. Four of the seven boats were extricated; the others were destroyed on the beach. Some one hundred men were captured, of which forty-one were marines. One marine was mortally wounded. It should be noted that the marines were not responsible for planning or executing this disaster.[6]

The assault on Fort Fisher, North Carolina, the last major Confederate coastal fortification, in January 1865, again saw the marines forming part of a combined landing force. In this instance it totalled about 2000 men, 400 of which were marines. They were to assault one bastion, while the army attacked a second and the navy shelled the remainder of the fortification. The attack, with the seamen armed with only cutlasses and pistols, was at least 800 yards across an open beach. As a survivor, Robley Evans (later Admiral Evans), described it: 'About five hundred yards... the column sudden stopped, and as if by magic, the whole mass of men went down like a row of falling bricks...at about three hundred yards, they again went down, this time under the effect of canister...'. A 'hail of lead' finally dissolved the assault at the base of the parapet. Casualties were severe, with some 61 of the 386 being marines. Thirty-five marines and sailors were awarded the congressional Medal of Honor in this action. Marines were later criticized for failing to provide sufficient cover for the poorly armed sailors.[7]

In the aftermath, it was claimed that the navy-marine assault provided a significant diversion, enabling the ultimate triumph of the army force over the defenders, but this apparently was an attempt to put the best face on an admitted fiasco.

Probably the only major naval-marine brigade action to avoid opprobrium occurred in the lowlands of South Carolina in 1864. A force of 500, including 150 marines, was detached from the South Atlantic Blockading Squadron and joined an army unit to force their way to the Charleston-Savannah railway and cut that artery. They were to establish contact with General William T Sherman's army coming from Atlanta – the famous 'March to the Sea'. From 29 November through 26 December 1864, the brigade was in nearly continuous contact with the enemy, though in what might be termed low intensity operations. The battles of Honey Hill, Tulifinny Crossroads, and Derang's Neck were fought, but with little effect, given the unit's lack of sufficient artillery. In the end, the brigade was re-shipped without destroying the railway or meeting Sherman. Twenty-two marines were lost in this unnecessary campaign.[8]

For better or worse, two other marine brigade incidents should be mentioned. In late 1862, the steamer *Ariel* was taken by the Confederate cruiser *Alabama*. On board was a battalion of marines en route to California. The *Ariel*'s captain surrendered his vessel, as

**O**n board ship, marines were commonly used to fill in when there were insufficient sailors to make up a gun crew. In many instances, marines were given a gun of their own. Shown here is the marine crew of the *Kearsarge*'s 30-pounder Dahlgren rifle. They were cited for their effectiveness in the confrontation with the *Alabama*. From Hobson's *Famous Cruise of the Kearsarge*.

well as the marines. And, in late 1863, the marines were detailed to restore order after the New York City draft riot. They proved competent and disciplined in this endeavour.[9]

Had the marines' Civil War reputation been built upon their role onboard ship, rather than on the results of their shore large-unit operations, the overall result would have been an ornament to their history.

Some ninety to one hundred naval vessels had marine guards, usually only the larger vessels – those which rated higher ranking commanding officers, and on high seas cruisers likely to call at foreign ports. There were none on the majority of the vessels, which in most instances were lightly armed merchantmen converted for blockade work.

In general, the marines' duties varied little from tradition. However, the practice of using marines to fill in at individual broadside guns when there was a manpower shortage saw a significant change. This was replaced by assigning guns to all-marine crews (as set forth officially in the naval regulations of April 1865). Again, this was probably the result of a shortage of personnel, but, as has been noted, during this war the scarcity of naval manpower was a persistent one and it was rare for any vessel to be at full complement. Although there were some objections to all-marine gun crews, in general it was received positively, and resulted in a bit of friendly gun-handling competition between the sailors and marines. Of course, individual marines were also assigned to gun crews when necessary, particularly on smaller vessels.[10]

There were marine gun crews in most, if not all, of the major naval engagements of the war. On *Kearsarge*, her 30-pounder rifle was marine-manned when she sank the raider *Alabama* in 1864; on Farragut's flagship *Hartford*, marines manned two of her broadside guns in the Battle of Mobile Bay. Of seventeen Medals of Honor awarded to marines during the war, thirteen were to members of gun crews, and it appears that in general the marines deported themselves well and with considerable elan in this role.[11]

To clarify a point, there was another 'Marine Brigade' associated with the Union forces on the western rivers. This unit had no connection with the marine corps, but was part of the War Department and their vessels were manned by army officers. It was a mixture of cavalry, artillery and infantry and attempted to inhibit Confederate guerilla activity against Union forces on the rivers (See next chapter).

Wartime marine losses were 148 officers and men killed in action. Probably the largest loss in battle occurred at the Fort Fisher debacle in 1865, where there were sixty-one killed, wounded or missing. Other non-battle marine deaths totalled 312.[12]

On balance, despite their poor showing in pitched battle, the marines exited the war with their image and circumstances relatively intact. The service had even survived an 1864 congressional resolution to merge it with the army. Vessel commanders remained insistent that the marine guard was a necessary part of the complement, in spite of the wartime evidence that the lack of such a guard (the situation on most vessels) did not lead to disorder and mutiny, and in the face of the long standing argument that they were merely ceremonial and as such, superfluous. In any event, though the corps was reduced with the coming of peace, the reduction was simply in proportion to the downsizing of the navy itself, with the personnel totals eventually reaching pre-war levels.

# Uniforms and Equipment

From the first, marine uniforms were distinct from their naval brothers. Certainly this was calculated to reinforce their shipboard police role, as well as the military aspect of their duties. Consequently, their dress was patterned after army practice, rather than the traditional seagoing bell-bottoms and jumpers.

Revolutionary War marine uniforms were distinguished by a green coat with white facings and silver buttons, plus a three-cornered hat. Facings were later changed to red, a color which recurred regularly through the many evolutions of their dress. It

should be noted that a black leather stock appeared early on, a peculiarity which engendered the marine's 'leatherneck' appellation. Though the stock was standard men's neckwear of the era, it was in stark contrast to the seaman's open collar.

The re-constituted 1797 marines were dressed in blue coats with red facings, and blue remained the predominant hue until 1834 when green was again prescribed. This reverted again to blue five years later, and has been retained, at least for dress uniforms, ever since. An exception to blue were the bandsmen's coats, which were red. The latter, worn with white belts, facings, and trousers, as well as a surfeit of gold buttons and lace, was sufficiently martial even for European tastes. It is noteworthy that such display, particularly in conjunction with equally brass-bound naval shipboard ceremony contributed to much criticism of the corps. Many charged that this pomp and circumstance was the 'real' reason the ranking naval officers, particularly those on foreign station, fought to retain their marines.

The marine's Civil War uniform was based on 1859 regulations, which in turn were developed from those of 1841. The full dress officer's coat was the basic blue frock, with two rows of eight 'large size Marine buttons' on each breast, and standing collar. The Colonel Commandant was authorized to wear the breast buttons arranged in pairs. Gold lace loops and buttons (two per side) decorated the collar, which was also piped in scarlet. Gold loops and small buttons also adorned the cuffs, with four of each indicating the Colonel Commandant and field officers, three for captains, and two for lieutenants. The skirts of the coat were to have two decorative 'pockets', with the vertically arranged flaps edged in red and each secured with three buttons, at top, middle and lower corners.

Dress trousers were sky blue, dark blue or white. Officers not serving with troops were authorized the dark blue; white was warm weather wear. A scarlet welt on the outside seam was to be sewn on dark blue and sky blue officer's pants, as well as on those of sergeant majors, quartermaster sergeants, and bandsmen.

Headgear varied with rank in full dress uniform. A 'French Pattern' chapeau was worn by the Commandant and field officers, with a yellow swan feather plume for the former and red cock or vulture feathers for the latter. On the front was a black velvet cockade and gold lace loop with a marine button.

Lower grade officers wore a French style medium height cap – a high, stiff version of the kepi – with forward tilted crown and small straight visor. A gold 2-inch diameter pompon was fixed by a wire to the fore part of the crown. The cap device, which measured about 4 inches high, was a bugle with the old English letter

**F**irst lieutenant, US Marines, service dress uniform. The marines were unique in their early use of shoulder knots. Note the bugle and 'M' kepi insignia. (US Navy)

'M' in its center, superimposed on a floral bordered United States shield, all within a half wreath. (The corps' familiar eagle, globe and anchor device was not developed until 1868.)

With the full dress uniform, officers wore ankle boots, white gloves and sash. The latter was buff for the Colonel Commandant and crimson for other officers. On 'officer of the day' duty, the sash was worn from right shoulder to left side.

Epaulets were gold and decorated with the corps device as described with the cap above. Silver rank insignia was on the strap and consisted of a star for the Commandant, an eagle for line colonel, silver leaf for lieutenant colonel, two bars for a captain, and one bar for a lieutenant. Majors and second lieutenants had no rank devices. The diameter of the epaulet fringe was larger for field officers; and lieutenant's fringe was shorter than that of the higher grades.

The officer's undress uniform was distinguished by a fatigue hat (the kepi), Russian style shoulder knots, and the frock coat minus collar and cuff lace loops. The hat device in this instance was the bugle and 'M' combination, with gold bugle and silver let-

ter, all on a scarlet cloth. The kepi's crown was decorated with a braid knot in quatrefoil pattern. The shoulder knots were of four cords for senior officers, three for captains and below, and were lined with scarlet cloth showing through the openings. Rank devices were as described for the epaulets. For summer, a white linen fatigue coat was authorized, made like the blue winter coat.

Additionally, there was a waist length, scarlet lined, fatigue jacket with shoulder knots for undress wear. This was single breasted, with sixteen small buttons down the front. The high collar and pointed cuffs were edged with ½-inch gold lace.

For cold climes a loose-sleeved 'coat cloak' was authorized. For officers, this was dark blue, lined with scarlet wool, fastened in front with four frogs. Black silk braid knots on the lower sleeves indicated rank. A black-lined cape could also be worn over the coat.

Unlike the army, the marine corps' full dress enlisted uniform coat was basically the same as that of the officer: a blue, double-breasted frock coat with standing collar. As with the officer coat, the collar had two lace loops with a button on each. Again there were loops and buttons on the cuffs: three for sergeant majors, and two for sergeants and below. Edges of the collar, sleeve slashes and skirt 'pocket flaps' were red. A red sash was authorized for first sergeants, sergeant majors and bandsmen.

As mentioned above, the bandsmen – drum majors and musicians – wore a red version of the frock coat. White substituted for red edging on this uniform for collars, etc.

Chevrons denoted rank on the uniform coat, and corresponded to army grades and designations. Chevrons were yellow silk lace on a scarlet ground, with three and an arc for the sergeant major, three and a tie for the quartermaster sergeant, and three and a tie with star in the center for the drum major. Sergeants and corporals had yellow worsted lace chevrons, again edged in red. Sergeants had three chevrons; first sergeants had a lozenge added below the chevrons. Corporals had two chevrons; privates, none.

Trousers were sky blue or, in warm weather, white. Musicians and sergeant majors and quartermaster sergeants wore a scarlet cord down the outer seam.

The full dress uniform cap was basically the same as the officer's, but with a 'bright' rather than gilt device. The pompon was to be red, 5 inches in circumference. The drum major wore a lambskin astrakhan with an even more imposing pompon.

The enlisted man's epaulets were unique to this service and were a combination of yellow metal crescent and scale strap with a removable bullion fringe. The object of this was to allow cleaning of the metal. Oddly enough, the scales were charged out to the

**M**arine enlisted uniforms of the Civil War era. Note the high French style kepi with elaborate wreath. Within the wreath was that era's marine device: a floral bordered US shield with bugle and 'M' in the center. Crossed white belts, epaulets and pompon on the hat were additional uniform distinctives. The marines have had a long history of remarkable uniforms. (USAMHI)

The most distinctive item in the marine's outfit was easily the crossed belts — a rarity in American military uniforms and most often occurring in ornate ceremonial band units. These were 2¼-inch wide white leather diagonals, with slightly narrower waist belt. Cartridge box, bayonet scabbard and cap pouch were suspended from the right, left, and waist belt respectively. An army eagle-pattern breast plate decorated the crossing of the belts; a convex brass waist plate, and a sword frog completed the regalia. It appears that under combat conditions, narrower, black leather versions of these belts were substituted.

Other accoutrements included a knapsack, haversack (or 'bread bag'), and canteen. The latter two were generally based on army quartermaster patterns or transferred directly from army stores, and were issued to the individual only when required. The knapsack was an elaborate, two-compartment item, unique to the marines; painted black and stencilled 'USM'.[13]

Marine corps long arms were regulation US Army weapons. The 1855 rifle musket was standard early in the war: a 56-inch long, .58 caliber muzzleloader with 18-inch bayonet and Maynard tape primer. These were made at Harpers Ferry and Springfield armories, as well as by contract with E Whitney at New Haven, Connecticut.

Later, Model 1863 and 1864 rifle muskets were issued. These differed from the earlier model in eliminating the Maynard priming mechanism and adding a spring to secure the ramrod.

It does not appear that there was an issued firearm for the officers. Navy-model Colt revolvers were known to have been carried, as well as pre-war single-shot muzzleloaders, such as the Model 1855 pistol-carbine. The latter was .58 caliber and equipped with a detachable rifle stock.

The army-pattern Model 1850 foot officer's sword was authorized as standard in the 1859 regulations. This weapon was 36 to 37 inches long with brass hilt and Phrygian helmet pommel. Grips were wood, covered with fish skin and wrapped with wire. The scabbard was black leather and brass. It should be noted that marine officers had, from the 1820s to 1859, carried a sword with Mameluke style hilt — without handguard basketwork. This item was brought back in the 1875 regulations and is now the traditional marine dress sword. Enlisted non-commissioned officers also carried the 1850 army pattern sword, but with a frog stud on the scabbard, rather than suspending rings. Bandsmen carried the army 1840 pattern NCO musician's sword, a straight-bladed weapon with brass hilt and grips, about 34 inches long.[14]

marine and returned at the termination of his enlistment — along with weapons and equipment. The diameter of the bullion on these epaulets increased with the wearer's rank.

The enlisted man's undress coat was a single-breasted kersey frock coat with seven-button front and standing collar with a red welt on the seam between collar and coat. Two small buttons decorated the cuffs and two additional were on the hips. A four-button fatigue sack coat was also available which was somewhat shorter than the undress coat and unlined. This lightweight garment was for service at sea and shore parties. The undress or fatigue hat was the kepi with bugle and 'M' device. A blue-gray overcoat with detachable cape and fastened with seven large buttons was issued for winter wear.

# Chapter Ten
# SHIPHANDLING UNDER STEAM AND SAIL

In contrast to the centuries in which the pure sailing vessel dominated the seaways and navies, the transition from sail to engine
power took up some sixty years, roughly covering the period 1820
to 1880. By the later date the sailing steamship was being margin-
alized by increasingly powerful ships with significantly more economical engines. By the late 1880s, even the navies of the world
had deleted the sailing rig on all but their colonial cruising vessels,
testimony to the fact that steam power had come to a point where
it could stand alone, without the need for an auxiliary sailing rig.

This short period in which the somewhat uncomfortable
amalgam of sails and steam power pre-dominated may explain
the dearth of major source materials dedicated to the handling

Sidewheel steamer *Mississippi*. Paddle wheels and sail formed an
uneasy alliance. Note the location of the funnel on this ship —
precisely where the main mast should have been. Though a
reliable steamer, she was a 'clumsy ship' under steam and sail.
From Stuart's *Naval and Mail Steamers of the United States.*

of these mixed-power vessels. For example, the seamanship
textbooks of the era rarely devoted significant space to the
subject. As late as the 1870s and 1880s, Stephen B Luce's various editions of his lengthy and detailed seamanship manual
included no more than forty pages so dedicated. Of course,
there has been little need for modern writers to broach the
subject at all. Hence, the following is not comprehensive by
any means, but is simply a digest of the material that is available from various widely scattered sources.

Because the subject of shiphandling under sail alone is a common item, I will concentrate here on the sail-plus-steam aspect. At
the other end of the spectrum, steam power without the benefit of
sails will be presented here only in the context of paddle-wheel
river operations.

The paddle-wheel warship was in vogue for barely half of the
transitional era. The sidewheel steamer obviously introduced
unique elements, and not all of them positive, to shiphandling.

Unlike the submerged screw, paddle wheels operated on the
surface of the water. Their efficiency was a function of such factors as the draft of the vessel, the sea and wind conditions, and
the angle of the blades' entry and exit from the water. As with
screw steamers, the windage presented by the vessel's sailing rig
was also a major consideration.

An 1851 engineer's report on the sidewheel frigate *Mississippi*
elucidated the windage problem with square-rigged vessels:

'The spars and sails of the "Mississippi" are too large; if they
were reduced to the proper size, her speed would be augment-

ed more than one knot per hour.... The engines not only have her vast hull to propel, but the great surface of spars.... When the winds are fair, a six knot breeze is required before the sails are of any use...conjointly with steam power; if the winds are strong, a large spread of canvas is dangerous. In a storm only a sufficient quantity is necessary to steady the ship, and this will of course be fore and aft sails. With light fair winds, the power of the engines will bring light airs ahead thus a steamer will most of the time have light airs ahead, or occasionally aft, but not in sufficient force to make her sails effective...the mainsail cannot be carried – the main topsail has seldom been used – steering sails have been useless – fore topsail useful – top-gal-lantsails seldom – fore-topmast staysail, and jib, useful. The useful sails are fore and main trysails, fore-topmast stay-sail, and jib, and occasionally, the spanker, with effect. With mod-erate, or fresh breezes ahead, the top-gallant masts are neces-sarily sent down; in strong head winds, lower yards and top-masts are also sent down. In fine weather, all these spars are again sent up to improve the appearance of the ship.'[1]

The engineer proceeded to note another drawback of paddle-wheel vessels as sailing ships. The main problem with the typical paddle-wheel design was the location of the main mast: the paddle wheel with its cross shaft, machinery and boilers, was of necessity where the main mast should have been located. Therefore, on the *Mississippi*, it was aft of the vessel's center of motion. Thus the main mast sails were exceedingly inefficient, except with the wind directly aft. The *Mississippi* was, for all the above reasons, 'a clumsy ship, hardly capable of handling herself', concluded the engineer.[2]

The paddle wheels and their 'floats' provided other sources of inefficiency. First, the floats were at their most efficient at the mid-point of the vessel's draft: if she was riding high the floats provid-ed little purchase on the water; if she was heavily laden, the paddles were overworked by the dragging of the paddle wheel arms and other non-essentials. Thus, the paddle wheel immersion would vary significantly in the course of a cruise. And, if the ship was under sail, there was the normal heel to leeward, giving that paddle more depth than that on the windward side.

Cross seas or winds created further difficulties. The rolling of the vessel in cross or quartering seas would put the paddle wheels in at differing intervals creating a 'corkscrew' effect on the vessel's direc-tion, and certainly creating discomfort for the crew. Heavy rolling could also bring one paddle completely out of the water. Furthermore, strong cross winds tended to catch under the wind-

**M**ississippi **in a typhoon. Rough weather aggravated shiphandling with sidewheels. In a cross wind the lee paddle would bury itself, while the windward wheel would often be raised totally out of the water to windmill uselessly. From** *Narrative of an American Squadron to the China Seas and Japan.*

ward paddle wheel housing, forcing the lee paddle farther into the sea. At the same time, with much of the efficacious engine power operating on the lee wheel and the windward wheel impotent, the vessel would be constantly driven up into the wind, giving her an excessive weather helm and thus making her nearly unmanageable. Only setting sail forward or shifting weights to windward could ameliorate this condition. All such uneven pressures on the paddles had detrimental effects on the engines as well as on forward progress.

When operating under sail alone, the paddle wheels were obvi-ous impediments to progress. Even when allowed to rotate freely, their drag was significant. Some ships' commanding officers oper-ated the engines at slow simply to facilitate progress, though this was wasteful of precious fuel. Another solution was to eliminate the drag altogether by detaching the lower floats altogether. This, however, was a dangerous task for the seamen, particularly in any kind of seaway.[3]

These problems coupled with the inconvenience of the side-wheeler's divided gundeck and vulnerable wheels and machinery, contributed to the service's search for a power delivery mechanism to replace the paddle wheel. The development of the screw pro-peller served to end the dominance of paddle-wheel warships. We will return to the paddle wheel in the discussion of riverboat operation below.

# Ship handling under screw propeller and sails

## Getting under way

In preparation for getting under way, steam was raised in the boilers. From lighting the fire to availability of adequate steam took up to two hours with anthracite coal; bituminous coal and forced draft could reduce this significantly. With banked fires, only twenty minutes were needed to spread them and generate useful steam. Unless planning to proceed under sail, the square sails were unnecessary in getting under way, but head sails and spanker were readied if needed to bring the vessel's head around to the desired course.

Once the cat block and fish hook were readied, the 'Up anchor' command was given and the capstan crew set to work. If necessary, to break out the anchor, the propeller was given a few turns ahead, but increased speed was delayed until the anchor was safely catted. When at a close berth, the stationary vessel could be turned outward by putting the helm hard over and going ahead slowly. The resulting water pressure on the rudder made the latter something of a pivot, turning the ship as if she were going ahead.

## Proceeding under sail and steam

When going ahead fast under steam alone, the direction of the wind was deceptive, with the forward motion imparted by the engine making it appear that the wind was farther ahead than it truly was. The first step was to determine, with a 'feeler' – the outer jib, trysail, or spanker – the true wind direction. If these stood well, the other fore and aft sails – jibs, staysails and trysails – could be employed. If the wind drew aft, the foresail could be brought on, then the other square sails. Only the mainsail was an exception, due to the location of the smokestack. Also, a watch was kept on the main topmast staysail to prevent its catching fire from exhaust sparks.

To reduce sail, and proceed under steam alone, the engineer was first notified to get up steam. If the vessel had a telescoping stack, it was raised; if her propeller was uncoupled from the shaft or raised out of the water for sailing, it was re-coupled or lowered into position. The latter operation, depending on the type of raising and lowering mechanism used, could require thirty minutes or more. When steam was up, the mainsail was hauled up and furled, fire buckets were sent aloft, and the remaining sails were taken in.

While under steam, care was taken to prevent ropes from towing overboard and fouling the propeller. The same caution was needed when heaving the lead. To reduce windage, as noted above, yards and upper masts were often sent down, depending on the strength and direction of the wind. Yards which remained were braced up sharp or pointed into the wind.

## Heaving to in bad weather

This was done head to the seas without sails, using a sea anchor, and operating the engines ahead slow. Under sail, the steam vessel, which was usually longer than a sailing ship, required a larger spread of sail to maintain position and steerageway with close reefed main topsail, main trysail, and storm mizzen or reefed spanker. Of course, sending down light yards and masts under these conditions was standard practice under sail or steam.

## Tacking under sail and steam

If the vessel was going ahead fast, she would have to slow before luffing around, preventing extreme strains on the fore and aft stays when the sails went aback. With engines running, the propeller-generated water pressure on the rudder easily brought the ship around and through the wind to the other tack.

In general, as steam engines became more efficient, the square-rigged steamer fell into more disfavor, as the rig was labor intensive and obtrusive. Also, wind conditions were rarely such that both power sources could be used together efficiently. As early as 1838, shiphandling manuals noted that under steam and sail square sail yards would be braced hard around at 5½ points from the wind, and all yards were sent down at 4 points from the wind. The increased dependence on fore and aft sails even on the square rigger was acknowledged early on, and resulted in the appearance of gaff sails on fore and main, in addition to the spanker. Called spencers at the time, these sails in effect transformed the square-rigged steamship into a motor schooner when conditions were appropriate.[4]

During the Civil War blue-water cruisers commonly were distinguished by relatively insignificant spread of square and prominent fore and aft sails. Of particular note in this regard were the vessels *Kearsarge* and Confederate *Alabama*, both of which had similar rigs, with the latter – designed specifically for long distance cruising – noted for her towering lower masts and attendant gaffs and spanker.

Replacement of paddle wheels with the submerged screw alleviated many problems of shiphandling. However, it was patently obvious that the square-rigged steamer rarely experienced conditions which allowed efficient use of square sails in addition to the propeller: usually the forward motion imparted by the screw prevented the square sails from filling completely. The result was extensive use of fore and aft sails, making these vessels auxiliary schooners. This is illustrated by the rigs of many of the Civil War ocean cruisers, both Union and Confederate. Shown is *Kearsarge* in 1864: note the fore and aft sails (spencers and spanker) bent on all three masts. (USAMHI)

The dominance of steam had another effect directly impinging on shiphandling itself. Steam power eliminated the necessity of many of the 'finer points' of seamanship under sail. Almost any given evolution, whether it be coming about, tacking, wearing, heaving to, scudding, and so forth, was deprived of its mystery or eliminated altogether by the availability of steam power. Often, in place of a complicated series of orders and dozens of sailors manning yards and lines, there was a simple order through the engine order telegraph or speaking tube to the engineer below. In the space of fifty years sail had precipitously declined in status from absolute necessity to somewhere between a not-always-expedient auxiliary and a positive encumbrance.

At this juncture, the subject of shiphandling under the steam-powered screw propeller alone might be considered. However, except for the modernization of the power source itself, from steam reciprocating engines to diesels or turbines, the principles remain unchanged to this day, and numerous volumes have been devoted to the subject, obviating the need to reiterate them here.

## Shiphandling on the western rivers

Operating a vessel on the rivers of the American west seemingly had little in common with ocean navigation. Not only were the ships a distinct breed, but the watery environment created conditions and hazards almost unknown to the seafarer. This was the state of affairs in 1861, when the US naval officers arrived on the scene where the army was preparing a fleet to accompany its movement down the nation's central river system.

The vessels – as described in detail in Chapter Four – were little more than scows: light draft, beamy, shallow hulls with lightly built wood superstructures and propelled by stern or side-mounted paddle wheels and simple but crude high pressure engines. The submerged screw propeller was a rarity on the rivers due to the myriad floating obstructions and snags. The wartime versions of these boats were simple conversions, replacing the superstructure cabins with heavy wood and sometimes iron bulwarks and shipping as many guns as the hull would support.

The river environment, usually the Mississippi and its tribu-

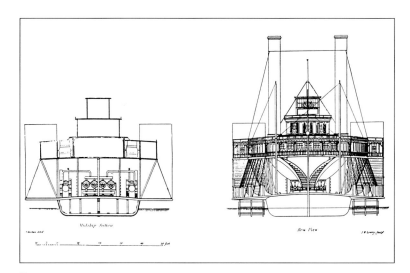

River steamboat cross sections, 1861. Extreme shallow draft and long flat bottoms were common riverboat characteristics, made necessary by shallow western streams. The same characteristics made these vessels susceptible to fast river currents and did not prevent the most prevalent type of river accident – 'snagging' on tree stumps or other obstructions in the waterway. From *Transactions of Naval Architects,* London, 1861.

taries, was an unstable one, characterized by immense variation in currents and ranges in depth. From the point of view of the navigator or pilot, both of these factors not only defined the path of the vessel but its safety as well.

The speed of the current impinged directly on the velocity of the vessel, whether up or down-stream. It commonly ranged from less than 1 mile per hour to 4 or 5 at flood stage, with 6 to 10 occurring at rapids and narrows.

The depth of water was inconstant both by virtue of season and sediment. High water occurred in the spring, along with the slashing currents. At low water, in places major rivers were un-navigable even to the shallowest boats. This factor, or at least its outworkings had major strategic implications throughout the war, and contributed to the loss of an entire campaign late in the conflict.

For the individual vessel, it was that which the current carried and deposited on the river bed that caused the most consternation. As the spring melt sent surges south through heavily wooded, soft alluvial soil, everything in its path went with it. The river's erosive power swiftly made new swaths through the wilderness, snapping trees like kindling. One observer reported that the 'continuous falling of trees, on some of the bends makes a noise resembling the distant roar of artillery'.

Trees became the notorious river snags, with their lower extremities wedged in the stream's bottom and upper ends aimed

at the poorly piloted riverboat. The soil or silt which accompanied the floods accumulated to form the other river menace – sand bars. These and other peculiarities of the rivers made this western war probably unique in history.

The techniques of riverboat handling – in war or peace – necessarily included dealing with the hazards noted above, and others which will be noted briefly. Snags, in addition to rocks, shoals, sunken boats, and sand bars, were part of the constantly changing river scene. A boat's pilot, if he wished to retain that position, maintained a working knowledge of a particular stretch of river, in addition to a general cognizance of clues given by the river itself – color gradations, visible eddies, currents – which betrayed hazards below. The encyclopedic knowledge and consummate skill required of good pilots on the western rivers resulted in their acquiring near legendary stature. (An excellent account of this era can be found in Mark Twain's *Life on the Mississippi,* as Twain (Samuel Clemens) was himself a pilot.) Such men were profoundly necessary to the Union cause during the war, particularly in view of the fact that it took but one substantial tree-trunk snag to impale and sink a major riverboat-turned-warship.

While snags were often fatal, sand bars presented variable challenges to the ingenuity of the river mariner. Avoidance was the obvious first step, with common sense measures such as sending out a yawl with a crew and sounding sticks to survey the length and depth of the obstruction. If the depth was not absolutely prohibitive, the pilot often resorted to brute force by pouring on full steam to propel the vessel across and at the same time batter down the built-up mass. If this method failed, the unfortunate vessel would probably be hard aground for some time by virtue of her pilot's efforts and the power of her engines.

If the thrashing of her engines, forward or aback, failed to break her loose, other methods were available. Towing by another vessel was often an option, if one was in the vicinity. Lightening the load was a second possibility. With warships, the weight of the guns and stores significantly affected the ship's draft. On the rivers, the shore was often near enough to allow off loading there, provided the enemy was not present. Once off the bar into a deep pool, she was re-loaded and the journey was continued. If it was low water season, the process might be regularly repeated in the course of the journey.

Warping and sparring were options utilizing the power of the vessel itself and its crew. The former involved sending the anchor ahead and securing it in the river bed (or attaching the line to a tree). The crew then hauled away at the capstan and, with the aid of the paddle wheels, dragged her — agonizingly — across the bar. It was a riverine variety of kedging; as *Constitution* had done to escape a British squadron when becalmed.

Sparring across a sand bar falls into the category of the unbelievable but true. Popularly known as 'walking the boat' or 'grasshoppering', this involved setting up long, stout spars in the shallow bottom ahead of the vessel, running lines from the top of the spar to the bows of the boat, and from thence to the capstan. When the crew heaved 'round on the capstan two things occurred: the bow was lifted up, and the riverboat was dragged forward a short distance towards the spars. With two spars in use, the process resembled so much as a boat on crutches and only a few feet of forward progress was gained with each hobble. The process would have to be repeated until the boat was in deep water. In all, the spectacle was probably quite entertaining for observers, though dangerous for the crew, should a tackle give way or spar break. By the Civil War era, steam-operated capstans were in use significantly reducing the manpower needs of both 'sparring' and 'warping'.

It should also be noted here that there were instances where the draft of water was such that the boat could be 'walked' across the bottom on her sidewheels. Though expedient, this no doubt caused significant injury to paddle wheels and shafts.[5]

## Operating the steam engine

With the steam engine's introduction into the ship came a redistribution of the labor involved in its operation as well as concentration of this labor into fewer hands. Necessary skills migrated from handling lines and sails to heaving coal, wielding oil cans and wrenches, and watching instruments.

The power plant and attendant duties was physically divided into boiler and engine rooms. The coal heavers were responsible for supplying coal from bunkers to the boiler room; the firemen raised the fires and maintained them. The engineers responded to orders from on deck, regulated the engine's operation accordingly and maintained and repaired the machinery.

Initial steps in preparing the engine for use were obvious ones: check all connections for tightness, oil all journals and moving parts, fill all mechanical oil reservoirs, etc. The flywheel was rotated manually to check the mechanism for loose — or over-tight — bearings and telltale rattles or knocks. Once the steam pressure was up to a predetermined point, the engine could be started, basically by opening the main steam valve, usually by a large handwheel.

Much as early automobiles required hand cranking, the initial steps were accomplished manually. The cylinder's steam inlet valve, whether a sliding D-valve or a circular 'poppet' comparable to today's gasoline engine valve, was opened until sufficient steam entered to generate starting power. It also might have been necessary to manually lever the flywheel around with a starting bar to bring the piston to the inward end of it's stroke and off 'dead center'. (Dead center was the point where the crank shaft and the connecting rod were in a straight line, so power from the piston simply forced the two to bind together, rather than transfer power.) Use of the starting bar, which was sometimes 10 feet long, had its dangers: if the steam built up unexpectedly, its power stroke might catch the bar and throw it — and the attached engineer — up and out of the engine room skylight — a larger version of the kickback common in the days of hand cranking autos.

Once the engine was in motion, the engineer re-attached the steam cut-off mechanism and allowed the valves to operate automatically. At this point, all the bearing surfaces and moving parts were checked and lubricated in preparation for getting under way.

Adjustment of the 'cut-off' was one of duties of the engineers. The cut-off was simply the point at which the steam entering the cylinder was shut off and allowed to expand to do its duty. A short cut-off allowed little steam into the cylinder, in expectation of significant expansion from the given amount. A long cut-off allowed more in and it 'followed' the piston farther until little expansion was needed. The former was more economical, at least in theory. However, at this stage of engine technology, the percentage of steam lost in the cylinder itself due to condensation, eviscerated the potential expansive power of this already small amount of steam. Engines with adjustable cut-off mechanisms could be run at various cut-off percentages and thus operated with a varying economy or power. (It should be noted that the question of the 'cut-off' was a controversial one throughout the Civil War era, with professional reputations made and destroyed on the question — not least in the navy's engineering corps.)

When orders came down to get under way, the engineer engaged a clutch mechanism transferring the engine's power to the propeller shaft, and the vessel went ahead. Reversing the engines was a matter of turning a hand wheel or throwing a lever. Of course, the initial stages of getting under way were busy ones, involving a series of orders necessary to break the anchor free, manoeuver away from the anchorage into the stream and possibly around other vessels to get to sea.

Once at cruising speed, the engineers tasks became routine provided there were no emergencies. Monitoring the engine and boilers involved careful attention both to instruments and the senses, with the latter, if well trained, often the more reliable and discriminating. If the ear was attuned to the sounds of a smoothly operating machine, the out-of-the-ordinary click, rattle, or knock might indicate an impending breakdown. The most likely form of mechanical failure usually involved lack of lubrication, which quickly transformed itself into unwanted heat at the source, usually a bearing surface. Lack of attention to this could cause the bearing to seize and self-destruct. Therefore, the lubrication system, whether it be by hand or mechanical oilers, was monitored constantly.

On the large 'walking beam' engines common to ferry boats and other coastal carriers, many of which were converted to navy use during the war, simple lubrication was a treacherous task, requiring a climb on the rocking beam high above the vessel's superstructure. Young boys were often assigned this work; hence, the story goes, the origin of the term 'grease monkey'.

The most dangerous and often unpredictable portion of the steam plant was the boiler. While a mechanical breakdown could stop the engines and create work and delays, the malfunction of a boiler could easily cause an explosion resulting in horrendous scaldings and death.

Ironically, these explosions at times occurred precisely when the boiler was doing its job – only too well. An excess of generated steam without an outlet was one obvious source of disaster; and the boiling away of the boiler water, thus lowering the water level, could accomplish the same result. The latter would be caused by the absence of the cooling effect of the water on the metal of the boiler, creating an unequal strain on various boiler surfaces.

This is not to say that an inefficient boiler was a safe one, however. The build up of scale, the development of cracks and thin spots, and weaknesses in soldered joints, all contributed to make boilers susceptible to breakdown. Such factors, accompanied by hard working, high pressures, and rapid temperature and pressure fluctuations, served to aggravate even the smallest defects and create a climate for disaster.

It should be noted here that in the early years of American steamboats roughly half of all vessel losses were due to boiler explosions, and most of these were accompanied by fatalities. The public outcry – generally directed at poorly trained engineers – resulted in one of the first instances of government industry regulations: a steam boiler inspection law of 1852.

Consequently, some of the most vital duties of the engineers

Engine room on the monitor *Catskill*. Dozens of moving parts and the prevalence of brass fittings gave the engine room personnel a continual task of lubricating and polishing. Though steam engines were simple in principle, mechanisms – particularly for screw steamers – were often complicated and in need of constant attention. (US Navy)

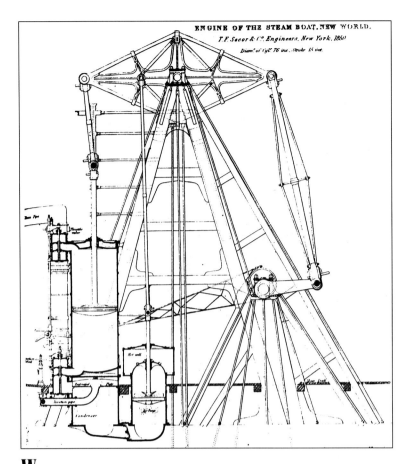

ENGINE OF THE STEAM BOAT. NEW WORLD.
*T. F. Secor & Cª Engineers. New York. 1850.*
*Diamʳ of Cylʳ 76 ins. Strokᵉ 15 feet.*

**W**alking beam engine, 1850. The walking beam itself was high above the highest deck and required a 'grease monkey' to lubricate its connections. From Tredgold, *The Steam Engine*, 1852.

involved monitoring the boilers, and in particular, their pressure and water levels. A dial-type instrument indicated pressure, and vertical glass tubes gave the observer an instant reading of the corresponding level in the boiler. Additionally, the mechanisms such as pumps and injectors by which water was supplied to the boilers, as well as blow-off and safety valves, were to be kept in good operating condition. Of course, regular maintenance would also require periodic cleaning and scaling of the boilers, a time consuming and dirty operation, and one which was easily neglected particularly if the vessel was to be an effective unit on the blockade. In this regard, repairs on the common horizontal tubular boilers involved draining the water only to the level of the defective tubes. In the navy's Martin-patent vertical tube boilers, any such work required draining the boiler in its entirety, a much more time consuming process. Furthermore, a thorough boiler cleaning required a person to crawl into the boiler itself for access to the far reaches of the unit. Small individuals were appropriate for this type of filthy work.

A few closing remarks might be made on the steam-powered ship in general. In principle, the steam engine was exceedingly simple. Many, many things could go awry with both boilers and engine, without resulting in a complete breakdown. Throughout the war, engineers and deck officers wrote distressingly acute reports of 'imminent breakdown', dangerous, leaking boilers, poor steaming performance, and so on. And the reports, for the same vessels, would continue in the same vein for months. All the while, the ship remained in service on the blockade, though as it were under protest. In reality, as long as the boiler was not totally sieved, and could retain the steam long enough to send it to the cylinders, the vessel could operate. It may have been slow, or uneconomical, or dangerous, but if steam could be developed and transmitted to the cylinder, then, barring a massive mechanical breakdown, the ship would move.

A 'massive mechanical breakdown' in the engine was usually caused by overheated bearing surfaces. If the overheating was not noticed, the heat would mushroom and the moving parts would seize up, destroying a major part of the machinery such as the crankshaft itself. In such cases, the engine was out of commission, regardless of the condition of the boiler or other appurtenances. Needless to say, crankshafts were not under the category of minor, on station repairs, and required a trip to a navy yard.

One other type of massive breakdown was caused by simple breakage. Poor maintenance, misalignments, and hard usage sometimes resulted in a major part of the machinery fracturing. Connecting rods were particularly apt to simply break. When this happened, the skill of the engineer on the spot determined whether the ship could remain on station or would be forced to retreat to the nearest repair facility. A spare part might be available, or one might be fabricated from scrap metal on hand. In either case, there would be some down time but not a trip to the yard.[6]

Finally, the simplicity of the steam engine and its ability to run under exceedingly poor circumstances and maintenance, resulted apparently in an unfortunate trade-off. Even when the vessels were on station, filling in their particular section of hostile shores, they were often, for the reasons stated above, incapable of sustained runs or high speeds. The results are obvious to anyone who has studied the wartime reports. Rarely was the runner simply to find an unoccupied stretch of coast. More often, there was a chase involved and the runner simply out lasted and outran the Union pursuer.

# Chapter Eleven

# NAVAL ORDNANCE AND GUNNERY

By the beginning of the Civil War, American naval ordnance was arguably the most advanced in the world. This was the direct result of the introduction of John Dahlgren's shell guns and Robert Parrott's rifled weapons during the last half of the 1850s. Their only serious contender was the British Armstrong rifled breechloader, a gun which proved too advanced for the metallurgy of the day and which was soon withdrawn. In any case, Dahlgren's and, to a lesser extent, Parrott's weaponry had become standard building blocks for all vessel batteries and construction before the war, and were part and parcel of the wartime ironclad program. It should also be noted that the 15-inch Dahlgren, introduced midway through the conflict, threw the heaviest projectile of any naval gun in existence.

## Shell guns

The shell gun, along with the ironclad and steam propulsion, had begun to wreak fundamental changes in naval warfare by the 1860s. Shell guns with their explosive projectiles not only punched larger holes than solid shot, they also added the danger of fire in an age when wooden ships were literally inbuilt with inflammables. Tar, in particular, could be found everywhere from the ship's keel to the sailor's hair.

Though shell-firing weapons had been in use as early as the War of 1812, their naval use had been limited. First, there was a constant danger of the explosive shell detonating prematurely, even within the gun when it was fired. Second, shell guns could not be used for firing solid shot. And it was still the era when bat-

tering the vessel to surrender and capture was preferred over destroying it by fire or otherwise. Furthermore, in the increasingly anachronistic chivalric tradition, shells were for some time quite seriously regarded as ungentlemanly weapons.

The first American shell guns were seen on the Great Lakes during the War of 1812 and were actually varieties of the army-designed gun called the columbiad. Few of these weapons were used and the last two were recorded in navy stocks in 1833.[1]

The next shell guns were introduced in 1841 after extensive testing on the steamer *Fulton II*. These were 64-pounders of 63 cwt, with an 8-inch bore and 32-pounder powder chamber. (Note: cwt indicates 'hundredweight', each one of which equals 112 pounds.) In 1842, a 10-inch version was introduced, firing a 104-pound projectile and weighing 86 cwt. In 1854 a larger 10-incher was cast, weighing 107 cwt and firing a 64-pound projectile. Some of each of these remained in the inventory during the Civil War. These guns, as well as the French Paixhans weapons which preceded them emphasized the explosive power of the weapon, to the detriment of both range and accuracy.

In the mid 1840s American naval ship batteries had been standardized with combinations of 32-pounders in broadside and 8- or 10-inch shell guns (or 64-pounder shot guns) in small numbers on pivot carriages on the spar deck. The shell gun, however, was still considered by many a poor substitute for a heavier, more accurate, long range, shot gun.[2]

John A Dahlgren soon undertook to rectify this situation. In May 1850, the first of his 9-inch smoothbore shell guns was delivered to Washington Navy Yard. The 9-inch gun fired a 72-

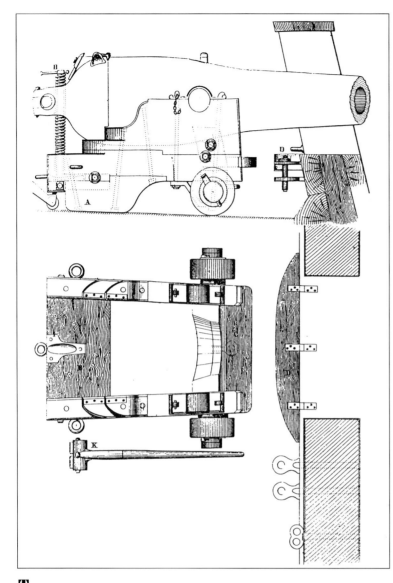

**T**he Dahlgren 9-inch smoothbore shell gun was the first of John Dahlgren's designs to see service. Previous shell guns did not have its strength or versatility. From the 1850s onward naval vessels were designed around the Dahlgrens or Parrot rifles. From *Ordnance Instructions*, 1860.

pound shell and weighed 9000 pounds; its soda-bottle shape resulted from maximizing the strength of the iron over the chamber itself. It is also obvious that Dahlgren had designed the weapon from a clean slate; discarding the traditional cannon shape (which had been merely modified by Paixhans and others) and letting scientific principles dictate the weapon's configuration.

Testing showed the gun to be exceedingly strong and a complete success. In one instance, after 1500 uneventful rounds, a 9-inch tube was filled with 10 shot (903 pounds) and 20 pounds of powder, which finally burst the weapon. With minor variations the 9-inch Dahlgren was used extensively during and beyond the Civil War.

Dahlgren's next gun was an 11-inch weapon, first made in 1851. This gun weighed 15,700 pounds and fired a 136-pound shell or 165-pound solid shot. This gun was used in the turret of the original *Monitor*. The standard charge for this gun was 15 pounds of powder. When these guns failed to penetrate the armor of the Confederate ironclad, Dahlgren tested increased charges for the 11-inch gun and determined that 20 pounds was acceptable, though no ill effects were seen in tests with 25 pounds. Thus the story that the *Monitor* was firing with reduced charges, to prevent concussive effects in the turret, is erroneous. Against wooden ships, however, the 11-incher was quite effective, even with the lesser charge. This was amply demonstrated in the *Kearsarge* versus *Alabama* fight.

Before war broke out, the 10-inch Dahlgren was also in service, firing a 97-pound shell or 130-pound shot. It was used in pivot carriages in lieu of the 11-inch gun and weighed 12,000 pounds.

Dahlgren envisioned a system in which the 9-inch guns would be the main deck battery and 11-inch guns would be on the spar deck of large frigates, in place of the usual battery of 32-pounders and 8- or 10-inch shell guns. The result, with Dahlgren's weapons, would be an entire battery of shell guns — all of which were also capable of firing solid shot.

In 1854, contracts were let for building one-hundred-and-fifty-six 9-inch guns and fourteen 11-inch and 10-inch Dahlgrens. These were for the new *Merrimack* class frigates. Each of the five navy-built ships were to have main deck batteries of 9-inchers, upper deck broadsides of 8-inch (old style) shell guns, plus a pair of 10-inch Dahlgrens as bow and stern chasers. (The sixth, *Niagara*, was given twelve 11-inchers on spar deck pivot rails.) These were the first naval vessels with batteries composed exclusively of shell guns. This, though, fell short of Dahlgren's desires, in that the old 8-inchers were incapable of firing solid shot. It would not be until the advent of *Warrior* in the 1860s that the Royal Navy would adopt a similar policy.[3]

To allay continuing resistance to shell guns and arguments that the larger weapon was too large and heavy to handle in any kind of seaway, Captain Dahlgren managed to secure the fitting out of a 'gunnery practice ship' in 1857. The vessel, the sloop of war *Plymouth*, was given four 9-inch Dahlgrens and one 11-incher. The results were positive. Among other things, 121 shots were fired from the larger gun without difficulty and the 9-inch gun was fired as fast as every forty seconds.[4]

Carriages for these guns were of necessity predicated on their great weight. The 9-inch gun was mounted on the Marsilly car-

**G**undeck, steam sloop *Hartford*, 1864. Nine-inch Dahlgrens formed the main battery, all on standard Marsilly carriages with 'dumb trucks' on the rear to reduce recoil. (US Navy)

riage, a French design having two forward wheels only. The rear 'dumb trucks' rested on the deck and their drag checked the recoil. The use of the roller handspike enabled relative ease in running out and training. Though the entire gun weighed some 5 tons, it could be moved from one side of the vessel to the opposite in less than two minutes. The complete crew for this weapon numbered sixteen men, though the manual spelled out normal operations with significantly fewer.

The 11-inch gun pivot carriage was a two part affair, consisting of a long slide with small wheels on the quarters to traverse on the deck rails, and an upper carriage, also on wheels, mounted on the slide. Screw compressors mounted on the upper carriage transoms applied friction to check the recoil. The entire assemblage weighed some 20,000 pounds, and the ordnance instructions called for a full crew of twenty-four men and a powder boy.[5]

Three more Dahlgren smoothbores were developed during the war, the 13-inch, 15-inch and 20-inch, all designed to be used against the Confederate ironclads. (In point of fact, the inability of the *Monitor*'s 11-inch guns to penetrate her adversary was a key factor in the development of the larger weapons.) The 15-inch gun was the earliest to be put in service. The weapon was rushed into production in 1862, and the first was delivered in the September. Weighing 42,000 pounds and firing 440-pound shot or 330-pound shell, it was specifically intended for the monitors where loading and handling were mechanised. The gun had a range of 2100 to 2420 yards, depending on the powder charge, and penetrated 4 inches of armor plate — as demonstrated by the capture of Confederate ironclad *Atlanta* in 1864. On the negative side, it required five or more minutes to reload.

Dahlgren himself favored the 13-inch gun over the 15-inch. This weapon did not appear until at least April 1864, in part because of the emphasis on the larger gun. It fired a 224-pound shell or 280-pound shot and weighed 36,000 pounds. In fact, the turret openings of the *Passaic* class monitors were designed for the 13-inch gun. Consequently, when the larger weapon was substituted, its muzzle was too large to protrude through the port.

The largest Dahlgren-pattern gun was the 20-inch smoothbore. This gun, which weighed 100,000 pounds, was cast in 1864

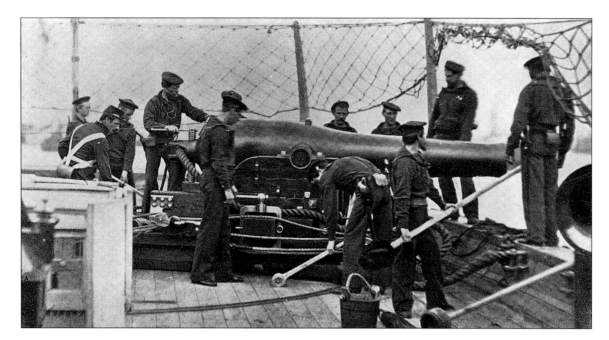

Gun practice, 11-inch Dahlgren. Note the crewman (fourth from left) at the elevating screw and another crewman (on this side of the weapon) at the compressor screw. Varying tension on the compressors dampened the gun's recoil. Note the marine (far left) as one of the crew. (US Navy)

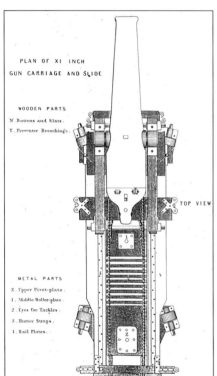

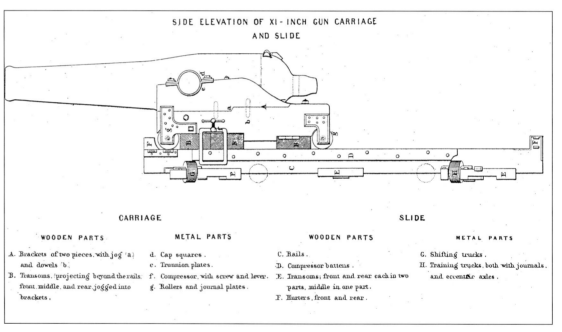

Two views of an 11-inch Dahlgren smoothbore on pivot carriage. This gun weighed over 8 tons and fired a 135-pound shell. From *Ordnance Instructions*, 1866.

but saw no service. It would fire a cored shot of 1080 pounds using a 100-pound charge. As with the 13- and 15-inch versions, this weapon was intended to punch through the iron sides of Confederate armorclads.

By the end of the war, several more varieties of the Dahlgren pattern gun had appeared. There was a 32-pounder, an 8-inch, and a heavier 10-inch weapon. The latter, as well as a heavier 9-incher were intended for shot alone. There were also rifled Dahlgrens (discussed below).

It is estimated that 1185 nine-inch guns were produced during the war and 465 of the 11-inchers. Of the larger guns, there were one-hundred-and-thirteen 15- and eleven 13-inch. None of the 9- or 11-inch guns burst in service, and they continued as standard broadside and pivot guns until the end of the old wooden navy. In the 1870s, a few 11-inchers were converted to 8-inch rifles by introducing a sleeve into the barrel. To take it further, Dahlgren-armed Civil War monitors remained in the inventory until 1908 – a full ten years beyond the Spanish American War.[6]

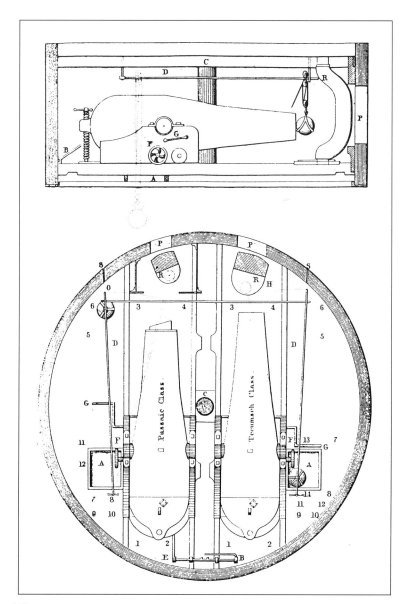

**M**onitor turret with two 15-inch Dahlgrens. 'F' is the handwheel for running the gun in and out. 'R' is the port stopper; 'D' is the travelling bar to move a 440-pound projectile to the gun's muzzle. As few as eight men could operate and fire this gun. From *Ordnance Instructions*, 1866.

# Rifled cannon

The principle of rifling, though used extensively in small arms, had found little acceptance in large ordnance – either military or naval. Certainly the traditional close-in ship-to-ship tactics called for mass firepower rather than pinpoint accuracy.

The most familiar Union rifled gun was that designed by Robert P Parrott in 1860, and built at West Point Foundry on the Hudson River in New York. The breech strength of these guns was provided by a wrought iron band which was heated, then cooled to shrink around the tube. The band itself was half the diameter of the gun's bore.

These guns were not introduced until mid 1861, with the first being 20- and 30-pounders (3.67- and 4.2-inch bore, respectively). Later, the 100-pounder came into the inventory, a gun which could fire a 6.4-inch projectile over 5 miles (at 35° elevation and with 10 pounds of powder).

The next larger Parrott was the 8-inch, referred to as the 150-pounder by the navy and 200-pounder by the army. This was comparable in weight to the 11-inch Dahlgren and was commonly used on pivot mounts. It fired a 152-pound shell on a charge of 16 pounds of powder.

For the most part, the Parrotts provided good service and reliability, and over 700 were used during the conflict. However, when several burst on firing during the Fort Fisher Expeditions late in the war, the 8-inch gun was withdrawn. It was determined that build up of residue in the bore contributed to the problem, but the reputation of rifled guns in general was again called into question.

Another large rifled naval gun was invented by General Charles T James. This was essentially a 42-pounder smoothbore (army pattern), rifled and firing 81.25-pound shot or 64.25 pound shells. These appeared in river service early in the war.

John Dahlgren also designed rifled ordnance, with bores of 4.4 inches (30 pounder), 5.1 inches (50-pounder), 6-inches (80-pounder) and 7.5 inches (150 pounder). Examples of both the 4.4-and 6-inch guns burst during early use and the majority of these and not one of the 7.5-inch guns saw service.[7]

Rifled ordnance was distinctly at a disadvantage during the Civil War. On shipboard, the long ranges possible with rifles was not particularly useful, and the rifled projectile lacked the ability to richochet inherent in the spherical smoothbore ammunition. That is, a ball fired at low angle would continue on course as it glanced off the water, whereas a similarly low rifled projectile would – much as a modern football – bounce unpredictably. Furthermore, it was found that the smoothbore Dahlgrens could withstand larger and larger charges – thus increasing their hitting power – whereas the rifle powder charges were necessarily smaller, reducing their effectiveness against armor.[8]

# Conventional cannon

In 1845, the US Navy adopted the 32-pound cannon as the standard shipboard weapon, in addition to the 8-inch shell guns already described. This was the result of a general trend in which major navies had worked to simplify ship's weaponry. Standardization eliminated other diameter and weight projectiles to decrease the possibility of confusion in the heat of battle.

This did not mean there was, after standardization, only one kind of gun on a given vessel. In fact, the American 32-pounder came in several sizes, including 27, 33, 42, 51, 57 and 61 cwt weapons. These ranged from 6 feet to nearly 10 feet long. All required different size powder charges for optimum efficiency and safety.

During the War Between the States, the conventional 32-pounder, though technically obsolescent, was much in evidence. Indeed, having been standard for some fifteen years, there were sufficient quantities available to fill in where the newer shell guns were in short supply.

It was often used in broadside, with some new vessels given 32-pounders and others of the same class mounting 9-inch Dahlgrens. Specifically, in the *Kearsarge* versus *Alabama* fight, the former had four 32-pounders (42 cwt) in addition to the two 11-inch pivots. The light 32-pounders were commonly used to arm the converted merchantmen for blockade duty, as they required less deck reinforcement than the larger guns.

The only other conventional broadside gun commonly in use during the war was the 24-pounder howitzer. Again, this gun was often seen in converted merchant vessels. It was also used extensively on the lightly built riverboats pressed into service in the inland river campaigns.[9]

# Mortars

The only mortar used extensively during the war was the 13-inch gun made by Charles Knap of Fort Pitt Foundry. This gun weighed 17,200 pounds and fired a 218-pound shell about 4200 yards (over 2 miles). Fired at an angle of 45°, differing charges determined the range of the 'bomb'. It typically was in the air some thirty seconds, and of course was not capable of pinpoint accuracy. It was not unusual for the shells to burrow 10 to 20 feet into the ground before exploding.

The mortar-loading procedure differed significantly from that of the long gun, particularly in the handling of the powder charge, and required a crew of thirteen. In the long gun, the cartridge (powder bag) was put into the chamber and pierced by the priming wire inserted through the vent. In loading the mortar, the measured powder was carried to the gun in

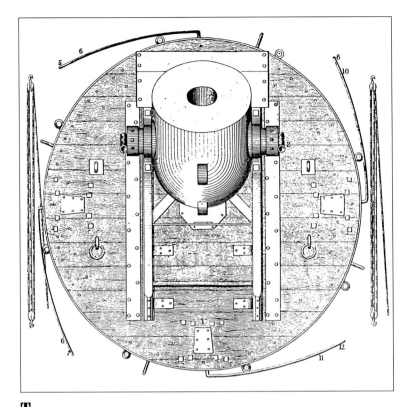

Thirteen-inch mortar. Note the iron carriage and wooden circular platform. The entire platform was moved to train the weapon, using block and tackles at each side. From *Ordnance Instructions*, 1866.

the cartridge bag, carefully poured into the chamber, and levelled with spatulas. The bomb was then lowered into the gun, keeping the fuze exactly in the axis of the bore. Obviously this was not a weapon to be used in close combat nor was it a fast operation. Typically it required five minutes per round, though it was possible to accomplish in just under three. For a complete description of this, see the section on gunnery.

Mortars were used extensively in the Mississippi River and coastal campaigns, mounted on schooners or scows. During the operations against New Orleans in April 1862, nineteen 13-inchers, mounted on mortar schooners, beseiged Forts Jackson and St Philip for six days and nights, firing over 8000 projectiles. (A twentieth schooner, *Maria J Carlson*, was sunk on the second day.) Despite the volume of fire, the inaccuracy and erratic detonation of these weapons was such that they contributed little to the eventual outcome.

The mortar scow was 45 feet by 28 feet with angled sides, made entirely of wood, towed into position, and often tied off to trees on the riverbank. Each mounted a single 13-incher. They were first used at Island No. 10 in early 1862 and saw continuous employment throughout the western river campaigns.[10]

Thirteen-inch mortar on the mortar schooner USS *Para*. Note the grappling hook in the foreground, used to lower the projectile, which weighed 218 pounds, into the muzzle. (USAMHI)

Mortar scow on the western rivers. These were essentially rafts, towed into position, and used frequently during the river campaigns. (US Navy)

# Boat guns

John A Dahlgren designed the navy's standard boat and field guns shortly after the Mexican War, during which army weapons had been pressed into navy amphibious use. There were four varieties of Dahlgren smoothbore howitzers, all of bronze: two versions of light 12-pounders, a medium 12-pounder, and a 24-pounder. Twelve- and 20-pounder rifles were also in service. The lightest 12-pounder weighed in at a mere 300 pounds; the heaviest 24-pounder at 1310 pounds (tube only). The medium 12-pounder with field carriage weighed 1250 pounds — about half that of the land forces' 12-pounder napoleon and carriage.

There were both boat and field carriages for these guns, and all except the 20-pounder were mounted with a loop beneath the gun. The 20-pounder had conventional trunnions. A gun mounted on the bow of a launch had a field of fire of 120° and could be easily transferred to a field carriage in amphibious operations. The field carriage was of iron and had a wheel on the end of its trail —

**D**ahlgren howitzers on boat carriage and field carriage. This weapon could be easily transferred from a ship's launch to the wrought iron carriage. The lightest gun, a 12-pounder, weighed 600 pounds. From *Ordnance Instructions, 1866.*

**S**ponging out the field howitzer, 1861. With a range of some 1200 yards and rate of fire of up to ten rounds per minute, these were popular and effective guns. From Frank Leslie's *Illustrated Newspaper.* (US Navy)

facilitating movement by manpower, rather than horsepower. The guns were to have a crew of twelve.

Ammunition for these weapons was shell, canister and shrapnel. Canister could be fired at a maximum of eight rounds per minute, but more typically, fifteen seconds per round. The range of the 24-pounder gun was 1308 yards with shrapnel and 1270 with shell at 5° elevation.

First made at Washington Navy Yard, the demand for these

howitzers was such that wartime production was expanded to the foundries of Cyrus Alger and Charles T Ames. At least 1087 12-pounders were cast during the war and 1009 24-pounders.

Though designated boat guns, a large number were retained on deck, particularly in riverine operations. They were also small enough for use in the fighting tops during close-in actions.

The Dahlgren howitzers were considered by some to be the best boat guns in the world. They continued in US naval service for many years following the war.[11]

# Army cannon

Early in the war, the flotilla on the western rivers was under the US Army Quartermaster Corps. This and the scarcity of naval ordnance in the west resulted in the City class ironclads (*Cairo*, et al), and a few other early ironclads being given batteries of mixed army and navy ordnance.

The *Cairo* and sister vessels all had up to four 42-pounder army rifles of 80 or 84 cwt. The largest number of these on a single vessel was seven, found on the ironclad *Benton*, the most formidably armed boat on the river. The army weapons on these vessels were all eventually replaced by navy guns.

# Gunnery

The sequence for firing broadside guns can be summarized as follows. For simplicity, the specifics of each crewman's job have been eliminated (though these were noted particularly in regulations and instructions). The gun in this instance is a 9-inch Dahlgren on Marsilly carriage.[12]

> Command: 'Silence! Man starboard [port] guns.'
> Command: 'Cast loose and provide!'

The gun crew removes the covers from the sights and tampion, remove or fold away the gunport covers, lower the gun's breech by quoin or elevating screw, and attach the training and side tackles to the appropriate bolts on the gun and deck. At hand were to be sponge, rammer, shot, wads, fire bucket and powder.

> Command: 'Run In!'

At this point, up to twelve men man the tackle to bring the gun muzzle out of the port.

> Command: 'Serve vent and sponge!'

The gun captain inserts the priming wire into the vent to ensure it is clear, and a moist sponge is rammed in, then brought out and examined for burning fragments. If needed, the sponging is repeated. Meanwhile, a powder charge (cartridge) and shell is in readiness.

Command: 'Load!'

The charge is placed in the muzzle by hand, then the rammer pushes it to the bottom of the bore. (A mark on the rammer handle indicates the proper depth.) The charge was not to be struck by the rammer. With the rammer clear, the shell is brought to the bore and the fuze cap removed. The shell is forced down the bore, again, to a mark on the rammer handle.

Command: 'Run Out!'

If the gun is to leeward and the roll is heavy, the number of men restraining the gun is larger than if it is to windward and rolling moderately. The captain heaves up on the roller handspike, raising the stern of the carriage, while the tackle-men pull it into the port on the front trucks. Once in place, the tackles are secured.

Command: 'Prime!'

The gun captain inserts the priming wire into the vent and into the charge (cartridge), then places a primer (fuse) into the vent.

Command: 'Point!'

The gun captain stands to the rear of the gun with lanyard in hand, sighting the piece. At 'Right' or 'Left' command by the gun captain, men on the tackles and hand- or roller-handspikes heave in the proper direction. One man at the quoin or elevating screw responds to 'Raise' or 'Lower' at the breech.

Command: 'Ready-Fire!'

The gun captain awaits the proper moment and roll of the ship, then 'Draws [the lanyard] promptly and firmly'. If the primer fails, another is to be quickly inserted. (A second failure indicated the charge was not seated).

Command: 'Cease Fire!'

If already primed, the primer is to be removed.

Command: 'Secure!'

Powder boy returns spare powder and passing boxes to the magazine. The gun is to be secured to securing bolts at the side of the ports, and the port lids replaced. All implements are returned to their places.

All the above commands and actions were carried out under normal circumstances, and as drilled. Many variations were possible. Quick firing, for instance, at the command 'Load in one motion!', combined ramming home both powder and shot together, and demanded less attention to aim. In fighting both broadsides of the vessel, the watches were distributed on all guns. Those who were not spongers, loaders or captains, were to alternate between port and starboard (and vice versa) guns at the command 'Change!'. When hot shot was used, the muzzle was elevated to allow the shot to roll home, and a wet wad was placed between the dry wad and the shot.[13]

Firing the pivot-mounted shell guns and rifles differed little in principle from the above. A greater number of men was needed and screw-down 'compressors' were utilized – in addition to breeching – to apply varying amounts of friction to ease or restrain the gun's movement along the slide. With carriage, the gun weighed about 20,000 pounds and too little friction at a critical point in the ship's roll would be disastrous. As the shell for the 11-inch gun weighed 135 pounds, two men and a 'ladle' were required to lift it to the bore for loading.[14]

In the monitor turrets were 150-pounder rifles, and 11- or 15-inch Dahlgren smoothbores. Due to the restricted space and other factors, mechanical aids were employed. At the 'Run Out!' command, the port stopper was opened, and a crank was used to move the weapon. To train the gun, the engineer at the starting bar revolved the turret. In practice, it was sometimes difficult to stop the turret exactly where it was needed. In these cases, the gun was sometimes fired while the turret was in motion. After the shot was fired, the turret was turned abeam to align the scuttle and allow ammunition to be passed up from below. A travelling bar was used to carry the 15-inch shell (weighing 440 pounds) across the turret to the muzzle. Though the standard crew for the 15-inch gun was fourteen men, it could be done with eight.[15]

The procedure for firing the 13-inch mortar has been alluded to above. This involved a thirteen-man crew who trained the weapon by tackles. The projectile was handled by a gun-tackle 'whip' rigged from a mast directly over the gun. In order to lessen the shock and concussion on the ear, the ordnance instructions directed the crew to 'stand on their toes...keeping at the same time their mouths and ears open' when the gun, with its 23-pound powder charge, was fired.[16]

## Chapter Twelve

# UNION NAVAL STRATEGY AND LOGISTICS OF THE CIVIL WAR

Bringing the Confederacy to heel was, in theory, as well as practice, an enormous undertaking. Simply in square mileage, the fledgling nation covered a substantial area with a seacoast of over 3500 miles. And the new nation had the advantage of internal lines of communications as well as the incentive inherent in defending the homeland from invaders. Only a protracted war of conquest would serve the purpose.

As daunting as this prospect was, Lincoln's army and navy had a precedent on which to build. Indeed, the only offensive war the young nation had experienced involved the conquest of Mexico – a subjugation accomplished with professionalism and without a major defeat on the battlefield. The war involved blockading the Mexican Gulf coast, amphibious landings, and a march directly to the capital of the country.

Winfield Scott, hallowed chief of the army in 1861, and the man who had dictated terms to the Mexicans, may have learned much in that previous conflict. However, the situation in the disintegrating Union required a more subtle strategic solution.

Scott's proposal was dubbed the 'Anaconda Plan' - and, like its namesake, was designed to defeat the states in rebellion by constriction. Scott actually envisioned the navy as the dominant component of the scheme: the Atlantic and Gulf coasts were to be blockaded, interdicting all Confederate overseas trade – particularly that of cotton. The second component was Union occupation of the Mississippi River corridor, severing the western states from the body of the Southern nation.[1]

'The last meeting between General Scott and the Cabinet.' General Winfield Scott (standing), was the author of the Union's only overall war strategy – the so-called Anaconda Plan, involving an economic strangulation of the South, with minimal military incursions. By late 1861 the latter element had been abandoned, and the naval blockade had been instituted. From *Harper's Weekly*. (US Navy)

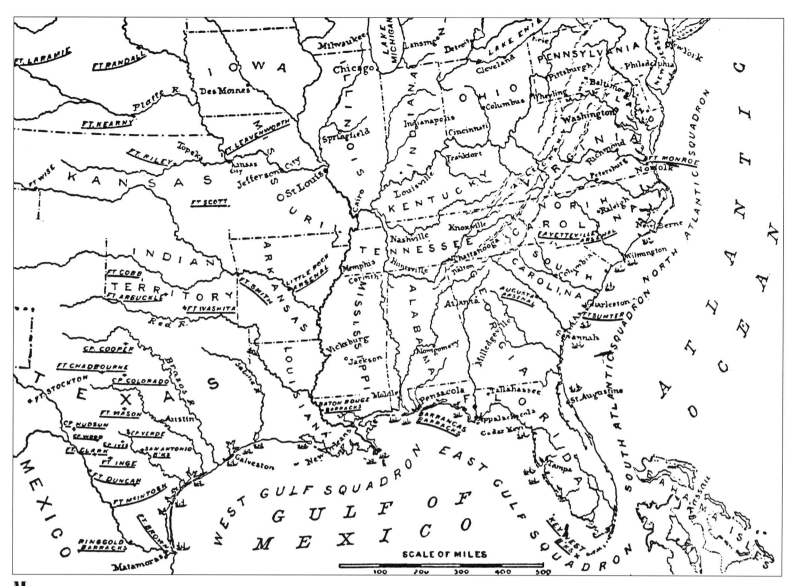

Map of the blockade of the southern coast, showing the respective areas covered by the four blockading units: North Atlantic, South Atlantic, East Gulf and West Gulf squadrons. From J R Soley's *The Blockade and the Cruisers.*

As originally envisioned, the only other incursions into the body of the Southern nation were to be the taking of selected strategic bases on the Atlantic from which the navy would operate its squadrons. In effect, the South was to be defeated by economic pressure and a minimum of bloodshed.

The plan was, of course, astoundingly unrealistic on two counts. It appeared to vastly underestimate the seriousness and resolve of the Southern states. This same strain of imagination brought the popular expectation of a ninety-day war – though Scott himself called for 300,000 men and three years – and of a rebel army which would run at the whiff of organized gunfire. As to the naval blockade, it is amazing that this proposed blockade

was expected to be practically watertight, particularly considering the size of the navy then in existence. The extent of this naivety was exemplified by the opinion held early on, by a maritime 'expert', that some fifty additional vessels, thirty of them sailing ships, were needed to 'complete the blockade'![2]

In any event, the Anaconda Plan as a whole was short lived, at least in its outworkings. Indeed, the reluctance to invade Southern territory fell by the wayside as early as the summer of 1861 with the penetration of Northern Virginia by Union forces. Scott himself resigned in November 1861.

The naval component of the strategy was initially formulated by the Commission of Conference, set up by Secretary Welles in June 1861 (see Chapter Two). The six reports of this group were instrumental in determining the priorities for naval operations, particularly in setting up the blockade. Once this board completed its work, overall war strategy apparently fell to the combined efforts of Lincoln, his cabinet and generals.

The board urged the seizure of strategic points along the Atlantic and Gulf coasts for use as naval bases to support the blockade, as well as to provide jumping-off points for later military incursions into the South. On the Atlantic, where the major ports used by blockade runners were Savannah, Charleston, and Wilmington, North Carolina, the preferred locations were originally Bull's Bay, north of Charleston, and Fernandina, north of Jacksonville, Florida. These were dropped in favor of Port Royal, South Carolina (between Savannah and Charleston), and Hatteras Inlet, North Carolina. On the Gulf of Mexico where New Orleans and Mobile, Alabama, were blockade-running havens, Ship Island, near Biloxi, Mississippi, and Head of the Passes, Louisiana were selected as potential bases. Key West, of course, remained in Union hands throughout the war, providing a much needed safe harbor between the Atlantic and the Gulf.

Carrying out the suggestions of the Commission of Conference (otherwise known as the Blockade Board) began with the fight at Hatteras Inlet in August 1861, a swift victory over two poorly prepared forts. Early in November, Port Royal was taken. Both operations were joint army-navy enterprises with light casualties.

Port Royal was blessed with one of the largest harbors in the southeast and quickly became the seat of the South Atlantic Blockading Squadron and a key to spreading Union control along the Atlantic coast. Hatteras was the first of several North Carolina strong points taken by army and navy forces, including New Berne and Roanoke Island. The latter controlled Pamlico Sound and the southern termini of the Dismal Swamp Canal and the Albemarle and Chesapeake Canal, both of which supplied Norfolk, Virginia. New Berne was significant as the railhead connection for materiel run through the blockade and en route inland. All these were in Union hands by early 1862.[3]

On the Gulf of Mexico, Ship Island and Head of the Passes, south of New Orleans, were seized by Union forces in 1861. They became the staging areas for David G Farragut's move up the Mississippi. Forts Jackson and St Philip, below New Orleans, were passed by Farragut's fleet in April 1862. Both forts and the city surrendered shortly thereafter. The South's largest port was then closed to blockade runners, and, more importantly, the stage was set for the Union move to rend the Confederacy on its north-south axis.

Two other major Gulf ports were Galveston, Texas and Mobile. The former was taken by Federal forces in the fall of 1862, but was lost again the first day of January 1863. Though it remained in Confederate hands for the balance of the war, the

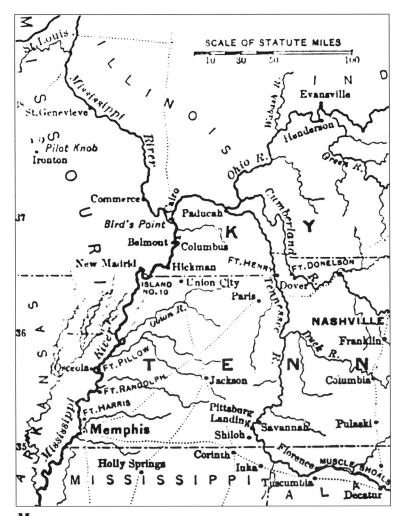

**M**ap of Union operations in the Upper Mississippi Valley, 1862. Forces moved in parallel down the Mississippi and Tennessee Rivers, with those operations on the Tennessee leading to the fall of Nashville and the eventual movement southeastward. The former movement, along with Farragut's drive northward from New Orleans would divide the Confederacy along the line of the great river. From *Battles and Leaders of the Civil War.*

eventual capture of the Mississippi and city of New Orleans effectively severed relations between the port and other areas west of the river, and the remaining states in rebellion. Mobile remained the only major open port on the Gulf. The delay in its capture was due to the fact that the army, whose cooperation was necessary, had priorities elsewhere.

In the Upper Mississippi Valley, the army was controlling the operations, with the navy initially supplying only gunboat expertise and officers and crews. Cairo, Illinois, at the confluence of the Mississippi and Ohio Rivers, was selected as a base of operations and General Ulysses Grant began the offensive which would carry the Union army and navy down the Mississippi and its tributaries.

Forts Henry, on the Tennessee River, and Donelson, on the Cumberland, both near the northern border of Tennessee, were the first objectives in a long string of army-navy battles gradually moving southward to eventually join with Union forces battling northward along the Mississippi. When both strongholds were taken by naval and army forces, under A H Foote and Grant respectively in February 1862, the Union gained control of these two important rivers, as well as effectively outflanked the Confederates at Columbus on the Mississippi River, which was abandoned shortly thereafter. Nashville, further up the Cumberland River, was then vulnerable to the advancing Union forces, and was evacuated less than a month after the fall of the two forts.

At this point, the Union movement southward was two-pronged, with one driving down the Mississippi, which forms the western border of Tennessee, while Grant's army was moving in parallel on the Tennessee River.

The next Union objectives on the Mississippi were Island No. 10, Fort Pillow and Memphis, Tennessee. Island No. 10 was bombarded by naval gunboats in March 1862. When the fort failed to yield, the gunboats ran past and cut it off, forcing its surrender. Fort Pillow suffered a naval bombardment but did not surrender until outflanked by Grant's army forces moving in parallel, south to Corinth, Mississippi. Memphis, the largest city on the Mississippi between St Louis and New Orleans, fell after a ram and gunboat battle in June 1862.

From this point onward the western flotilla was a major element of Grant's year-long Vicksburg campaign, with the secondary target being Port Hudson, a few miles above Baton Rouge, Louisiana. Both strongholds fell in July 1863 – coinciding with the Union victory at Gettysburg. These victories effectively allowed the Mississippi to finally flow, in Lincoln's words, 'unvexed to the sea', and denied the Confederacy the benefits of its use.

The only other western campaign which deserves mention was the ill-conceived Red River Expedition of 1864. This was an army-designed affair, though enthusiastically supported by Admiral Porter. The objective was the capture of Shreveport, Louisiana, a major supply depot for Confederate forces in Texas. The effort was marked by poor planning and nearly resulted in significant naval losses due to the rapid falling of the river. In all it was a waste of resources for a questionable strategic rationale. Indeed, it delayed U S Grant's plan to attack Mobile, Alabama

and move eastward rather than west into territory already severed from the Confederacy.[4]

On the Atlantic and Gulf coasts the remainder of the war can be summarized in three names: Charleston, Mobile and Wilmington. Of these three, Wilmington was the most strategically important target: it was the most accessible point for blockade runners making the short run from Bermuda and Nassau, and its rail connections to Virginia provided critical supplies for Robert E Lee's Army of Northern Virginia. It was, for these reasons, exceedingly well defended – or was by the time the Union brought its forces to bear.

Taking Wilmington had been one of the suggestions of the Blockade Board as early as September 1861. At that early date, its defenses were minimal. However, in addition to difficulties obtaining army forces for the operation, the main obstacle in any naval assault was the shallowness of the waters: close-in action against the defenses would require vessels of less than a 12-foot draft. After March 1862 the navy had only one armored vessel which met this criteria and that was Ericsson's *Monitor*. By the end of 1862 more monitors were entering the inventory and serious plans were being made for a combined naval and army assault. The new monitors, however, were found to be deeper than the original ship – making their usefulness in the effort questionable. Then *Monitor* herself sank in a gale in December 1862. At that juncture, the Wilmington attempt was cancelled and almost immediately the target was changed to Charleston.[5]

The Union attack on the defences of Charleston, April 1863. Politically, the city was a popular target. This particular effort failed, and the city did not succumb until late in the war. From *Harper's Weekly*. (US Navy)

**A**ttack on Fort Fisher, North Carolina, January 1865. The largest Union fleet ever assembled eliminated the fort and deprived blockade runners of their most useful port – Wilmington, North Carolina. (US Navy)

Charleston was the politically popular objective, though its strategic value was negligible. The city was considered the hotbed of the rebellion, and had been the focal point of secession fervor since the Nullification Controversy of 1832. Further incentive to take Charleston was provided in January 1863, when the Confederate fleet temporarily drove off part of the blockading fleet. In April 1863, a fleet under S F Dupont attacked the forts in Charleston harbor. This failed, and subsequent bombardments were equally unsuccessful. The Confederate forces evacuated in February 1865, only after W T Sherman's army, moving northward from Savannah, cut off its communications.

Meanwhile, both the West Gulf and North Atlantic Blockading Squadrons were more successful. In August 1864, Farragut took Mobile Bay. Then, in January 1865, naval and army forces attacked Fort Fisher at Wilmington. This success proved to be a factor leading to Lee's surrender in April 1865.

It appears that naval war strategy was less brilliant than the caliber of its leadership might have indicated. It is remarkable that the naval successes on the Atlantic coast were never exploited as part of an overall strategic plan. Given the navy's amphibious capability and demonstrated prowess, it is amazing that a major invasion force was not put ashore – most profitably in North Carolina – to threaten Richmond from the south. Of course such a move would have been predicated on substantial army cooperation, which may have been unlikely for many reasons, including the long-standing reluctance to detach significant forces from the defense of Washington. In any event, the gains made on the Atlantic remained only holding actions.

These accomplished little except to prevent some local defense forces from reinforcing the more important theatres of the war, and, of course, to close long portions of the coast to blockade runners. If this strategic summary leads to the conclusion that Union strategy was, after Vicksburg, quite unclear, many authorities are agreed. One summed it thus: 'Strategic Planning was almost non existent.'[6]

# Naval logistics

Logistics seems to hold as analogous a position in the military as economics holds in academia: a dismal science. It rarely appears in popular history and space devoted to it is never in proportion to its importance in any given war. The Civil War is no different: precious little has been written on naval logistics in that conflict. The majority of the following has been culled from Dr Robert Browning's recent study of the North Atlantic Blockading Squadron.

Of course the basis for logistics was the acquisition of supplies, whether it was coal, food, or clothing. Most of the materiel was purchased by contract, via advertisements and the lowest bidder. In some instances, particularly when time was of the essence, the purchases were made on the open market – with no guarantees of low or fair pricing. The materials were divided into forty-five categories or classes for convenience of bidders.

The Bureau of Provisions and Clothing handled all materiel purchasing and distribution for the department, with the exception of coal, which fell to a navy agent in Philadelphia, and munitions, which fell under the Bureau of Ordnance. More on this later. Paymaster Horatio Bridge, head of the bureau, proved an able man for the job. At the beginning of the war, he restructured procedures to eliminate the agents and their commissions and made contracts directly through the department.

Distribution points were necessary to facilitate the navy's access to supplies. In the west, the first depot was at Cairo, Illinois, followed by others set up as the navy moved south. The most important of these was at Memphis, Tennessee. Along the hostile coast, only Key West remained a Union strong point and supply depot. As has been described above, other distribution points were seized, including New Berne and Beaufort, North Carolina (note that there was also a Beaufort, South Carolina, also in Federal hands), Port Royal in South Carolina, Ship Island, and, later, New Orleans and the re-taken Pensacola Navy Yard.

Two major categories of goods had to be dealt with by Bridge

Port Royal, South Carolina. A huge protected harbor made this an ideal base of operations and a depot for the blockading squadrons. (US Navy)

Ship Island, west of Mobile, was seized early in the war and became a staging area for operations against New Orleans. From *Harper's Pictorial History of the Civil War.*

and his bureau. On one hand were clothing and dry goods, for which spoilage was not a major problem. On the other were fresh beef and vegetables for the men. These perishables required prompt delivery and constant replenishment.

In the fall of 1861, the navy instituted regularly scheduled supply steamers, running the length of the blockade and carrying fresh beef and vegetables, as well as mail, personal parcels, and sutlers. Initially, the large steamers *Supply*, *Rhode Island* and *Connecticut* were used for this purpose, with *Massachusetts* and *New Berne* later added to the schedule.

An innovation was a 'chill room' on the *Connecticut*. This refrigeration compartment carried 59,000 pounds of beef and 125 tons of ice. The beef quarters were hung on hooks rather than stowed between ice layers.

These steamers loaded at New York, Boston, Philadelphia and Baltimore and became an important fixture in the maintenance of the blockade. As the number of blockaders increased, the system was strained to its limits, and eventually *Rhode Island* and *Connecticut* were reserved for the Gulf squadrons; *Masschusetts* for the Virginia-to-the-Keys vessels.

It was soon obvious that one supply vessel for the two Atlantic squadrons was simply impracticable. The interval between supply ships for the North Atlantic squadron increased to four to six weeks, forcing blockaders to go off station to obtain supplies and resulting in breakdowns in communications with the north. The result, in 1863, was the addition of the *New Berne*, a screw steamer strictly for supplying the North Atlantic blockaders.

Non-perishables had a more prosaic path from supplier to blockader. In the North Atlantic squadron, they went to the storeship *Brandywine* at Hampton Roads, from whence they were sent, usually by chartered vessels, to New Bern or Beaufort. On their arrival, they were parcelled out directly from the transport to the blockaders close at hand. Chartered schooners were utilized to trans-ship supplies from the transport to blockaders at extremities of the squadron's cruising grounds. Unfortunately, by the time the schooners reached the outer limits, there was likely to be little left in their holds – the leavings, as it were.

To preserve the levels of non-perishables, particularly clothing, storage facilities were maintained by the squadrons. In the North Atlantic squadron, there were schooners chartered for the long term, as well as storage warehouses at New Berne, Morehead City and Fort Macon, North Carolina. The North Atlantic squadron also obtained fresh beef via the army commissary at Roanoke Island.[7]

Two problems harried the navy's supply system for the North Atlantic squadron: the high cost of demurrage (the fees paid for allowing a vessel to remain on station until she was unloaded) and losses due to spoilage. One schooner on the North Carolina Sounds cost the navy $23,000 for her presence basically as a storeship for over two-and-a-half years. The *William Badger*, the main storage hulk on the Sounds, leaked, was rotten, and infested with rats. In this condition she remained on station from 1862 to the end of the war.[8]

Ordnance supplies were ordered from the Bureau of Ordnance, and the naval ordnance officer at Fort Monroe, Virginia supervised shipping the munitions via chartered schooner to the storage facilities to the south. Shortage of storage warehouses at Fort Monroe created a situation where storage schooners were employed for most of the war. Again, demurrage charges were a constant drain on funds, and some of the schooners leaked badly. Furthermore, the small hatches to their holds made access difficult and offloading time consuming. The only advantage of schooner-storage over warehouse accommodations was its tow-ability.

In the steam navy, coal was a constant need. The previous war with Mexico had not prepared the navy to deal with the amounts of coal necessary and the distances over which it would be transported during the War Between the States. Early in the Civil War it was thought that five sailing vessels would suffice for all the supplies of the blockading squadrons including coal.[9] Such unrealistic thinking was soon discarded and the department, encouraged by the Bureau of Steam Engineering, determined that southern coaling bases were necessary. Fort Monroe was the first base to be so utilized, though it did not have adequate wharfage for efficient loading. Coaling stations were later established at various points along the coast – usually coinciding with the other supply facilities mentioned above.

The coal supply for the blockade was the responsibility of one man: John S Chambers, navy agent at Philadelphia. He oversaw contracts purchasing a regular supply from mines in Pennsylvania, as well as transportation to the wharves in Philadelphia and New York. Coal companies, railroads and canals profited immensely from the navy's wartime coal needs.

Though there was never an actual shortage of coal, there were significant stoppages in its supply during the war. A particularly destructive storm in the coal region, for instance, interrupted deliveries for two to three months in 1862. A major miners' strike closed the mines in 1863, and the threat of Confederate military action in July of the same year delayed shipments from the

Coaling on the James River, 1864. The collier schooner USS *Zeta* is alongside monitor *Canonicus* with a tug awaiting completion of the loading operation. In the steam navy, coal was a strategic element of the first order and its availability was critical for all operations, routine or otherwise. (US Navy)

Pennsylvania mines. During the winters, ice often obstructed the Delaware River, further hampering deliveries.

The operation of coaling itself was fraught with difficulties. When a wharf was not available, which was the usual situation with the blockading squadrons, coal was loaded from the collier. Rough weather would prevent a collier from laying alongside to discharge her cargo, and such conditions could prevent small boats from being used to trans-ship the coal. Poor weather was a seemingly unavoidable difficulty in North Carolina's Cape Fear and vicinity.

Coaling generally was done with wheelbarrows, carrying about 200 pounds each, or various types of buckets or tubs, the largest of which might handle 375 pounds. At six to ten containers to the ton, coaling a 150-ton capacity gunboat would require 900 containers. This could consume a significant part of a day or longer — leaving open the possibility that worsening weather could halt the process.

Pre-planning to determine the need for coal was also an inexact science. A major variable was the widely disparate rates at which various types of vessels consumed it. Even within the same type of vessel, coal use could vary by 20 to 30 per cent, depending upon the skill of the firemen in its economic use.

Coal usage also was a function of the type of steaming being done on station. As the vessels ranged further out, coal usage increased, if their station allowed little movement, the opposite was true. In shallow waters, many steamers could not accept a full load in their bunkers. Consequently, these ships exhausted their supply quickly, and their time off station at a collier or wharf ballooned. Similarly, shallow waters often hampered the colliers themselves: if their draft was too deep, lighters might be required to offload their cargo simply to allow passage over a bar or sandbank.[10]

The navy never completely solved the coal logistics problems during the Civil War, particularly in North Carolina waters, where all the problems listed above intersected graphically: legendarily poor weather, high coal usage due to the number of blockade runners in that vicinity, and shallow waters which hampered both blockaders and heavily laden colliers. In consequence, the blockade was probably the least effective in those waters.

Further south and in the Gulf, the weather generally moderated, but distance to the Pennsylvania coal supply increased. The coast further south also provided an increasing number of sheltered coves and inlets where coaling could be accomplished in smooth waters.

The subject of Civil War naval logistics has not been studied in its entirety. Though it does not have the glamour of combat and heroism, the impact of logistics on the war effort cannot be underestimated.

# Chapter Thirteen
# CIVIL WAR NAVAL TACTICS

The swift advance in naval technology, had not, at least by 1861, spawned a comprehensive study of the impact of these developments on battle tactics. To that date, there had been three significant tactical studies: the French Admiral Bouet-Willaumez's *Batailles de Terre et de Mer*, Sir Howard Douglas's *Naval Warfare under Steam*, and Commander James H Ward's *A Manual of Naval Tactics*. In the last of these three, Ward, an American naval officer, quoted en masse from Douglas's work, and expanded but little upon it. Though these studies addressed steam warships and shell guns, the latest of them (Ward's) was written in 1859, three years before the *Monitor*'s turret came into being and the *Warrior* took to the seas.[1]

As Commander Ward stated: 'So recent is the introduction of steam into the navies of the world, that no maritime battle, and but little experience of any kind, is afforded from which to draw examples and illustrations...'.[2] The Civil War naval vessel or flotilla commander did not have a significant body of work to draw upon when going into battle. Consequently, the tactics utilized during the war were in many instances common sense solutions made by the commanding officer on the spot, with due consideration of the strengths and weaknesses of his own and his adversary's position and warships, in addition to general maxims handed down from the Nelsons and Bainbridges of the age of sail.

The following descriptions cover the engagements of several types fought during the war, with emphasis on the tactics actually employed. If possible, historical precedents will be related, as well as the battle's implications for the future of naval warfare.

To begin with, it would be appropriate to present highlights of Sir Howard Douglas's work and a few other observations on the state of naval tactics in 1861.

Douglas went to great lengths explaining the sailing tactics which had been negated by the appearance of steam. Steam, he wrote, 'entirely annuls all the limitations and disabilities imposed by the wind...and opens the whole surface of the ocean as a battle-field.' Furthermore, he stated, a fleet in line ahead, if penetrated by the enemy, would not be thrown into 'that inextricable disorder' common in the days of sail, and, in fact, such a penetration might now be prevented by the skilful use of steam power for manoeuvering.[3]

Much of Douglas's work — seconded by Commander Ward — dealt with fleet-versus-fleet actions at sea and the steamers' capability of manoeuvering with the precision of army formations. The Confederacy's lack of a seagoing battlefleet thus made much of his theorizing purely academic in discussing the Civil War. However, use of steam power to enable precise movements — regardless of the wind's direction — was practiced assiduously by wartime commanders on both sides.

Douglas repeatedly voiced the dangers of loose and dragging lines on screw-propelled sailing vessels, even advocating 'submarine armor' to prevent these from fouling propellers. Then he turned the idea on end and suggested firing on the adversary's rigging to foul his screw, then close in and aim for the hull.

Douglas was enamored by steam, it appears, in that it would allow the more powerful and fast steamer to take the advantage (formerly the weather gauge in sailing parlance) and close in. And by closing in, he meant to grapple and board, and, by extension, win by capturing the enemy vessel. This was the traditional viewpoint supported by centuries of naval warfare in which sinking the enemy vessel was the exception rather than the rule.

Douglas made one assumption which was to be disproved repeatedly in the Civil War and afterwards. With screw steamers, he wrote, 'their masts may be shot away, but the submerged machine by which they are moved, if kept free from entanglement, is inaccessible to shot.' In context, Douglas is discussing giving chase to a flying enemy after an indecisive action. However, he did not take into consideration the longer range and greater destructive power of the shell gun, and therefore did not visualize the possibility that a sea battle between relatively well matched ships would be resolved by concentrating aim on the hull and it's machinery and sinking the adversary. Though boarding would occur in the Civil War, it was more a function of the confines, riverine and littoral, in which it was generally fought. On the bluewater, the norm would soon be long range confrontations, and destroying the vessel, rather than its personnel.[4]

Probably Douglas's most applicable statement in regard to the War Between the States was his reiteration of Henri Paixhan's observation 'that a few steamers, with little or no sailing power, might destroy or capture any ship if properly attacked...', though Douglas added that this would be true only 'in calms and [in] operations in inland seas and waters, in which fleets of large ships of war can neither manoeuvre, nor follow vessels of small draught of water into shallow creeks or channels'.[5]

Interestingly, neither Douglas nor Ward mentioned two subjects which became crucial factors in the Civil War: armored vessels and ramming tactics, despite the increasing popular interest in the latter subject and the appearance of the ironclad floating batteries in the Crimea. As early as the 1830s, Captain Matthew C Perry had suggested adapting a ram to a fast and heavy paddlewheel warship and, at the same time advocated thick, angletopped, iron-protected bulwarks for the vessel. The pre-Civil War decades would see variations on these ideas, usually projected by inventors and entrepreneurs, but generally ignored – until the Crimea – by naval authorities.

The American Civil War would provide the world with examples of armored vessels in battle, both in ship-to-ship encounters and against fortifications. It would also give ram advocates much ammunition, though many failed to see that effective ramming was usually limited to engagements at close quarters, rather on the open seas.

The following is a presentation of the three types of Civil War naval actions: fleet versus shore fortifications, single-ship duels, and fleets of various sizes versus single ironclads. Additionally, tactics used on the blockade will be presented. This will not be a comprehensive study of all Civil War naval battles; rather I have chosen examples which illustrate the tactics of the era.

It was axiomatic – at least before the Crimea – that naval ships were no match, gun for gun, for shore fortifications. If the vessels stopped to aim, they made excellent targets for the stationary guns

**P**oorly defended Hatteras Inlet fell to seven ships and 158 guns in August 1861. Under steam, the fleet circled and began firing when within range. (US Navy)

*Second days action at Hatteras inlet*

Mohican.    Augusta.    Unadilla.    Pawnee.    Ottawa.  Curlew  Seneca.
Susquehanna.    Wabash. (Flag ship)    Bienville.    raking the fort

FORT BEAUREGARD.    TRANSPORT FLEET IN THE DISTANCE.    FORT WALKER

Parsons, del.    W. Ridgway

ashore; if they moved to avoid damage, their own aim was degraded.

It was not long into the war that several examples called the axiom into question. On the Atlantic, actions against Hatteras Inlet, North Carolina and Port Royal, South Carolina pitted large Union fleets against four Confederate forts, two in each engagement. In each instance, the ships were unarmored and, for the most part, steam powered.

At Hatteras Inlet in August 1861, seven ships with 158 guns, plus transports and troops, attacked Forts Hatteras and Clark. The forts mounted only 25 guns, and were poorly constructed and defended in the bargain. The larger naval vessels, under Flag Officer Silas Stringham, used the innovative tactic of steaming in a circle, firing while in motion, while the smaller ships towed surf boats with their infantry to within rowing range of the shore. The latter was a common practice during the Mexican War. (It is also noteworthy that the sailing frigate *Cumberland* was towed through this engagement.)

The forts, which mounted no cannon heavier than 32-pounders, were overwhelmed by the 9-, 10- and 11-inch guns on the Union vessels and surrendered, obviating the need to use ground troops.[6] It was an easy victory, with only one Federal casualty, and the Hatteras Inlet action heavily influenced future Union tactics against shore fortifications.

The action against Port Royal was in some ways a scaled up version of Hatteras Inlet. In this instance, the two Confederate forts, Beauregard and Walker, faced each other some 2½ miles across Port Royal Sound and mounted a total of 43 guns, some of which were 8- and 10-inch Columbiads and rifles. The forts themselves were significantly more substantial than those at Hatteras.

The Union fleet totalled seventy-seven ships, sixty of which were transporting over 12,000 troops. The seventeen warships mounted 157 guns, and all save one were steamers.

The plan of attack, formulated by Captain Samuel F DuPont, called for emphasis on Fort Walker, the larger of the two, on the west side of the sound. The five smaller vessels, mounting some 32 guns, were in a flanking position in the event the small Confederate squadron entered the action. The bulk of the fleet (now 125 guns counting only weapons larger than 12-pounders) was arranged line ahead with one ship length between each.

The fleet steamed due north, slowing to fire on both forts, passing some 2½ miles north of them before reversing course, passing them again, this time closer to Fort Walker, on the west. Once south of the forts, the fleet reversed, repeating the ellipse as needed.

Again, the fight was signally one-sided, with the four-hour bombardment killing or wounding fifty-nine Confederates; Union casualties were about half that number, and none of the vessels were significantly damaged.

The Confederates, it seems, were uniformly astounded at the regularity, even mechanical precision of the steam-powered fleet, passing at unvaried intervals, sending its deadly projectiles — and not visibly harmed by their response.[7] It was a well executed plan, and one which shook the old three-shipboard-guns-equals-one-ashore axiom. It was also a tactical performance which would have been impossible under sail.

The famous axiom was not necessarily applicable to two of the most well-known encounters between Union fleets and fortifications at New Orleans and Mobile Bay. In these instances, the objective was to successfully pass the forts with the expectation that they would fall when cut off from their sources of support and supply. In both instances, major cities were the eventual prizes, and, in each case, there was a Confederate naval force in attendance, leading to a fleet encounter.

New Orleans lay some 75 miles upstream from its two most formidable defensive works at Forts Jackson and St Philip, mounting 126 guns, and located advantageously at a bend in the Mississippi. To delay the passage of the enemy fleet at the worst possible place for the ships, a raft of logs and hulks was chained across the river under the fort's guns, and fire rafts were prepared to drift down onto the attackers and create further havoc. Nature assisted the defenders with a 3½ knot current working against the Union fleet.

The Confederate naval force numbered eighteen vessels, most of which were converted tugs and merchant vessels and were of

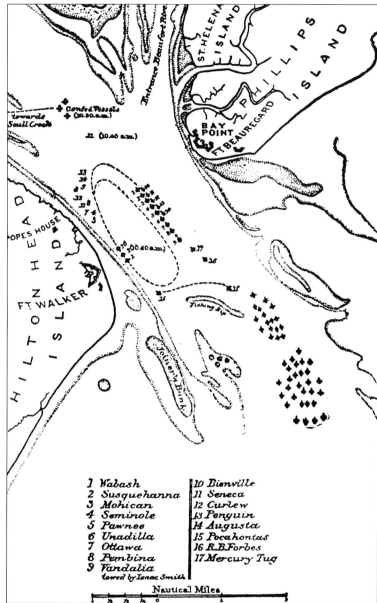

| 1 Wabash | 10 Bienville |
| 2 Susquehanna | 11 Seneca |
| 3 Mohican | 12 Curlew |
| 4 Seminole | 13 Penguin |
| 5 Pawnee | 14 Augusta |
| 6 Unadilla | 15 Pocahontas |
| 7 Ottawa | 16 R.B.Forbes |
| 8 Pembina | 17 Mercury Tug |
| 9 Vandalia | |

*Towed by Isaac Smith*

Nautical Miles

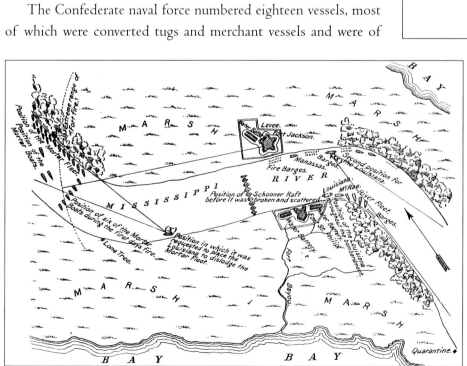

**M**ap of the Port Royal attack. The regularity and ferocity of the Union bombardment astounded the Confederates and put both forts out of action in four hours. From *Battles and Leaders of the Civil War.*

**T**he New Orleans campaign opened with a massive six-day bombardment of the defending forts by mortar boats, as shown here. Their overall effectiveness was doubtful. From *Official Records of the Union and Confederate Navies in the War of the Rebellion.*

marginal naval value. One, however, was the ironclad *Manassas*, which, though only carrying one 32-pounder, had a low profile and a formidable ram bow – which had already punctured, though not fatally, the Union steam sloop *Richmond* in October 1861. Another ironclad, *Louisiana* was incomplete and remained moored throughout the battle, firing on targets of opportunity.

Against this array was the Union fleet under David G Farragut, consisting of twenty-three steamers and twenty mortar boats. Each of the mortar boats carried a single 13-inch mortar, firing a 200-pound shell. They were towed into their firing positions by six of the smaller gunboats. The seventeen steamers which were to pass the forts mounted 192 guns.

There was much disagreement among Farragut and the other principals planning the campaign, particularly concerning the efficacy of the mortars in 'softening up' the forts, and the question of whether the forts would fall if the fleet was successful in passing them. Should they not, the fleet would find itself with an armed enemy to its rear.

In the event, the mortar boats, their masts disguised with tree branches, were brought into position close to the river bank on 18 April 1862, and proceeded to inundate the forts at the rate of over 100 shells an hour for six days. The forts, however, were well sand-bagged and lost as few as eighteen men and 7 guns in this unprecedented bombardment.

The mortars had indeed provided a distraction for two of Farragut's steamers which were sent in to make a break in the river barrier. The effort succeeded by dint of one of the vessels ramming her way through and making a narrow passage on the left bank of the river.

On the 24th, Farragut began his ascent past the forts and other barriers. His original intent was to lead in with the largest vessels, take on the forts, break through the remaining barrier, and meet the Confederate fleet. He was dissuaded from this by his subordinates and, instead, one of the small gunboats was given the lead position as the fleet advanced in line ahead. The heaviest steamers, including Farragut's *Hartford*, were roughly in the center of the line.

Preparations for the passage were well thought out. As the event was to be under darkness, the sides of the ships were daubed with mud, while their decks were white-washed to make objects on deck easily distinguishable. The sides of each ship, alongside the boilers, were draped with anchor chain, to 2 feet below the waterline, with each bight overlapping, resembling the ancient's chain mail. Of course, the upper masts and yards were sent down, with

some of the gunboats even unshipping their lower masts.

Farragut further instructed that guns be mounted on the poop and topgallant forecastle, noting that fore and aft fire would be at a premium in dealing with the enemy vessels and forts. Any great sheer of the helm to bring a broadside to bear forward would place the vessel in danger of losing control to the power of the strong current. Farragut also directed that the ships be trimmed by the head, 'so that if she touches the bottom, she will not swing head down the river'.

The passage itself began in line ahead formation. Once his vessels were beyond the barrier and became targets for the brunt of the fort's guns, the fire rafts and the rebel fleet, all semblance of a line disappeared and a mêleé ensued. In some instances the ships pressed as close as 100 feet to the shore under the guns of the forts; close enough for the ship's gun crews to be singed by enemy gunpowder, and, by the same token, too near for the enemy guns to be depressed for good effect.

The fleet action subsequent to the passage of the forts was a brawl marked by the Confederates' emphasis on ramming – at least two of their fleet were specially built with ram bows. The ram was obviously considered the weapon with which they hoped to counter the Union vessels' overwhelming firepower.

Given the Union fleet's superiority in vessels and guns, 'victo-

Once past the barriers, Farragut's fleet faced the fire of the two forts, fire rafts, and the Confederate fleet, which included two ironclads. Fort St Phillip is in the background here, with the moored ironclad *Louisiana* seen almost in the center. The ironclad *Manassas* is to the left, approaching the steam frigate *Mississippi*. From Wood and Edmonds, *Military History of the Civil War*.

ry' in the fleet engagement at New Orleans had less to do with destroying the Confederate flotilla than with bringing those guns and vessels through relatively intact. The Union vessels generally were in a defensive mode: determined to break through rather than necessarily carry the fight to the enemy. Late in the fray, one of the larger ships, though not built with a ram bow, attempted to run down the *Manassas*. The attempt itself was unsuccessful, but it drove the pestiferous ram aground and ended her career.

Despite predictions to the contrary, the fleet's passage by the forts was successful, with some 180 Union casualties and the loss of one vessel and one mortar schooner. Confederate losses in the forts numbered fifty-two men; and at least seven vessels were destroyed. Three days later the forts' garrisons mutinied, leading to the surrender of the citadels. The city itself followed suit.[8]

The Battle of Mobile Bay led to the capture of one of the last Southern port cities. Again, the battle was in two phases: a passage by fortifications and a fleet contest afterwards, though the latter was dominated by a brawl between the Confederate ironclad *Tennessee* and the entire Union squadron under Admiral Farragut. Unlike New Orleans, there were now ironclads on both sides of the contest.

The defenses of Mobile centered around Fort Morgan, guarding the eastern side of the entrance of the bay. Some 3 miles distant, on the western side of the bay's entrance, was Fort Gaines. Morgan, which would take the brunt of the Union attack, mounted 69 guns, ranging upwards to 8-inch rifled cannon and 10-inch smoothbores. Twenty-nine of these were in exterior works, including a water battery with 7 heavy guns. Fort Gaines was of secondary importance to the battle, and mounted 27 guns.

Of major significance, in addition to the guns, were mines seeded strategically across the bay's entrance. Approximately 180 of these 'torpedoes' effectively limited safe access to the bay to an area some 100 yards wide directly in front of Fort Morgan. Though Civil War torpedoes were about as likely to misfire as not, with a charge of as much as 100 pounds of black powder each, they were not minor annoyances.

Nor was the ironclad *Tennessee* a minor consideration for the fleet. Though mounting only six rifled cannon, the *Tennessee* was exceptionally well protected, with 5 to 6 inches of armor on her sloping sides, as well as down, on a reverse angle, to several feet below the waterline. All this was backed by at least 2 feet of oak and pine. Her prow was fashioned as a ram — which was rendered less effective by her feeble engines.

The remaining Confederate 'fleet' was to prove the least effec-

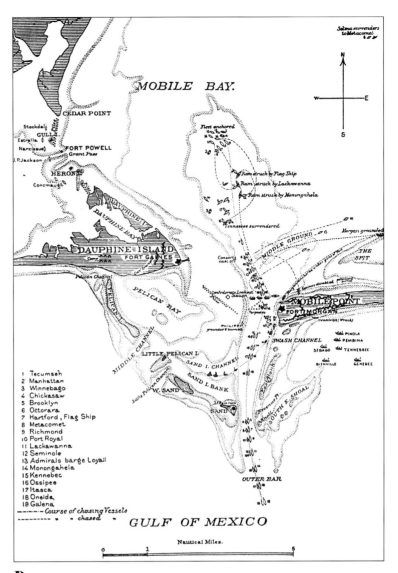

**B**attle of Mobile Bay, August 1864. Farragut ordered his wooden ships to be lashed in pairs to pass the forts. This protected the smaller vessels in the lee of the larger, and provided two sets of machinery should one ship's engines be disabled. The scheme worked exactly as planned. From *Battles and Leaders of the Civil War*.

tive element of the rebel defenses. The three wooden gunboats were hastily contrived and mounted an aggregate of 16 guns on their open decks. Their usefulness ended when the line of torpedoes no longer restricted the oncoming Union vessels to bow-on fire, and their broadsides could be brought to bear.

The Union fleet consisted of eighteen ships, four of which were monitors. In all there were 199 guns, including four 15-inch smoothbores on two of the monitors. These were the largest guns used in the battle.

As at New Orleans, there was no question of destroying the forts: Farragut's objective was to the enter the bay with his fleet intact, expecting the subsequent fall of the forts and the city. Thus his battle plan emphasized compacting the length of his formation as much as possible and doing the utmost to eliminate the possibility of mechanical or other damage which might impede their progress through the Confederate gauntlet. Given the number and size of the enemy guns at Fort Morgan, any lengthy delay at the head of his column could prove fatal to his wooden ships. Concentration of his line would also increase the volume of fire available to batter down the fort's guns and their crews.

To achieve his objectives, Farragut ordered an attack in two parallel columns. The relatively invulnerable ironclads would be in the column nearest the fort, interposed between it and the wooden vessels. The wooden ships were lashed in twos, immediately halving the length of the line. This disposition accomplished two other objectives: the smaller, less well armed ships were sheltered behind the big steam sloops; and each pair had two sources of motive power in the event that one was disabled by shot or accident. Farragut had used this arrangement previously, passing the guns at Port Hudson on the Mississippi in 1863.

It is noteworthy that the fleet's only three paddle-wheel steamers were paired with the largest steam sloops at the head of the column. This may well have been to capitalize on the extra turning capability of sidewheel ships, in the event that one of the lead vessels should be disabled or need assistance in quickly pulling out of the line. It will be seen that this capability was to prove useful at a critical point in the battle.

Other factors which Farragut considered were tide and wind conditions. To aid in swift passage, it was planned at flood tide; to provide clear sight for his gunners, a west wind was desired. These conditions coincided on typical August mornings on the Gulf.

Preparing his ships again involved sending down upper masts and spars, mounting additional forward guns, protecting the ships' sides with anchor cables, and decks with sandbags. On *Richmond* over 3000 sandbags were piled on her starboard side - stem to stern as well as athwartships fore and aft.

Instructions to the gunners were simple. Once in range, fire as fast as possible. They were to begin with shell and shrapnel and, at 300 to 400 yards, switch to grape shot. This was obviously not intended to destroy the forts or guns, but to decimate or drive off the Confederate gun crews while the fleet was at its most vulnerable point in the passage.

On 5 August 1864, the fleet weighed and steamed into Mobile Bay, the fourteen wooden ships lashed together in pairs led by *Brooklyn* (and sidewheeler *Octarara*), with Farragut on *Hartford* (lashed to *Metacomet*), second in line. *Tecumseh* led the four ironclads, in the column between the wooden ships and Fort Morgan.

As Farragut had feared, events at the head of his columns nearly condemned the squadron to ignominy. Reaching a point slightly beyond the fort, *Tecumseh*, leading the ironclads, suddenly lurched and sank before the eyes of the entire fleet. In less than thirty seconds she was an eddy in the bay. The sight — sudden evidence of the capability of the underwater bombs — was probably unprecedented in naval warfare and nearly brought about a greater disaster. *Brooklyn*, leading the second column, immediately stopped and backed, bringing her port quarter across *Hartford*'s path, and all this directly under the galling fire of Fort Morgan, as well as the raking fire of the Confederate squadron ahead. It would be a catastrophe to remain and potential disaster to proceed. But *Brooklyn* was too close for *Hartford* to clear by simply bringing the helm over. Farragut ordered his sidewheel consort *Metacomet* to back hard, and, simultaneously, *Hartford* went ahead. Thus *Hartford*'s bows were, in Alfred Thayer Mahan's words, 'twisted short round' and she was clear to proceed. Farragut then uttered his immortal words, usually rendered: 'Damn the torpedoes. Full speed ahead!', but which were more likely: 'Damn the torpedoes...Four bells' — full ahead — and the passage by the fort was completed successfully.

The only major loss was the disabling of the machinery of the *Oneida*, which was last in the line, by a shot to her boilers. As per Farragut's plan, her consort, *Galena*, shepherded her through, but not without casualties. This event probably brought the most serious criticism of Farragut's battle arrangements: his placing of all the heavier ships at the line's head, leaving the less well armed vessels at the rear. By the time the rear-most ships were at the forts, the Confederate gunners had recovered from the pounding they had received earlier, and pounced upon them with renewed ferocity.

Leaving the now-sidelined fort behind, the fleet faced the Confederate ironclad and gunboats. *Metacomet* and *Hartford* made short work of two gunboats and a third grounded out of the action. Only the formidable *Tennessee* remained, and, contrary to good sense, the courageous ironclad, under veteran Franklin Buchanan, took on the entire Union fleet.

The order of the day was to ram. In preparation, the bows of two of the faster Union steam sloops, *Lackawanna* and *Monongahela*, had been given ad hoc iron plating, no doubt in the hope that sufficient speed and the momentum of their tonnage (over 2000 each) would at least dent the *Tennessee*. The combat began when both steamed at the ironclad at full speed, landing well-aimed blows which only succeeded in damaging their own bows. (It is noteworthy that the *Monongahela* rammed the ironclad while still lashed to the gunboat *Kennebec*, adding yet more to her momentum.) Next *Hartford* delivered a glancing blow, also without noticeable effect.

The monitors joined the fray and the remainder of the battle was played out at point blank range. Eventually the *Tennessee*'s exposed rudder chains were shot away, her stack was riddled, and gunport shutters were disabled. Most of the damage was apparently inflicted by the 11-inch guns of the monitor *Chickasaw*, which dogged her stern at 50 yards for a half-hour, pounding away at her plating. She surrendered literally surrounded – gunwale to gunwale – by five of Farragut's fleet.

On 17 August Fort Morgan surrendered, followed a week

**T**he lone Confederate ironclad *Tennessee* took on the fleet, shown here engaging with *Hartford*. **Ramming tactics came into play, but point-blank gunfire alone ended *Tennessee*'s career. (US Navy)**

later by Fort Gaines. The Federal forces then controlled the bay, though a serious effort to capture the city itself would come only later in the war.[9]

The above examples describe successful Union efforts against coastal fortifications, involving first wooden vessels, then combined fleets of ironclads and conventional ships. The other side to the story was seen at Charleston, South Carolina in April 1863. Here a fleet comprised wholly of ironclad vessels was repulsed in less than an hour.

The determination to attack Charleston was based less on strategic considerations than to quash the Confederate seat of rebellion. Taking the city was not to be simple. Much Confederate treasure had been spent in expectation of this very event. The key to the harbor defenses was Fort Sumter, dominating the center of its entrance. Second in importance and size was Fort Moultrie on the northern side of the entrance, and four smaller batteries completed the defenses. At the time of the Federal attack at least 69 heavy guns came into play, 33 at Fort Sumter. A significant por-

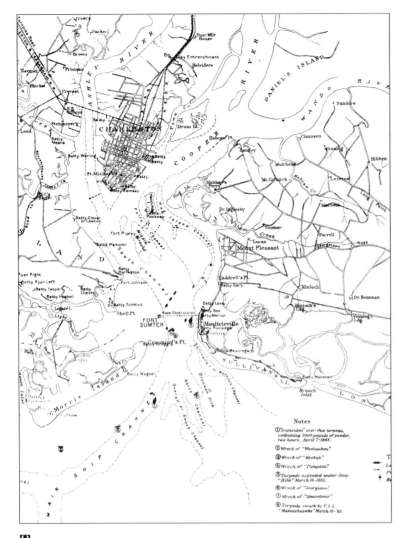

**T**he defences of Charleston were formidable – the product of years of preparation. In addition to heavy guns arranged to catch any foe in crossfire, there were obstructions and torpedoes in artfully contrived locations. Some of the latter were operated by remote from the shore. Note Fort Sumter in the center of harbor entrance, with batteries on either side and beyond. From *Official Records....*

tion of these were rifled 7-, 8- and 10-inch weapons. The disposition of these weapons was such that there were few locations in or near the harbor where attacking vessels would not be caught in a crossfire.

The defenders missed no opportunity to further enhance the trap they were laying for any invading fleet. Obstructions, buoys and torpedoes made the harbor and its approaches a deadly obstacle course for anything afloat. Obstacles included pilings, rope, cable, and net obstructions designed to entangle the enemy's propellers. Three concentric circles of buoys were set out at predetermined distances from Fort Sumter specifically as aiming aids for

their gunners, and various types of torpedoes were strategically placed in the harbor, in some instances in conjunction with the obstructions. Some of the larger torpedoes, made by filling iron boilers with powder, were electrically operated from shore points, to be detonated when an enemy vessel parked itself unknowingly above.

Two ironclads, *Chicora* and *Palmetto State*, were also available if needed. They were not.

Admiral Samuel F DuPont had at his disposal the most advanced warships ever devised by man. Seven were *Passaic* class monitors, improved versions of Ericsson's original 'cheesebox', each with one 11- and one 15-inch gun in the turret. One was the broadside armorclad *New Ironsides*, with fourteen 11-inch Dahlgren smoothbores, two 150-pounder and two 50-pounder rifles. She would prove to be the most invulnerable ironclad produced by the Union. The unfortunate *Keokuk* completed the flotilla: she carried an astonishly fragile armor cladding with two 11-inch guns in non-rotating 'turrets' or barbettes. An aggregate of 34 guns afloat were delivered into a what proved to be a cauldron of fire.

DuPont's plan was for the fleet to advance line ahead to the north and northwest of Fort Sumter between that fort and Fort Moultrie. They were to 'take up a position' at '600 to 800 yards' and concentrate slow and deliberate fire on the northwest face of that fort, which was considered its weakest wall. This area of the harbor was also that which was least subject to the Confederate batteries' crossfire.

*New Ironsides*, the flagship, took position in the center of the line, to enable vessels at both extremes to see her signals. The lead ship, monitor *Weehawken*, was pushing an unwieldy timber raft-like contraption designed to sweep a clear path through the mines. For reasons unknown, the weak *Keokuk* was last in line.

The attack began the afternoon of 7 April 1863, and was initially delayed some two hours when the torpedo 'rake' became entangled with *Weehawken*'s anchor cable. Once under way again, *Weehawken* led as far as an imaginary line drawn from Fort Sumter to Fort Moultrie. Unfortunately, this demarcation point was not intangible, but proved to be a formidable 'boom' composed of net, ropes, and cable, held afloat by doubled casks, and rendered lethal by torpedoes. For good reason, *Weehawken* halted and the followers proceeded to crowd in on her, equally stymied by the unholy objects floating ahead. At this juncture, as at one signal, the Confederate torrent was unleashed.

By all reports, the volume of rebel fire was indescribable. No observer was able to avoid hyperbole in attempting to convey the

Positions of the ironclads at Charleston. Mine-laden obstructions stopped their advance and held them when the Confederate batteries opened fire. Note the position of *Keokuk* ('K') – this untried and poorly armored vessel was quickly dispatched by the barrage. From *Official Records*....

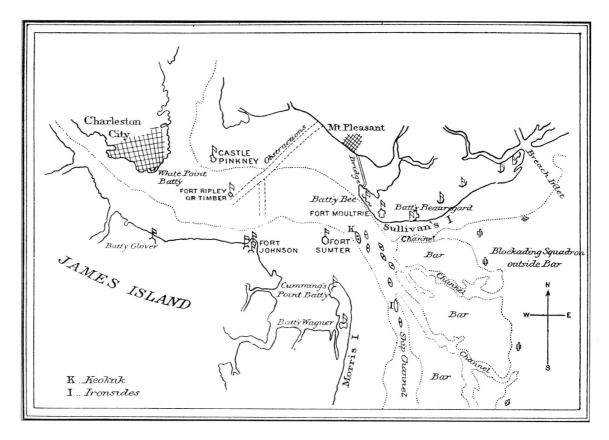

impression made by the Confederate cannonade. In the space of less than one hour Charleston's defenders fired an estimated 2200 projectiles, with some reports claiming 3500. Even the lower number averaged about 36 shots per minute. And the fire was – as should have been expected – exceedingly well directed.

One of monitor *Passaic's* officers reported fifteen shots passing in a few seconds – and those were ones that missed. She was hit thirty-five times and *New Ironsides* took ninety-three hits. There were fifty-three identifiable shot dents on the *Weehawken*. The poor so-called ironclad *Keokuk* had the misfortune to find herself as close as any of the others (about 500 yards) and sustained ninety hits, nineteen of which perforated her hull near the waterline.

DuPont's fleet replied spasmodically: a total of 139 shots were fired, no more than 25 from any one vessel. This can be attributed to the typical slow rate of fire for the monitors. The turrets on two monitors were jammed by enemy projectiles, and two others lost the use of one of their 2 guns. *Keokuk* fired three shells before succumbing to the intense fire and pulling out of the action. *New Ironsides*, whose deeper draft placed her farther from Sumter, was carried about by the current and forced to anchor twice to prevent being put ashore. She fired one token broadside before the engagement was terminated by DuPont.

It was DuPont's intention at the end of the day to re-engage the following morning. On calling his ships' commanding officers

to confer, however, he learned of the damage already sustained by the vessels and determined that the odds were too greatly skewed to warrant a renewal of the fight.[10] Though the Federal fleet – and ground troops – would continue to hound, harass and beseige this 'contumacious city', it would not fall until early 1865.

DuPont, however, quickly fell from grace due to his 'failure', and he was soon replaced. In fairness, however, he had long been reluctant to attack the city and essentially had been pressured into a project which, realistically, could not succeed as constituted in April 1863. It is probably significant that DuPont's replacement, John A Dahlgren, an a expert in naval ordnance, did not attempt a purely naval assault. Rather, a series of combined naval-army actions began, aimed at capturing some of the smaller batteries, and provide land bases for Union artillery.

Finally, it is amazing that a fleet mounting 34 guns could have been expected to make any significant mark on forts with twice that number of cannon. This illogic can only be explained by the 'monitor fever' rampant in the land since the original *Monitor* had checkmated the *Virginia* at Hampton Roads. The 'fever' was one of the earliest examples of the 'magic' of technology when applied to war. Overestimation of the efficacy of sophisticated technology is a continuing thread, particularly in the history of American warfare. One is reminded of the Second World War's famous Norden aircraft bombsight, or sonar – new

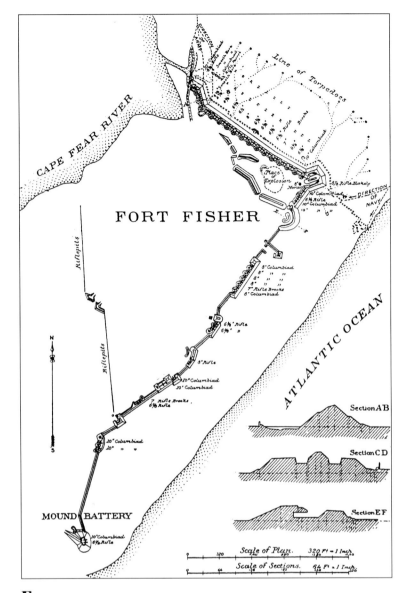

**F**ort Fisher, North Carolina. Guarding the most important blockade running southern port – Wilmington – Fort Fisher's defences had been continually strengthened through three years of war. Its earthworks and bomb-proofs were effective against the largest shell guns: unlike masonry, the exploded earth could simply be filled back in. From *Battles and Leaders of the Civil War.*

and overrated technology which accomplished significantly less than hyperbole would have had it.

Monitor fever was also based on a totally erroneous understanding of the vessel and its designed mission, which was solely to take on Confederate ironclads in shallow waters. Ericsson never claimed it was the tool with which to batter down shore fortifications. Unfortunately, he failed to actively emphasize this aspect of his vessel's shortcomings and the 'fever' went unabated with predictable results.

While the attack on Charleston was woefully under-armed, the Union's final assault, in December 1864 and January 1865, on a major coastal fortification saw the largest American fleet in action until the Second World War. Appropriately, the target was Fort Fisher, North Carolina, protecting Wilmington, the last remaining open Confederate port. (Charleston would be evacuated in February, 1865.)

Wilmington had been a long-standing thorn in the side of the Union: it not only remained uncaptured, it was by far the most convenient port to blockade runners from Bermuda. Strategically, if it fell, the rebel army's position at Richmond would soon be untenable.

The first assault on Fort Fisher, in late 1864, was a miscarriage involving poor planning and dissension between the army and navy commanders. It only served to warn the Confederates that worse was soon to come.

Fort Fisher itself was an 'L' shaped work with the intersection of the two sides on the sea side of the peninsula separating the Cape Fear River from the Atlantic. The longer side of the 'L' paralleled the sea and the shorter face ran athwart the width of the peninsula, about ½ a mile, the whole facing northeastward. The sea face ran about 1 mile in a southwestward direction.

In contrast to pre-war masonry works, Fisher was entirely of earth, which was found to absorb projectiles whose craters were simple enough to re-fill with a bit of industry on the part of the defenders. There were some seventy cannon at intervals along the two sides, arranged individually or in pairs, divided by traverses. This series of 'mounds', each some 12 feet above the parapet, provided protection from enfilading fire and contained 'bomb-proofs' with passageways and shelter for the gun crews. The land face was further protected by a palisade and an extensive minefield.

The Union fleet gathered to take Fort Fisher was commanded by David Dixon Porter and numbered fifty-nine ships mounting 627 guns. Of these ships, forty-four would shell the fort, while the remainder waited in reserve. Five ironclads were in the assaulting fleet, including one twin-turret monitor and the *New Ironsides*. The shore forces, landed beforehand, numbered 8000 army troops, plus some 1600 marines and sailors.

This was to be a set-piece battle, as far as the navy was concerned: the vessels were to take pre-determined positions, anchor, and deliver their fire on command. The warships were in line ahead with the column extending over 2 miles from end to end. In general, the vessels were arranged in descending order by armament with the weakest batteries at the ends and the most powerful

Bomb-proof at Fort Fisher sheltered gunners and ammunition from lateral and plunging fire. Un-hit guns could quickly be re-manned and brought back into action. (USAMHI)

as close to the northeast bastion (the intersection of the two faces) as possible. The four monitors formed their own rank to the inside of the main line of wooden ships and were the nearest Union vessels to the fort. Porter's instructions indicate that the vessels were to be spaced as close as feasible without interfering with each other's line of fire.

The campaign began on 13 January with landings by the army, and with the ironclads and gunboats moving in to cover their disembarkation. Porter had given specific instructions: 'The object is to lodge the shell in the parapets, and tear away the traverses under which the bombproofs are located.' He discouraged simply firing at the flagstaff, but more rather to 'pick out the guns', particularly on the fort's land face, where the land force would later launch their attack. The level of detail of Porter's plan can be deduced by the fact that each vessel was assigned specific targets along the fort's face. With *New Ironsides* and the monitors as close as 800 yards and given a reasonably calm sea, the destructive effect was considerable. By the same token, the fort's return fire was, on the first day, disconcertingly accurate: monitor *Canonicus*, for example, took thirty-six hits. By the close of the first day most of the guns on the land face were disabled and visible damage was evident on the palisades and traverses. Some 200 boats had landed the troops successfully, along with ammunition and supplies.

A steady but reduced fire was maintained overnight to prevent the defenders re-establishing their positions. The following day, the smaller, shallower draft gunboats, mounting 11-inch guns, were brought in – closer than those on the first day – firing with deliberate aim to complete the demolition of the heavy guns on the land face. At the same time, the larger vessels maintained rapid fire to prevent the enemy working the guns. The Confederate commander estimated some 200 casualties on the first two days of the attack, and when the battle was over it was found that all of the

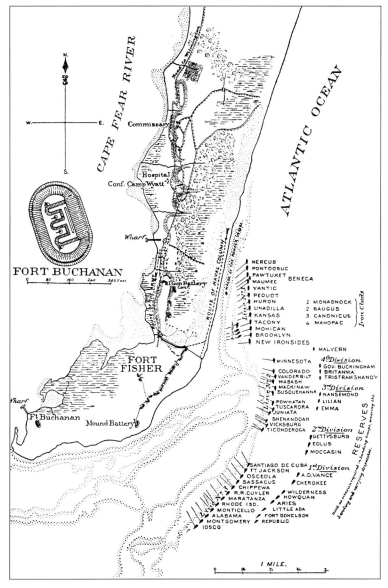

Plan of the Federal attack on Fort Fisher, January 1865. This was the largest concentration of American naval might to that date, and would not be matched in numbers of vessels until the Second World War. The most invulnerable vessels – the monitors – were arranged closest to the northeastern angle of the fortification. *New Ironsides* due to her deeper draft was head of the second line of vessels. The vessels were as close to each other as their lines of fire permitted. From *Battles and Leaders of the Civil War*.

guns on the land face had been disabled during the first two days.

The land assault came on the third day, 15 January, in the afternoon, again after several hours of shelling from well-aimed naval guns. (Some Union vessel commanders reported that they chose a specific target, fired, waited for the smoke to clear to determine if they had been effective, then repeated the process.) In a preview of scores of landings in the Pacific in the Second World War, it was found that the disabling of the guns simply drove the defenders into the bombproofs, waiting for the ground troops to press their attack.

At Fort Fisher, the seamen and marines assaulted the seaward end of the land face, with their numbers, some 1600, confronted by the strongest part of the fort and largest portion of its defenders. After a ½-mile charge across an open field, they were driven back from the very base of the bastion. The carnage was intense, but apparently with some effect, in that the Confederates were surprised when the army forces appeared at their rear, at the river end of the land face.

In the ensuing five hours, the army fought its way from traverse to traverse, gradually forcing the defenders down the sea face. The *New Ironsides* and others fired through the traverses in advance of the men, assisting in clearing the defenders, though their shell and shrapnel did not preclude some of the most vicious hand-to-hand combat of the war. Though contemporary writers credit the navy with remarkably accurate fire in this process, it would have been difficult for it to have been accomplished without some 'friendly' casualties, though specific numbers were not mentioned at the time.

After an expenditure of some 19,000 projectiles and a navy-marines casualty list some 350 names long, Fort Fisher and its satellite batteries were taken. It was subsequently found that nearly every artillery piece in the fortification was dismounted or seriously injured. Most of the Union casualties occurred during the land assault, but not as the result of Confederate artillery fire. This was the last major coastal operation of the war.[11]

Before turning to ship-versus-ship tactics, some general comments are in order concerning operations on the western rivers. Two factors dominated river tactics: end-on fire and the effects of the current. Regarding the former, it would be most unlikely that river gunboats pitted against shore forts would be allowed the luxury of turning broadside on and maintaining that position for any length of time, to deliver the full force of their broadsides. And, in any event, fortifications would naturally be able to fire on the oncoming vessels long before the vessel's broadsides came to bear. By the same token, their sterns would be vulnerable if they successfully passed. Hence, the importance of substantial firepower on the bows, and sterns, of river warships.

The river current, generally ranging upwards from 3½ knots, was such that significant deviation from its flow would quickly catch the vessel and wind it around with little regard to its rudder. And the gunboats, in particular the ironclads, were vastly underpowered as a group, and barely able to stem the tide, no less maintain great control against it.

The design of the ironclad gunboats reflected these factors. Fortunately, the width of the rivers allowed the construction of wide hulls, on which it was possible to mount 3, sometimes 4, heavy guns across the bows, and equally as many firing astern. Furthermore, in order to conserve weight, many of the gunboats were only armored on the bow and fore quarters. Also, the width of paddle wheels was a significant advantage over screw propellers when dealing with these currents.

The first two major actions on the rivers, in February 1862, will serve to illustrate tactics used in this milieu. Flag Officer A H Foote approached both Forts Henry, on the Tennessee River, and Fort Donelson, on the Cumberland, using similar tactics.

Fort Henry was a small, poorly positioned earthwork, mounting 17 guns, only 11 of which were useful in the event of an attack by water. Foote's plan of attack began with dividing his force into two: four ironclads and three wooden gunboats. The former would lead in the approach and maintain a line abreast formation, placing their 11 guns mounted on their armored bows in the forefront of the action. The wooden boats were also to be in line abreast, astern and inshore to the ironclads, firing over the latter. Foote encouraged slow but accurate fire, directed primarily at the guns.

Firing began at 1700 yards and quickly became general. Some twenty minutes into the fight a shot burst the boiler on one of the armored vessels, and she was allowed to drift with the current out of the action. The remaining boats continued a slow advance, firing, as Foote had ordered, slowly but with effect. In less than an hour-and-a-half, the armored vessels were hit at least fifty-nine times, but the fort capitulated. The majority of the Union casualties were due to the boiler explosion.[12]

Less than three weeks later, six of the river fleet struck at Fort Donelson, a larger work in a stronger defensive location. Foote duplicated his Fort Henry tactics, advancing slowly with the four armored vessels line abreast, while the two wooden gunboats brought up the rear.

Firing began at about a mile from the fort, with a slow advance to within 400 yards. The Confederate fire was galling, putting no less than twenty shots into each of the ironclads. The fight ended when Confederate fire disabled the steering on two of the ironclads, leaving them at the mercy of the current. The flotil-

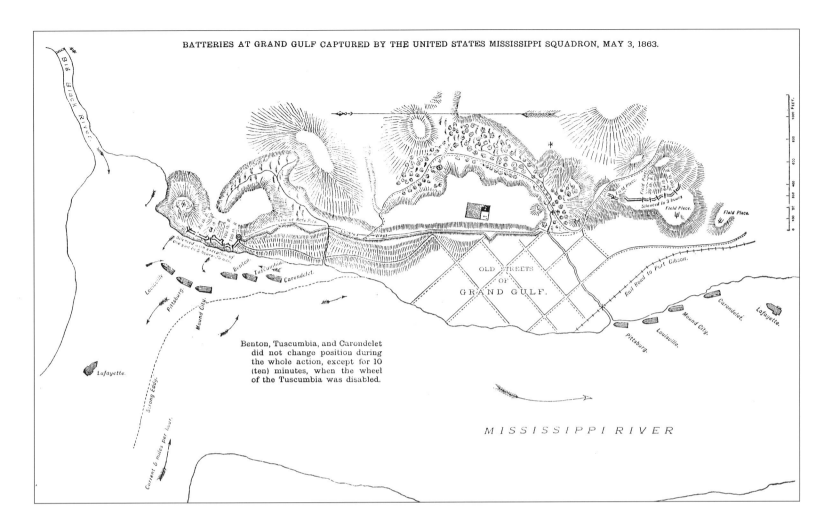

BATTERIES AT GRAND GULF CAPTURED BY THE UNITED STATES MISSISSIPPI SQUADRON, MAY 3, 1863.

Benton, Tuscumbia, and Carondelet did not change position during the whole action, except for 10 (ten) minutes, when the wheel of the Tuscumbia was disabled.

MISSISSIPPI RIVER

**P**lan of attack at Grand Gulf on the Mississippi. In common with most other river actions, the navy here faced Confederate guns as well as contrary and strong river currents. Gunboats were directed to use stern batteries whenever possible. At one point in the five-hour bombarbment, the current forced *Benton* out of the action and turned her completely around. Her commander ended her free fall by running her into the bank downstream. From *Official Records....*

la then withdrew. Two days afterwards, Fort Donelson was taken by the army under US General Grant.[13]

The action against Grand Gulf, Mississippi in 1863 is illustrative of both the tactics used and the problems encountered in the riverine war.

Grand Gulf lay some 20 miles south of Vicksburg, on the Mississippi River, and its fortifications had a reputation for invulnerability. The four Confederate batteries mounted 13 heavy guns and a few field pieces. The main work (referred to as the 'upper battery') had 4 heavy guns and lay some 80 feet above the river. A half mile down river were the 'lower' batteries where 9 guns were

placed on the brow of a hill some 150 feet above river level. Field pieces were emplaced in other works, also high over the Mississippi. Entrenchments allowed free movement of reinforcements among the works. The navy's problem was compounded by a 6 mile per hour current with strong eddies and countercurrents, arising in part from the nearby confluence with the Black River.

The attack was made in daylight, by seven ironclads, which Admiral Porter divided into two groups: four concentrating on the lower batteries and the remainder on the upper fort. First the lead four were to pass the upper battery, firing as they went, and were to round to with one each concentrating on the next two batteries, and two on the most formidable work. At the upper fort, one of the ironclads was to use her broadside guns, and the other, her bow guns. (Due to the current, all the vessels were to engage with bows up-river.) The seventh vessel was to engage from 600 yards *above* the upper work and use her stern guns. Porter also ordered the two vessels at the upper works to fire their stern guns on the lower batteries when they came to bear. Porter directed that whenever possible, the vessels should form a line abreast and thus 'bring all the bow guns to bear on one place'. The vessels mounted a total of 80 guns. Of these, some 20 were mounted in the bows.

The attack was made 27 April 1863 with the intention of silencing the guns to make way for landing troops. At the upper battery, the elevation was such that the gunners resorted to aiming at the muzzles of the enemy guns as they were run out. However, the current and eddies made it difficult for the underpowered and unwieldy gunboats to maintain their positions. The *Tuscumbia* reported she fired from 'positions above, below, and abreast of it, as the current and eddy made it necessary'. She later lost an engine for one of her paddle wheels, was no longer able to stem the current with her remaining screw propellers and one paddle, and dropped out to find an anchorage. The *Benton*, one of the larger vessels, was caught in an eddy, forced out of position, and turned completely around in the current – even then firing with port and stern guns as they would bear. She dropped down 1500 yards and was obliged to run into the bank to finally turn around, returning to action some thirty-five minutes later.

The Confederate gun crews at the lower batteries deserted first, after one of the vessels at the upper works was sent down to assist. However, the Confederates at the upper fort redoubled their efforts and soon the entire flotilla regrouped to concentrate their effort there. After over five hours, fire from the upper work had slackened little and the attack was terminated.

Though no vessels were lost, the Federal ships were mangled by the accuracy and volume of enemy fire. Two, *Tuscumbia*, and *Benton*, which had been at the upper battery, were the hardest hit: the former with eighty-one hits; the latter, seventy. Although the upper battery was not silenced, it's fire dwindled sufficiently to allow passage of the troop transports later in the day – covered by the guns of the flotilla. The works were then flanked by the army and were abandoned within a few days after the gunboats' assault. Grand Gulf was one of the last major Confederate bastions on the Mississippi.[14] Vicksburg was the final fortress, and this town fell in July 1863 after a lengthy and arduous combined army-navy campaign.

Engagements between individual vessels were rare during the Civil War. Certainly the battle between *Monitor* and *Virginia* (ex-*Merrimack*) has long dominated the popular view of the conflict. Though the significance of this confrontation has been exaggerated, particularly by American popular historians, it was indeed the first engagement between ironclad vessels, as well as the first appearance in combat of the armored gun turret. From a tactical point of view, however, a few facts are significant. *Monitor*'s com-

mander, John Worden, had an immediate objective: prevent the *Virginia* from attacking the steam frigate *Minnesota*, which lay vulnerable and hard aground. As had been demonstrated the previous day by the destruction of the frigates *Congress* and *Cumberland*, no wooden ship could withstand the onslaught of the *Virginia*, and thus the entire wooden Union blockading squadron was at risk. Worden's task was not an inviting one. The little ironclad had narrowly escaped sinking three days before on her passage from New York to Hampton Roads; she was untried in combat, and, indeed, was unlike any warship ever built. More specifically, *Monitor* mounted only 2 guns, though both were 11-inch Dahlgren smoothbores. *Virginia* had 10 guns, 4 of which were rifled. Furthermore, if ramming came into play, the *Virginia* would carry enormous momentum and power: she had over three times the tonnage of Ericsson's vessel.

Worden entered the fight intending to capitalize on the advantage provided by his rotating turret, as well as the smaller vessel's greater manoeuverability. The former enabled *Monitor* to fire from nearly any direction – the only exception was directly forward and a few degrees either side of the bow, due to the blast effect on the pilot house. In addition, the *Monitor*'s relatively small size would make it theoretically possible to avoid the enemy's broadside at will.

With these factors in mind, Worden went into the battle intending to circle his opponent, firing as his guns were available. He was indeed able to deflect the *Virginia* from the frigate and, at one point, attempted to ram *Virginia*'s propeller but failed. Later, the *Virginia* went aground, an accident which could well have been significant had it been capitalized upon, as the Confederate ship was considerably deeper than the *Monitor*. Also, observers on the *Virginia* suggested that if Worden had remained in one position and delivered a continuous fire into one portion of the enemy's armor, she may well have penetrated it and taken the advantage. As a counterpoint to this, it should be noted that *Monitor*'s rate of fire was two shots every eight to ten minutes – certainly a very long time to remain stationary in close proximity to a hostile armorclad.

In any event, after some four hours of sparring, the two vessels drew apart, each without dealing a decisive blow to the other. Both had only succeeded in denting, but not penetrating, the other's armor, and each was quite capable of renewing the fight immediately, if necessary. In the short run, Worden and the *Monitor* had accomplished the primary goals of preventing the sinking of the *Minnesota* and parrying the Confederate

Hampton Roads, showing the locations of Union vessels *Cumberland, Congress,* and the steam frigate *Minnesota.* The last of these was the intended third victim of the Confederate ironclad on 9 March 1862, when Ericsson's *Monitor* arrived on the scene. From *Battles and Leaders of the Civil War.*

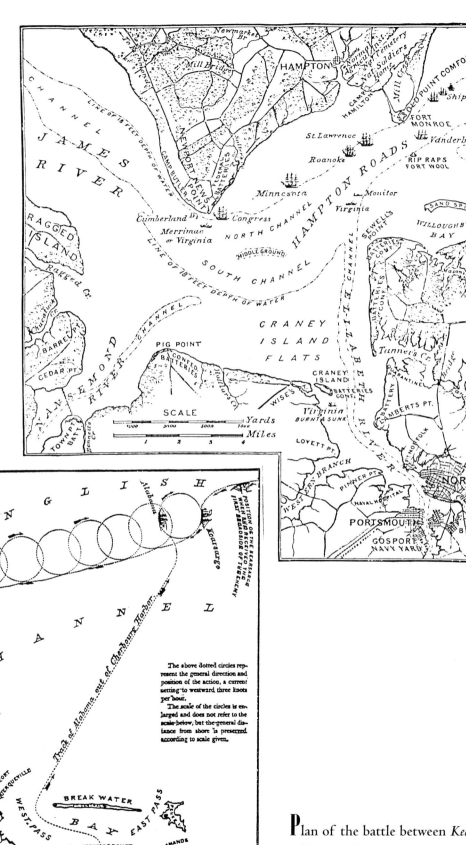

Plan of the battle between *Kearsarge* and *Alabama,* July 1864. Winslow's relentless attempts to rake the Confederate's stern, and *Alabama*'s sheering off, put the two steam sloops into a series of circles. From *Battles and Leaders of the Civil War.*

**S**inking of the Confederate cruiser *Alabama*. The well placed fire of 11-inch pivot smoothbore shell guns pierced the Confederate's hull and ended her career. Painting by Xanthus Smith. (Mobile Convention and Visitors Corporation and AmSouth Bank Collection)

thrust at the Union blockading fleet. The action went down in history as a tactical draw.[15]

From a tactical standpoint, the lessons learned by the Union from this famous duel were probably the wrong ones, and were in a sense less tactical in nature than a general attitude toward Ericsson's wonderful invention. The *Monitor*'s invulnerability in this action, combined with her dramatic arrival to save the Union fleet, created a sensation not often surpassed during the war. The monitor became a panacea. Despite Ericsson's original intent – simply to counter Confederate ironclads in shallow coastal waters – whole

classes of monitors were expected to take on all comers, in particular the enemy's coastal fortifications. This impression led to the debacle of April 1863, just over a year after Hampton Roads, when 34 guns, most of them on Ericsson monitors, took on 69 well emplaced pieces defending Charleston, South Carolina, and withdrew badly mauled in less than an hour. (See earlier in the chapter.)

The final action to be looked at in terms of battle tactics was that between the Union steam sloop *Kearsarge* and the Confederate cruiser *Alabama* off Cherbourg in 1864.

The British-built *Alabama* had wreaked havoc on American merchant shipping on the high seas for nearly two years. In that time she took sixty-four prizes and sank the Union gunboat *Hatteras* in a short and one-sided fight in 1863. *Alabama*, as well as her cohorts, has been blamed for much of the decline of American merchant shipping during this era.

The Union navy's response to the *Alabama* was to dispatch a

*Kearsarge* after the battle. The fore end of the planked over chain 'armor' can be distinguished just forward of the funnel. Winslow recognized the importance of the steam engine both in his vessel and the adversary's. His gunners aimed for the hull; *Alabama*'s almost consistently fired high. (US Navy)

series of cruisers specifically to find and destroy her. These were screw sloops such as *Kearsarge* and *Tuscarora* – barque-rigged 1400-ton vessels capable of extended blue-water cruising. *Kearsarge* was armed with two 11-inch Dahlgren smoothbores on centerline pivot mounts, capable of firing 136-pound projectiles, four 32-pounders, and a 30-pounder rifle on the forecastle.

The *Alabama* seemed an appropriate match. She was nearly the same size and tonnage, with no great differential in speed or crew size. She was heavily armed for a commerce raider, carrying six 32-pounders in broadside, a 68-pounder and a 100-pounder rifle on pivots. Though *Alabama*'s broadside was about 100 pounds less than that of *Kearsarge*, her British Blakely 100-pounder rifle was theoretically more accurate than the big smoothbores on the Union warship.

Captain John A Winslow of the *Kearsarge* chose the battle site. When the Confederate raider came out of Cherbourg, Winslow, then some 3 miles off, turned away, leading the *Alabama* to a point over 6 miles from shore, with the double purpose of assuring that

there was no question of French jurisdiction, as well as lengthening the *Alabama*'s direct line of escape to the French coast. At that point, Winslow 'turned short around' and steered at full speed for the adversary, intending to run her down or close in with her, as circumstances dictated.

Captain Raphael Semmes of the *Alabama*, on seeing the *Kearsarge* reverse course, immediately sheered to present his starboard side and, at about a mile distant, fired the first of three unanswered broadsides. At about 900 yards, faced with *Alabama*'s raking fire, *Kearsarge* sheered and opened with her starboard broadside.

At this stage, the object of Winslow's preparations became apparent. His two 11-inch pivot guns had been run out to starboard in anticipation of his eventual port helm. Once his battery opened, his gunners were directed to fire deliberately with direct aim. The heavy 11-inchers were to concentrate 'below rather than above the water line' while the 32-pounders and rifle were to 'clear the deck'.

Winslow's attempts to close as well as rake *Alabama*'s stern were frustrated when Semmes repeatedly sheered off, keeping both vessels on a circular course with starboard broadsides engaged. An observer on shore described the scene as resembling two flies circling the lip of a glass, as the series of turns extended to seven complete circles in just over an hour, by which time *Alabama* was sinking rapidly by the stern.

Winslow's instructions had been both prescient and effectively executed. Firing 173 rounds put the *Alabama* in sinking condition with large apertures near and below the water line, while the heaviest casualties were among her gun crews. The crew of her after pivot gun, for instance, was renewed four times, with nearly every man disabled. Conversely, it appears that of over 370 rounds fired by the *Alabama*, fewer than 35 actually struck the Union ship, and, of those, only 14 lodged in the hull. (This despite the fact that *Kearsarge* was low on coal and thus high in the water.)

Much has been made of another precaution taken by Winslow: the use of anchor chain cable to 'armor' the sides of his vessel. Semmes, of course, later protested vociferously about the unfairness of it all. However, the *Kearsarge*'s damage report indicates that, of the thirteen hits in the hull, only two struck the chain cables, and those were fairly high on her sides, well above boilers and machinery. Therefore, the presence or absence of chain 'armor' had little bearing on either the accuracy of the winner's fire or the haphazard character of the loser's.[16]

This writer has not found any specific indication of Winslow's intentions on entering this battle – whether his priority was capturing or sinking the *Alabama*. However, his instruction to fire for the water line supports the latter course. The captain of the *Kearsarge*, then, had realized that a sweeping reordering had occurred in naval tactics with the introduction of steam propulsion. He had realized that the *Alabama*'s barque rig was of only passing importance, and firing to dismast in the traditional manner would be a waste of ammunition: the adversary would still have the wherewithal to escape. The sole alternative was to disable the steam engine, a process scarcely separable from sinking the hull in which it was located.

The fight between *Alabama* and *Kearsarge* thus marked a significant change in naval tactics. Boarding and capturing along with the emphasis on dismasting the enemy vessel, would soon no longer be viable options. The combination of large guns, steam propulsion and armor made the future of naval warfare one in which sinking the enemy was the norm, rather than the exception.

# Tactics on the blockade

As with nearly every aspect of naval warfare, blockading assumed new dimensions with the advent of steam power. If anything, freedom from the tyranny of the wind made the life of the blockader more complicated: no longer could the direction or speed of the wind determine when a blockade runner would make its run. The

blockader needed to maintain a constant vigilance in all but the worst of weathers.

In the age of Nelson, the typical blockade was two-fold. One part of the squadron was kept close-in, the other no farther than signal distance outside the port. Usually, the vessels maintained constant movement, tacking when necessary due to the winds. With both blockaders and runners subjected to the same winds, the options for both were limited to the detriment of the latter's chances of escaping without being forced ashore. With steam vessels, the wind was demoted to a lesser role and speed became the key factor in one's chances to elude the pursuers.

The tactics used by the Union blockading squadrons can be exemplified by those of the North Atlantic Blockading Squadron at various times during the war. The squadron probably had the most difficult part of the southern coast to deal with: the weather off Hatteras and vicinity was often atrocious, the waters close in were treacherously shallow, fog was common, and the Confederate batteries at Fort Fisher and elsewhere were quick to come into action if a blockader strayed within their range.

Under squadron commander S P Lee, the Union vessels were initially in two groups, inshore and out, and generally moved very little. As more vessels were added to the squadron, Lee's options increased and a larger number of shallow draft vessels were available for duties close to shore. He also attempted to reduce the visibility of his vessels. First, they were painted a dull grey, then the inshore vessels were ordered to remove their masts and yards.

By 1864, Lee was able to expand the blockade to four lines of ships. As close as possible to the two outlets of the Cape Fear River were the 'bar tenders'. These were usually small, very shallow draft vessels, whose duty was to signal when a runner was spotted attempting to run out. The second line of vessels was constantly in motion and gave chase. A third line of fast gunboats supported ships of the second line. The line farthest out included the fastest steamers. Their location was determined by the distance a vessel could steam from twilight to dawn. This worked out to about 160 miles from the coast. Generally, the larger the vessel, the farther out it was stationed. In heavy weather, the deep draft blockaders on the far line had an advantage over the light blockade runners.[17]

Lee was replaced in 1864 by D D Porter, who reduced the lines to three. He was given more vessels – and faster ones – for the purpose. Porter allowed the bar tenders to chase the quarry, mainly because he had faster shallow draft vessels on hand. Porter's dispositions included twenty vessels close to the bars, twenty in a semicircle about 12 miles out, and the fastest

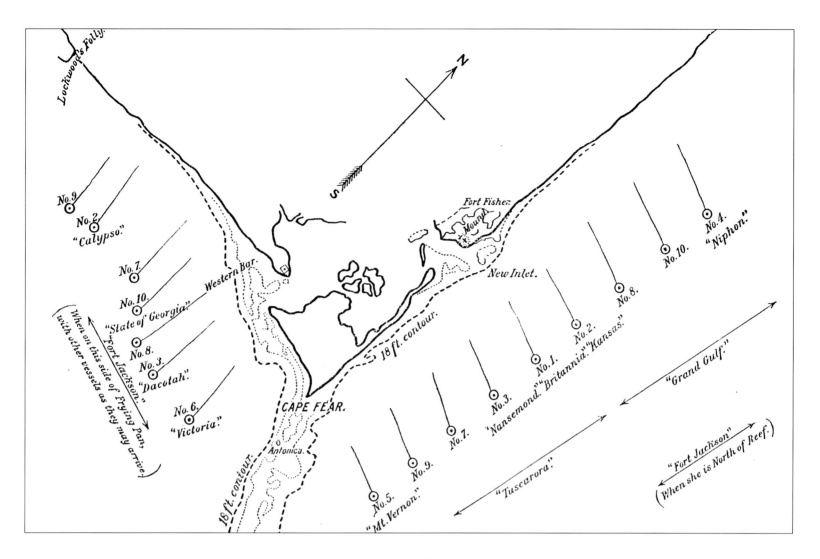

Lockwood's Folly.

N

S

No.9.

No.2.
"Calypso."

No.7.

No.10.
"State of Georgia."

No.8.
No.3.
"Dacotah."

No.6.
"Victoria."

*(When on this side of Frying Pan, with other vessels as they may arrive.)*

"Fort Jackson."

Western Bar.

CAPE FEAR.

Antonica.

No.5.
"Mt. Vernon."

18 ft. contour.

18 ft. contour.

No.9.

No.7.

No.3.
"Nansemond."

No.1.
"Britannia."

No.2.
"Kansas."

No.8.

New Inlet.

Fort Fisher.
Mound.

No.10.

No.4.
"Niphon."

"Tuscarora."

"Grand Gulf."

"Fort Jackson."
*(When she is North of Reef.)*

vessels about 12 miles apart in a crescent-shaped line about 120 miles out.[18]

The various manners in which the blockaders were arranged as well as the increased numbers of faster ships, changed the pattern of captures somewhat but never thoroughly stopped the runners. As the war progressed, captures were made farther out at sea and faster runners were taken. But as the blockade runners always had the advantage of an offensive posture and were generally faster ships than their pursuers, the blockade was never totally successful.

Plan of the blockade off Cape Fear, North Carolina. Three lines of vessels can be seen. The shallow draft ships were close in (bar tenders); the second line was about 12 miles out, and the third were the long-legged, fast steamers, positioned as far as 120 miles from shore. This part of the southern coast was possibly the most difficult to seal off: bad weather, shallow approaches and enemy guns all conspired to aggravate the essentially defensive position of the Union squadron here. (*Official Records...*)

## Chapter Fourteen
# ASSOCIATED UNION MARITIME SERVICES

In terms of engaging the enemy in battle and blockade, the US Navy formed the predominant proportion of the wartime marine service. However, a comprehensive study of the maritime aspect of the war cannot overlook the contributions of four other arms of President Lincoln's waterborne forces: the US Revenue Marine, the US Coast Survey, the Quartermaster Department of the US Army, and the anomalous and idiosyncratic unit known as the Mississippi Marine Brigade.

Both the Revenue Marine and Coast Survey were small in numbers of ships and men and figured only tangentially in the outcome of the conflict. They continued to pursue their pre-war tasks but in a wartime context. The army's navy, operated by its Quartermaster Corps, on the other hand, was vast in numbers. From a logistical and transportation standpoint this fleet certainly was a critical element in the Union army's war effort on the coasts and western rivers. The Marine Brigade was *sui generis*: an awkward amalgam of riverboats, infantry, light artillery and cavalry, which seems to have had little to contribute to the war save originality of concept.

## United States Revenue Service

Early in the history of the republic, the US Treasury Department recognized the need for a maritime force to patrol the American coasts enforcing customs laws. The upshot was a flotilla of ten small schooners and sloops authorized in 1790, and thus predating both the army and navy in the US Government under the Constitution. This service was called, with some inconsistency

**G**allatin, typical revenue cutter of the 1850s. For the purpose of enforcing revenue laws, these small vessels were appropriate; for war purposes they were too small to be of use. (US Coast Guard)

even in official documents, the Revenue Service, Revenue Cutter Service and Revenue Marine at various times in the nineteenth century. It became the Coast Guard in 1915.

Although the original cutters were unarmed and had limited responsibilities, it was soon obvious that other missions were easily subsumed into their purview. Co-incident with the outbreak of undeclared war with France in 1798, a new generation of cutters was built, again, ostensibly for the protection of the revenue. However, their 14-gun armament, as well as their immediate operational assignments, made it obvious that they were to augment

At various times during the war, cutters saw service as VIP barges. This view, on deck of the steam cutter *Wayanda* purportedly shows President Lincoln (blurred) to the right in top hat. Secretary of State William H Seward is in a white hat, seated. Note the pair of Dahlgren howitzers on deck. (US Coast Guard)

the new naval fleet – vessels such as the *Constitution* – in a real shooting war. Thus began the Revenue Service's traditional role as a wartime adjunct to the navy. (It is also worth noting that these heavily armed cutters, reverting to revenue service after the war, were quickly replaced by smaller ships.)

In the early decades of the nineteenth century, the service obtained, officially or otherwise, other roles. As agencies of the Federal government they patrolled government naval timber reserves on the southern coasts to prevent widespread poaching by lumbering interests. In the 1830s, after a series of harsh winters at sea, the cutters were ordered to maintain winter patrols in the northeast, for the protection of mariners. During the same decade, it appears that an informal arrangement was developing with the Federal lighthouse establishment, in which the cutters irregularly

made supply runs to the various beacons and transported light-house keepers to remote stations when needed.[1]

The ships for these missions continued to be small sloops or topsail schooners, rarely over 100 feet long, but usually with a good turn of speed. The only exception to this before 1858 was a class of iron-hulled steamers a few of which had experimental and horrendously unsuccessful machinery - horizontally mounted pad-dle wheels. Massive amounts of departmental money were swallowed up by these vessels, none of which remained long with their original engines, and most of which were discarded as soon as was quietly possible. The embarrassed Revenue Service did not build another steamer until 1858 with the *Harriet Lane*. At the outbreak of the Civil War, this extremely competent 180-foot, 650-ton paddle wheeler was the lone steamer among twenty-three sailing

At the outbreak of the war, *Harriet Lane* was the Revenue Service's only modern ship. Under Revenue Service officers she cooperated with the navy until late 1861, when the navy took her over. Confederates boarded and captured her in 1864, ending a useful naval career. Illustration by John Tilley. (US Coast Guard)

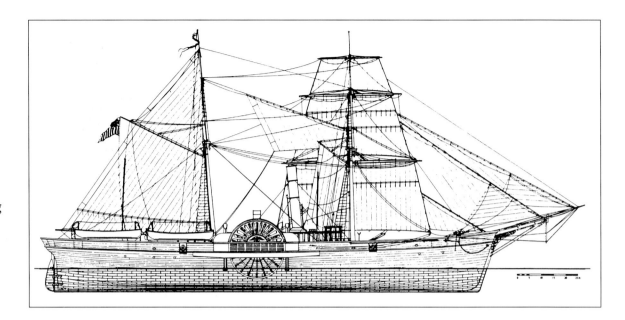

cutters, most of which were less than 150 tons and 100 feet in length. Furthermore, the cutters were dispersed throughout the United States, including several on the Great Lakes and three on the west coast.[2]

At the beginning of the Civil War, the service, headed by Secretary of the Treasury Salmon P Chase, numbered less than 400 men. The officers ranked from third to first lieutenant and captain, and of course had military uniforms, which were little more than the naval styles and color, substituting the Revenue Service emblem – a national shield – for naval devices. Pay was comparable with that of the navy. However, service conditions were quite different. It was quite possible to enlist in the Revenue Marine and remain in one port city, assigned to the same cutter for years at a time. Unlike the navy, the cutters rarely went to sea – their assigned tasks for the most part lay within sight of the major port cities, or at least of the coast itself. The ultimate in 'home assignment' was on the Great Lakes, where the cutters were laid up every winter and the crews released. Crews, in any event were small, only sufficient to support a boarding without denuding the vessel entirely. Thus the typical cutter carried one officer and no more than ten ratings. Only enough weaponry was mounted to intimidate with a shot across the bow of a suspected smuggler or other miscreant. Most cutters had a single 32-pounder pivot gun. Only the *Harriet Lane*, with a crew of about fifty, was capable of handling a large battery, though she did not do so in peacetime. The coming of secession caught the cutters on southern stations in what abruptly became foreign port cities. Six were seized by local authorities and lost to the service. Some became revenue cutters in the newly formed Confederacy; others became

Revenue Service officer in uniform. Except for buttons and insignia, the uniform was identical to that of the navy. Note the Treasury Department shield below the anchor on the service cap. (US Coast Guard)

blockade runners or dropped out of sight. Of course, as with the navy, many revenue officers went over to the South.

In any event, to compensate for the loss in cutters, in late 1861 five of the six cutters on the Great Lakes were ordered to the east coast. Captain Douglas Ottinger set out from Milwaukee, Wisconsin on the last day of October with the first cutter, and, gathering the rest as he went eastward, brought his flotilla to Boston by the last week in December. It proved to be a saga of snow, gales and wholesale desertions by cold, reluctant seamen, not to mention re-rigging the vessels which had already been laid up for the winter months. It was not without cost, with the smallest cutter piling onto the rocks off Cape Ann, Massachusetts. The other four took stations in New England and one later served in the sounds of North Carolina, after the capture of that coastal area by Union forces. Living up to the service's long-standing tradition of frugality, the cost to transfer the five vessels was $801.69.[3]

Unlike other wars, in the Civil War the Revenue Service was not taken over or utilized to any extent by the navy. The most obvious explanation for this is probably the fact that all except the *Harriet Lane* were too small for naval use, and all except that vessel were sailing ships. Furthermore, it seems that the normal port collection, inspection and emergency distress duties of the Revenue Service were quite enough to occupy them throughout the war. Statistics indicate that there were an average of 115 Revenue Service search and rescue operations annually during the war years.[4]

Some cutters were pressed into an unusual variety of revenue enforcement, particularly along the Virginia-Maryland border on the lower Chesapeake Bay. They were patrolling for contraband – including escaped slaves – crossing the frontier. In addition, a special contingent of four cutters served to enforce revenue laws and contraband regulations in the sounds of North Carolina, where again both normal customs duties were in effect, as well as military restrictions on trade in what was essentially an occupied territory.[5]

As might be expected, the revenue cutters rarely came under hostile fire. Only the *Harriet Lane* participated in any of the navy's major coastal operations. She was a unit of the fleet which took Forts Hatteras and Clark off North Carolina in mid 1861 and was commended for effective use of her four 32-pounder guns in the action.[6] At the time she was still a Revenue Service vessel, but shortly thereafter she was turned over permanently to the navy, which obviously saw her as a valuable asset.

**L**oss of revenue cutter *Caleb Cushing* off Portland, Maine. In a daring raid, Confederate Lieutenant Charles Read of the cruiser *Tacony* towed her out of the harbor. Authorities gave chase and Read blew her up. (*Harper's Weekly*)

Only one cutter was lost due to enemy action. In one of the more unusual incidents of the war, the schooner *Caleb Cushing*, in port at Portland, Maine, was boarded at night by Confederates from the cruiser cum commerce raider *Tacony*. With no wind available they towed her out behind two boats. When local authorities made chase in two steamers the Confederates blew up the revenue cutter. There were no Revenue Service casualties.

The only other set-piece battle with Revenue Service participation was at Drewry's Bluff on the James River, some 8 miles from Richmond, where Ericsson's *Monitor*, the ironclad *Galena*, and the Revenue Steamer *E A Stevens* shelled a Confederate position in May 1862. The *Stevens*, also known as the 'Stevens Battery' or *Naugatuck*, was a 100-foot experimental screw steamer donated to the service by the Stevens family of New Jersey. She was a test bed designed to demonstrate features of a large ironclad they had laid down in the 1840s, and had continued to build with a series of Congressional appropriations. At the outset of the Civil War a naval committee had recommended dropping the project as impracticable. The Stevens' response was that this vessel incorporated features of the larger ship: a large Parrott rifle which was loaded from beneath the deck, obviating the need for an exposed gun crew; water ballast tanks with pumps to lower the vessel's profile in combat; and independently operating twin screws, to provide great maneouverability.

The *Stevens* had a short, anticlimactic career: her Parrott rifle burst - some say on the first round fired in this engagement. She was relegated to revenue service in New York where about a year later, her (new) large gun also burst, wounding seven. The proposed large ironclad version of the Stevens battery was never completed.[7]

The only Revenue Service war casualty occurred under more mundane circumstances. A cutter's commanding officer took it upon his vessel to chastise the Southern sympathies of a village in the lower Chesapeake Bay, and shelled the town with his pivot gun - possibly a 12-pounder. The populace on shore retaliated with small arms fire, killing the captain and wounding a second crewman.[8]

By the end of the war, the Revenue Service consisted of thirty-three vessels: twenty steamers and thirteen sloops or schooners. (Wartime necessity had overcome the previous reluctance to acquire steam vessels.) Other than the incidents related above, the cutters and men had rarely been in harm's way. However, they had continued their tradition of service in their assigned tasks — sometimes in difficult circumstances arising from wartime conditions. Moreover, then, as now, the services rendered were often far beyond simple enforcement of the revenue laws. Reading contemporary accounts one finds revenue cutters delivering mail, supply-ing lighthouses in remote areas, carrying supplies for the army and navy, assisting in Coast Survey work, carrying runaway slaves to freedom, intercepting contraband goods going south, and, of course, aiding those in peril at sea. Certainly their efforts, though rarely trumpeted, were necessary and vital to the Union war effort.

# The United States Coast Survey

The US Coast Survey had been formed to chart and sound the American seacoast, ports and inlets. It was a scientific organization, with close ties to the Smithsonian Institution — its Director, A D Bache, a descendant of Benjamin Franklin, was a regent on the original Smithsonian Board in 1846. It's ties to the navy were also significant, for that service was one of its major clients, and, indeed supplied many of its ships' officers, usually on detached

**US** Coast Survey vessel *Bibb*. These vessels often went ahead of the naval fleet, surveying the coast and waters and setting out buoys where necessary. *Bibb* was damaged by a Confederate torpedo in 1864, but remained in service until 1868. (US Navy)

duty. Before the war, the Revenue Service had also lent officers and, frequently, appropriate vessels for their work.

For all practical purposes, the Survey vessels continued their assigned mission throughout the war, with wartime needs receiving the appropriate priority. Some served as advance units before the fleet went into action – setting out buoys to mark Confederate obstructions and as range markers for gunnery. At the war's outbreak, the Survey's previous work was invaluable for the committees recommending locales most likely to provide shore bases for the naval blockaders. This information became part of the basis for the Union's overall war strategy.

Thirty-one vessels operated with the Coast Survey during the war. Only five were steamers: *Bibb*, *Walker*, *Hetzel*, *Vixen* and *Corwin*. *Hetzel* and *Vixen* were turned over to the navy in August 1861, and saw considerable active service; *Bibb* and *Corwin* served with the Revenue Service for a short time the same year. All were sidewheel vessels, less than 150 feet in length and 500 tons, and generally had no deck guns. Though neither ship ever engaged in combat, *Bibb* was damaged at Mobile Bay by a Confederate torpedo late in the war and *Corwin* took two blockade runners as prizes in 1862.[9]

Of the sailing vessels – most of which were small schooners – three also were on short term loan to the Revenue Service in 1861 and two more went to the navy. The schooner *Petrel* was seized by Confederates, converted into a 'privateer' and sunk by the US Frigate *St Lawrence* in July 1861.

# United States Army Quartermaster Corps

It would be difficult to overestimate the contribution of the army's fleet of vessels, both seagoing and riverine, to the ultimate triumph of the Union cause. Though much has been made of the importance of the railroads to the war effort, several facts should be kept in mind:

1 Bulk commodities, such as coal, hay, flour, etc., are always carried more economically and in larger loads by sea.

2 The railroads of the 1860s had significantly less capacity, in terms of tonnage per freight car, and number of cars per train, than their modern counterparts.

3 The rail network of the era was not nearly as geographically inclusive as it would be until long after the war.

4 When the war expanded into Southern territory, the rail systems there were found to be exceedingly poor – and indeed had been prior to the war – in terms of track, network, rolling stock, and maintenance, forcing the army's continued reliance, where possible, on riverine transport.

5 All army coastal operations, both supported by the navy and otherwise, relied on oceangoing transport.

6 Even a cursory study of the army's operations in 'seat of the war' in Northern Virginia reveals that the Union efforts there were always predicated on the army's access to the rivers and the supplies carried thereon.

Thus it can be seen that the railroads, though used in innovative ways by the military – not the least being the quick movement of troops – were secondary to the sea and rivers in terms of the bulk of the supplies necessary for immense armies.

The exact size of the fleet eventually utilized by the Army's Quartermaster Corps has never been exactly determined. Absence of complete and centralized records, particularly early in the war, prevent absolute conclusions in this area. A recent compilation has been made by Charles Dana and E Kay Gibson in *The Army's Navy Series*, and is probably as close as the records allow. They enumerate 4033 vessels operated, owned, seized, or chartered by the army during the conflict. Though this number includes those built or obtained for combat use – armorclads, timberclads, gunboats and rams – the vast majority were transports.

Of this total number of vessels, 2927 were acquired through purchase or formal charter, and the remainder were 'affreightment' hires, with no charter, or were temporarily seized. Only 448 were purchased or built by the War Department: 343 for the coastal operations; 105 on the rivers.

By type of vessel, the total number of steamers was 1966; sailing ships 2003. Sixty-four were miscellaneous or unknown types, including one horsepowered ferry. Of the sailing ships, 1571 were schooners, and 114 were fully rigged ships.[10]

This was an extraordinary effort. Early in 1865, at the peak of Grant's Virginia Campaign, when the army was at its highest numerical strength, the chief of the army's Ocean and Lake Transport Division reported that 'nearly all the seagoing steamers of the country have been employed [by the Quartermaster]'. (Quoted by Charles Dana Gibson from the Army *Official Records*.) It is difficult to put the total number used by the army in context with the Union's total commercial tonnage, as most available figures are based on the total for the undissolved nation, and most

Quartermaster Corps tug boat *W W Wotkyns;* a typical utility-type vessel of that era. Most operated under charter for the corps. (National Archives)

only include vessels engaged in foreign trade. However, it is noteworthy that both in the Virginia Peninsular campaign of 1862 and Grant's late war campaigns, mentioned above, the Quartermaster Department was experiencing extreme difficulty in locating vessels to meet the army's needs for water transportation.

At least 140 Quartermaster Corps vessels were lost during the war. However, many of these were marine casualties or vessels sunk as obstructions, rather than combat losses.

Needless to say, the careers of these vessels were generally unremarkable, at least in terms of engaging the enemy. They were indispensable for support of the army, as troop transports, supply ships, prisoners-of-war transport, dispatch vessels, coaling hulks, and so forth.

A few examples will suffice to give some scale to the numbers of vessels utilized by the army for specific battles or needs. As early as March 1862, at least seventeen river steamers were employed to support the capture of Forts Henry and Donelson on western rivers. Shortly thereafter, at the battle of Shiloh, Tennessee, where a major union force was engaged, 174 vessels were involved in the build-up, support and follow-up for that engagement. It is noteworthy that a large contingent of reinforcements arrived by steamer between the first and second day's fighting, enabling Grant to retrieve his position and prevent a disastrous loss in this critical battle.[11]

Later in the war, ninety-nine ships were chartered to supply General Sherman's forces after their arrival at the sea near Savannah – following his famous march through Georgia.[12]

Another instance saw a major troop movement involving both river and rail transport. In 1865, the the army's XXIII corps was transferred from Paducah, Kentucky, on the

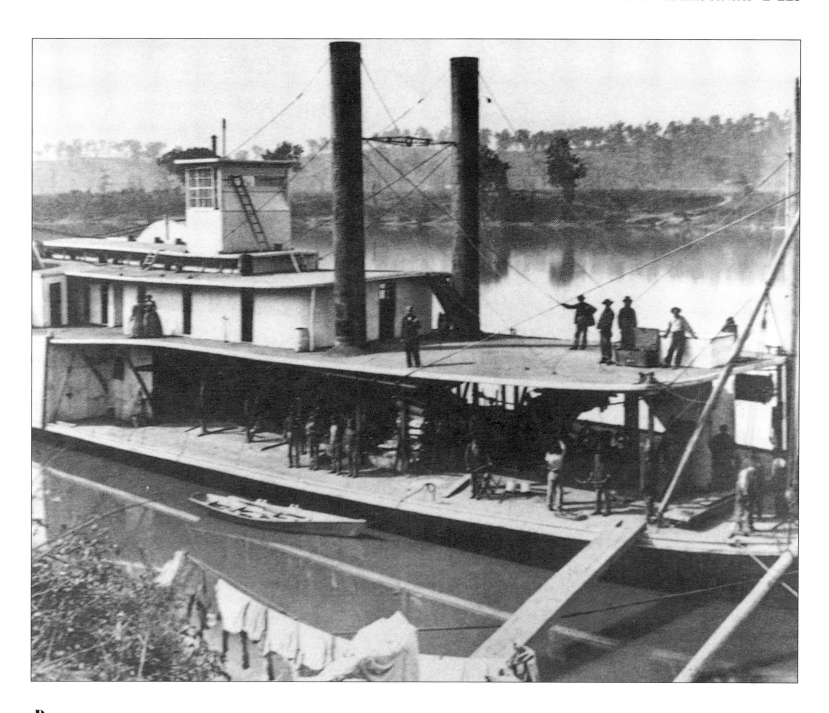

Riverboat *Chickamauga*, Quartermaster vessel in the west. She was a typical sidewheel transport vessel, most of which were chartered for military use. (National Archives)

Mississippi River, to Annapolis, Maryland. Fifty-two steamers were chartered to transport the men to the rail head at Cincinnati, despite fog and ice on the river. Trains completed the transfer to Annapolis, with the men eventually arriving at Fort Fisher, North Carolina, by sea, on 9 February 1865. The total time in transit was seventeen days for the 20,000-man corps. It is noteworthy that the railroads involved were worked well past their capacity in this operation, employing all avail-

able passenger cars plus a substantial number of freight cars for this troop movement.[13]

In addition to the army-built ironclads which eventually became the navy's western rivers squadron, and the Ellet rams, there was another group of army vessels specifically built for combat. These little-known ships were designed by Norman Wiard, who also had developed a type of rifled cannon. It is believed that six of these were built, four in New York and two slightly smaller versions at Bridgeport, Alabama.

The design of these vessels, as recorded in letters in the *Official Records* of the navy and documents in the National Archives, was for shallow-draft river operations and had side paddle wheels and

Scene on deck of a small transport on the James River. Note the 'US' marked crate in the foreground and crude wooden berths. (National Archives)

identical ends, and were similar to, but smaller than, the navy's double-ended gunboats. Dimensions were 160 feet long by only 21 feet 6 inches breadth (35 feet over the paddle-wheel guards), and intended to draw only 3 feet of water. The ends were protected by light (¼-inch) iron and they attained 8 knots with two-cylin-der engines and three locomotive type boilers. They were to be armed with six howitzers and carry six heavy launches.

*General Burnside*, *Reno*, *Parke* and *General Foster* were built at New York, and two were constructed in Alabama. The latter pair were thought to have been named *Augusta* and *Savannah*, with one possibly called *Grant* or *General Grant*. They were roundly derided by navy critics, who nicknamed them 'Japanese Wheelbarrows', due to their very light construction and lack of protection for their steam drums.[14] Despite this, they were apparently used in 'combat patrols', landing reconnaissance parties on the coasts of North Carolina and Virginia in 1864 and 1865. Little else, and no plans or illustrations, has been found of these ships.

# The Ellet ram fleet and the Mississippi Marine Brigade

One of the more controversial aspects of the war on the western rivers was the Mississippi Marine Brigade. This unit was formed in October 1862 and incorporated the Ellet ram fleet in its operations. The latter force had been organized by Colonel Charles Ellet in the spring of 1862, under army auspices and was composed of nine steam rams, intended to destroy the Confederate naval force on the river. Though otherwise unarmed, the fleet took on the rebel force at Memphis (June 1862) and thoroughly decimated it, resulting in the capture of the town.

The Mississippi Marine Brigade was an amphibious force, designed to search out and destroy Confederate guerillas preying on Union forces along the river. It was the brainchild of Rear Admiral David D Porter, commander of the navy's western gunboat flotilla (later called the Mississippi squadron), and was composed of infantry, cavalry, and a full artillery battery, totalling some 1500 military men plus about 500 civilians. The majority of the army personnel were from other army units, and the civilians included many contrabands, mostly enlisted as deck hands. Of the blacks, twenty-seven were female 'chambermaids' – probably the first black females attached to an American combat force.[15]

Porter, it is said, had ulterior motives in organizing this unit. By incorporating Ellet's ram fleet into it, and placing the entire brigade under naval (Porter's) direction, it would eliminate the Ellet organization as an independent naval river force.

Porter's opposition to the unit's independent operations was sufficient to limit its usefulness, but it remained in existence until mid 1864. In addition to the rams, it included ten other steamers, three of which were tugs and one a hospital vessel.

The brigade was active in Tennessee, Mississippi, Arkansas, and Louisiana, taking part in the Red River Campaign and battles at Port Gibson and Lake Chicot. However, its primary use was in smaller scale actions, among them escorting transports up and down the guerilla-infested rivers.

The seventeen-month history of the brigade was marred by

Colonel Charles Ellet, in brigade uniform. Note the bugle cap device, but without the marine corps's center 'M'. (USAMHI)

continual army-navy sniping, much of it instigated by Admiral Porter. The reputation of the unit was tarnished by a poor disciplinary record early on and by the loss of rams *Queen of the West* and *Lancaster*. A mutiny on board three vessels, caused by the lack of food, and by the family squabbles among the Ellets – four of whom were senior officers – further undermined the unit's credibility. (At one point in 1863, Brigadier General Alfred Ellet had his colonel-brother arrested.)[16]

The brigade was a rather modern concept, both in terms of interservice cooperation, and innovative use of modern technology – steamers as the basis for a quick reaction force. Under more circumspect and canny leaders, it might have proved more effective and might have survived in the murky waters of interservice relations.

# Chapter Fifteen
# US NAVAL CASUALTIES AND VESSEL LOSSES

Little has been written about naval casualties and vessel losses during the Civil War. The general belief is that the naval casualties were minuscule compared to the army's, even when taking into consideration the vast disparity in total manpower in each case. As to vessel losses, the very nature of the war, and the imbalance between the size of the Union and Confederate navies kept the numbers of battle (and other losses) to a minimum.

Determining the veracity of the above statements, particularly concerning personnel losses, is not simple. Even the very basic fact – how many men served in the army and navy – is not easily determined. The only relatively reliable figures are the numbers in each service at given dates, and the total number of enlistments through the course of the war. For the army, the disparities are enormous: there were over 2.66 million enlistments, but the largest one-time total was 1 million in May 1865. Statistics do not show the number of individuals who enlisted more than once, which was a common practice, particularly with volunteer regiments. Estimates of the actual number of individuals who served in the army range from 1.5 to 2.1 million.[1]

As to the sea services, there were 118,044 enlistments in the navy and marines. However, the largest number recorded in any one year was 51,500, in 1865; growing from around 7500 to 22,000 by the end of 1862 and thence upward.[2] To hazard a guess at the actual number of individuals who served is dangerous, but for the sake of a baseline, we will say 75,000.

Losses are somewhat less ambiguous figures, with the army counting 110,000 battle deaths, 224,580 disease-related, and 275,000 wounded, for a total of about 609,000 casualties. Naval combat mortalities numbered 1804, plus 3000 deaths by disease, and 2226 wounded. Included in the combat killed were 342 by scalding and 308 by drowning. The overal total was 7030, killed, wounded or died of disease.[3]

If the 1.5 million overall number is used for the army, total casualties were nearly 40 per cent; if 2.2 million is the basic figure, then casualties were about 27 per cent. In battle deaths alone, the percentages range from 5 to 7 per cent. For the navy, using the 75,000 overall total, combat deaths were 2.4 per cent; all casualties, 9 per cent. Consequently, it appears that the navy and marines were nearly three times as 'safe' as the army, in terms of battle deaths and wounds, as well as succumbing to disease.

Considering the number of casualties, the work done by the navy was enormous. In surveying the major operations, it is amazing to note the light casualty count, vis-à-vis the fruits of the operations in question. This is particularly noteworthy in the following instances, where naval losses were in all but one case, less than ten killed.

The operation against Hatteras Inlet, North Carolina, in August, 1861 cost the navy no casualties. Forts Hatteras and Clark were captured, with 700 prisoners, securing the navy's first toehold on the South's Atlantic Coast.

On 7 November 1861, Port Royal Sound was attacked, taking Forts Walker and Beauregard. Naval losses were eight killed; thirty-three wounded, giving the Union a substantial base of operations between Savannah and Charleston.

Even more impressive was the expedition to Roanoke Island in February 1862, where five forts and 2000 prisoners were taken with a naval loss of six killed, seventeen wounded and two missing. The accompanying army force lost around 250 men. This North Carolina island was a strategic threat both to Norfolk and all of eastern North Carolina.

Of course, Farragut's New Orleans operation was the most significant example of the navy's string of low-casualty victories. Forts Jackson and St Philip were taken, eight Confederate vessels were lost, and the way to the largest Gulf port was opened. Naval losses were thirty-seven killed, and 147 wounded.

On the western rivers, the capture of Fort Henry cost seven killed and twenty-seven wounded; the Battle of Fort Donelson resulted in eleven navy deaths and forty-three wounded. These secured part of Tennessee and Kentucky for the Union. Later, at Memphis, a naval fleet mêlée cost four wounded, one mortally. Confederate losses were seven war vessels and five transports. This victory secured both the city and a well equipped navy yard.

Other notable successes with few losses were *Kearsarge* versus *Alabama* (three wounded) and Union monitor *Weehawken*'s capture of ironclad *Atlanta* with no Federal losses. Probably the ultimate in human cost-effectiveness was Lieutenant William Cushing's astonishingly bold sinking of the formidable ironclad *Albemarle* in 1864, with fourteen men, a spar torpedo and a picket boat. Two were drowned, eleven were captured, and the Union presence in North Carolina was re-secured.

Other major operations were of course not so easy, but in proportion, the results were substantial. At Mobile Bay, the South's last Gulf port was closed with the loss of 145 killed, 170 wounded and two missing. Of these, ninety-three were lost with the mining of the monitor *Tecumseh*. Finally, at Fort Fisher, North Carolina, two assaults resulted in 101 navy and marine killed and a total of 386 casualties. The majority of these losses were in a ground attack by marines and sailors.

The above were naval, or sometimes naval and army combined victories. The reverses, of course, involved larger numbers, and sometimes were for questionable or unworthy reasons.

In the latter category was the Red River Expedition, a massive joint army-navy campaign seemingly without a cogent justification. The navy lost 120 men and three vessels in the process, and significant forces were drawn away to northern Louisiana from other more worthwhile pursuits.

Another abortive, but smaller, effort was the attempt to invade south Texas at Sabine Pass in 1863. Four gunboats attempted to take a small 6-gun earthwork. Two grounded immediately under fire and struck their colors, and the others

**T**he largest casualty list from a torpedo was the sinking of *Tecumseh* at Mobile Bay in 1864. Ninety-three men went down with the ship. (US Navy)

withdrew. There were about twenty Union killed, and an equal number wounded.

At least one disaster was directly related to primitive attempts to employ iron armor. At Drewry's Bluff, Virginia, in 1862, the ironclad *Galena*, with an experimental rail-type armor, was held under plunging Confederate fire for nearly three hours, despite immediate evidence that the enemy projectiles easily pierced her sides. Indeed, some passed through both sides of the vessel. Thirteen were killed and eleven wounded before her ammunition was exhausted and she withdrew.

As can be seen, even in defeat navy combat losses rarely numbered over one hundred in any given engagement — even aggregate losses in a fleet encounter. There was one exception to this: 8 March 1862, the first day of the Battle of Hampton Roads, when the ironclad *Virginia* destroyed the wooden warships *Congress* and *Cumberland*.

While popular interest and attention focussed on the *Monitor-Merrimack* (*Virginia*) clash of the following day, for the navy, the losses of *Congress* and *Cumberland* signalled the end of the wooden navy and an uncertain future at the mercy of iron monsters operated by engineers. In fact, these two vessels were the first naval ships lost in combat in this war (the strange riverboats were not in any way in the same category), and the first lost to an enemy since the War of 1812. The losses in men in a single day were not to be exceeded in the navy for decades to come.

*Congress*, a 50-gun frigate, with a crew of 434, lost 120 killed or

The first day at the Battle of Hampton Roads, 8 March 1862, saw the sinking of *Cumberland* (above) by the Confederate *Virginia*, with 121 killed, and *Congress* (left) with 120. The former had more killed than any other vessel in the war and no other day of the war saw as many seamen killed in action. From *Battles and Leader of the Civil War*. (US Navy)

missing and 25 wounded. *Cumberland* lost 121 of a crew of 376. Thus *Congress* had the single largest combat casualty list of any vessel of the war, with *Cumberland* a close second. The *Tecumseh*'s sinking was third. In number of men killed, this was the largest loss of life in any single battle of the war: Mobile Bay was second with 145 killed. (It should also be pointed out that these numbers do not include six killed and about thirty-five wounded on four other vessels scourged by the CSS *Virginia* that day.)[4] And the circumstances were extraordinary: the survivors attest to the helplessness of both wooden vessels and their hapless crews in the face of an impersonal and impenetrable iron behemoth. The trauma of 8 March 1862 would haunt the Union navy for the remainder of the war.

As far as this writer can determine, there has been no attempt to calculate the naval ship losses of the Civil War. As the conflict was not primarily naval, the general impression is that losses, particularly in ship-to-ship actions were relatively few.

In fact, a survey of the listing of vessels in the *Official Records of the Union and Confederate Navies...* (Series II, Vol. 1), reveals that 114 ships were lost by the Union navy during the war's four years. This was over 15 per cent of the maximum number recorded in the fleet (671) in December 1864.

This is a raw number, of course, and comprehends both losses due to enemy action as well as to natural causes, such as foundering, collision, fire, weather, and so on. In the latter category, forty-four ships were lost. Of these, one is particularly significant: the sloop of war *Bainbridge*, lost at sea in 1863, carried over a hundred to their deaths, ranking with the *Tecumseh* lost at Mobile Bay, as the third or fourth largest personnel loss during the conflict. Also included in the accidental losses was one tug run down by an ironclad, riverboats 'snagged', according to the *Official Records*, on underwater obstructions, and several sunk in Atlantic storms.

Under the heading of losses due to the enemy were those lost in action, to floating torpedoes (mines), captured, destroyed to prevent capture, and those destroyed by the Union navy at Norfolk Navy Yard – also to prevent their falling into enemy hands. There were a few vessels which were severely mauled in action and 'destroyed to prevent capture' by their own crews; these I have included in 'action' losses. (Note: I have not included those which were sunk, then re-floated and returned to service.)

The largest proportion within this category were those captured and those lost in action: nineteen of the former; twenty of the latter. Confederate torpedoes took a toll of fifteen ships and eight were destroyed to prevent capture, not including those lost at Norfolk Navy Yard. In all categories in which enemy action or threat of action played a part, the total was seventy. It should be noted that some of the vessels, particularly the ships of the line lost at Norfolk may well have never participated in the war, even had they not been destroyed to prevent their capture. Similarly, the steamer *Fulton II*, though lost when Pensacola Navy Yard was taken, was completely dismantled and not included in this listing. In a lone category was the *Housatonic*, first warship destroyed by action of a submersible vessel, but I have termed her 'lost in action'.

These statistics could be analyzed further, but for our purposes only a few other observations will suffice. First, about forty vessels were lost on the western rivers, of a total of about three hundred in

Fifteen Union ships were lost due to enemy torpedoes (mines). *Commodore Barney*, shown here, was mined but survived: two men were drowned in this incident. From Frank Leslie's *Illustrated Magazine*.

those campaigns. The balance were lost on the Gulf or Atlantic squadrons, which numbered 471 ships in December 1865.

Of particular interest in this era would be the losses to the ironclad fleet and their causes, and the number of conventional vessels lost to enemy ironclads. There were eleven ironclads lost, of which nine were due to enemy action. Seven of these were torpedo victims – one at the Battle of Mobile Bay. Only the *Keokuk* and *Indianola* were lost to gunfire. *Monitor* was lost at sea and *Weehawken* sank at her moorings. Three wooden ships in the coastal campaigns were destroyed by Confederate ironclads: *Cumberland*, *Congress*, and *Southfield*. One vessel, the *Mercedita*, was forced to surrender by the ram *Albemarle*, then was 'paroled'. She returned to duty, however, and is not included in these statistics.

The following is a list of vessel losses derived from two sources: the *Official Records*, Series II, Vol. I, and a related listing of all Civil War era shipwrecks obtained at the Naval Historical Center. There are inaccuracies in the *Official Records*, some stemming from vessel name inconsistencies, particularly on the western riverboats. The 'commissioning' of vessels on the rivers seems to have often been quite informal and the transferring of vessels from the army to the navy (and vice versa) supplements the confusion. This list should therefore be considered a starting point for the whole subject, rather than a definitive catalogue.

## CIVIL WAR UNION NAVAL LOSSES

### KEY

**Loss Codes**

| | |
|---|---|
| WR | Wrecked (accident/act of God) |
| ACT | Lost in action |
| TOR | Lost due to torpedo (mine) |
| CAP | Captured |
| BPC | Burned/destroyed to prevent capture |
| NVA | Lost at Norfolk Navy Yard, 1861 |

| Vessel name | Loss code | Vessel name | Loss code |
|---|---|---|---|
| Adirondack | WR | Bainbridge | WR |
| Albemarle | WR | Baron de Kalb | TOR |
| Althea | TOR | Barataria | WR |
| Amanda | WR | Bazely | TOR |
| Anna (Annie?) | WR | Black Hawk | WR |
| Antelope | WR | Bloomer | WR |
| Arizona | WR | Brandywine | WR |
| Aster | WR | Buffalo | WR |

| Vessel name | Loss code | Vessel name | Loss code |
|---|---|---|---|
| Cairo | TOR | Mississippi | ACT |
| Champion No. 5 | BPC | Monitor | WR |
| Clifton | CAP | Monarch | WR |
| Columbia | WR | Morning Light | CAP |
| Columbus | NVA | O M Petit | WR |
| Columbia | NVA | Osage | TOR |
| Columbine | CAP | Otsego | TOR |
| Commodore Jones | TOR | Patapsco | TOR |
| Conestoga | WR | Pennsylvania | NVA |
| Congress | ACT | Peterhoff | WR |
| Courier | WR | Petrel | CAP |
| Covington | BPC | Philipi | ACT |
| Crocus | WR | Preble | WR |
| Cumberland | ACT | Queen City | CAP |
| Dai Ching | ACT | Queen of the West | CAP |
| Dan | WR | R B Forbes | WR |
| Diana | CAP | Raritan | NVA |
| Dolphin | NVA | Rattler | WR |
| Eastport | TOR | Reliance | CAP |
| Elfin | ACT | Rodolph | TOR |
| Ellis | BPC | Sachem | CAP |
| G L Brockenboro | WR | Sally Woods | CAP |
| General Hunter | TOR | San Jacinto | WR |
| Germantown | NVA | Satellite | CAP |
| Glide | WR | Sciota | TOR |
| Granite City | CAP | Shawsheen | WR |
| Harriet Lane | CAP | Shepherd Knapp | WR |
| Harvest Moon | TOR | Sidney C Jones | BPC |
| Hatteras | ACT | Signal | ACT |
| Henry Andrew | WR | Southfield | ACT |
| Housatonic | ACT | Sumter | WR |
| Ida | TOR | Sumter | WR |
| Indianola | ACT | Switzerland | ACT |
| Iron Age | BPC | Tecumseh | ACT/TOR |
| Isaac Smith | CAP | Tawah | ACT |
| Island Belle | BPC | Tigress | WR |
| Keokuk | ACT | Tulip | WR |
| Key West | ACT | Underwriter | CAP |
| Kingfisher | WR | Undine | CAP |
| Kosciusko | ACT | Union | BPC |
| Lavender | WR | United States | NVA |
| Linden | WR | Varuna | ACT |
| Madgie | WR | Violet | WR |
| Maria J Carlson | ACT | Water Witch | CAP |
| Merrimac | WR | Wave | CAP |
| Merrimack | NVA | Weehawken | WR |
| Milwaukee | TOR | Westfield | BPC |
| Mingo | WR | Whitehall | WR |

# SOURCES

A bibliography and set of footnotes are listed for each chapter.
(Note: there are no footnotes for Chapters One and Four.)

## Chapter One

Bailey, Thomas A, *The American Pageant* (2 vols), New York: D C Heath, 1971.

Beach, Edward L, *The United States Navy: 200 years*, New York: Henry Holt, c.1986.

Bryant, Samuel W , *The Sea and the States*, New York: Crowell, 1947.

*Causes of the Reduction of American Tonnage*, Washington: Government Printing Office, 1870.

Chapelle, Howard I, *The History of American Sailing Navy*, New York: W W Norton, 1949.

Coletta, Paolo E, ed., *American Secretaries of the Navy* (2 vols), Annapolis: Naval Institute Press, 1980.

*Conway's All the World's Fighting Ships: 1860-1906*, London: Conway Maritime Press, c.1979.

Grant, Bruce, *Captain of Old Ironsides*, Chicago: Pellegrini & Cudahy, 1947.

Knox, Dudley W , *A History of the United States Navy*, New York: G P Putnam, c.1936.

Morison, Samuel Eliot, *'Old Bruin': Commodore Matthew Calbraith Perry*, Boston: Little, Brown & Co., 1967.

Morison, Samuel Eliot, *The Oxford History of the American People*, New York: Oxford, 1965.

Paullin, Charles Oscar, *Paullin's History of Naval Administration, 1775-1911*, Annapolis: Naval Institute Press, 1968.

Scharf, J Thomas, *History of the Confederate States Navy*, New York: Crown Press, 1977 (reprint).

Silverstone, Paul H, *Warships of the Civil War Navies*, Annapolis: Naval Institute Press, 1989.

Sprout, Harold and Margaret, *The Rise of American Naval Power, 1776-1918*, Annapolis: Naval Institute Press, 1966.

Still, William N Jr, *Iron Afloat*, Columbia, SC: University of South Carolina Press, 1985.

Wise, Stephen, *Lifeline of the Confederacy*, Columbia: University of South Carolina Press, 1988.

Special thanks to Kevin Foster for his assistance on the subject of Confederate Blockade Runners.

## Chapter Two

*Annual Reports of the Secretary of the Navy*, 1860 through 1865.

Bennett, Frank M, *The Steam Navy of the United States*, Pittsburg, PA: Warren & Co., 1896.

Browning, Robert M Jr, *From Cape Charles to Cape Fear*, Tuscaloosa, AL: University of Alabama Press, 1993.

Canney, Donald L, *The Old Steam Navy* (2 vols), Annapolis: Naval Institute Press, 1990 & 1993.

Church, William Conant, *The Life of John Ericsson* (2 vols), New York: Scribner's, 1911.

Coletta, Paolo E, ed., *American Secretaries of the Navy* (2 vols), Annapolis: Naval Institute Press, 1980.

McCartney, Clarence Edward, *Mr Lincoln's Admirals*, New York: Funk & Wagnalls, 1956.

*Navy Register of the United States*, 1862, Washington: Government Printing Office, 1862.

*Official Records of the Union and Confederate Navies in the War of the Rebellion* (30 vols), Washington: Government Printing Office, 1894-1921.

Paullin, Charles Oscar, *Paullin's History of Naval Administration, 1775-1911*, Annapolis: Naval Institute Press, 1968.

Sloan, Edward William III, *Benjamin Franklin Isherwood, Naval Engineer*, Annapolis: Naval Institute Press, 1965.

Soley, James Russell, *The Blockade and the Cruisers*, New York: Scribner's, 1881.

Still, William N Jr, *Iron Afloat*, Columbia, SC: University of South Carolina Press, 1985.

Sullivan, William J, 'Gustavus Vasa Fox and Naval Administration, 1861-1866' (dissertation), Catholic University of America, 1977.

West, Richard S Jr, *Gideon Welles: Lincoln's Navy Department*, New York: Bobbs-Merrill Company, 1943.

West, Richard S Jr, 'The Morgan Purchases', *Proceedings of the US Naval Institute*, January 1940.

Williams, Harry, 'The Navy and the Committee on the Conduct of the War', *Proceedings of the US Naval Institute*, December 1939.

1  Paullin, p.211
2  IBID, p.266
3  IBID, p.267; McCartney, p.150
4  West, 'The Morgan Purchases', pp.76-77
5  Sloan, p.66-67
6  Church, Vol.2, p.20-33; Sloan, pp.71-72
7  Bennett, p.263-72
8  SECNAV Rpt 1861, p.18
9  Paullin, pp.299-300
10  Previous iron USN ships were *Michigan* (1843) and *Water Witch* (1844)
11  Coletta, p.349
12  Paullin, p.261
13  Sloan, pp.56-58; Church, Vol.2, pp.13 & 36
14  Paullin, pp.264-65
15  IBID, p.263
16  Bennett, Appendix B
17  SECNAV Rpts 1861-65; Browning, pp.190-97
18  Browning, p.150
19  Canney, Vol.2, p.85
20  Canney, Vol.2, p.25
21  Sloan, pp.130-31

### Chapter Three

*Annual Reports of the Secretary of the Navy*, 1859 through 1869.

Bennett, Frank M, *The Steam Navy of the United States*, Pittsburg, PA: Warren & Co., 1896.

Browning, Robert M Jr, *From Cape Charles to Cape Fear*, Tuscaloosa, AL: The University of Alabama Press, 1993.

Butt, Marshall W , *Norfolk Naval Shipyard*, Portsmouth, VA: Public Information Office, 1951.

Canney, Donald L, *The Old Steam Navy* Vol.2, Annapolis: Naval Institute Press, 1993.

Carse, Robert, *Department of the South: Hilton Head Island in the Civil War*, Columbia, SC: The State Printing Company, 1961.

*Causes of the Reduction of American Tonnage*, Washington: Government Printing Office, 1870.

Coletta, Paolo, ed., *American Secretaries of the Navy* (2 vols), Annapolis: Naval Institute Press, 1980.

*Dictionary of American Naval Fighting Ships* (9 vols), Washington: US Navy, 1959-91 (DANFS)

Fentress, Walter E H, *Centennial History of the United States Navy Yard, Construction and Repair, at Portsmouth, N.H.*, Portsmouth, VA: O M Knight, 1876.

Hamlin, P W LTJG, *History of the Boston Naval Shipyard, 1800-1937*, Boston: 1948.

Lott, Arnold S, *A Long Line of Ships*, Annapolis: Naval Institute Press, c.1954.

Lull, Edward P, *History of the United States Navy-Yard at Gosport, Virginia...*, Washington: Government Printing Office, 1874.

Malone, Dumas, *Jefferson the President: First Term, 1801-1805*, Boston: Little, Brown, & Co., 1970.

*National Historic Mechanical Engineering Landmark*, American Society of Mechanical Engineers, 22 March 1975.

*Navy Register of the United States*, Washington: Government Printing Office, 1860-65 (annual).

'Navy Yards Board of Navy Officers – Evidence Taken Before Them', Executive Document 71, 36th Congress, 1st Session, US House of Representatives, April 1860.

*Official Records of the Union and Confederate Navies in the War of the Rebellion* (30 vols), Washington: Government Printing Office, 1894-1921.

Paullin, Charles Oscar, *Paullin's History of Naval Administration, 1775-1911*, Annapolis: Naval Institute Press, 1968.

Pearce, George F, *The U.S. Navy in Pensacola*. Pensacola, FL: University Press of Florida, 1980.

Preble, George Henry, *History of the United States Navy Yard, Portsmouth, N.H.*, Washington: Government Printing Office, 1892.

*Report of the Secretary of the Treasury*, 'Commerce and Navigation', 1855, Washington: A.O.P. Nicholson, 1855.

Ritter, A H, comp., *A Brief History of the Philadelphia Navy Yard from its Inception to December 31, 1920*, (typescript manuscript), 1921.

*A Short History of the New York Navy Yard*, (Commandant's Office), New York Navy Yard, 23 February 1941.

Stuart, Charles B, *The Naval Drydocks of the United States*, New York: Charles B Norton, 1852.

Tucker, Spencer, *Arming the Fleet*, Annapolis: Naval Institute Press, 1989.

Young, Lucien, *A Brief History of the United States Navy Yard and Station, Pensacola, Florida and its Possibilities*, (typescript, n.d.).

1  Coletta, p.71
2  A naval station at Whitehall, New York, on Lake Champlain existed from the War of 1812 to *c.* 1823 (National Archives, Record Group 45)
3  Canney, Vol.2, p.20
4  DANFS, Vol.VI, p.103-5
5  Bennett, Appendix B
6  Preble, pp.6-13
7  IBID, pp.80-90
8  SECNAV Rpt 1869, pp.222-31; 'Navy Yard Boards', pp.273-78
9  SECNAV Rpt 1869, pp.222-31
10  Stuart, Pt 2, pp.29-33
11  Nat'l Eng. Landmark, 1975
12  SECNAV Rpt 1869, pp.222-31; 'Navy Yard Boards', pp.273-78
13  *Causes...*, p.262
14  Stuart, Pt I, pp.59-64
15  SECNAV Rpt 1869, pp.222-31
16  Sec. Treasury Rpt, p.356

17  SECNAV Rpt 1869, pp.222-31
18  Stuart, Pt 1, pp.9-50
19  SECNAV Rpt 1869, pp.222-31;
    'Navy Yard Boards', pp.59-61
20  *Short History...New York...*, pp.74-78
21  Bennett, Appendix B
22  *Short History...New York...*, p.44
23  IBID; Browning, pp.162-65
24  *Short History...New York...*, p.44
25  Paullin, p.115
26  Bennett, Appendix B
27  Stuart, Pt 2, pp.7-20
28  Bennett, Appendix B; DANFS, Vol.V,
    p.862
29  Browning, pp.161-65
30  Paullin, p.296
31  Malone, p.263
32  Tucker, pp.234-36; SECNAV Rpt
    1869, pp.222-31
33  SECNAV Rpt 1869, pp.222-31
34  Browning, pp.161 & 165
35  Butt, p.45
36  'Navy Yards Board...', pp.107-12
37  Bennett, p.242
38  Browning, pp.160-61
39  Stuart, Pt 2, pp.35-40
40  Pearce, p.80
41  IBID, p.92
42  Paullin, p.223; SECNAV Rpt 1860,
    p.82
43  Stuart, Pt 2, pp.23-26
44  Browning, pp.162-63
45  IBID pp.170-71
46  Paullin, pp.294-95
47  Carse, pp.76-80
48  SECNAV Rpt 1860, p.67
49  SECNAV Rpt 1860, p.351
50  Browning, pp.164-66

## Chapter Four

*Annual Reports of the Secretary of the Navy,*
    *1861-65.*
Bauer, K Jack and Stephen S Roberts,
    *Register of Ships of the U. S. Navy, 1775-*
    *1990,* Westport, CT: Greenwood
    Press, 1991.
Bennett, Frank M, *The Steam Navy of the*
    *United States,* Pittsburg, PA: Warren &
    Co., 1896.
Boynton, Charles, *History of the Navy during*
    *the Rebellion,* New York: Appleton,
    1868.
Canney, Donald L, *The Old Steam Navy* (2
    vols), Annapolis: Naval Institute Press,
    1990 & 1993.
*Official Records of the Union and Confederate*
    *Navies in the War of the Rebellion* (30 vols),
    Washington: Government Printing
    Office, 1894-1921.
Silverstone, Paul H, *Warships of the Civil War*
    *Navies,* Annapolis: Naval Institute
    Press, 1989.
Soley, James Russell, *The Blockade and the*
    *Cruisers,* New York, Scribner's, 1881.

## Chapter Five

Bauer, K Jack and Stephen S Roberts,
    *Register of Ships of the U. S. Navy, 1775-*
    *1990,* Westport, CT: Greenwood
    Press, 1991.
Canney, Donald L, *The Old Steam Navy* (2
    vols), Annapolis: Naval Institute Press,
    1990 & 1993.
Chapelle, Howard I, *History of the American*
    *Sailing Navy,* New York: W W Norton,
    1949.
Church, William Conant, *The Life of John*
    *Ericsson* (2 vols), New York: Scribner's,
    1891.
Desmond, Charles, *Wooden Ship-building,*
    New York: Vestal Press Ltd, 1984.
'The Ericsson Battery', *Scientific American*
    Vol.5 No.21, 23 November 1861.
'Ironclad Vessels', *Harpers New Monthly*
    *Magazine* Vol.XXV, September 1862.
Isherwood, Benjamin F, *Experimental*
    *Researches in Steam Engineering* (2 vols),
    Philadelphia: R Hamilton, 1863-65.
National Archives Record Group 19, US
    Navy, Bureau of Construction and
    Repair: Doc. 80-11-26, Specifications
    of USS *Monitor.*
National Archives Record Group 19, US
    Navy, Bureau of Construction and
    Repair: Plans of *Merrimack, Wabash,*
    *Colorado* and *Roanoke,* 1854-56.
Patterson, Howard, *Patterson's Illustrated*
    *Nautical Dictionary,* New York: Howard
    Patterson, 1891.
Stuart, Charles B, *The Naval and Mail Steamers*
    *of the United States,* New York: C B
    Norton, 1853.
Thompson, Stephen C, 'The Design and
    Construction of USS *Monitor*', *Warship*
    *International,* No.3, 1990.
'Trial Trip of the United States Steam
    Frigate Merrimac', *Journal of the Franklin*
    *Institute* Vol.61, p.274-9, April 1856.
Wilson, Theodore D, *An Outline of*
    *Shipbuilding, Theoretical and Practical,* New
    York: John Wiley & Son, 1873.

1   Canney, Vol.2, pp.25-31; Thompson,
    pp.226-27
2   'Ironclad Vessels'
3   IBID
4   Thompson, pp.226-27
5   *Monitor* description from: Canney, Vol.2,
    pp.25-31; Thompson, pp.222-27;
    'Ironclad Vessels'; and Ericsson's
    Specifications (National Archives, RG
    19)
6   Canney, Vol.2, pp.60-62
7   *Roanoke* construction from: Canney,
    Vol.2, pp.60-62; 'Ironclad Vessels'
8   Wooden ship construction from:
    Desmond; Patterson; Wilson; Chapelle
9   *Merrimack* construction from: National
    Archives, RG 19, Vessel Plans; 'Trial
    Trip...'; Wilson
10  Canney, Vol.1, p.43
11  Bauer & Roberts, p.68

## Chapter Six

'Civil War Small Arms', reprints from
    *American Rifleman* magazine, 1948-
    1960.
Davis, Rollin V Jr, *U.S. Sword Bayonets:1847-*
    *1865,* published by author, Pittsburg,
    PA: 1962.
Hickox, Ron G, *Collector's Guide of Ames U.S.*
    *Contract Edged Military Weapons 1832-*
    *1906,* published by author, Tampa, FL:
    1992 (rev. ed.).

Katcher, Philip, *The Civil War Source Book*, New York: Facts on File, 1992.

McAulay, John D, *Carbines of the Civil War*, Union City, TN: Pioneer Press, 1981.

McAulay, John D, *Civil War Pistols*, Lincoln, RI: Andrew Mowbray, 1992.

National Archives Record Group 74: Bureau of Ordnance: Entry 6, Letters and Telegrams from Chief of Ordnance.

Rankin, Robert H, *Small Arms of the Sea Services*, New Milford, CT: N Flayderman & Co., 1972.

Rankin, Robert H, *Uniforms of the Sea Services*, Annapolis: Naval Institute Press, 1962.

*Schuyler, Hartley & Graham's Illustrated Catalogue of Arms and Military Goods* 1864, Greenwich, Connecticut: N Flayderman, 1961 (reprint).

Tily, James C, *The Uniforms of the Unites States Navy*, New York: Yoseloff, 1964.

Todd, Frederick P, *American Military Equipage, 1851-1872*, New York: Scribner's, 1980.

Winter, Frederick R, *U.S. Naval Handguns 1808-1911*, Lincoln, RI: Andrew Mowbray Publishers, 1990.

A special thanks to Steve Selenfriend, whose collection of Civil War Union Naval small arms is unmatched.

1   Katcher, pp.182-83; Tily, pp.103-15
2   Tily, pp.117-28
3   Tily, pp.128-54; *Schuyler, Hartley & Graham*, pp.91-103; Todd, Pt 2, pp.528-50
4   Tily, pp.128-54 & 187-94
5   McAulay, *Pistols...*, pp.42-76 & 161-62
6   McAulay, *Pistols...*, pp.123-26
7   McAulay, *Pistols...*, pp.128-30
8   Todd, Pt 2, pp.556-57; McAulay, *Pistols...*, pp.22, 32-34 & 40-41
9   McAulay, *Pistols...*, pp.102 & 106; Winter, pp.55-59
10  McAulay, *Pistols...*, pp.60-61
11  McAulay, *Pistols...*, pp.158-62 & 74-84
12  'Civil War Small Arms', pp.18-21
13  IBID; Interviews by the author with Steve Selenfriend, 1995-96
14  (Interviews); McAulay, *Carbines...*, p.72
15  Todd, Pt 2, pp.556-57; Rankin, *Small Arms...*
16  Todd, Pt 2, pp.554-56; McAulay, *Carbines...*, pp.51 & 95
17  (Interviews); Davis; Todd, Pt 2, pp.556-60
18  (Interviews); Todd, Pt 2, pp.556-60

## Chapter Seven

Ammen, Daniel, RADM USN, (Ret.), *The Old Navy and the New*, Philadelphia: J B Lippincott Company, 1898.

*Annual Report of the Secretary of the Navy*, December 1855, Washington: Beverley Tucker, 1855, (various publishers, through 1865).

Bennett, Frank M, *The Steam Navy of the Unites States*, Pittsburg, PA: Warren & Co., 1896.

Browning, Robert M Jr, *From Cape Charles to Cape Fear*, Tuscaloosa, AL: University of Alabama Press, 1993.

Coletta, Paolo E, ed., *American Secretaries of the Navy* (2 vols), Annapolis: Naval Institute Press, 1980.

Daly, Robert W , LCDR USCGR, 'Pay and Prize Money in the Old Navy', *Proceedings of the US Naval Institute*, August 1948.

*General Orders and Circulars, 1863-1887*, Washington: Government Printing Office, 1887.

Jones, C C, *From the Forecastle to the Pulpit*, New York: N Tibbals, 1884.

Jones, Virgil Carrington, *The Civil War at Sea* (3 vols), Wilmington, NC: Broadfoot, 1990.

Katcher, Philip, *The Civil War Source Book*, New York: Facts on File, 1992.

Langley, Harold D, 'The Sailor's Life', *Fighting for Time* (*The Image of War*, Vol.IV), New York: Doubleday & Co., c.1983.

Langley, Harold D, *Social Reform in the United States Navy, 1798-1862*, Chicago: University of Illinois Press, 1967.

Long, E B, with Barbara, *The Civil War Day By Day*, New York: Da Capo Press, 1971.

Luce, Stephen B, *Text-book of Seamanship, The Equipping and Handling of Vessels Under Sail or Steam*, (revised and enlarged by Aaron Ward, USN), New York: D Van Nostrand, 1884.

McCartney, Clarence Edward, *Mr Lincoln's Admirals*, New York: Funk & Wagnalls, 1956.

Merrill, James M, 'Men, Monotony and Mouldy Beans: Life on Board a Civil War Blockader', *American Neptune* Vol.XVI, June 1956, pp.49-59.

*Navy Register of the United States*, 1862, Washington: Government Printing Office, 1862.

*Official Records of the Union and Confederate Navies in the War of the Rebellion* (30 vols), Washington: Government Printing Office, 1894-1921.

*Ordnance Instructions for the United States Navy*, Washington: Government Printing Office, 1866.

Paullin, Charles Oscar, *Paullin's History of Naval Administration, 1775-1911*, Annapolis: Naval Institute Press, 1968.

Randall, J G, and David Donald, *The Civil War and Reconstruction*, Boston: D C Heath and Company, 1965.

*Regulations for the Government of the United States Navy: 1863*, Washington: Government Printing Office, 1863.

*Regulations for the Government of the United States Navy, 1865*, Washington: Government Printing Office, 1865.

Roe, F A, *Naval Duties and Discipline*, New York: D Van Nostrand, 1865.

Silverstone, Paul H, *Warships of the Civil War Navies*, Annapolis: Naval Institute Press, 1989.

Stedman, Charles Ellery, *The Civil War Sketchbook*, (biography and commentary by Jim Dan Hill), San Rafael, CA: Presidio Press, 1976.

Symonds, Craig L, ed., *A Year on a Monitor and the Destruction of Fort Sumter*, by Alvah F Hunter, Columbia, SC: University of

South Carolina Press, 1987.

USN Ships' Muster Rolls, National Archives Record Group 45.

*United States of America Congressional Medal of Honor Recipients*, Columbia Heights, MN: Highland House, 1994.

Watch and Quarter Bills (USS *Richmond?*), 1865, National Archives Record Group 45, Subject File NA.


1   Paullin, p.304
2   Langley, 'The Sailor's Life...', p.361; USN Regs 1865, p.179
3   Browning, p.201; Katcher, pp.96-97
4   Browning, p.201; Katcher, pp.97-98
5   Coletta, p.350; USN Regs 1865, p.182
6   USN Regs 1865, pp.179-83
7   Browning, p.201; National Archives RG 45 USN Ship Deck Log, USS *Niagara*
8   *Navy Register*, 1862, pp.3-7 & 15-21
9   Paullin, p.233; Langley, 'The Sailors Life...', p.373
10  Browning, p.263; USN Regs 1863, pp.245-51
11  SECNAV Rpt 1865, p.393; USN Regs 1863, pp.261-67
12  USN Regs 1865, pp.330-33
13  Silverstone, p.125
14  USN Regs 1865, pp.184-87
15  National Archives, RG 45, Subject File
16  *Ordnance Inst.*, pp.16-21
17  Luce, pp.294-96
18  USN Regs 1865, pp.106-107
19  USN Regs 1865, p.107
20  SECNAV Rpt 1855, pp.15-16
21  USN Regs 1865, pp.221-28
22  Langley, *Social Reform...*, p.279
23  Ammen, pp.386-99
24  Luce, p.299; USN Reg 1865, p.84
25  Luce, p.606; USN Reg 1865, p.85
26  Luce, p.617
27  USN Regs 1865, p.105
28  Roe, pp.159-62; Bennett, p.86
29  Luce, p.295
31  Langley, 'The Sailors Life...', pp.367-68
32  Stedman, pp.46-53
33  Luce, p.619

34  Merrill, pp.50-58
35  Browning, p.210
36  Merrill, p.51
37  IBID
38  Merrill, p.56; Langley, 'The Sailors Life...', pp.367-69
39  Jones, *Forecastle...*, pp.485-91
40  McCartney, p.78; Jones, *Civil War at Sea*, Vol.I, p.372
41  Merrill, pp.54-56
42  Merrill, p.58
43  Figure from Dr Joseph Reidy, Howard University, Black Sailors Project
44  National Archives, RG 45, Ships Muster Rolls
45  *ORN*, Ser. I, Vol.25, p.326
46  Phone conversation with Dolly Nash, descendant of Smalls.
47  *Circulars*, pp.7, 9, 15, 22, 25, 33-34; *Congressional Medal of Honor Recipients*


## Chapter Eight

*Annual Reports of the Secretary of the Navy*, 1855 & 1860.

Bennett, Frank M, *The Steam Navy of the United States*, Pittsburgh, PA: Warren & Co., 1896.

Browning, Robert M Jr, *From Cape Charles to Cape Fear*, Tuscaloosa AL: University of Alabama Press, 1993.

Coletta, Paolo E, ed., *American Secretaries of the Navy* (2 vols), Annapolis: Naval Institute Press, 1980.

*General Orders and Circulars, 1863-1887*, Washington: Government Printing Office, 1887.

Johnson, Robert Erwin, *Rear Admiral John Rodgers 1812-1882*, Annapolis: Naval Institute Press, *c*.1967.

McCartney, Clarence Edward, *Mr Lincoln's Admirals*, New York: Funk & Wagnalls, 1956.

Merrill, James M, 'Men, Monotony and Mouldy Beans: Life on Board a Civil War Blockader', *American Neptune* Vol.XVI, June 1956, pp.49-59.

Morison, Samuel Eliot, *'Old Bruin': Matthew Calbraith Perry*, Boston: Little, Brown &

Co., 1967.

*Navy Register of the United States* 1862, Washington: Government Printing Office, 1862.

Paullin, Charles Oscar, *Paullin's History of Naval Administration 1775-1911*, Annapolis: Naval Institute Press, 1968.

*Regulations for the Government of the United States Navy, 1863*, Washington: Government Printing Office, 1863.

*Regulations for the Navy of the United States* 1865, Washington: 1865.

Roe, F A, *Naval Duties and Discipline*, New York: D Van Nostrand, 1865.

Sloan, Edward William III, *Benjamin Franklin Isherwood, Naval Engineer*, Annapolis: Naval Institute Press, 1965.

Soley, James Russell, *The Blockade and the Cruisers*, New York: Scribner's, 1881

Tily, James C, *The Uniforms of the Unites States Navy*, New York: Yoseloff, 1964.


1   Paullin, p.297; Coletta, p.348; Morison, Appendix
2   Paullin, p.297
3   IBID, p.299
4   IBID, p.401; Tily, p.117
5   USN Register 1862, pp.3-7
6   Tily, p.131
7   Morison, p.162; Coletta, p.220
8   Bennett, pp.656-67
9   *Circulars*, p.22; USN Regs 1865
10  *Circulars*, p.56
11  IBID, p.22
12  Merrill, p.50; Browning, p.209
13  *Circulars*, p.56
14  USN Regs 1865, pp.52-84
15  IBID, pp.11-15
16  National Archives, RG 19, Ship Plans
17  USN Regs 1865, pp.42-50
18  Paullin, pp.238-39 & 360; USN Regs 1865, pp.93-97; *Register* 1862, pp.24-28; Tily, p.126-127 & 158-59
19  USN Regs 1865, pp.42-50 & 97-101
20  Bennett, p.185
21  IBID, p.401
22  IBID, p.200-10

23  USN Regs 1865, pp.87-93; Roe,
    pp.160-65, 46-49 & 497
24  USN Regs 1865, pp.101-102; *Register*
    1862; Paullin, p.298


## Chapter Nine

*Battles and Leaders of the Civil War* Vol.IV,
    Secaucus, NJ: Castle Press, 1971
    (reprint).
*Civil War Naval Chronology: 1861-1865*,
    Washington: Government Printing
    Office, 1971.
Collum, Richard S, *History of the United
    States Marine Corps*, New York: L R
    Hammersly Co., *c*.1903.
Jones, James P, and Edward F Keuchel, eds,
    *Civil War Marine*, Washington: History
    and Museums Division, US Marine
    Corps, 1975.
Katcher, Philip, *The Civil War Source Book*,
    New York: Facts on File, 1992.
Katcher, Philip, *Union Forces of the American
    Civil War*, London: Arms and Armour
    Press, 1989.
Langley, Harold D, 'The Sailor's Life',
    *Fighting for Time* (*The Image of War* Vol.
    IV), New York: Doubleday & Co.,
    1983.
Long, E B, with Barbara, *The Civil War Day
    by Day*, New York: De Capo Press,
    1971.
Metcalf, Clyde H, *A History of the United
    States Marine Corps*, New York: G P
    Putnam, 1939.
Millett, Allan R, *Semper Fidelis: The History of
    the United States Marine Corps*, New York:
    Macmillan Publishing Co., 1980.
*Official Records of the Union and Confederate
    Navies in the War of the Rebellion* (30 vols),
    Washington: Government Printing
    Office, 1894-1921.
Paullin, Charles Oscar, *Paullin's History of
    Naval Administration, 1775-1911*,
    Annapolis: Naval Institutes Press,
    1968.
Rankin, Robert H, *Uniforms of the Sea
    Services*, Annapolis: Naval Institute
    Press, 1962.

*Regulations for the Navy of the Unites States*
    1865, Washington: Government
    Printing Office, 1865.
*Schuyler, Hartley & Graham's Illustrated
    Catalogue of Arms and Military Goods
    1864*, Greenwich, Connecticut: Norm
    Flayderman, 1961 (reprint).
Todd, Frederick P, *American Military Equipage,
    1851-1872*, New York: Scribner's,
    1980.
*United States of America's Congressional Medal of
    Honor Recipients*, Columbia Heights,
    MN: Highland House II, 1994.

1   Collum, pp.41-105
2   Katcher, *The Civil War Source Book*,
    pp.192-93; Paullin, p.304
3   Katcher, *The Civil War Source Book*, p.192
4   Metcalf, p.405
5   Collum, pp.116-20
6   Collum, pp.154-58; Metcalf, pp.208-
    209
7   *Battles & Leaders...*, Vol.IV, pp.642-61
8   *ORN*, Ser.1, Vol.21, pp.98-111;
    Collum, pp.177-80
9   Collum, pp.151-52; Metcalf, pp.217-19
10  USN Regs 1865, pp.173-75
11  *Congressional Medal of Honor...*; *ORN*,
    Ser.1, Vol.21, p.425 ff
12  Katcher, *The Civil War Source Book*, p.193
13  Rankin, p.145; Todd, pp.570-80;
    Katcher, *The Civil War Source Book*,
    pp.193-95
14  Todd, pp.500-501; Rankin, pp.262-66


## Chapter Ten

Brown, David K, *Paddle Warships*, London:
    Conway Maritime Press, 1993.
Gardiner, Robert, ed., *The Advent of Steam*
    (*History of the Ship*), London: Conway
    Maritime Press, 1993.
Hunter, Louis C, *Steamboats on the Western
    Rivers*, New York: Dover Publications,
    1993 (reprint).
Lucas and Hawkins, *Questions and Answers
    for Marine Engineers*, New York: Audel &
    Co., *c*.1903
Luce, Stephen B, *Text-book on Seamanship: The*

*Equipping and Handling of Vessels Under Sail
    and Steam* (revised and enlarged by
    Aaron Ward, USN), New York: D Van
    Nostrand, 1884.
Stuart, Charles B, *The Naval and Mail Steamers
    of the United States*, New York: C B
    Norton, 1853. (Appendix D: Letter
    from Jesse Gay, Chief Engineer, USS
    *Mississippi*).
Winton, John G, *Modern Steam Practice and
    Engineering*, London: Blackie & Son,
    1883.

1   Stuart, pp.164-66
2   IBID
3   Brown, pp.71-76; Gardiner, pp.16-19
4   Luce, pp.537-50
5   Hunter, pp.244-56
6   Steam engine operation: Lucas and
    Hawkins; Winton; other expertise pro-
    vided by Ladd L Canney


## Chapter Eleven

Canfield, Eugene, 'Civil War Naval
    Ordnance', *Dictionary of American Naval
    Fighting Ships* Vol. III, Washington:
    Government Printing Office, Reprint,
    1977.
Dahlgren, J A, 'Report on Cruise of
    Ordnance Ship Plymouth', *The U.S.
    Nautical Magazine and Naval Journal*, Vol.7,
    No.3, (1857).
Gardiner, Robert, ed., *Steam, Steel and Shellfire*
    (*History of the Ship*) London: Conway
    Maritime Press, 1992.
Gibbon, John, *The Artillerist's Manual*
    (1860), Westport, CT: Greenwood
    Press, 1970 (reprint).
Knowles, A J, 'The Development,
    Adoption, Use and Decline of the
    Parrott Gun: An Overview', term
    paper, East Carolina University, 1992.
*Ordnance Instructions for the United States Navy,
    1866*, Washington: Government
    Printing Office, 1866.
Simpson, Edward, *A Treatise on Ordnance and
    Naval Gunnery*, New York: 1862.
Tucker, Spencer, *Arming the Fleet*, Annapolis,
    Naval Institute Press, 1989.

1　Tucker, p.184
2　IBID, pp.184-96
3　Canfield, pp.798-801; Tucker, pp.198-216
4　Dahlgren Report
5　*Ordnance Inst... 1866*, p.45; Canfield, p.815
6　Canfield, p.800-802 & 805-806
7　IBID; Tucker, pp.225-39
8　Tucker, p.238
9　Canfield, p.802; Tucker, pp.142 ff & 218
10　Tucker, pp.239-42; Canfield, pp.807 & 816; *Ordnance Inst....*, pp.113-21
11　*Ordnance Inst....*, Pt 2, pp.6-24; Canfield, pp.807-808
12　*Ordnance Inst....*, pp.46-60
13　Simpson, p.617; *Ordnance Inst....*, pp.56-60
14　*Ordnance Inst....*, pp.61-73
15　*IBID, pp.108-12*; Canfield, pp.805-806
16　*Ordnance Inst....*, pp.113-127

## Chapter Twelve

Anderson, Bern, RADM USN, 'The Naval Strategy of the Civil War', *Military Affairs* Vol.XXVI, Spring 1962, p.11-21.

Boynton, Charles B, *The History of the Navy During the Rebellion* (2 vols), New York: D Appleton and Company, 1867.

Browning, Robert M Jr, *From Cape Charles to Cape Fear*, Tuscaloosa, AL: University of Alabama Press, 1993.

Coletta, Paolo E, ed., *American Secretaries of the Navy* (2 vols), Annapolis: Naval Institute Press, 1980.

Faust, Patricia L, ed., *Historical Times Illustrated Encyclopedia of the Civil War*, New York: Harper & Row, 1986.

Gibson, Charles Dana and E Kay, *Assault and Logistics, Union Army Coastal and River Operations, 1861-1866*, (*The Army's Navy* Vol.II.), Camden, Maine: Ensign Press, 1995.

*Official Records of the Union and Confederate Navies in the War of the Rebellion* (30 vols), Washington: Government Printing Office, 1894-1921.

Paullin, Charles Oscar, *Paullin's History of Naval Administration, 1775-1911*, Annapolis: Naval Institute Press, 1968.

Randall, J G, and David Donald, *The Civil War and Reconstruction*, Boston: D C Heath and Company, 1965.

Soley, James Russell, *The Blockade and the Cruisers*, New York: Scribner's, 1881.

Welles, Gideon, *Diary of Gideon Welles* (3 vols), New York: W W Norton, 1960.

West, Richard S Jr, *Gideon Welles: Lincoln's Navy Department*, New York: Bobbs-Merrill, 1943.

1　Anderson, p.15; Gibson, p.xxi
2　Boynton, Vol.I, p.89
3　Coletta, pp.333-35
4　Faust, p.619
5　Welles *Diary*, Vol.I, p.216
6　West, p.269
7　Browning, pp.170-179
8　Browning, p.183
9　Soley, p.2
10　Browning, pp.185-98

## Chapter Thirteen

Ammen, Daniel, *The Atlantic Coast*, New York: Scribner's, 1882.

*Battles and Leaders of the Civil War* (4 vols), Secaucus, NJ: Castle Press, 1971 (reprint), originally published 1887-88.

Baxter, James Phinney, *The Introduction of the Ironclad Warship*, Cambridge, Massachusetts: Harvard University Press, 1933.

Beach, Edward L, *The United States Navy: 200 Years*, New York: Henry Holt and Company, *c*.1986.

Boynton, Charles, *History of the Navy During the Rebellion* (2 vols), New York: D D appleton & company, 1868.

Browning, Robert M Jr, *From Cape Charles to Cape Fear*, Tuscaloosa, AL: University of Alabama Press, 1993.

*Civil War Naval Chronology, 1861-65*, Washington: Government Printing Office, 1971.

Jones, Virgil Carrington, *The Civil War at Sea* (3 vols), New York: Holt, Rinehart and Winston, 1962.

Lossing, Benson J, *Pictorial History of the Civil War* (3 vols), Hartford: T Belknap, 1868.

Mahan, Alfred Thayer, *Admiral Farragut*, New York: Haskell House Publishers Inc., 1968 (originally published 1892).

Mahan, Alfred Thayer, *The Gulf and Inland Waters, The Navy in the Civil War* Vol.III, New York: Scribner's, 1882.

Morison, Samuel Eliot, *'Old Bruin': Commodore Matthew Calbraith Perry*, Boston: Little, Brown & Co., 1967.

*Official Records of the Union and Confederate Navies in the War of the Rebellion* (30 vols), Washington: Government Printing Office, 1894-1921.

Parker, Foxhall A, *Squadron Tactics Under Steam*, New York: D Van Nostrand, 1864.

Porter, David D, *Naval History of the Civil War*, New York: Sherman, 1886.

Robison, Samuel S and Mary L, *A History of Naval Tactics from 1530 to 1930*, Annapolis: Naval Institute Press, 1942.

Scharf, J Thomas, *History of the Confederate States Navy*, New York: Crown Press, 1977 (reprint).

Soley, James Russell, *The Blockade and the Cruisers*, New York: Scribner's, 1881.

Stern, Philip Van Doren, *The Confederate Navy, A Pictorial History*, New York: Doubleday & Co., 1962.

Ward, James H, *A Manual of Naval Tactics*, New York: D Appleton & Company, 1859.

1 Ward, pp.143-204
2 IBID, p.137
3 Douglas, quoted in Ward, p.150
4 IBID, pp.156, 198 & 200
5 IBID, p.157
6 Porter, pp.45-47
7 Ammen, pp.23-28; Porter, pp.53-62

8 *Battles and Leaders...*, Vol.2, pp.22-89; Lossing, Vol.2, pp.328-39

9 Porter, pp.565-600; *Battles and Leaders...*, Vol.4, pp.379-409; Mahan, pp.256-93; Beach, pp.309-16

10 Porter, pp.367-98; *Battles and Leaders...*, Vol.4, pp.32-47 & 74

11 Lossing, Vol.3, pp.484-91; Porter, p.710-747; *Battles and Leaders...*, Vol.1, pp.358-72

12 Porter, pp.142-47; Lossing, Vol.2, pp.200-203; *Battles and Leaders...*, Vol.1, pp.358-72

13 Porter, pp.149-58; Lossing, Vol.2, pp.206-220

14 Lossing, Vol.2, pp.603-604; *Chronology*, Vol.3, pp.72-73; Boynton, Vol.2, pp.392-99

15 *Battles and Leaders...*, Vol.1, pp.692-730; Beach, pp.294-97; Stern, pp.80-89; Lossing, Vol.2, pp.364-66

16 Boynton, Vol.2, pp.552-65; Lossing, Vol.3, pp.436-37; Stern, pp.190-96; Scharf, pp.797-80

17 Browning, pp.223-46 & 260-62

18 IBID, pp.246-48

## Chapter Fourteen

Abel, Christopher A, 'Marines under Fire', *Civil War Times Illustrated*, May 1996, pp.54-61.

Canney, Donald L, *U.S. Coast Guard and Revenue Cutters, 1790-1935*, Annapolis: Naval Institute Press, 1995.

Evans, Stephen, *The United States Coast Guard, 1790-1915*, Annapolis: Naval Institute Press, 1949.

Faust, Patricia L, ed., *Historical Times Illustrated Encyclopedia of the Civil War*, New York: Harper & Row, 1986.

Gibson, Charles Dana and E Kay Gibson, comps, *Dictionary of Transports and Combatant Vessels Steam and Sail Employed by the Union Army, 1861-1865, The Army's Navy* Series, Camden, ME: Ensign Press, c.1995.

Gibson, Charles Dana, and E Kay Gibson, *Assault and Logistics Union Army Coastal and River Operations, 1861-1865, The Army's Navy* Series Vol.II, Camden, ME: Ensign Press, c.1995.

Katcher, Philip, *The Civil War Source Book*, New York: Facts on File, 1992.

Kern, Florence, *U.S. Revenue Cutters in the Civil War*, Washington: US Coast Guard Historian's Office, n.d. (1989?)

King, Irving, *The Coast Guard Under Sail, 1790 to 1865*, Annapolis: Naval Institute Press, 1989.

Long, E B, *The Civil War Day by Day*, New York: De Capo Press, c.1971.

*Official Records of the Union and Confederate Navies in the War of the Rebellion* (30 vols), Washington: Government Printing Office, 1894-1921.

Silverstone, Paul H, *Warships of the Civil War Navies*, Annapolis: Naval Institute Press, 1989.

1 Canney, Vol.1, p.2

2 IBID, pp.27-28

3 Kern, 9-1 thru 9-7

4 Evans, p.78

5 Kern, 9-7

6 Kern, 7-3 thru 7-7

7 IBID, 13-4 & 13-5

8 IBID, 15-6 & 15-7; the casualty was Captain Thomas M Dungan

9 Silverstone, p.195

10 Gibson, *Dictionary...*, p.viii

11 Gibson, *Assault...*, pp.67-78

12 IBID, pp.450-54

13 IBID, pp.467-71

14 IBID, pp.411-13; *ORN*, Vol.25, pp.699 & 741; National Archives, RG 19, E64 Report on Wiard Vessel

15 Gibson, *Assault...*, pp.236-42

16 Faust, p.501

## Chapter Fifteen

*Battles and Leaders of the Civil War* (4 vols), Secaucus, NJ: Castle Press 1986 (reprint).

Browning, Robert M Jr, *From Cape Charles to Cape Fear*, Tuscaloosa, AL: University of Alabama Press, 1993.

*Civil War Naval Chronology, 1861-65*, Washington: Government Printing Office, 1971.

Coletta, Paolo E, ed., *American Secretaries of the Navy* (2 vols), Annapolis: Naval Institute Press, 1989.

Faust, Patricia L, ed., *Historical Times Illustrated Encyclopedia of the Civil War*, New York: Harper & Row, 1986.

Long, E B, with Barbara, *The Civil War Day by Day*, New York: Da Capo Press, 1971.

*Official Records of the Union and Confederate Navies in the War of the Rebellion* (30 vols), Washington: Government Printing Office, 1894-1921.

1 Long, p.705; *Battles and Leaders...*, Vol.4, p.767

2 Coletta, p.348; Browning, p.200

3 Long, pp.710-11

4 *ORN*; *Battles and Leaders...*, vols 1-4

# INDEX

Page references in *italics* refer to illustrations, and those in **bold** to tables.

Adams, John Quincy 16
*Adirondack*, USS 62–3, **220**
Africa Squadron 1, 10, **10**, **17**, 33, 55
*Agamemnon*, HMS 67
*Agamenticus*, USS 72–3
*Alabama*, CSS 16, 18–21, 32, 52, 60–2, 136, 139, 157–8, 163, 170, 174, *201–2*, 202–4, 217
*Alabama*, USS 122
*Albemarle*, CSS 18, 21, 81, 217, 220
*Albemarle*, USS **220**
*Algonquin*, (uncommissioned) 44
*Alligator*, USS 12, 81
*Althea*, USS **220**
*Amanda*, USS **220**
*America* (US) 67
Ammen, Lt Daniel 127
'Anaconda Plan' 19, 178
   *see also* blockade policy
*Anna*, USS **220**
*Antelope*, USS **220**
*Ariel*, USS 157
*Arkansas*, CSS 18–20, 181
armies *see* Confederate Army, US Army
arms, personal
   long arms 111–14, *111–14*, 160
   small arms 106–11, *107–11*, 160
*Aroostook*, USS *59*
Aspinwall 55
*Aster*, USS **220**
*Atlanta*, CSS 71, 81, 171, 217
Australia 12
*Avenger*, USS 76

Bache, Alexander Dallas 24, 29, 210
*Bainbridge*, USS **17**, 219, **220**
Bainbridge, William 4, 140
Baltimore navy yard 9, 34, 44, 52, 55, 137–8, 184
Bancroft, George *142*
*Barataria*, USS **220**
Barbary States 2–3, 5, 9, 154
Barnard, Major J G 24
Barney, Cdre Joshua 7
*Baron de Kalb*, USS 78, **220**
Baton Rouge 20
battle-axes 116, *116*
bayonets 115
*Bazely*, USS **220**

Beaufort (N.C.) naval station 52, 137, 182, 184
*Benton*, USS 78, 200
*Bibb* (US) *210*, 211
*Black Hawk*, USS 76, **220**
Bladensburg, battle of 155
Blair, Montgomery 140
Blake, Robert 139
blockade policy 15, 18–20, 24, 27, 30, 32, 35–6, 48, 52, 55, 57, 135, 141, 178–82, *179*, 184, 200, 204–5, *205*, 206
blockade runners 18–19, 21, 121, 180–1, 196, 208
Blockade Strategy Board 24, 179–81
*Bloomer*, USS **220**
Board of Naval Commissioners 8–9, 14, 22
boilers 30, 71, 83, 167–8, 192
*Bonhomme Richard* (US) *3*
Borie, Adolph 147
Boston 7, **17**, 184
   navy yard 30, 33, 36–7, 39–42, *40*, 44, 55, 137–8, *154*
*Boxer*, HMS 6
*Brandywine*, USS 52, 184, **220**
Brazil 12, 17, 55
   Brazil Squadron **17**, 33, 55
*Brazileira*, USS 136–7
Brazil Squadron 10, **10**
Bridge, Horatio 29, 182, 184
Britain 1–3, 6, 8–10, 12, 16, 18, 66, 153, 155
   shipbuilding 18–19, 98, 202
   supplies to Confederacy 16, 18–20, 202–3
   *see also* War of Independence, War of 1812
*Brockenboro*, USS **220**
Broke, Captain Philip 7
*Brooklyn*, USS **17**, *56*, 63, 65, 192
Brooklyn naval yard *see under* New York
Buchanan, Admiral Franklin 19
*Buffalo*, USS **220**
Bull Run, battle of 156
Bureau of Construction and Repair 22, 25–6, 37–8, 40–1, 86, 145
Bureau of Equipment and Recruiting 37–8
Bureau of Medicine and Surgery 22, 33, 37, 149

Bureau of Navigation and Hydrography 22, 37, 39
Bureau of Ordnance 22–3, 37, 39, 41, 48, 182, 184
Bureau of Provisions and Clothing 22, 28–9, 37, 39, 43, 182, 184
Bureau of Steam Engineering 25–6, 37–8, 41, 48, 184
Bureau of Yards and Docks 22, 32, 37

Cadmus, HMS 63
*Cairo*, USS 77, 78, 176, **220**
Cairo naval station (Ill.) 52–3, 180, 182
*Caleb Cushing*, USS 19, *209*
California 9, 11, 13, 50–2, 70
   *see also* San Francisco
*Camanche*, USS 52, 70
Canada 5, 8, 54
*Canandaigua*, USS 62, 98
*Canonicus*, USS 71, *71*, 197
   class 71
Cape Fear 185, 204–5, *205*
*Carondelet*, USS 78
*Casco*, USS *72*
   class 72
*Catawba*, USS 71
*Catskill*, USS 70, *70*, 167
*Cayuga*, USS 59, **59**
Chambers, John S 184
*Champion No 5*, USS **220**
Chandler, William A 30
Charleston 19, 39, 63, 139, 180–2
   attack on 20–1, 70–1, 73, 138, *181*, 193–6, *194–195*, 202
Charlestown Navy Yard *see* Boston Navy Yard
charts and hydrography 23–4, 28
Chase, Salmon P 208
Cherbourg 21, 202
   *see also* Kearsage, Alabama
*Chesapeake*, USS 2–3, 6–7
Chesapeake Bay 7, 32, 209–10
*Chickamauga* (US) *213*
*Chickasaw*, USS 81, 193
*Chicora*, CSS 156, 194
*Chilicothe*, USS 78
China 9, **10**, 12, 60
*Chippewa*, USS *59*
*Choctaw*, USS 79, *79*, 81
*Chocura*, USS *59*

*Cincinatti*, USS 78
City class 78
*Clifton*, USS **220**
coal and coaling 24, 30, 52–5, 129, 182, 184–5, *185*, 211
*Colorado*, USS **17**, 56, 65–7
*Columbia*, USS **17**, **220**
*Columbia* (2), USS **220**
*Columbine*, USS **220**
Columbus 181
*Columbus*, USS **17**, **220**
commerce raiders 15, 18–20, 32, 52, 81, 158, 202, 209
Commission of Conference *see* Blockade Strategy Board
*Commodore Barney*, USS *219*
*Commodore Jones*, USS **220**
*Commodore Perry*, USS *75*
*Conestoga*, USS 78, **220**
Confederate Army 81, 179, 181, 184, 198–200
Confederate Navy 1, 18–19, 52, 57, 79, 186, 189
   fleet size 18–19
Congress 24–5, 28, 30, 32, 36, 50, 52, 60, 120, 126, 141–2, 155
   naval affairs committees 23
*Congress*, USS **17**, 66, 200, *201*, 217–18, *218*, 220, **220**
Congressional Medal of Honour 139, 157
*Connecticut*, USS 184
*Constellation*, USS (1797) 2–4, *4*, **17**, 33, 140, *154*
*Constellation*, USS (1854) 9, 60, 63, 74
*Constitution*, USS 1–3, 6, *6*, 8, 33, 40, 57, 65, 93, *142*
contract administration 26–7, 30–2
   Confederate 26
*Corwin* (US) 211
*Courier*, USS **220**
*Covington*, USS **220**
crew 2, 15, 58, 69, 117–39, 152, 216–19
   black 118, 120, *134*, 138–9, 215
   conditions and duties 122–39, *123*, *129–32*, *134*, *136–7*, *154*, *167*, 176–7, 185
   Confederate 19
   recruitment 28, *117*, 117–21, *118–20*, 138, 216

training 122, *122*, 130, *131–2*, 133, *172*
uniforms 99, *99*, 101–2, 105, *105*
*see also* officers
Crimean War 16, 26, 53, 70, 187
*Crocus*, USS **220**
*Crusader*, USS **17**, 67
*Cumberland*, USS **17**, 49, 66, *74*, 188, 200, *201*, 217–18, *218*, 220 **220**
Cushing, Lt William B 21, 81, 148–9, 217
*Cyane*, HMS 6

Dacotah, USS **60**, 61
Dahlgren, Captain John A 14, 26, 29, *29*, 48, 62, 112–13, 195
   shell guns 14, 48–9, 58–61, 65–7, 69–71, 73, 78–9, 113, 125, 169–77, *170*, *172–3*, *175–6*, 187, 194, 200
*Dai Ching*, USS **220**
*Dakota*, USS **17**
*Dale*, USS **17**
*Dan*, USS **220**
Dana, Richard Henry 126
'David' class submersibles 19, *21*
Davis, Cdr Charles H 24, 26, *26*, 29
Decatur, Stephen 4, 140
*Decatur*, USS 12
*Delaware*, USS **17**
*Demologos*, USS *see Fulton*
Derang's Neck, battle of 157
*Diana*, USS **220**
*Dictator*, USS *56*, 71
*Dolphin*, USS **17**, **220**
Drewry's Bluff 73, 209, 217
*Dunderberg*, USS 81
DuPont, Flag Officer Samuel F 20, 24, 53, 136, 156, 182, 188, 194–5

Eads, James B 78, 81
East Gulf Squadron 50, *179*, 184, 220
East Indies Command 10, **10**
East Indies Squadron **17**, 33
*Eastport*, USS 79, 81, **220**
*Elfin*, USS **220**
Ellet, Colonel Charles 215, *215*
   rams 213, 215
*Ellis*, USS **220**
engines 13, 57–9, 61–2, 65–6, 69, 83, 166–8, *168*
   construction and repair 25–6, 29–31, 35–6, 48, 55
   and shiphandling 161–8, *164*
   *see also* steam
*Enterprise*, USS 6
*Eolus*, USS 121
epaulets 100, 103, *104*, 159–60
Ericsson, John 27, 29, 83, 86
   guns *13*, 29
   ship design 13, *13*, 17, 26–7, 31, 69–72, 196, 202
   turrets 25–6, 56, 66, 71–3, 81, 86–7
   *see also Monitor*, monitors
*Essex*, USS *37*, 78, 140
European Squadron 55
Evans, Admiral Robley 157
exploration 12–13, 15

Falkland, HMS 37
Farragut, Admiral David G 50, *51*, 60, 65, 68, 136, 139, 142
   Mississippi campaign 19, 62, 180, 192
   at Mobile Bay 21, 158, 182, 191–3
   at New Orleans 20, 59, 190, 217
Faxon, William 24
ferries 75, 78
Flamborough Head action 2, *3*
fleet sizes 8, **10**, **17**, 18–19, 81, 188
floating batteries 16, 26, 187
floating dry docks 38, *38–9*, 45
Florida 9, 48, 50
*Florida*, CSS 20, 32, 61
food supplies 22–4, 28–9, 52–3, 55, 135–6, 182, 184, 211, 215
Foote, Flag Officer Andrew H 10, 12, 20, 53, 136, 181, 198
*Forbes*, USS **220**
Fort Beauregard 216
Fort Donelson 20, 181, 198–9, 212
*Fort Donelson*, USS 76
Fort Fisher 21, 60, 63, 66, 73, 156–8, 182, *182*, *196–7*, 196–8, 213, 217
Fort Henry 20, 181, 198, 212, 217
Fort Jackson 174, 180, 189, 217
Fort Monroe 52, 184
Fort Morgan 21, 191–3
Fort Pillow 181
Fort St Philip 174, 180, 189, *190*, 217
Fort Sumter 1, 19, 23, 25, 107, 139, 156–7, 193–4
Fox, Gustavus Vasa 19, 25, 32, 86, 88
France 3, 16, 21, 53, 73
   *see also* Cherbourg
Franklin, Sir John 13
*Franklin*, USS 37–9, 45, 66
Fulton, Robert 13
*Fulton*, USS 13, 50
*Fulton II*, USS *13*, 169, 219

Galatea, USS 75
*Galena*, USS 27, 57, 69, 73, *74*, *89*, 192, 209, 217
*Gallatin* (US) 206
Galveston 19–20, 55, 180
*General Burnside* (US) 214–15
*General Foster* (US) 214–15
*General Hunter*, USS **220**
*Georgia*, CSS 67
*Germantown*, USS **17**, **220**
Gettysburg 181
*Glaucus*, USS 75
*Glide*, USS **220**
*Gloire* (Fr) 16
Gosport Navy Yard *see* Norfolk Navy Yard
Grand Gulf 21, *199*, 199–200
*Granite City*, USS **220**
Grant, General Ulysses S 20–1, 180–1, 211–12
Great Lakes 5, 7–8, 10, 14, *14*, **17**, 33–4, 54, 169, 209
Greece 9
Gregory, R/A Francis 25
*Guerriere*, HMS 1, 6, *6*, 8

Gulf of Mexico 11, 21, 53, *179*, 180
   *see also* East Gulf Squadron, West Gulf Squadron
gunboats 5, 7, 18–19, 55, 68, 138, 197, 217
   ninety-day 30–1, 56, *56*, 88–98, *95*
   *see also Unadilla* class
guns 3, 49, *49*, 60–3, 71, 116, 169–77, 184, 220
   cannon 173–4, 176, 191
   carriage guns 57–8, 71, 170–1
   construction and fitting 35, 41, 48, 53, 56, 60–1, 68, 170, 172
   gunnery 13, 27–8, 187, 200
   pivot guns 57–63, 68, 171, 202–3, 210
   rifled 14, 65, 172–3
   *see also* Bureau of Ordnance and under Dahlgren, Parrott

Hamilton, Alexander 3
Hampton Roads 12, 44, 52, 184
   battle of 15, 20, 27, 31, 70, 86, 195, 200–4, *201*, *202*, 217–18, *218*
*Harriet Lane*, USS 68, 75, 207–8, *208*, 209, 220
Harris, Colonel John 155–6
*Hartford*, USS **17**, *51*, 60, *64*, *132*, *153*, 158, *171*, 190, 192–3
   class 60, 63–5
*Harvest Moon*, USS **220**
*Hatteras*, USS 19, 202, **220**
Hatteras Inlet 20, 70, 180, *187*, 188, 216
Hawaii 12
Henry, Joseph 27, 29
*Henry Andrew*, USS **220**
Hilton Head naval station *52*, 53
*HL Hunley*, CSS 19, 21, 63
Home Squadron 10, **10**
Honey Hill, battle of 157
Hong Kong 12, 55, 59
*Hope*, CSS 121
*Hornet*, USS 6
*Housatonic*, USS 21, 62–3, 219, **220**
*Hudson*, USS 9
Hull, Captain 8
Hull, Cdr J B 25, 140
Hull, Isaac 4
Humphreys, Joshua 93
Humphreys, Josiah 3, 6–8
*Hunchback*, USS 138
*Huron*, USS *58*, **59**

Ida, USS **220**
*Idaho*, USS 31
*Independence*, USS 8, 122
*Indianola*, USS 78–9, 220, **220**
*Insurgent* (Fr) 4
*Iron Age*, USS **220**
iron armour 13, 19, 31
ironclads 14–17, 20, 26–7, 31–2, 44, 46, 52, *56*, 56–7, 63, 69–73, 76, *77*, 78, 81, 135, 192–4, 196–7, 200
   Confederate 18, 20–1, 26–7, 63, 67, 69, 71, 73, 81, 156, 171–2, 181, 191, 196, 217, 220
   construction of 26–7, 33, 36, 82–6, *83–5*, 86–8

*see also* individual ships' names
iron hulls 13–14, 19, 25, 31, 36, 68–9, 73
*Iroquois*, USS **17**, **60**, 61–2, *62*
*Isaac Smith*, USS **220**
Isherwood, Benjamin F 29, *30*, 62, 86
*Island Belle*, USS **220**
*Itasca*, USS **59**

Jackson, General Andrew 8
Jacksonville 180
James, General Charles T 173
James River 73, 209, *214*
*Jamestown*, USS **17**
Japan 13, **17**, 61, 67, 111
*Java*, HMS 6
Jefferson, Thomas 2, 4–5, 7–8, 46, 48
*John Adams*, USS **17**
Jones, Captain John Paul 2, *2*
*Juniata*, USS 62–3

Kalamazoo, USS
   class 73, 81
*Kanawha*, USS **59**
*Kansas*, USS **60**
   class 59–60
*Katahdin*, USS **59**
*Kearsarge*, USS 19, 21, 36, 60, **60**, 61–2, *103*, 136, 139, 158, 163, *164*, 170, 174, *201–3*, 202–4, 217
*Kennebec*, USS 59, **59**, 193
*Keokuk*, USS *56*, 73, *74*, 194–5, 220, **220**
*Key West*, USS **220**
Key West naval station 32, 50, 52–3, 180, 182
*Kineo*, USS 59, **59**
*Kingfisher*, USS **220**
Knox, Henry 3
*Kosciusko*, USS **220**

Lackawanna, USS 62–3, *63*, 192–3
*Lafayette*, USS 79–81
Lake Champlain 7
Lake Chicot 215
Lake Erie 7, 54
   battle of 7, 8
*Lancaster*, USS **17**, 63–5, *65*, 215
Latrobe, Benjamin 46–8, *47*
*Lavender*, USS **220**
law and litigation 30–2, 75
Lawrence, Captain 7
Lee, Cdr S P 204
Lee, General Robert E 181–2
*Lehigh*, USS 70
Lenthall, John *29*, 86
*Leopard*, HMS 6
*Levant*, HMS 6, 12
*Lexington*, USS 78
Liberia 10, 12
*Lily*, USS 81
Lincoln, President Abraham 19, 49, 139, 141, *179*, *207*
   and naval administration 24
*Linden*, USS **220**
*Little Belt* (Br) 140

Los Angeles 11
*Louisiana*, CSS 190, *190*
Louisiana Purchase 50
*Louisville*, USS 78

**M**acdonough, Cdre Thomas 4, 7–8
*Macedonian*, HMS 6
*Madgie*, USS **220**
*Maedonian*, USS **17**
Magruder, G A 29
*Mahopac*, USS 71
Mallory, Stephen A 18, 26
*Manassas*, CSS 190–1
*Manayunk*, USS 71
*Manhattan*, USS 71
*Marblehead*, USS **59**
Mare Island Navy Yard 33–4, 36, 38, 50–2, *51*, 62
*Maria J Carlson*, USS 174, **220**
*Marietta*, USS 81
marines 5, 8, 11, 37, 39, *153–4*, 153–60, 216
'Marine Brigade' 158, 164–6, 206, 215
uniforms and arms 158–60, *159–60*, 160
*Marion*, USS **17**
*Martha* (US) 10
Maryland naval station 52
*Massachusetts*, USS 184
*Maurnee*, USS 60, **60**
Maury, Matthew Fontaine 19
McClellan, General George B 20
Mediterranean Squadron 9, **10**, **17**, 33
Memphis *180*
capture of 20, 54, 181, 215
naval station 33, 52, 54, *54*, 182
*Mendota*, USS *68*
*Mercedita*, USS 220
merchant ship conversions 16, 19, 35, 44, 57, 76, 79
Merrick and Cramp 73
*Merrimac*, USS **220**
*Merrimack*, USS 8, **17**, 20, 26, 40, 49, 56–7, 60, 65–6, 88–96, **220**
class 38, 49, 57, 65–7, 93, 170
*see also* Virginia, CSS
*Metacomet*, USS 192
*Meteor*, USS 138
Mexican War 9–10, *11*, 11–12, 44, 50, 111, 140, 155–6, 175, 178, 184, 188
Mexico 16, 32, 50
*see also* Gulf of Mexico, East Gulf Squadron, West Gulf Squadron
*Miantonomah*, USS 72–3
*Michigan*, USS 10, 14, *14*, **17**, 54, 68
*Milwaukee*, USS **220**
class *80*, 81
mines 78, 81, 191–2, 194, 219, *219*, 220, **220**
*Mings*, USS **220**
*Minnesota*, USS **17**, 65–7, 148, 200, *201*, 202
*Mississippi*, USS 13, **17**, 45, 68, *68*, 161–2, *161–2*, *190*, **220**
Mississippi Marine Brigade 158, 164–6, 206, 215
Mississippi River 9, 34, 53
campaign 19–21, 36, 62, 68, 178,

180, *180*, 180–1, 192, 213
*see also* Grand Gulf
Mississippi Squadron 18, 32–3, 76–81, 107, 110, 144, 174
Mobile 180–1
Mobile Bay 61, 182, 211, 217
battle of 18, 21, 63, *64*, 65, 81, 158, 189, *191*, 191–3, 218–20
*Mohawk*, USS **17**, 67
*Mohican*, USS (1859) **17**, 60, **60**, 61–2
class 67
*Mohican*, USS (1885) 62
*Mohongo* class (US) 68–9
*Monadnock*, USS 72–3
*Monarch*, USS **220**
*Monitor*, USS 18–20, 25, 27–8, 31, 56, *56*, *69*, 69–70, **70**, 73, *82*, 82–6, *125*, 170–1, 181, 195, 200, *201*, 202, 209, 217, 220, **220**
rig 26
monitors 17–18, 20–1, 32, 39, 42, 44, 46, 52, 69, 72–3, 81, 172, *173*, 181, 193–4, 196
'Light Draft Monitors' 26, 32, 71–2
'monitor fever' 25–6, 32, 73, 195–6, 202
*Monongahela*, USS 60, 62–3, 192–3
Monroe Doctrine 16
*Montauk*, USS 70, *147*
Monterey 11
Morgan, George D 24–5
Morgan Iron works 30
*Morning Light*, USS **220**
mortars 20, 174, *174–5*, *189*, 190
*Mound City*, USS 78
Mound City naval station 34, *35*, 52–3
*Muscoota*, USS 68–9
*Mystic*, USS **17**, 67

**N**ahant, USS 70
*Nantucket*, USS 70
Napoleonic Wars 3–6, 16
*Narragansett*, USS 60, **60**, 61
Nashville 181
*Naugatuck*, USS *see* 'Stevens Battery'
naval administration 2, 4–5, 8–10, 14–15, 22–32, *32*, 147
bureau system 22–3, 25–6, 28–9, 32, 147
*see also* individual bureaux
naval yards and stations 14, 22–3, 25, 28–30, 32–52
Confederate 54
*see also* individual yards, stations and rendezvous, and under shipbuilding
*Neosbo*, USS 81
*Nereus*, USS 75
Netherlands 9
New Berne 52, 180, 182, 184
*New Berne*, USS 184
*New Hampshire*, USS 57
New Hampshire navy yard 33
*New Ironsides*, USS 27, 35, 57, 69, 73, 84, 194–6
New Orleans 7–9, 36, 39, 50, 65, 139, 180, 182
fall of 20–1, 53, 59, 174, 180, *189*, 189–91, 217

naval station 34, 52
*New Orleans*, USS (uncompleted) 54
New York 13–14, **17**, 25, 30, 31, 42, 52, 84, 108, 120, 155–7, 184, 210
naval yard 33, 36–7, 40, *42–3*, 42–4, 55, 88, 111, 137–8, 213–14
*New York*, USS **17**
*Niagara*, USS **17**, 65, *66*, 67, 121, 136, 170
*Nipsic*, USS **60**
*Nipsis*, USS 48
Norfolk Navy Yard 27, 33–4, 37, 41, 44, 48–50, *49*, 52, 55, 66, 180, 219
captured by Confederates **17**, 20, 26, 34, 36, 46, 49, *49*, 50, 57
North Atlantic Squadron 33, 44, 46, 48, 50, 52, 55, *179*, 182, 184, 204, 220
*Nyack*, USS **60**

**O**achita, USS 76
*Ocean Queen* (US) 127
*Octorara*, USS 68, 192
class 68
officers 1–2, 8, 15, 23–4, 27–8, 48, 126–7, 138, 140–52, *150*, 209
conditions and duties 50, 53, 145–52
Confederate 19, 140–1
recruitment 15, 28, 141
training 15, 43–4, *142–4*, 142–5
uniforms *99–100*, 99–106, *102–5*
*see also* crew, US Naval Academy
Old Port Comfort 52
*Oneida*, USS **60**, 61, 192
*Oneota*, USS 71
*Onondaga*, USS 21, 72, 72–3
*Ontario*, USS 9–10
*Osage*, USS 79, 81, **220**
*Ossipee*, USS 62–3, *123*
class 2–3
*Otsego*, USS **220**
*Ottawa*, USS **59**
Ottinger, Captain Douglas 209
*Ouachita*, USS *77*
*Owasco*, USS **59**
*Ozark*, USS 81

**P**acific Squadron 9–10, *10*, **17**, 33
paddle steamers 13, 16, **17**, 52, 54, 56–7, 60, 67–9, 76, 78, 138, 161–2, 166, 174–5, 187, 192, 200, 213–14
*Palmetto State*, CSS 194
*Para*, USS *175*
*Parke* (US) 214–15
Parrott, Robert 14
Parrott rifles 14, 58, 60, 62, 67, 73, 78, 169, *173*, 188, 194, 209–10
*Passaic*, USS 70, 195
class 20, 70–1, 194
*Patapsco*, USS 70–1, **220**
Paulding, Captain Hiram K 13, 26
*Pawnee*, USS **17**, 60, *66*, 67
*Peacock*, HMS 6
*Pearl*, HMS 63
Peck, Joachim 139
Peck, Oscar F 139
*Pembina*, USS **59**
*Pennsylvania*, USS 9, **17**, 57, 74, **220**
*Penobscot*, USS **59**

*Pensacola*, USS **17**, 48, 50, 63–5
Pensacola Navy Yard **17**, 33–4, 36, 38, 50, *50*, 55, 182, 219
captured by Confederates 34, 36, 50
*Pequot*, USS 60, **60**
Perry, Cdre Matthew Calbraith 10, *12*, 13, 15, 44, 67, 107, 111, 140, 142, 187
Perry, Cdre Oliver Hazard 7, 140
*Perry*, USS *10*, **17**
*Peterhoff*, USS **220**
*Petit*, USS **220**
*Petrel*, USS 211, **220**
Philadelphia **17**, 28, 52, 182, 184
navy yard 33, 35–6, 44, *44–5*, 44–6, 137–8
*Philip*, USS **220**
pikes 116
*Pinola*, USS **59**
*Pittsburgh*, USS 78
pivot guns *see under* guns
*Planter*, USS *139*
*Plymouth*, USS **17**, 113, 170
Plymouth (N.C.) 21
*Pocahontas*, USS 58, 67, 148
Pook, SM 78
Porter, Admiral David Dixon 4, 20, 138, 140, 147, 149, 181, 196–7, 199–200, 204–5, 215
Porter, William 140
Port Gibson 215
Port Hudson, battle of 68
Port Royal 137, 180
captured 20, 53, 59, 66, 188–9, *188–9*, *189*, 216
naval yard 34, 52, *52*, 182, *183*
*Portsmouth*, USS 12, **17**
Portsmouth Navy Yard (N.H.) 33, 36–40, *37–9*, 44, 48, 73
*Potomac*, USS 10, **17**
Potomac River 19, 32, 48
flotilla 32
*Powhatan*, USS 13, **17**, 67, *67*
Preble, Edward 4, 140
*Preble*, USS **17**, **220**
*President*, USS 2–3, 140
*Princeton*, USS 11, 13, *13*, 45
privateers 2–3, 7
*Proteus*, USS 75
*Pulaski*, USS **17**
*Puritan*, USS 71, 81

**Q**ueen City, USS **220**
*Queen of the West*, USS 215, **220**
*Quinnebaug*, USS 46
Quintard, G W 72

**R**ams and ramming 19, 21, 67, 79, 81, 187, 190–1, 193, 200, 213, 215
*see also under* Ellet
Rapahannock River 32
*Raritan*, USS **17**, **220**
*Rattler*, USS **220**
Read, Captain 19
Red River Expedition 21, 81, 181, 215, 217
*Reindeer*, HMS 6
*Reliance*, USS **220**

*Relief*, USS **17**
*Reno* (US) 214–15
repair facilities 22, 28, 35–6, 41, 43–4,
    48, 50, 52–3, 55
    time spent in 55, 79
*Rhode Island*, USS 184
*Richmond*, USS **17**, 36, 63–5, 124, 190, 192
Richmond (VA) 20–1, 196
Rio de Janeiro 55
river ships and warfare 1, 16, 19–21, 34,
    56–7, 57, 62, 67–8, 76–81, 117, 138,
    164–8, *165*, *175*, *219*
    *see also* Mississippi campaign, Mississippi
      Marine Brigade
*Roanoke*, USS **17**, 44, *56*, 65–6, 73, *73*,
    84, 86–8, *86–8*
Roanoke Island naval station 52, 180,
    184, 216–71
Rodgers, Cdre John 76, 78, 136, 140
*Rodolph*, USS **220**
rope-making 41, *41*
Russia 16–17

**S**abine, USS **17**
Sabine Pass 217
*Sachem*, USS **220**
Sackets Harbor naval station 33–4, 54
*Saco*, USS **60**
*Sacramento*, USS 62–3
    class 62–3
*Sagamore*, USS 59, **59**
*Saginaw*, USS **17**, 68
sail-alone 20, 74, 76, 162, 186, 211
*Sally Woods*, USS **220**
*Sandusky*, USS 81
San Francisco 11, 39, 50, 73
    navy yard 33
*Sangamon*, USS 70
*San Jacinto*, USS **17**, 67, **220**
San Juan de Ulua 11
*Santee*, USS 9, **17**, *142*
*Saranac*, USS **17**, 68
*Saratoga*, USS **17**
*Sassacus*, USS 68
    class 68, *68*, 68–9
*Satellite*, USS **220**
*Saugus*, USS 71
Savannah 180, 212
*Savannah*, USS **17**
*Sciota*, USS 59, **59**, **220**
Scott, General Winfield 24, 178, *178*, 179
screw propulsion 13–14, 16–17, **17**,
    30–1, 44, 57–8, 60, 65–7, 73, 75, 79,
    81, 161–8, 200, 203
    and tactics 186–7
Seattle 12
*Seminole*, USS **17**, 50, 60, **60**, 61
Seminole Wars 9, 50, 111, 156
Semmes, Captain Raphael 202
*Seneca*, USS **59**
*Serapis*, HMS 2, *3*
*Shannon*, HMS 7
*Shawmul*, USS **60**
*Shawsheen*, USS **220**
shells 60, 65–7, 169–72, 187, 190

**T**aborna, USS **59**
*Tacony*, CSS 19, 209

*Shenandoah*, CSS 19, 21
*Shenandoah*, USS 62–3
*Shepherd Knapp*, USS **220**
Sherman, General William T 157, 182, 212
Shiloh, battle of 212
shipbuilding 4–5, 9, 14, 16, 22, 25–8,
    31, 33, 35, 37–8, 41–2, 56–7, 76,
    81–98
    Confederate *18*, 18–20, 27
    contracted-out 28, 33, 36, 40, 56, 58,
      67, 69–70, 84
    in naval yards 36, 39–40, 43–4, 46,
      48–50, 52, 58–67, 73
Ship Island naval station 52–3, 180, 182,
    *183*
ship purchases 24–5, 67, 74–6
shore batteries and fortifications 1,
    187–94, *188*
Shreveport 181
*Sidney C Jones*, USS **220**
*Signal*, USS **220**
Sloat, John 11
Smalls, Robert 139, *139*
Smith, Cdre Joseph 26, 29
*Somers*, USS 15
South America 9–10, 12, 16, 71
    *see also* Brazil, Mexico, Mexican War
South Atlantic Squadron 33, 44, 55,
    156–7, *179*, 180, 220
*Southfield*, USS 220, **220**
Spain 9–10, 48
spar torpedoes 19, 21, 35, 81, 217
    Confederate 19, 36
Spezia 55
steam, introduction of 13, 19, 186, 189,
    204, 207–8, 210
Steers, George 67
Stevens, Captain Henry K 19
Stevens, Robert L 14, *15*
'Stevens Battery' 14, *15*, 27, *56*, 81, 209–10
*Stevens* (US) *see* 'Stevens Battery' under
    Stevens above
Stimers, Alban 26, 72
*St Lawrence*, USS **17**, 211
St Louis 25
*St Louis*, USS **17**
Stockton, Robert 11
Stoddert, Benjamin 4, *4*, 33
'stone fleet' 24, 81
*Stonewall*, CSS *18*, 67
St Paul do Loando 55
Stringham, Flag Officer Silas 24, *28*,
    138, 188
submersibles 19, 21, 57, 81, 219
*Sumter*, USS **220**
*Sumter*, CSS 61
*Sumter*, USS **17**, 67, **220**
*Supply*, USS **17**, 184
*Susquehanna*, USS 13, **17**, 44, 67
*Suwannee*, USS 68–9
*Switzerland*, USS **220**
swords *115*, 115–16, 122, *132*, 160

Tattnall, Joseph 12
*Tawah*, USS **220**
*Tecumseh*, USS 71, 192, 217, *217*,
    218–19, **220**
*Tennessee*, CSS 18–19, 21, 63, 81, 191,
    193, *193*
Texas 107, 181
*Ticonderoga*, USS 62–3
*Tigress*, USS **220**
timberclads 76–8, *77*, 138
tinclads 76
*Tippecanoe*, USS 71
*Tonawanda*, USS 72–3
torpedo vessels 57
training ships 57, 67
*Trent*, CSS 67
Trent's Reach 21, 73
Tripoli 5, *5*, 140, 154–5
Truxton, Captain Thomas 154
tugs 75–6, 81, 121
Tulifinny Crossroads, battle of 157
*Tulip*, USS **220**
Turkey 9
turrets 57, 69–71, 76, **80**, 81, 85–7
    *see also under* Ericsson
*Tuscarora*, USS 46, **60**, 61, 203
*Tuscumbia*, USS *78*, 78–9, 200
*Tyler*, USS 78, 138

**U**nadilla, USS 59, **59**
    class 58–9, *59*, **59**
*Underwriter*, USS **220**
*Undine*, USS **220**
uniforms 22
    *see also* Bureau of Provisions and
      Clothing, and under crew, marines,
      officers
*Union*, USS **220**
*United States*, USS 2–3, 6, **17**, **220**
Upshur, Abel P 14, *14*
US Army 2–3, 8–9, 11–12, 18–21, 24,
    28, 52, 76, 78, 107, 109, 127, 140–1,
    154–7, 164, 175–6, 180–2, 197–8,
    199, 216–17
    Quartermaster Corps 206, 211–15
US Coast Survey Service 75, 148, 174,
    206, *210*, 210–11
US Naval Academy 14–15, 23, 33, 44,
    57, 100, 140, 142, *142*, 145, 148
US Naval Observatory 23, 33
US Revenue Service 9, 18–19, 68, *74*,
    75, 206–10, *208*, 211

**V**alparaiso 55
*Vandalia*, USS *97*
*Vanderbilt*, USS 75, *75*, 136
*Varuna*, USS 139, **220**
*Vengeance* (Fr) 4
Vera Cruz 11, **17**
*Vermont*, USS 53, 57, 122
Vicksburg 19–21, 181, 199–200
Vicksburg (Miss.) 20
*Vincennes*, USS **17**
*Vindicator*, USS 76

*Violet*, USS **220**
Virginia 30, 49
*Virginia*, CSS 18, 20, 26–7, 66–7, 69–70,
    86, 171, 200, 217–18
*Virginia II*, CSS 73
*Virginia* (uncompleted) 42
*Vixen* (US) 211

**W**abash, USS **17**, 65, *65*, 66–7, 94
*Wachusett*, USS **60**, 61
*Walker* (US) 211
*Wampanoag*, USS 81
War of 1812 1, 5, 7–8, 16, 48, 140,
    155, 169
War of Independence 1–2, 6–7, 16,
    39–40, 48, 140, 158
*Warrior*, HMS 28, 82, 170
Washington, George 2, 15
*Washington*, USS 8
Washington (D.C.) **17**, 32, 182
    burning of 7–8, *47*, 48, 155
    navy yard 5, 33, *34*, 41, 44, 45, *46–7*,
    46–8, 52, 55, 109, 137–8, 169, 176
*Wasp*, USS 6
*Waterre*, USS 68
*Water Witch*, USS 12, **17**, 68, **220**
*Watkyns* (US) *212*
*Wave*, USS **220**
*Wayanda* (US) *207*
*Weehawken*, USS 70–1, 193, 195, 217,
    220, **220**
Welles, Gideon 16, 19, *23*, 23–4, 25–6,
    28–32, 46, 50, 60, 106, 127, 138,
    140–1, 179
Westervelt, Jacob 63
*Westfield*, USS **220**
West Gulf Squadron *179*, 182, 184, 220
West India Squadron 9
West Indies 9, 32, 48, 62, 181
Whelan, William 29
*Whitehall*, USS **220**
Wiard, Norman 213–14
Wilkes, Cdr Charles 12, 32
*William Badger*, USS 184
Wilmington 21, 180–2, 196
*Winnebago*, USS 81
*Winona*, USS 59
Winslow, Captain John A 136, 203
Wise, Henry A 29
*Wissahickon*, USS **59**
wooden hulls 18–20, 28, 35, 39, 42, 44,
    49, 56, 56–5, 73, 81–2, 86–8,
    135, 191, 193, 198, 200, 217
    construction of 88–97, *89–97*
Worden, Captain John 200
*Wyandotte*, USS **17**, 67
*Wyoming*, USS **60**, 61

**Y**antic, USS 60, **60**
Yazoo River 78
Yorktown 1

**Z**eilin, Colonel Joseph 156